Caesarism in the
Post-Revolutionary Age

Europe's Legacy in the Modern World

Series Editors: *Martti Koskenniemi and Bo Stråth (University of Helsinki, Finland)*

The nineteenth century is often described as Europe's century. This series aims to explore the truth of this claim. It views Europe as a global actor and offers insights into its role in ordering the world, creating community and providing welfare in the nineteenth century and beyond. Volumes in the series investigate tensions between the national and the global, welfare and warfare, property and poverty. They look at how notions like democracy, populism and totalitarianism came to be intertwined and how this legacy persists in the present day world.

The series emphasizes the entanglements between the legal, the political and the economic and employs techniques and methodologies from the history of legal, political and economic thought, the history of events, and structural history. The result is a collection of works that shed new light on the role that Europe's history has played in the development of the modern world.

Published

Historical Teleologies in the Modern World, Henning Trüper,
Dipesh Chakrabarty and Sanjay Subrahmanyam
Europe's Utopias of Peace, Bo Stråth
Political Reform in the Ottoman and Russian Empires, Adrian Brisku
European Modernity: A Global Approach, Bo Stråth and Peter Wagner
The Contested History of Autonomy, Gerard Rosich

Forthcoming

Social Difference in Nineteenth-Century Spanish America: An Intellectual History,
Francisco A. Ortega
Orientalism, Philology, and the Illegibility of the Modern World, Henning Trüper

Caesarism in the Post-Revolutionary Age

Crisis, Populace and Leadership

Markus J. Prutsch

BLOOMSBURY ACADEMIC

LONDON • NEW YORK • OXFORD • NEW DELHI • SYDNEY

BLOOMSBURY ACADEMIC
Bloomsbury Publishing Plc
50 Bedford Square, London, WC1B 3DP, UK
1385 Broadway, New York, NY 10018, USA

BLOOMSBURY, BLOOMSBURY ACADEMIC and the Diana logo are
trademarks of Bloomsbury Publishing Plc

First published in Great Britain 2020

Cover image: Statue of Napoleon, Cherbourg. Normandy, France
(© Doug Scott/Getty Images)

A catalog record for this book is available from the British Library.

A catalog record for this book is available from the Library of Congress.

ISBN: HB: 978-1-4742-6754-0
        ePDF: 978-1-4742-6756-4
        eBook: 978-1-4742-6755-7

Typeset by RefineCatch Limited, Bungay, Suffolk
Printed and bound in Great Britain

To find out more about our authors and books visit www.bloomsbury.com
and sign up for our newsletters.

Contents

Preface

To be able to say "thank you" is undoubtedly the most pleasant task related to the finalization of a long-term project as work-intensive as this present monograph. At the same time, however, there is the inherent risk of not taking adequate note of each and every one who has contributed in one way or another. I owe my thanks to a great many people for helping me in the various stages of researching and writing this book and the underlying habilitation thesis submitted at Heidelberg University in early 2018, on which its findings are largely based. Even if I fail to mention all of them here by name individually, my gratitude is no less sincere.

I would like to express my profound and collective thanks to all the colleagues, friends and companions who over the last few years have made the present study possible with their generous advice and support, be it in the form of valuable recommendations regarding structure and content, suggestions for sources and literature, or their active help in commenting on, revising and editing the draft manuscript. A special acknowledgment in this context to: Roisin Boyd, Deborah Fölsche-Forrow, Kelly L. Grotke, Urban Kirchler, Lars Lehmann, Andrea Nicole Maier and Johan Rooryck.

I am particularly indebted to the European Research Council, which supported my preparatory work on this book in the context of the research project *Europe 1815–1914* at the University of Helsinki, and to Volker Sellin, who has accompanied my academic life since the beginning of my university studies, and who as the diligent mentor of my habilitation continued to be the committed and conscientious while at the same time unassuming teacher I have always perceived him as.

Above all, my thanks go to my entire family, who have been an immeasurable mainstay for my research, above all Lisa, Valentin and Alva: *Danke von Herzen* for everything. Insufficient though this may be to compensate for the stresses and strains they were prepared to shoulder for this book to reach the stage of publication, I would like to dedicate my humble work to them.

Brussels, March 2019

1

Introduction

1.1 Object of Research

Debates about the "legitimacy" and "essence" of political rule and the search for "ideal" forms of government have been at the very heart of political thought ever since its beginnings in the Ancient World. Discussions on how a balance between "just" and "effective" government might best be achieved have been particularly intense and controversial, as have those on the need and danger of dictatorship, the scope and limits of democracy, and on whether there might be some sort of "natural" sequence of regime types. The latter view, for example, was articulated within the various cyclical theories of political evolution (*anacyclosis*), the first of which date back to Greek and Roman constitutional theory.

The richness of these debates stands in contrast to an often astonishingly simplistic and ahistorical view on these matters in the post-Second World War era. The idea that today's Western world represents the outcome of a more or less linear development towards liberal and representative democracy, in which specific inalienable values are upheld, and that the rest of the world is inescapably animated by and moving towards that model, has become deeply entrenched in Western political rhetoric and public debate since 1945. In other words, that view that the nature of (Western) democracy is essentially geared towards some sort of finality antithetical to "dictatorship" has become commonplace. Even so, the teleological assumption of a long-term breakthrough of liberal democracy from the eighteenth century onwards is one-sided and at the same time problematic, because it disregards the complexity of historical developments, and also neglects both the explicit and the implicit tensions, contradictions and conflicts that (Western-style) democracy continues to face even today.

The shortcomings of what may be labelled a "democratization imperative" are evident in the difficulty of providing persuasive explanations for the totalitarian experiences of the twentieth century, since they construing them simply as temporary aberrations or "historical exceptions" that prove the "democratic rule" is far from satisfactory. On a contemporary global scale, they are also empirically mirrored by the fact that political systems considered undemocratic or only partly democratic still outnumber those regarded as fully democratic, with a clear tendency toward diminishing global democracy over the last few years,[1] thus putting into perspective how pervasive the charms of democracy might have been beyond the frontiers of the "West". However, shortcomings are also palpable in the West, since the image of today's

Western world as a group of mature and stable democratic states is itself dangerously deceptive. Europeans and Americans alike must allow for critical questions to be raised with regard to their own political systems and ideals: Does "formal democracy" necessarily guarantee "real democracy", so that democratic institutions and practices actually function where they are claimed to exist and have been implemented? Is it always possible to make a clear distinction between pluralistic and autocratic regimes? Do liberal society and economy on the one hand, and authoritarian polity on the other, mutually exclude each other? And, perhaps most important, do the "masses" really desire "democracy" as if by nature, to the exclusion of other possibilities?

On closer examination, the borderline between democracy and "non-democracy"— to use the perhaps least prejudiced counter-term—seems less clear than might first appear, as does the appeal of democracy as such. It can plausibly be argued that we are living through a distinct crisis of democracy in its liberal-representative form, something evident in growing alienation from parliamentarism, as indicated by widespread public distrust towards parliamentary institutions and procedures. However, also democracy as such is exposed to constant and serious threats. Subtle encroachments on public and political liberties, as well as more or less obvious attempts to steer public opinion by instrumentalizing the media may be cited as examples, alongside widespread susceptibility to populist politicians claiming to be the "voice of the people" or the "crisis manager" nations need, which frequently corresponds with openness to "strong leadership".

Such openness is not exclusively found on the "periphery", where the examples of Russia, Ukraine or Turkey demonstrate the fragility of democracy in states often described as "transitional" by social and political scientists. Even in the very heart of "the West", including the European Union, the crisis—or rather imponderability—of democracy is manifest. Hungary and Poland are cases in point, where the respective governments have successfully pushed for curtailing oppositional forces in politics and society by restraining media pluralism, politicizing the judiciary, or revising the constitutional order to benefit the ruling party. Whether one is inclined to regard these policies as autocratic or just as a means for more "efficient" governance:[2] it remains the case that these developments have been undertaken by democratically elected governments entrusted with a majority in parliament. One might argue that politics does not necessarily reflect what electorates originally wanted their governments to accomplish, or that it is merely specific conditions such as a brief experience of post-dictatorial government that favor the authoritarian. But the most convenient explanations are not always the most sustainable ones. To contrast an innocent—or possibly inexperienced—electorate with a disobedient government, or to portray Hungary, Poland and other "sinners" as special cases, is one such convenient view and does not reflect the intricacies of our contemporary world, where (liberal) democracy has been put on the defensive.

Evidence speaks a clear language: the desire and preparedness for authoritarian forms of government is now widely present throughout the globe, including in Western democracies. In Europe, for example, the results of a study published in early 2011 show that in Portugal, which was hit particularly hard by the public debt crisis, no less than 62.4 percent of respondents expressed their active support for the idea of authoritarian leadership, and also in long-established democracies like Great Britain and France more than 40 percent took the view that their country needed a "strong man" in power regardless of parliament or election results (41.8 percent and 43.2 percent respectively). Even in Germany with its traumatic experience of National Socialism one third of the sampled population (32.3 percent) was of the same opinion.[3]

What can be deduced from such empirical findings? If nothing else, they are a reminder that our present age is not far from the brink of authoritarianism: not only are reckless politicians advocating for it out of personal lust for power, whatever the desires of the people might actually be, but a considerable number of citizens long for authoritarianism or are at least indifferent towards it even in Western democracies. "Natural" distinctions between "good democracy" and "bad dictatorship" seem to fade in the presence of widely-felt anxiety about the future, which is nurtured by dissatisfaction with the current state of affairs and the almost omnipresent sense of "crisis", be it economic, political or cultural, real or imagined. Yet is the relativization of such distinctions really a particularly "modern" phenomenon? Hardly so. Consequently, an historical analysis of palpably ambivalent attitudes towards authority seems a promising, and possibly indispensable, starting point for attaining a better understanding of present-day conditions and the future prospects of (democratic) politics.

World history exhibits a continual and dynamic clash of values, rather than a gradual creation and preservation of clear normative commitments; over time, these clashes have occasioned a range of theoretical and institutional compromises that have resulted in stability and fragility alike. This may be said of all periods of history, but perhaps the nineteenth century in particular; an age, in which fundamental departures from traditional understandings of society and politics were discernible, as manifest in the shift from a monarchical and dynastic to a democratic concept of legitimacy. It was also an age in which a multitude of clashes among different value systems became manifest within intellectual production and political action on a global scale, prefiguring much of our contemporary world. Against this background, the present enquiry sets out to challenge simplistic assumptions of smooth political-institutional development and overly optimistic democratization narratives by problematizing anew the complex relation between democracy and dictatorship, notably from the late eighteenth century onwards. More concretely, it aims to analyze the extent to which democracy emerged as compatible with dictatorship in political thought and practice during the revolutionary period and its aftermath.

Claims for potential compatibility between democracy and dictatorship might appear daring in view of the strict "illegitimacy" ascribed to the latter in political theory after the Second World War, but this is much less the case when earlier usage is taken into account. In 1923, for example, the German jurist Carl Schmitt (1888–1985) argued in his *Die geistesgeschichtliche Lage des heutigen Parlamentarismus* that a democratic concept of legitimacy could be perfectly compatible with the establishment of dictatorship. An individual leader could act, or at least decide, in the name of those represented no less than a representative parliamentary body could:

> [...] The notion of parliamentarism appears to be something essentially democratic. But despite all its coincidence with democratic ideas and all the connections it has to them, it is not [...] If for practical and technical reasons the

representatives of the people can decide instead of the people themselves, then certainly a single trusted representative could also decide in the name of the same people. Without ceasing to be democratic, the argument would justify an antiparliamentary Caesarism.[4]

At the time Schmitt made this statement, his contentious claim that democracy and rule of the one were not incompatible had a long and intricate intellectual history behind it; a history, that is part of a more general debate about the nature and viability of modern statehood, the relationship of modern society, constitutionalism and representative government to classical forms of rule, and—more abstractly still—the potential links between the ancient and the modern world. That debate was a product of the kinds of experiences being opened up by the emergence of modernity, and the political options conceived to manage it. The term used by Schmitt in 1923 to characterize an alternative system of government, situated somewhere between democracy and dictatorship, reflects the struggle to make sense of the (modern) present by relating it to the (ancient) past: "Caesarism". It refers to the regimes of the Roman Emperors created out of the late Republic and more particularly to the person of Julius Caesar, but also evinces intrinsic "novelty" because the term was only coined in the nineteenth century. Contemporary lexicographic entries widely reflect that dual and ambiguous nature of "Caesarism".[5]

"Caesarism"[6] assumes the guiding conceptual role within this study because of this inherent ambivalence, alongside the term's suitability in comparison with other alternatives. That said, what follows will not offer any clear-cut definition of the term, and neither will it provide a straightforward "conceptual history" (*Begriffsgeschichte*). While both approaches have their strengths, they have immanent flaws, too: to agree *a priori* on an authoritative definition and classification of Caesarism and thus create an "ideal type" might provide a handy list of features against which certain historical phenomena and statesmen could be easily "checked" as to whether they match the model or not. Yet any pre-definition of what Caesarism actually means would inevitably be highly constructed and overlook the dynamic history of the Caesarism discourse, hence de-historicizing the results obtained.[7] A "lexicographic" history of "Caesarism" focused on the changing uses of the concept over time would set out a clear research agenda, but at the same time run the risk of failing to encompass instances in which the same issues might have been addressed using another terminology, such as "Bonapartism". In other words, focusing exclusively on one term disregards the fact that active usage of a specific term does not necessarily coincide with its full conceptual range or its membership within a family of related concepts. This also holds true for Caesarism, which is embedded in an extensive semantic field of both adjacent and oppositional concepts and has a far longer lineage than its sudden appearance as a discrete word in the 1840s might suggest.[8]

With this in mind, the present inquiry will take a less straightforward approach to the analysis of "Caesarism", which will neither be understood as a rigidly fixed category nor as a particular form of government characterized by unequivocal features; rather, it will be shown to be as a "floating" and "open" political concept describing certain visions of political rule positioned amidst the conflicting priorities of "effective rule" and "political mass participation", and at the crossroads of dictatorship and democracy more generally. Why "Caesarism" and related concepts of rule and government became central at particular historical moments in the wake of the "revolutionary experience", what they basically signified, and which hopes and fears were associated with them by contemporaries are all key concerns in what follows.

Notwithstanding the need to underscore the fluid and often ambiguous nature of seemingly lucid political concepts, a basic preconception of Caesarism is indispensable: defining the conceptual framework conditions helps to reify the object of research and avoid the danger of indulging in "whateverism". Against this background, **three main traits** will be considered integral to the concept of Caesarism within this study:

I.   Caesarism as a political and politico-theoretical phenomenon incorporating both "democratic" and "dictatorial" elements. More particularly, it is assumed that Caesarism combines authoritarian leadership by one with an underlying democratic—usually "plebiscitary"—legitimization by the people, with intermediary representative bodies either absent or neutralized. Accordingly, Caesarism has an intrinsically anti-parliamentarian dimension.

II.   Caesarism as an essentially (post-)revolutionary phenomenon. While the desire to reconcile monocratic[9] and democratic premises surfaces in human history throughout the ages, it was only with the radical shift away from a traditional and toward a predominantly democratic legitimization of rule under the slogan of "popular sovereignty" in the American and especially French Revolution—a period accompanied by fundamental economic, social and cultural changes—that this challenge became politically and conceptually pivotal. This claim also substantiates the starting point chosen for the investigation: the late eighteenth century.

III. Caesarism as embedded in a pronounced and fundamental "crisis". Regardless of whether this crisis is real or constructed, Caesarism is inseparable from the perception of an acute "moment of danger" and "exception(ality)". The most widespread arguments in favor of dictatorial forms of government have coincided with a "state of exception(ality)" and crisis, blazing the trail for "unconventional" regimes to assume power. At the same time, however, it is the (potential) excesses of power accompanying or following in the wake of such a "state of exception(ality)" that have also provoked outright rejections of Caesarism as a viable political alternative.

What is to be expected from an inquiry revolving around the concept of Caesarism as categorized above? Ideally, a more nuanced and realistic understanding of the nature of politics in the "modern age", and of the delicate intricacies of democracy in particular.

The idealized narrative of political-institutional progress from absolutism to parliamentary democracy, with monarchical-constitutional systems perhaps seen as a temporary stepping-stone between the two, clearly disregards the complexity of historical development; especially the fact that multiple alternatives to transform politics existed in the (post-)revolutionary period, including one in the direction of autocratic yet genuinely modern-style leadership. While the democratic spirit invoked by the American and French Revolutions in the second half of the eighteenth century was increasingly difficult to ignore, there was a continual risk that constitutional law, parliamentarian control mechanisms or liberal values would lose out to a distinctively monocratic element assuming comprehensive power. This was particularly the case in times of increased susceptibility to radical political "solutions" such as revolutionary upheaval, economic calamity or rapid socio-economic change; in short: in times of "crisis".

Traditional divine-right and absolutist monarchy was increasingly less likely to be a sustainable model in the longer term, since its foundations had been shattered by enlightened philosophy and revolutionary experience had deprived it of its mystique. Even so, the monarchical element had by no means lost all of its significance by the early nineteenth century. The increasing complexity of social and political life generated a desire for new forms of "rule by one" and "personalized leadership" that differed considerably from the pre-revolutionary period. Regimes that reinterpreted the old idea of rule essentially being "monarchical" and "by one" in ways that were in line with the spirit of the time had particular appeal: regimes managing to make the "rule of the one" fit with the demands of the "modern age", political participation of the "people" (however defined), progress, innovation, national power and social welfare. One potential means to bring these demands together was a democratic-plebiscitary form of autocratic leadership, to be subsumed under "Caesarism". For such Caesarism to work, however, a suitable leader was required. But who would best fit the role of a new type of leader in an age geared more towards the future than the past?

The decline of tradition and customs as *the* classical basis for legitimate rule together with mounting public expectations regarding politics made alternative forms of legitimacy all the more important. According to Max Weber's classical distinction of "pure" sources of political legitimacy, these were mainly rational-legal and charismatic forms, both of which can legitimately claim to be revolutionizing powers.[10] The growing rational-legal underpinning of rule found its clearest expression in the wave of legal codifications taking place throughout Europe from the second half of the eighteenth century onwards, above all in the many constitutions enacted in the wake of revolutionary upheaval, which made people such as the German liberal Karl von Rotteck (1775–1840) declare the nineteenth century to be "the age of constitutions".[11] Alongside rational authority, based on the popular perception that a government's power derives from established (constitutional) norms, charismatic authority was also becoming potentially more important, embodied by individuals who seemed to be natural leaders and guarantors of progress or stability by their sheer personal magnetism and their exceptional attributes.[12]

It was not impossible for traditional monarchs to assume—or, if "charisma" is taken as an integral element of any kind of political rule, to reinforce—the role of a "charismatic leader" and adapt their style of government accordingly, as a number of nineteenth century figures such as the Russian tsar Alexander I illustrate. Yet even more than the rational-legal it was the charismatic element that created possibilities for newcomers and *homines novi* from outside the established political class unseen before in history. The road to power was paved by gaining the status of a popular hero or national saviour; a process favored by the growing political "mass market" and its corresponding media serving as a tool for the charismatization of the leader and as the link between him and the "people". In combination with a democratic-plebiscitary underpinning, charismatic rule wielded potential advantages: while it incorporated the "popular moment", it promised better decision-making capacities than either parliamentary democracy, which was still struggling against the reproach that it tended towards anarchy, or constitutional monarchy with its systemic dualism between monarch and parliament. Charismatic-plebiscitary forms of rule also implied an ability to transcend existing boundaries, legal, ethical or otherwise, provided the leader successfully managed to argue that it was for the benefit of the "nation" or "whole". The option of abandoning—at least temporarily—conventions and the rule of law, whether to justify a "necessary" *coup d'état* or to declare a state of emergency, was not least due to the pseudo-religious traits of charismatic leadership. If charismatic leaders were seen as the "prophets" of a new era, chances were high that their political ambitions and promises would be perceived more as a creed than a simple political program, especially in the (post-)revolutionary age. There, the "cult" of heroic leadership—which could even nurture Messianic traits and the notion of a community of fate—compensated for traditional forms of religiosity that were increasingly exposed to secularizing tendencies.

It therefore seems vital to maintain charisma as a key category of Caesaristic discourse and government, even if the term itself only gained analytical relevance in the twentieth century. Charisma also applies to those two figures in modern history who are regarded as *the* representatives of what many sharp-eyed analysts of European politics have seen as a qualitatively new type of rule growing out of the Revolution and at the same time representing a reaction against it: Napoleon I and Napoleon III. It was their seizure and exercise of power that essentially triggered an interest within nineteenth-century political theory and philosophy about the issue of "Caesarism". For this reason alone, these two assume a pivotal role in the present inquiry.

1.2 Scope of Study

While in twentieth- and partly also twenty-first-century scholarship different national variants of "Caesarism" and especially French "Bonapartism" have been examined in some detail,[13] works focusing on the broader European context and theorizing in-depth studies on the background of and impetus for the phenomenon and its repercussions have largely remained a *desideratum*. This gap seems all the more astonishing in view of the considerable interest in the topic on the part of nineteenth-century observers, but it can be explained by at least two things: first, Caesarism does not fit into the aforementioned Western *topos* of long-term democratization and parliamentarization; second, the totalitarian experiences of the twentieth century have absorbed much of the attention in research Caesarism might otherwise have continued to receive.[14] More recently, a growing scholarly interest in Caesarism can be observed,[15] spurred on by political developments that challenge long-established narratives of political progress and pose anew the question of whether and to what extent democracy and authoritarianism are mutually exclusive. Nevertheless, the current discusssion has not yet reached anything like the intensity of the debates about Caesarism throughout the nineteenth and early twentieth century. Moreover, the rediscovery of Caesarism has mainly yielded works focusing on the intellectual and conceptual history of the term, therefore addressing only one—albeit crucial—dimension of the phenomenon and largely leaving aside the dynamic relation between political discourse and "real politics".

With this in mind, the present study will deliberately refrain from an individual case study method, nor will it attempt an exhaustive comparative analysis of various national facets of "Caesarism". Instead, it will elaborate on general trends in interpretation and perspectives of development and present a broader picture of Caesaristic discourse *and* politics in a European framework. The approach chosen for this task is "theoretical", and simultaneously explicitly "historicizing". The assumption is that "Caesarism" can be perceived as something contingent upon concrete conditions at specific moments in history, that is a political, social or economic phenomenon in the narrower sense, but not exclusively so because the phenomenon is also rooted in broader spiritual-intellectual currents indicated by the term "modernity". Regardless of more particular explanations of the phenomenon that may be put forward, the challenges of the modern age remain evident, especially regarding the realm of politics and the underpinning legitimations of rule. In this context, the study aims to help delineate the underlying structures, contingencies and contradictions that generated Caesarism as a particular expression of "political modernity".

While this enquiry is intended to supplement existing explanations of "Caesarism" by analyzing the phenomenon at a more general level, this does not necessarily imply abstraction. Rather, the specificity of the subject within its particular time period will be emphasized in order to explain broad tendencies and long-term implications. Contemporary definitions of "Caesarism" and related concepts will be drawn upon to provide insight into the extent to which these terms and concepts were connoted in a negative or positive way, and whether—and why—there was craving for Caesaristic rule among contemporaries. The underlying assumption is that the "signature" of an era can best be grasped by taking the debates and intellectual discourse, that is the "self-diagnoses", of the time as a starting point.[16] These shed light on existing concepts of "future" and perceptions of "historical development" during the period.[17] Within this framework, a two-fold standpoint on the subject will be taken: on the one hand an "internal", focusing on the understanding and legitimization of Caesarism by rulers and politicians commonly associated with the term; on the other an "external", dealing with the perception and theorization of Caesaristic forms of government by contemporary political observers. What will have to be shown in this context is that right from the beginning debate was exceedingly heterogeneous. While the implications of a putatively new regime type embodied by Napoleon Bonaparte and others would occupy politicians and theorists for the rest of the nineteenth century and beyond, there was no agreement at all as to the actual benchmark to be used in assessment, nor even about the actual terminology referring to the phenomenon: whether it might best be characterized as "Napoleonism", "Bonapartism", simply "dictatorship", or perhaps "(modern) Caesarism"; whether it was foremost a national, particularly French, phenomenon, or a universal *signum* of the era, characteristic of all post-revolutionary societies; whether it was a transient aberration on the path of history or more its *ultima ratio;* whether it was more about "progress" than "regression"; and whether it was a rescue from anarchy and revolution, and thus the salvation of "reason", or rather a hindrance and misdirection of development.

No matter how rich the self-diagnoses of the time might be, however, their study remains superficial without an accompanying "**historical analysis**", which explores and judges the past from the present. Historical distance from our objects of research might carry a risk of retrojection, with former epochs being interpreted and understood according to today's standards and methods; nevertheless, distance also affords the opportunity to assess historical phenomena differently and sometimes perhaps also more astutely than contemporaries of the period. Caesarism is no exception, since the experiences of the twentieth and twenty-first century have provided us with abundant material for insight and reflection unavailable to nineteenth-century observers.

In the present volume, the importance of a "historical analysis" is understood in yet another, perhaps more pragmatic respect: dealing with Caesarism primarily as an intellectual and "ideological" problem runs the risk of emphasizing just one aspect while neglecting the Machiavellian moments, material interests and actual politics—components without which the phenomenon cannot be adequately grasped. In order to minimize this danger and strengthen the "historical" dimension of the inquiry, the theoretical focus will be contextualized to underscore the specific configurations in which Caesarism came into being and was debated: not only by referring to (geo-) political, social and economic framework conditions in which debates took place, but also by addressing institutionalized forms of Caesarism and the policies of such regimes—though without any claim to offer exhaustive accounts of these regimes. Not only does this approach add a complementary dimension, it demonstrates the interplay of political discourse and political practice, as well as their reciprocal contingency. "Political ideas" and "concepts" are accordingly understood as embedded in and affected by existing settings, and part of an ongoing communicative process in actual historical moments inasmuch as the result and object of concrete political action and institutions. The present study is less a conceptual history or history of political thought *sensu stricto*, than it is a political history seeking to bridge political theory and political practice. Factoring in "concrete politics" is essential, since the role of empiricism for theory formation has tended to be neglected in Caesarism scholarship, increasing the risk of Caesarism becoming an empty formula for all kinds of "authoritarian rule".[18]

With regard to the **temporal and spatial limits of the present study**, there are no clear-cut "natural boundaries". This permits a certain degree of freedom, but also potential reproach for arbitrariness. As for the temporal limitation, preceding comments on Caesarism being an essentially (post-)revolutionary phenomenon fix a starting point in the late eighteenth century; a period, in which older lines of discourse (republicanism, absolutism, Enlightenment) clashed with a set of new ones.[19] More specifically, the examination will start with the French Revolution, taken as a culmination point of the Revolutionary Age in which the collision of democratic and monocratic imperatives was demonstrated even more distinctly than in the preceding American Revolution. It was from the French Revolution that Napoleon Bonaparte emerged as a key point of reference for most subsequent analysts of Caesarism. Setting a temporal endpoint is perhaps more difficult, since it could be argued that we are still living in a version of "post-revolutionary modernity". Nevertheless, rather than expanding the analysis to encompass the whole twentieth century, the First World War and the 1920s will serve as a general terminus: firstly, since the Great War and its political repercussions are widely accepted as a historical caesura; secondly, because the debate on Caesarism declined with the growing scientification of the term and the ensuing discourse on totalitarianism, respectively. Nevertheless, in what is conceived as an outlook chapter, the relation between Caesarism and totalitarianism as well as the long-term legacies of the Caesarism discourse will be examined, if only in outline.

A particular challenge has been setting spatial limits. Given the underlying understanding of Caesarism as an essentially universal phenomenon, it would certainly be desirable to investigate it in a pan-European or even global perspective, allowing for a well-balanced analysis of Caesaristic languages and practices employed in various national contexts. But even within a collaborative project this would hardly be manageable, particularly not for a timespan encompassing more than a century. For this reason, my focus will be on two national cases: France and Germany, which were both formative for the Caesarism discourse in the nineteenth century. This focus allows for the examination of patterns of transfer and reception between the two cases, though an "entangled history" of France and Germany in the proper sense of the word cannot be offered. Other national cases in specific periods will occasionally be taken into consideration as well, with an aim to providing a more complete picture of the significance of Caesarism in the (post-)revolutionary age.

In summary, the following issues of the (post-)revolutionary age emerge as **central research objects** of this study:

- The ambivalent heritage of the Revolution, popular and monarchical sovereignty, processes of democratization and radicalization, change and preservation, and the resulting problems and strategies of political legitimization.
- The changing foundations of political legitimacy and the shifts between traditional, rational and charismatic forms of rule; developments taking place within the context of changing patterns of "faith" and expectations of salvation characterized by an increasing desire to *Immanentise the Eschaton*,[20] that is to create a sort of "heaven on earth" within history.
- The importance of an emerging "public sphere"—as manifest, for example, in the emergence of mass media and political parties—for negotiating power, setting new frameworks for the exercise of power and promoting the emergence of new styles of government.
- The repercussions of industrialization and social change, as well as nationalism and imperialism on the organization of rule and political institutions.

In order to shed light on these issues in a structured manner, the inquiry is specifically arranged around the following **research questions**:

1. What was the context in which discourse on Caesarism developed and grew?
2. To what extent and by the use of which arguments was Caesarism seen as a specifically "new" form of political rule by contemporary observers and politicians, and what flaws and perils, but also possible strengths and promises, were considered inherent in Caesaristic regimes?

3. How great is the convergence and/or divergence between the politico-theoretical discourse on Caesarism on the one hand, and "Caesaristic politics" as well as institutionalized expressions of such politics on the other?
4. What is the long-term legacy of nineteenth- and early twentieth-century discourse on Caesarism, and its relevance for the contemporary world?

2

Revolution and Crisis

The adoption of the Federal Constitution on September 14, 1787 by the *Constitutional Convention* in Philadelphia and the successful—even if controversial—ratification of the document in the single states brought the American Revolution to a formal close.[1] At the same time, however, the "revolutionary-constitutional spirit" had already infected Europe and one country in particular: France. It was in the French Revolution that the radicalization of justifications for the organization of politics and society, and the replacement of traditional by new forms of political legitimacy—characterized by a language of "political suitability"—came to a climax.

2.1 The French Revolution: Sovereignty, Legitimacy and Radicalism

Perhaps the most fundamental single question dominating the debates of the French Revolution, which can reasonably be said to have begun on July 5, 1788, when King Louis XVI agreed to summon the Estates General (*États généraux*), was that of the definition of the "nation", to which the government was accountable. This question was answered in a both systematic and radical way in the most celebrated pamphlet of the period: Abbé Sieyès' *Qu'est-ce que le Tiers-Etat?*[2]

In "What is the Third Estate?", Sieyès expanded his earlier criticism of the traditional social order to a fundamental condemnation of the *Ancien Régime* as such and offered a new definition of "nation" and "sovereignty", which became the manifesto of the French revolutionary movement. According to Sieyès, the essence of the nation was based on the equality of citizens and the universality inherent in their exercise of a common will, thus reflecting two key premises of the American Revolution. For Sieyès, anyone who refused a common civic status automatically excluded himself from the political order. Therefore, in order to guarantee one general will, the three existing estates had to be abolished in favor of one common representation of the nation, symbolized by the Third Estate which up until then had been neglected: "What is the Third Estate? Everything. What has it been hitherto in the political order? Nothing. What does it desire? To be something."[3]

What Sieyès essentially did was to establish *la Nation* as a primordial political reality and invent a radical doctrine of national sovereignty clearly following from Rousseau's rhetoric of "popular sovereignty", but also marking a significant departure:

whereas Rousseau had interpreted representation as a feudal legacy inconsistent with the exercise of the general will, Sieyès saw representation as the quintessence of modern government. In both cases, however, constitutionalism was clearly subordinate to the principle of "popular" and "national sovereignty", respectively. For Sieyès, as for Rousseau before him, rule could only be legitimized by the people, this purpose dictating the constitution. According to this understanding, the nation also exists without a constitution and is—as *pouvoir constituant*—always set higher than the constitution: it is the nation that distributes and limits power, but above all safeguards its own fundamental rights.

The Constitution of 1791[4] reflected Sieyès' doctrine of unrestricted popular sovereignty coinciding with a highly hierarchical view of powers, not fundamentally different from the *Ancien Régime*: a nation absolute in its sovereignty was now at the top, taking the place of the former absolute monarch, whose rule had been based on the fundamental claim that "the sovereign power in his kingdom belongs to the king alone".[5] French revolutionary constitutionalism had shifted away from the idea of "popular sovereignty" and "separation of powers" prevalent in the American Revolution. There, both doctrines were interpreted in a rather restrictive and "protective" way. Remembering the powerful English legislature, the revolutionary elite in America considered a legislature unlimited in its power as the greatest danger to liberty. Separation of powers was therefore conceived as a system of mutual monitoring by each branch of government and as a means of preventing unrestricted majority rule. Thus, the dogma of popular sovereignty remained subservient to the principle of separation of powers and the idea of "limited government".[6] In France, the situation was quite the opposite, and separation of powers subordinated to popular sovereignty; there, historical experience dictated that the power of the executive be limited and the controlling power of the people strengthened. Separation of powers was therefore introduced to check an otherwise dominant executive through an even more powerful legislative.[7]

Yet no systemic stability derived from the Constitution, quite the contrary: with war beginning and extreme forces coming to the fore in the National Assembly, the French "republican monarchy"[8] established in 1791 soon proved to be unworkable. Among the main reasons for the failure of the first written French constitution was the unsolved problem of closing the gap between the claim for popular sovereignty and its representation; that is, who should actually represent the general will and translate it into actual policies.

On account of this ambiguity, the political thought of the Revolution became increasingly radicalized and the constitutional monarchy finally destroyed. The erosion of the monarchy, ultimately resulting in its abolition, was effectively accompanied by the progressing symbolic destruction of traditional kingship during the early years of the Revolution. The political imagination that solemnity and authority of state and nation were inseparably linked to and represented by the person of the king had long suffered under the influence of the Enlightenment.[9] From 1789 onwards, the delegitimization of (absolutist) monarchical rule accelerated dramatically, with the dismantling of divine-right monarchy taking place at multiple levels. Under the new Constitution, for example, the king was no longer addressed as "King of France and Navarre" (*Roi de France et de Navarre*), but "King of the French" (*Roi des Français*), thus making the reversal of claims for sovereignty obvious. No less important than the political-institutional disparagement was the people's symbolically taking possession of the monarch. When the royal apartments in the Tuileries were invaded by an armed populace on June 20, 1792, who forced the King to put on the *bonnet rouge* with the tricolor national cockade, Louis XVI was no longer a "ruler", nor even a "king of the people", but a powerless puppet at the mercy of the new sovereign.

Considering the symbolic demystification of king and "monarchy", the suspension of Louis XVI in August 1792 followed by his dethronement and the proclamation of the Republic in September appear somewhat inevitable. At this stage of the French Revolution it was no longer necessary for nor even desired by the political actors to follow a legalistic argument for this radical regime change. This made the events of 1792 distinct not only from the Glorious Revolution of 1688, but also from the American Declaration of Independence. In the latter case, the American Continental Congress in 1776 had at least justified the deposition of George III by legal arguments. In contrast, the French Legislative Assembly based its decision to suspend the king and call for a new constituent assembly on August 10, 1792 on far more general considerations such as "the dangers to the fatherland" and the "suspicions that the conduct of the head of the executive authority has aroused".[10] Clearly, a new criterion of legitimacy was developing, oriented primarily towards political rather than juridical reasoning: a criterion which was to become a characteristic feature of the nineteenth century and the concept of Caesarism in particular. For a ruler to be accepted by his subjects, more was needed than legalistic behavior. He also had to live up to certain expectations of "good" and "appropriate" policies, which might vary over time. In the critical situation of 1792, Louis XVI had obviously not managed to meet such expectations.

The overthrow of the constitutional monarchy by the "Second Revolution" of August 10, 1792[11] marked the beginning of a dramatic radicalization of the political and social sphere in France. Legal and moral arguments were almost entirely replaced by reasoning in terms of "political will" and "reign of virtue". Under the aegis of Maximilien Robespierre (1758–1794), a *de facto* dictatorship was set up by the Jacobins, the central organ of which was the Committee of Public Safety (*Comité de salut public*) founded on April 6, 1793. Established as the unchallenged executor of the popular will and considering itself to be an "emergency government" in a national crisis, the Committee not only postponed the enactment of the constitutional draft of June 24, 1793,[12] which had been ratified by popular vote in early August, but also suspended the rights guaranteed by the 1789 Declaration of the Rights of Man and of the Citizen. The Committee members reasoned that the *terreur* had to be continued relentlessly until the final victory over the Revolution's enemies, both foreign and domestic. Accordingly, thousands of executions against real and supposed enemies of the young Republic were carried out, while anti-revolutionary resistance—flaring up all around the country—was suppressed with utmost brutality.

In view of sustained terror and unrest in the country, domestic opposition against the Jacobins' rule grew, as was the demand for stable government and legal security. Shortly after the decisive victory over the Coalition Army at the Battle of Fleurus (June 26, 1794), Robespierre together with other radical revolutionaries was overthrown by the Thermidorian Reaction on July 27 (9 Thermidor).

Due to the negative experience of Jacobin rule, radical democratic concepts had lost much of their appeal. The new political rulers had no interest in enforcing the Constitution of 1793, and therefore initiated a new constitutional draft which entered into force in August 1795 ("Constitution of the Year III"). It was more conservative than its abortive predecessor and established a liberal republic with a franchise based on the payment of taxes, similar to that of the first French Constitution of 1791; a Constitution which it shared other important systemic similarities, too, despite the abandonment of unicameralism in favor of a bicameral system.[13]

Constitutional practice, however, soon proved to be sobering. Like its predecessor of 1791, the new Constitution failed to create any kind of durable constitutional stability. Though realizing the acute dangers of unrestricted popular sovereignty when carried to its extremes, the Thermidorians' attempt to find a solution was not promising: instead of reducing the omnipotence of the state, they tried to reduce the omnipotence of the people by introducing bicameral legislation and restricting suffrage. All they achieved was to create a disequilibrium of power which resulted in the renewed dominance of the executive branch. The four years of the Directory,[14] which tried to steer a course between conservative and radical-revolutionary aspirations, was a time of chronic disquiet. Continuous conflict between the directors and the chambers, but also within the executive, widespread corruption among the members of the directorate, and general maladministration as well as persisting legal uncertainty and arbitrariness heightened the unpopularity of the government, which was only able to maintain its power with the active support of the army.

Even by the second half of the 1790s, the state of exception and emergency, with which revolutionary France had been confronted since the late 1780s, was anything but over. This was manifest in the continuous wars against other European powers as much as in the continued incapacity to establish a durable political and institutional order domestically. Under such circumstances it is no wonder that the call for a stabilizing factor became louder, especially after new electoral success for the Jacobins in 1799 heralded another radical rule of the chambers. What was at stake was nothing less than finding a way out of the fundamental crisis, in which the Revolution found itself *en permanence*.

The challenge of the time was striking a balance between "liberty" and "order"; or, to put it another way: to continue the Thermidorian Reaction in a more sustainable way than the Directory had been able to do. Paying tribute to the legacy of the Revolution essentially meant preserving the tangible socio-economic improvements a considerable part of French society had enjoyed since 1789, but also acknowledging the Revolution's core political principle of popular and national sovereignty. What had in fact shaped the French Revolution during all its phases from 1789 onwards was the doctrine of the absolute sovereignty of the people and its *pouvoir constituant*. To subscribe to these principles in one way or other was hence the *conditio sine qua non* for every political regime claiming to be "progressive" and keen to distance itself from traditional forms of political legitimacy personified by monarchists and reactionaries at home and abroad. It was in this particular context that Napoleon Bonaparte achieved power and that the debate about a "new Caesar", which had started almost immediately after the outbreak of the Revolution, moved to the center of political discourse.

Before turning to Napoleon Bonaparte and examining the political regime that was to become lastingly associated with his name ("Bonapartism"; "Napoleonism"), it may be worthwhile to briefly explore in more abstract terms the "Dilemma of the Revolution" as a project of radical change, out of which the quest for strong personalized leadership and a "new Caesar" developed its dynamics at the end of the eighteenth century.

2.2 The Dilemma of the Revolution and the Quest for Leadership

While utopianism and progressivism helped to intellectually propel the "project of modernity" from the Middle Ages onwards, it was revolutionary activism which finally guaranteed "modernity" its political breakthrough and helped to anchor it as the age of ideologies and secularization in the collective consciousness. The "Great Revolutions"[15] and the French Revolution in particular were characterized by a radical change of political organization, marked by the removal or fundamental reformation of existing forms of rule and culminating in new political rules, symbols, and sources of legitimacy. The attempt to renew the body politic along the lines of certain ideas of a "just" body politic to allow the people to participate in politics as present in the Great Revolution(s) was nothing entirely novel. What was new, however, was linking these recurrent protest themes with specifically "modern" elements such as the belief in progress, argued to be "universal", or the claim for unrestricted access to the center of political power. What was innovative, too, was combining such themes with general utopian visions of political and social renewal regarded to be politically possible; visions that—intellectually prepared by the cultural project of the Enlightenment— were often propagated with missionary zeal.

Running parallel to changing patterns in what was politically acceptable and desirable was a far-reaching downgrading of established concepts of legitimacy. Tradition and the idea of an "authority of the past", which had long served as a regulator for social change, were replaced by "renewal" as a cultural orientation benchmark and the decisive component of legitimacy, thus fundamentally changing the character of politics: it was no longer possible to found rule exclusively upon faith in what previously existed;[16] political institutions were now forced to assert their legitimacy by continuous activism and innovation. In point of fact, the more rational and economic the understanding of political institutions was, the more replaceable the rulers became if they did not meet public expectations. The destiny of Louis XVI was a highly instructive example in this respect.

This was a favorable situation for new political elites to assume power, and especially leaders disposing of what was later to be termed "charisma"; leaders who due to their sheer strength of personality and the extraordinary abilities ascribed to them might seem to fulfill the kinds of expectations created by the Enlightenment and the Revolution. Full of utopian-visionary vigor, they personified the aspirations of the "new era" and promised to fill at least partly the vacuum created by the supersession of the transcendental God. Susceptibility to monocratic leadership in general was favored by the fact that—despite the universalization of the principle of popular sovereignty—the centuries-old experience of rule by one was too pervasive to be replaced *in toto*. This was all the more the case due to the pragmatic reasoning that the decision-making procedure was faster if made by an individual than by a group: an argument particularly important in a period of domestic tumult and foreign-political danger.

The desire for a "hero" and "saviour", representing revolutionary principles and dynamism but holding out at the same time their finality had existed before Napoleon's rise to power. Since 1790 demands for an end or at least a stabilization of the Revolution had increasingly set the tone of political discourse.[17] Given that the figure of the traditional monarch was ousted as a political alternative, while the desire for a "personification of power" was still manifest, the dilemma now was how a collective and sovereign "nation" could be personified by an individual. One potential solution to this dilemma was the blueprint of Roman Caesarism, reflecting a remarkable change in the perception of the historical figure and political deeds of Julius Caesar.

For many centuries—with the history of the Greek and Roman world continuing to be an ever-present point of reference, furnishing a storehouse of symbols, allegories, arguments and archetypes—*Caesar* had always aroused strong feelings among intellectuals. Some of these feelings were laudatory; but over time another discourse became dominant, namely that of political "republicanism", envisaging Caesar as a historical symbol for some of the most dangerous tendencies a polity could experience.[18] In the context of republican depiction from the early fifteenth to the end of the eighteenth century, Caesar was repeatedly summoned as the gravedigger of the Roman Republic. Structural fissures in the Republic had provided him, and to a slighter extent precursors such as the Gracchi brothers or Marius, with opportunities which had been exploited rigorously.

Caesar's conduct was used time and again to illustrate the contrast to actions motivated by true republican values and, above all, political liberty, envisaged as freedom from tyranny and the right to take an active part in political decision-making. Both Niccolò Machiavelli (1469–1527) and Francesco Guicciardini (1483–1540) invoked the "detestable and monstrous" Caesar,[19] and Montesquieu in the eighteenth century did not see much worthy of praise, particularly when comparing Caesar with other figureheads of the Ancient World such as Alexander the Great. While Caesar had sought monarchy as an ornament of ostentation, wishing to "imitate the kings of Asia", and while the Romans had "conquered all in order to destroy all", Alexander's purpose had been "to conquer in order to preserve all": "in every country he entered, his first ideas, his first designs, were always to do something to increase its prosperity and power".[20] Montesquieu, however, was also able to identify the faults of republican government preparing the ground for a Caesar, namely the spirit of extreme equality which was not at all the true spirit of equality: where such a spirit prevailed, Montesquieu argued, a republic would open itself up to demagogues who "speak only of the people's greatness".[21]

However, envisaging him not only as an abominable tyrant marking a transformation of types of government, but also as a systemic product of ill-guided (republican) government, heralded a shift in the interpretation of Caesar, who could be seen as an example of syndromes to which all political systems were prone, perhaps even as a "necessary evil". Attempts to cast a slur on Caesar by emphasizing his misconduct and by contrasting him with "republican heroes" such as Cato the Younger continued to be prominent in England, America and France at the time of their revolutions, but by the eighteenth century the ground had been cleared for a more sympathetic assessment of Caesar's accomplishments.[22] This was particularly the case with respect to his role of guaranteeing order and lawfulness, actually an interpretation in line with some older tradition, according to which Caesar had imposed the discipline and sound government Rome required.

Facilitated by this change in perception it was even before 1789—with the legitimacy crisis of the *Ancien Régime* aggravating in view of enlightened philosophy, acceleration of social change in the wake of proto-industrialization, disintegration of the state, and the disruption of public finances—that the myth of a "new Caesar" gained ground.[23] For pre-revolutionary writers such as Anne-Robert-Jacques Turgot (1727–1781) and Simon-Nicholas Henri Linguet (1736–1794) the legitimacy of a new Caesar derived from the fact that he would leave the old (feudal) order behind and save society from civil war, based on the premise that a state of civil war was already latently evident.[24] The ways in which the "new Caesar" and his role were portrayed remained sketchy and inconsistent, though: for Turgot, the main task of the *chef d'état* was to assume a moderating role between antagonistic classes of society; Linguet, on the other hand, envisaged a radical concentration of power in the hands of a *bon roi*, advocate of the suppressed, who would fulfill the middle classes' craving for a strong state order.[25] Yet despite the fact that appraisals of a "new Caesar" were certainly in the minority and found only limited public resonance, visions like those of Turgot and Linguet demonstrated that there was potential for a "popular dictatorship" based on the principles of progress and stability. At least at a theoretical level, the role of some kind of Caesaristic "saviour of society" had already been defined, even before the *Ancien Régime* plunged into the vortex of revolutionary upheaval.

It is against the background of a shifting "Caesar" discourse—hand in hand with the incremental development of a "negative great parallel" between the ancient and modern world[26]—that observers of the time tried to make sense of the events of the French Revolution. Among them was Edmund Burke, whose critical analysis of the Revolution in his *Reflections on the Revolution in France*[27] soon became an object both of fervent admiration and animosity.[28] As early as 1790 he famously predicted that at the end of the war France would not only become a republic, but that a victorious general would seize unlimited power. In line with his central argument that the French Revolution had to end in disaster because it was based on abstract notions purporting to be rational but in fact ignoring the complexities of human nature and society, Burke anticipated that instability and disorder would make the army:

> mutinous and full of faction, until some popular general, who understands the Art of conciliating the soldiery, and who possesses the true spirit of command, shall draw the eyes of all men upon himself. Armies will obey him on his personal account. [...] But the moment in which that event shall happen, the person who really commands the army is your master; the master (that is little) of your king, the master of your assembly, the master of your whole republic.[29]

Burke's prediction was not only the result of the belief that the army was the only institution that would come out intact from revolutionary turmoil, but also of widespread historical analogy with ancient Caesarism: "dictatorship" in its ancient manifestation represented a potential and indeed familiar construct of rule which might bring about "personal rule". This element of the "negative great parallel" was often interlinked with the argument—common not only among conservative critics of the Revolution—that the very concept of republicanism was illogical or anachronistic under modern conditions, and the idea of "popular government" a mere chimera. In this vein, Joseph de Maistre (1753–1821) declared in his *Considerations on France* of 1796 that:

> [. . .] the efforts of a people to obtain a goal are precisely the means that [Providence] employs to keep them from it. Thus, the Roman people gave themselves masters while believing they were opposing the aristocracy by following Caesar. That is the image of all popular insurrections.[30]

The vision of dictatorial rule by a charismatic military leader raised fears, but expectations as well: no matter how unconstitutional the prospect of such rule might be *per se*, there was also hope that the temporary transfer of power to a "new Caesar" could secure the Constitution in the long term. This concept was close to what Carl Schmitt was later to characterize as "commissarial dictatorship":[31] declaring a state of emergency in order to save the legal order. Based on the Roman precedent, Schmitt defended this type of dictatorship as a "crisis mode" of rule that would suspend legality solely for the protection of society at large and, once the danger was over, restore the *status quo ante*. Such a "commissarial" dictatorship stood in contrast to "sovereign" dictatorship, in which law was suspended not to save an existing Constitution, but to found an entirely new social and political order with unlimited powers for those ruling. From a legal-philosophical perspective, commissarial dictatorship is thus a vital means to provide endangered "normality" with the stability vital for the application and effectuality of law: dictatorship restores the unison between *Sein* ("Is") and *Sollen* ("Ought") by suspending the legal norm temporarily in order to allow for the *Rechtsverwirklichung* ("realization of law").

In the early period of the French Revolution, the man most likely to represent some sort of a "commissarial dictator" was Marquis de La Fayette (1757–1834), "hero of two worlds"[32] with the status of a public idol. The Parisians adored him and his vision of a new and stable nation, with prosperity guaranteed by a constitution and the powerful National Guard under his command, and it was not just Mirabeau who claimed the mantle of a "modern-day Caesar" for La Fayette.[33] In the end, however, all speculation about La Fayette seizing power was unjustified: not so much due to insurmountable practical difficulties or the polemics of his enemies, but because of his personal reluctance to take the reins of state power into his own hands. La Fayette stunned friends and enemies alike in 1790 by rejecting the post of "national commander", which had been offered to him, just as he had rejected political power in the National Assembly before, declaring that nationwide control of the Guard would provide too much power for one man and risk replacing royal autocracy with a military autocracy.[34] Like his former American comrade in arms (and in many ways inspiring example) George

Washington (1732–1799), La Fayette, too, defied the temptation to seek the role of a "new Caesar". In common with his American paragon, La Fayette was convinced that the principles of liberty, equality and justice could best be guaranteed by personal commitment to strict legalism and adherence to the existing constitution.

Maximilien Robespierre had fewer scruples about setting up a personal dictatorship. He had no reservations whatsoever in propagating the idea that the nation—torn apart by internal power struggles, (anti-revolutionary) riots and social conflicts—was in dire need of a firm hand. What Robespierre was able to offer was revolutionary ideology and rhetoric, the evocation of axiomatic "principles" and the warning of the "enemy". Rule of "reason" and "virtue" by the *terreur* was the underlying principle of the Jacobin regime, which Robespierre combined with personal moral authority. The rule of the Committee of Public Safety had none of the characteristics of a commissarial dictatorship. Rather, Robespierre's regime had clear features of "sovereign dictatorship", to refer to Schmitt's terminology, unlimited in its parameters and seeking to perpetuate itself, even if it used its power under the pretense of merely "temporary" circumstances. But the "charisma" of Robespierre—which was more the charisma of the revolutionary principle of reason than a genuine personal one[35]—shattered the moment the domestic and foreign threat to the "revolutionary nation" attenuated. Under the auspices of "normalization", the methods of his Reign of Terror were no longer acceptable in the pursuit of a legitimate political order, and in July 1794 Robespierre lost both power and life within a matter of three days.

The quest for a charismatic "saviour", however, did not stop. This was all the more so since the Directory succeeding the *terreur* was far from capable of fulfilling such expectations: neither with respect to its character as a collective body, nor concerning the actual personality of its leaders and their policies, which caused widespread disappointment in the French public. At this very historical moment the conditions were favorable for a military leader with fewer personal scruples than a La Fayette, but a less radical agenda than Robespierre, to assume power: a chance, Napoleon Bonaparte eventually seized.

2.3 Napoleon Bonaparte: Saviour or Despot?

Hardly anyone in world history has attracted as much attention as Napoleon Bonaparte,[36] and the immense number of literary, artistic and scholarly works dealing with his life and heritage bears witness to this fact.[37] Up to the present day, the interpretation of Napoleon and his achievements is controversial and ranges from seeing him as the progressively-minded trailblazer for a modern Europe to characterizing him as nothing more than a power-hungry and egomaniacal despot. However, no matter how much views may differ over Napoleon's character—the followers of "The Man of Destiny" and the "tragic exile of St. Helena" camps clashing with the "sheep-worrier of Europe", "Corsican Ogre" and "talented thug" schools of thought—, one personal quality is rarely questioned even by critics: his skills as a leader and as a virtuoso of power.

What is of interest here is not whether Napoleon is a person to be admired or despised, but the question as to the foundation stones and instruments of his regime later termed "Napoleonism" or "Bonapartism", and how his rule was interpreted by contemporaries. Let us first turn to Napoleon's rise to power and his—and his regime's—legitimization strategies and self-display.

2.3.1 Rise to Power, "Great Parallel" and Legitimacy

"Men of genius are meteors destined to be consumed in illuminating their century", wrote the then as yet unknown Napoleon in 1791,[38] but it was not until his first military victories as commander in charge in Italy that Napoleon started to think of himself as one of them.[39] By then, Napoleon had moved on from a supporter of Robespierre,[40] after whose fall he had been briefly imprisoned, to become a protégée of the most powerful man in the Directory, Barras, whose confidence he had gained after the suppression of the royalist revolt on *13 Vendémiaire* (October 5, 1795).[41] The successful Italian Campaign, resulting in the Treaty of Campo Formio in 1797, which guaranteed the French "Sister Republics" in Italy, extended the borders of France up to the Rhine, the Nette and the Rur and rang in the collapse of the First Coalition, marked the beginning of the "legend" of Napoleon. His military, diplomatic and administrative achievements had made him not only a public hero, but an influential figure in French politics, too. Even the less fortunate course of the Egyptian expedition could not lastingly damage his reputation as the "undefeated general" and "peacemaker", which was also due to the fact that Napoleon continued to demonstrate his talent as a master of propaganda. Even in February 1797 he had launched the Parisian *Le Journal de Bonaparte et des hommes vertueux*, whose title could be seen as a challenge to the moral character of the government itself and bore testimony to Napoleon's growing confidence. The foundation of the *Courrier de l'Armée de l'Italie ou le patriote français à Milan* and *La France vue de l'armée d'Italie* followed a couple of months later: ostensibly for the troops, but widely circulated in France as well, serving as a vehicle for praising Bonaparte and conveying his political ideas to the larger audience back home.[42]

In view of Napoleon's growing popularity, together with his rising political clout, it was long before the events of 18 Brumaire that contemporaries regarded him as "the man to be": not only observers in France, but also abroad, including the German writer Christoph Martin Wieland (1733–1813). In 1777 Wieland had already vindicated a "natural" right to rule for the most vigorous in a body politic, arguing that human nature was characterized by an "innate instinct to recognise that one as our natural superior, leader and ruler and be willingly guided and mastered by him, whose authority we feel".[43] He viewed hereditary monarchy as the most gentle and indeed most common form of such authority, but not the only one. Human history and particularly periods of civil war had proved over and over again that there was always a man making his way to the top of the political order, for which Caesar and Cromwell were mentioned as historical examples. It was against the background of this unconventional theoretical reasoning, by which hereditary monarchs were functionally at no other level than any other kind of "leader", that two decades later Wieland predicted not only the end of the French Republic, as Burke had before him, but named Bonaparte the man who was destined to become "the saviour of the entire world ". In his prognosis for a "Lord Protector" and "Dictator" in March 1798, Wieland—despite his personal reservations—declared Napoleon a man "of the sort one rarely sees in a century, and whose genius discerns how to be respected by all others and to overpower them",[44] and who alone was able to transform the "democracy tottering amidst so many parties and factions" into a stable political system.[45]

While the moment for an open coup had not yet com, Napoleon himself became more active in reflecting on the need to transform and reorganize the French political system. In a confidential letter written to the newly appointed foreign minister Talleyrand in autumn 1797,[46] Napoleon openly questioned why the legislative branch should be entrusted with comprehensive rights in a nation based on the principle of popular sovereignty, mentioning the right to declare war and peace as a practical example: "why, in a government whose whole authority emanates from the nation; why, where the sovereign is the people, should one include among the functions of the legislative power things which are foreign to it?" In his opinion, governmental power "ought to be regarded as the real representative of the nation, governing in virtue of the constitutional charter and the organic laws", and should therefore be considerably strengthened in its powers. In such a system, the legislative branch—effectively restricted—"would have no ambitions, and would not inundate us with thousands of ephemeral measures, whose very absurdity defeats their own ends, and which have turned us into a nation with 300 law books in folio, and not a single law".[47]

Tellingly, in his letter Napoleon asked Talleyrand to present his ideas solely to Sieyès: the man, who two years later was to play a decisive part in preparing the 18 Brumaire. It was the "Failure of the Liberal Republic"[48] and the sustaining political instability which provoked Sieyès—who had returned to politics with the Directory— to consider a *coup d'état* in order to paralyse the domestic political adversaries on the right and left, and to "terminate the Revolution"[49] while safeguarding its achievements. That the army should play a decisive role merely underlined the fact that the military had become a key political force since 1789, and it was perhaps the first time since the English Civil War and Oliver Cromwell that power in a major European state lay so clearly with the armed forces. However, Sieyès and his fellow conspirators still envisaged a "parliamentary coup" with the army just as abettor, and Napoleon did not originally play a leading role in the conspiracy, nor was he even the Brumairians' first choice.[50] In the end, the 18 Brumaire turned out to be not so much an individual endeavor by Napoleon, but a "joint venture", as Isser Woloch puts it,[51] arranged by an elite who had done financially well out of the Revolution and wanted to protect themselves and their economic, social and political position against royalist reaction as well as against Jacobin egalitarianism.

The success of the attempted seizure of power, which had been prepared well in advance, was anything but certain and could have easily ended in disaster. This was particularly true since Napoleon did not personally shine in the coup which would eventually bring him to power. Above all, it was his brother Lucien's presence of mind that saved the day.[52] In the official version of the coup, however, which was posted in Paris and reprinted in the *Moniteur*, no mention was made of Lucien nor Sieyès. Rather, the events of 19 Brumaire—resulting in the Council of Ancients (upper house) passing a decree which adjourned parliament for three months, appointed Napoleon,

Sieyès, and Ducos provisional consuls, and named two Legislative Commissions—were contorted and portrayed as a plot against Napoleon's life. Napoleon managed to gain center stage, and the proclamation reveals how he perceived himself and wanted to be perceived: as someone who was above party politics and as the restorer of moderation.[53]

The use of military force in the coup and the official presentation of the events had strengthened Napoleon's hand *vis-à-vis* Sieyès and the other conspirators, an opportunity he seized to accomplish his "coup within the coup". Despite sobering experiences made with weak and collective executives during successive phases of the Revolution, Sieyès still feared the concentration of power in one man alone. He believed in a strong, yet divided and layered executive branch, and therefore proposed installing a *grand électeur*—designated for life—as head of state, whose sole governing function was to appoint and dismiss the two chief executive officers of the state. But Napoleon dismissed the proposition to install himself as grand elector, and thus Sieyès' intricate design to stymie the young "general of action".[54] Instead, Napoleon had his vision of concentrated executive power accepted in the drafting committee for a new constitution, with supreme authority to be vested in a "first consul" for a ten-year term, who would be backed by a second and third consul meant to provide advice and help, but whose consent was otherwise not necessary for any decision. In the end, although much of the nomenclature of the Consulate could be associated with Sieyès's thought, the spirit of the regime derived from Napoleon's will.

The lack of public reaction after Brumaire could be interpreted as implicit support for the events, and encouraged Napoleon to proceed in organizing and institutionalizing his power. While Jacobin resistance was quickly quelled in the provinces,[55] the commissions proceeded in drawing up the "Constitution of the Year VIII".[56] When Dominique Joseph Garat (1749–1833)—a man of liberal convictions and an active revolutionary throughout the 1790s—brought the drafting process to a closure on 23 Frimaire (December 14) with an address celebrating the new Constitution's achievements, the ascendancy of Napoleon Bonaparte had become a *fait accompli*:

> For the execution of the laws you intended to give to the laws a power which is as powerful as the laws are sacred; an executive power which, by its unity, is always in action and in accord; by its speed, reaches everything; by having initiative in lawmaking, can assimilate into the republic's code all the fruits of experience and all positive enlightenment about government; by its irresponsibility [*sic*!] is an immutable fixed point, around which everything becomes solid and constant.[57]

The new constitutional order was clearly tailored to fit Napoleon as First Consul and entrusted him with comprehensive powers. While the executive branch was concentrated in one person, the character of the legislature was diffuse, with three distinct houses: a *Sénat conservateur* of 80 men, a *Tribunat* composed of 100, and a *Corps législatif* with 300 members. The power of the legislature was not only weakened by this institutional separation and limited rights, but also by a complicated system of indirect elections being introduced, allowing the executive to exert its influence on the composition of the three houses. Even more importantly, the legislature could no longer claim to have any direct popular legitimacy. The only political institution that could lay claim to representing the popular will was the First Consul. This was by means of an instrument which was to become archetypal not only for Napoleon's rule, but also later regimes associated with "Bonapartism" or "Napoleonism": plebiscites. Being its only true electoral acts, plebiscites were both anchor point and main source of legitimacy for the complex system of the Consulate, and indeed a novelty in modern French—and generally Western—politics and democratic constitution making.

After its adoption on September 17, 1787 by the Constitutional Convention in Philadelphia, the United States Constitution had been ratified by conventions in each of the thirteen founding states acting in the name of the people rather than by popular vote. Similarly, the French Constitution of 1791 had been adopted by decision of the *Assemblée nationale constituante* and directly enacted with its acceptance by Louis XVI, without any further approval of the document by the nation. The immanent logic of the procedure was that the constitutions had been created by the elected representatives of the nation anyway and thus did not require any further endorsement. After the downfall of the monarchy in 1792, France had trodden new paths in legitimizing constitutions democratically. Under the National Convention (*Convention nationale*) as the country's elected new constitutional and legislative assembly from September 20, 1792 onwards, both the Constitution of 1793 (which was never actually enforced) and that of 1795 were subjected to a referendum after being passed. Thus, strictly speaking the Convent actually changed its character from a constituent to a constitution-suggesting body. Yet if it was only by the vote of the nation that a constitutional draft could obtain legal force, one might also conclude that the elaboration of such a draft could also be left to a body not elected by the nation. This was the case with the Consular Constitution drafted under the aegis of Napoleon.[58] After its public proclamation on December 15, the new Consular Constitution was enacted on December 24, without prior public confirmation in a referendum. What Art. 95 provided, however, was that "The present constitution shall be offered immediately for the acceptance of the French people". This happened in February 1800 and hence only after a couple of weeks in which the Constitution had already been in force, lending the vote of the nation no longer a constitutive, but only an acclamatory character.[59]

Thus, the popular vote on the 1799 Constitution was not a referendum as those on the Constitutions of 1793 and 1795, but a plebiscite; a distinction in terminology which has to be made, even though it does not quite reflect the use at the time, since the referenda under the National Convention were formally called *plébiscites*, while the plebiscite of Napoleon was termed *appel au peuple*.[60] The differences between referendum and plebiscite are quite obvious, despite the fact that both are essentially enquiries directed at the "sovereign nation": the referenda of 1793 and 1795 were initiated by the National Convention as effective part of the constitution-making process. In contrast, the plebiscite of February 1800 was called by the First Consul for an *ex post* legitimization not only of a constitutional framework already in force, but especially the person of the First Consul after his seizing of power. The character of a "personal vote of confidence" was manifest in that the Constitution of 1799—unlike its two predecessors—mentioned the heads of state (namely the Consuls) by name.

Much was at stake for Napoleon in February 1800, when he utilized this new but also potentially powerful instrument of democratic legitimization for the first time. A negative outcome of the plebiscite with eligibility to vote approximating universal male suffrage was not an option and had to be prevented at all costs. Accordingly, all necessary arrangements were made to guarantee the desired result, above all by putting a suitable voting procedure in place: unlike in the referenda of 1793 and 1795, in 1800 voting took place by writing one's name in official registers. With the prospect of being filed as a "No" voter, many potential critics were well-advised not to openly challenge the new regime, and the number of dismissive votes proved to be marginal. However, with roughly 1.6 million votes the number of those endorsing the Constitution remained clearly under what had been expected, particularly since eligibility to vote had approximated universal male suffrage. Wishing to bolster the Consulate's—and above all Napoleon's—image with a stronger mandate than the 2 million votes recorded for the Jacobin Constitution of 1793, the government and especially Lucien Bonaparte as Minister of the Interior therefore falsified the results by adding 900,000 fictitious "Yes" votes and creating around 500,000 military votes out of thin air. As a result, more than 3 million official *oui* were announced.[61] Thus, even the first "Bonapartist" plebiscite demonstrated both the fragility of plebiscitary legitimacy and the manipulative ways in which political leadership could influence the desired outcome.

No matter how much fraud had been involved, the plebiscite served its purpose to demonstrate democratic legitimization for the First Consul. At the same time, the confirmation of the new constitutional order in February 1800 marked the ultimate success of the Brumaire coup and the definite end of the "radical Revolution". The "conservative"—or rather "conservatory"—character of the new regime was obvious in several respects,[62] including the recourse to the terminology of the Roman Republic. Referring to the ancient institutions of "Consul", "Tribune" and "Senator" communicated stability, order and peace: the Consulate was still a republic based on the will of the people, but one which followed well-tried historical traditions rather than dangerous "republican experiments" as during the Jacobin rule. However, in invoking analogies with antiquity, another, somewhat ambiguous parallel to Roman history seemed to be even more compelling for contemporaries, namely the one between Napoleon and Caesar. Bonapartist propaganda soon realized the potential in instrumentalizing Caesar and presenting the new First Consul as the "successor" of the man who had brought an end to the civil war and crisis of the Roman Republic: an analogy which might strengthen Napoleon's political position and prepare the ground for the institutionalization of his power.

Soon after the plebiscite on the Consular Constitution, Lucien Bonaparte commissioned a 16-page pamphlet—published anonymously, but most likely drafted by Louis-Marcelin de Fontanes (1757–1821)—tellingly entitled *Parallèle entre César, Cromwell, Monck et Bonaparte,* in which Napoleon's achievements were linked with those of Caesar while distinguished from other leaders in world history.[63] The pamphlet starts with a comparison of Napoleon with Cromwell and finds no parallels between the two men whatsoever, with the two described as diametric opposites. Cromwell is presented as a revolutionary zealot and tyrant, the leader of a bloodthirsty faction, a conqueror only in civil war, and a barbarian who had ravaged the Universities of Cambridge and Oxford. The "heir" of Cromwell in the French Revolution was Robespierre. In contrast, Bonaparte is portrayed as someone who with immense glory has washed away the crimes that were not his, who has abolished the barbaric party instituted in honor of the regicide, and who has put an end to the horrors of revolutionary fanaticism. Nor were any similarities found between Bonaparte and General George Monck (1608–1670), a key figure in the restoration of Charles II in England, whose vulgar vanity was contrasted with the grandeur of France's hero of Brumaire: "It is to the Martels and the Charlemagnes, not to the Moncks, that Bonaparte should be compared."[64] The only proper and legitimate historical analogy was the one between Bonaparte and Caesar, albeit obvious differences had to be acknowledged:

> They were both born in the midst of civil wars, and both ended those wars. But Caesar did so by overwhelming the fairest faction, and Bonaparte by rallying citizens against the brigands. In this, Bonaparte and Caesar, while similar as men of war, differ as politicians.[65]

While "Caesar was a usurper and tribune of the people, Bonaparte is a legitimate consul".[66] Nevertheless, parallels in character and destiny could not be denied, including their capacity as leaders to be almost superhuman in nature. Bonaparte and Caesar, as well as Alexander the Great, "often had the same theatrical sense of glory; all three triumphed through their lieutenants; all three brought the arts and the sciences to barbarian lands". The two heros of antiquity had a great influence on the future, the pamphlet stated, but "will the influence of the French hero last as long?"[67] The actual political concern of the pamphlet was how Napoleon's "genius" could be institutionalized long term. The author examined the political alternatives in the event of the sudden death of Bonaparte: rule by a parliamentary body, a military dictatorship, or a counter-revolutionary government, none of which would actually be desirable. The pamphlet's conclusion was therefore clear-cut: in order to avoid future chaos and arbitrariness, Napoleon's rule should be made "immortal".[68] This was basically an open invitation for some kind of hereditary rule to be established.

Public reception of the widely-distributed propaganda pamphlet, however, was overwhelmingly negative.[69] Napoleon, who, it seems, had approved and most likely copyedited the pamphlet, dissociated himself from it, and laid all blame on his brother Lucien, effecting a breach between them.[70] This was a lesson for Napoleon, who became cautious not to overdo the "great parallel" between Caesar and himself in public. He realized the danger involved in equating the new First Consul with the Roman general, particularly since the latter could be seen as the "terminator" of the Roman Republic rather than the bringer of stability and order. Even on 19 Brumaire he had been openly denounced in the Council of Five Hundred (lower house) as "Caesar, Cromwell, Tyrant", and had had to struggle to defend himself against such accusations.[71] In the years to come, Napoleon therefore abstained from publicly giving the impression of his striving to become a "new Caesar". At the same time, however, he continued to make use of the comparison in more intimate moments. Five years after the coup, for example, he promised his first wife Joséphine: "I will take you to London, madam [...] I intend the wife of the 'modern Caesar' shall be crowned at Westminster."[72] At their meeting in Erfurt on October 2, 1808, Napoleon later advised Goethe:

to write a tragedy about the death of Caesar—one really worthy of the subject, a greater one than Voltaire's. That could be the finest task you undertake. You would have to show the world how Caesar would have been its benefactor, how everything would have turned out quite differently if he had been given time to carry out his magnificent plans.[73]

The negative reception of the pamphlet demonstrated the ambivalence of the Caesar analogy, but also the danger of a sudden break with the republican tradition in favor of monarchical rule. It was one thing to argue for a new constitutional order with a strong executive to overcome political instability, but it was an entirely different matter to establish a formal hereditary monarchy. Revealingly, *de jure* the Consular Constitution of 1800 remained in force until 1814 and was formally only amended, but it was exactly those "amendments" which reflected Napoleon's consistent—eventually successful—efforts to strengthen his personal power. The first step was the extension of Napoleon's authority by making him First Consul for Life ("Constitution of the Year X");[74] the second the establishment of the hereditary Empire ("Constitution of the Year XII").[75]

On his way from Consulate to Empire, Napoleon could depend on the help and support of active collaborators, who wished to see Bonaparte's power further enhanced.[76] In backstage lobbying for a lifelong Consulate, Napoleon skillfully made use of the argument that this new arrangement assured the stability and durability of the Consulate and placed the first consul on a level with foreign sovereigns. Behind the facade of the Senate and Council of State, Napoleon effectively pushed for a plebiscite on the question[77] and personally outlined the proposition to be voted on by the French people: "Shall Napoleon Bonaparte be named first consul for life?" The plebiscite of 1802 was the second instance whereby Napoleon sought public confirmation of his policies, but it was the first time the vote was exclusively concerned with Bonaparte's personal title and power. The results were reassuring and reflected the impressive progress in popular acceptance of Napoleon's power: unlike two years before, the announced turnout of about 3.6 million "Yes" votes—to only 8,374 "No" votes—was in the main accurate, surpassing the absolute majority of eligible voters.[78] Even though one can conjecture that most critics of Napoleon did not even cast their ballot, this was an impressive acknowledgement of Napoleon's popularity, resting on indubitable domestic and foreign political achievements.

In his first two years as head of the French state, Napoleon had not only provided security for the middle classes, who had profited both from social advancement and the purchase of the *biens nationaux*, but also for the peasantry interested in guarantees for their new legal status and the durable preservation of their property. Moreover, he had also gained the workers' trust in fighting high inflation during the Directory and creating new jobs by boosting the economy, while reaping the gratitude of many former *émigrés*, whose return to France was made possible due to the moderation of domestic politics and improvements to the security situation in the country. Economic and fiscal recovery and success in fighting hunger and unemployment was perhaps more important for the population than the military victories so enthusiastically celebrated by Bonapartist partisans. But they, too, were important building blocks in promoting the First Consul's popularity and creating the "Napoleonic legend", particularly, since the triumphs on the battlefield and France's ascent to a hegemonic power in Europe not only flattered national pride, but also helped to promote domestic prosperity.

Popular support for the new "man of courage" was actively promoted by massive propaganda and the instrumentalization of the *beaux-arts*, museums, architecture, design and music, which in return profited from government gratuities and state sponsorship. Due to the fact that the whole political regime was almost exclusively adjusted to the First Consul, a personality cult started to take shape, and gradually an idealized public image of Napoleon as the nation's saviour emerged: a development, however, which did not always meet with Napoleon's approval, since he had no desire to nourish Jacobin and royalist opposition.[79] The fact that the political construction of the Consulate stood and fell with Napoleon favored his transformation into a public hero, but this raised the question as to what would happen in the event of his sudden death. This question was no less urgent even with the successful plebiscite on a lifelong consulate.

The conversion of the Republic into a quasi-monarchy was heralded by significant changes in the ceremonies of power, manifest, for example, in Napoleon residing at the *Palais du Luxembourg* and reinstating a court with highly formalized etiquette and dress codes, in which the revolutionary-egalitarian *tu*-form was abandoned. As regards the fundamental matter of succession, however, Napoleon displayed a rather unclear attitude at the beginning, most likely because he had no natural offspring and male heir so far and could not see any of his brothers being potential candidates. On one earlier occasion he had emphasized that "heredity has never been instituted by law [...] it has always been established by fact [...]", concluding that "the French at this moment can only be governed by me" and that "my natural heir is the French people".[80]

But the situation changed in 1804: a thwarted royalist conspiracy under the leadership of Georges Cadoudal (1771–1804) and the danger of assassination not only served as a pretext to toughen censorship and repression, but also became the catalyst for establishing an empire and solving the problem of succession at the same time. As before, Napoleon left the initiative to others. Michel Regnaud de St. Jean d'Angély (1760–1819) and the four presidents of the Council of State's other sections emphatically linked their proposal to an hereditary empire with a reaffirmation of the Revolution's basic gains, arguing that "the stability and force of hereditary power and the rights of the nation that will have voted for it must be inseparably guaranteed in the same act [...]".[81] This move did not meet with the undivided approval in the Council, but resistance was soon debunked as hypocritical, as the case of Théophile Berlier (1761–1844) demonstrates. As the staunchest republican in the Council, Berlier still criticized the move, but had no reservations later on to continue and intensify his collaboration with Napoleon after the Empire had become a *fait accompli*, and even actively defend the obvious breach with the republican tradition. Berlier's political memoirs, written decades later, provide a sketchy glimpse into the motives of the French political class—including declared revolutionaries and republicans—in delivering themselves up to the Napoleonic cause and thus providing a mainstay for the new regime. With respect to the prevailing attitude in 1804, Berlier noted that citizens who had been:

prior partisans of the Republic, but fatigued by the oscillations suffered for several years, ended up being persuaded that in the heart of an old and monarchical Europe, the best France could reasonably hope for definitively was a representative government under a new dynasty, whose power would be limited by liberal institutions.[82]

However, he also candidly admitted that it was not only the lack of an agreeable alternative together with a lingering confidence in Napoleon's commitment to the revolutionary legacy which prevailed over republican sensibility, but also plain financial interests of a man "without any patrimonial fortune":[83] interests, which Napoleon skillfully served with the prospect of social mobility and a generous system of benefits and gratuities.

It was the same combination of pragmatism, credulity and tangible self-interest which guaranteed broad support for the motion of a hereditary empire not only in the Council of State, but also in the *Tribunat*, even if in the Consulate's most independent institution criticism was formulated in a more explicit way. The most prominent opponent of the motion was Lazare Carnot (1753–1827), the "organizer of victory" in the French Revolutionary Wars, who had already voted against the establishment of Napoleon's Consular powers for life. In his speech, Carnot acknowledged the need for a temporary concentration of authority at the time of the 18 Brumaire to rescue the Republic from "the edge of an abyss". But the very success of Brumaire now provided the opportunity "to establish liberty on solid foundations". To erect a stable and prosperous republic—referring to the United States—was the only reasonable alternative in today's circumstances, since, as Carnot warned, "it is less difficult to form a republic without anarchy than a monarchy without despotism".[84]

Carnot, however, ploughed a lonely furrow, with an overwhelming majority of the tribunes defending the plan to set up a hereditary monarchy.[85] The arguments put forward were numerous: some invoked Jean Bodin on the superiority of hereditary over elective monarchy, and argued that the guarantee of liberty endured in the legislature's power over taxation (Ambroise-Henry Arnould, 1757–1812), others argued that unlike a king, the new emperor would not be the owner of the country: he was the chief of the French by their wish, and his domain was moral, so no legal servitude could arise from such a system (Henri de Carrion-Nisas, 1767–1841). Some voices stressed that only a fixed order of succession would put an end to Bourbon aspirations, while others, such as Michel Carret (1752–1818), praised the end of anarchy and the prospect of avoiding factionalism.[86] In a resolution presented to the Senate, the *Tribunat* even declared that the Revolution had never set out to abolish the monarchy, and that it was only the Bourbon's conduct which had forced the nation into a democratic government producing anarchy. Under Bonaparte's "government of one", France had finally recovered its tranquillity at home and gained glory abroad. A hereditary Empire would definitively end any threat to the new order, return France to the path envisaged in 1789, and "preserve all the advantages of the Revolution by choosing a dynasty [...] interested in maintaining those advantages".[87] In the same vein, Jean Albisson (1732–1810) expressed his hopes that the goal of 18 Brumaire "to end the Revolution by fusing it to the principles with which it began [i.e. hereditary executive power; MJP]" would be realized at last.[88] The chorus of enthusiasm expressed both in the Council of State and the *Tribunat* was complemented by a mass of petitions from army units across the country demanding the establishment of an imperial order. This—partly spontaneous, but for the most part government-controlled—initiative was designed to demonstrate public support, but at the same time suggested in a subtle way the scenario of "military intervention". While most petitions reflected familiar arguments, welcoming the Empire either as a reconfiguration of the Consulate that would thwart the counter-revolution definitively and guarantee the future of liberty and equality, or as the final burial of the Revolution's legacy of anarchic disruption, one could also discern a new "vision"; one, which no longer revolved around the revolutionary past, but looked forward to a generically new order acknowledging military glory and Napoleon's "destiny" to rule.

Considering the broad support for the movement toward hereditary government, it was a mere formality that the Senate endorsed the transition to empire as well. The Senate's official response delivered by Nicolas François de Neufchâteau (1750–1828) declared that this new government would "defend public liberty, maintain equality, and dip its banners before the expression of the sovereign will of the people", guaranteed by the fact that imperial power would be vested in a family "whose destiny is inseparable from that of the Revolution".[89]

In order to honor the "sovereignty of the people", effusively upheld throughout all the debates, the government again fell back on the well-tried instrument of a plebiscite. The official results of the 1804 plebiscite were almost identical to the vote in 1802, with 3,572,000 votes cast (of which only 8,272 were "No"). But no matter how impressive the renewed affirmation of Napoleon certainly was *prima facie* and especially when applying today's standards, there was ambivalence in the result, too. Considering the fact that France was more extensive in 1804 than two years before, the overall turnout had in fact fallen considerably. One can only speculate whether the charisma of Napoleon—who had memorialized himself a couple of months earlier with the enactment of the *Code civil des Français*—was showing first signs of a weakening or "routinization"[90] of his charisma. What can be assumed is that with the transition to Empire the popular opinion on which Bonaparte relied for his legitimacy was stagnating rather than growing.

Revealingly, the plebiscite of November 1804, which blazed the way to Napoleon's pompous coronation as Emperor of the French on December 2,[91] was the last act of the sovereign people until 1814. The plebiscites had served their purpose in legitimizing Napoleon's rise to power, and from the perspective of the new Emperor there was neither sense nor reason to fall back on this precarious tool any longer. In the same way as Napoleon's rule had become hereditary, the delegation of popular power was henceforth considered as "permanent". The dictum so extensively used at the time even by Napoleon's supporters that "the people's authority is bound only by its own interests"[92] now rang hollow, and the Emperor's right to rule was no longer defined exclusively with reference to the Revolution. This was clearly demonstrated in Napoleon's coronation ceremony.

In his oath, he presented himself in a familiar manner as the crowned representative of the Revolution and guarantor of its legacy.[93] But this was just one component of the political staging, and certainly not the most powerful in symbolic terms: the ritual benediction of Napoleon by the Pope impressively revived the tradition of divine right monarchy, while the act of self-coronation was a powerful expression of his personal sovereign power. In evoking "classical monarchy" and blending Roman imperial pageantry with the purported memory of Charlemagne,[94] Napoleon revealed that he regarded himself as much more than just the governor of the revolutionary nation: a ruler *sui generis*.

Meanwhile, the system of government was undergoing considerable change. In 1802 there were already signs of political repression, with the reorganized administrative apparatus and the system of prefects serving as the strongholds of centralism and authoritarianism. The constitutional amendment following Napoleon's confirmation as First Consul for Life (*Sénatus-consulte organique de la Constitution du 16 thermidor an X*)[95] had further marginalized the legislative bodies and restricted personal liberties, especially by limiting the right to vote and taking first steps towards censitary suffrage.[96] After the transition to empire, repression became all the more common, and Napoleon's rule a personal dictatorship to an even greater extent.[97] Napoleon ceased to consider the legality of his political actions, while the chambers and the Council of State lost their remaining powers; a technocratic form of government gained the upper hand, with the bureaucratic machinery serving as a complacent executing instrument of imperial orders. These changes in politics corresponded with changes in Napoleon's personality discernable in his political actions and utterances, both verbal and written: egoism, propensity to violence, and blind trust in his own abilities gained the mastery; even if Napoleon had originally respected the idea of popular sovereignty, the longer he was in power the more he lost sight of it. In 1814 he declared in a letter to his brother Joseph:

> You like flattering people, and falling in with their ideas. I like people to please me, and to fall in with mine. Today, as at Austerlitz, I am the master. [...] [there is] a difference between the times of La Fayette, when the people was sovereign, and the present moment, when I am [...][98]

As megalomania increased and Napoleon lost sense of what was feasible, he became less sensitive to public opinion. The establishment of a new nobility alienated not only former revolutionaries who had fought for the principle of equality, but also the notables, who saw their status as the political and economic elite fading away. Napoleon thus lost the support of the Brumairians, who had paved his way to power, while the new Napoleonic aristocracy degenerated into a group of sycophants predominantly concerned with the preservation of their assets rather than being a stabilizer for the dynasty. The general public was once again burdened by continuous war efforts and the rigid practice of conscription, necessitated by the fact that "war" had become a permanent condition and increasingly "total".[99]

The government aimed to counteract public discontent both by toughening censorship and intensifying propaganda, which was now assuming the guise of a cult. Through literature, art, and public festivities the achievements of Napoleon were elevated and his person idealized.[100] But even though republican reminiscences became fewer and fewer, while references to Roman Caesarism became more explicit—minting of imperial coins, portraying Napoleon in Caesar-like manner with a laurel crown on his head, or introducing the legionary eagles in the army[101]—Napoleon remained cautious with regard to the "great parallel". He made an effort to keep up the semblance of a "republican emperor" and a "crowned Washington" rather than a "new Caesar", and even turned down a request from the *Institut de France* to award him the titles of *Augustus* and *Germanicus* in 1809, explaining his decision as follows:

> The only man, and he was not an emperor, who distinguished himself by his character and by many illustrious deeds was Caesar. If there was any title the Emperor should desire, it would be that of *Caesar*. But the name has been dishonoured (if that is possible) by so many petty princes, that it is no longer associated with the memory of the great Caesar, but with that of a mob of German princelings, as feeble as they were ignorant, not one of whom has left a mark on history. The Emperor's title is *Emperor of the French*. He wishes to be associated neither with *Augustus*, nor *Germanicus*, nor even with *Caesar*.[102]

With the French Empire and the emperor himself at the zenith of their power following the defeat of Austria in the War of the Fifth Coalition, Napoleon dismissed being identified with Caesar not only because of potentially negative connotations, but also because he deemed it redundant, if not offensive, to be compared with any other world-historical character. This growth in self-confidence went hand in hand with Napoleon's occasional criticism of Caesar, whom he chastised as having overdone his efforts to appeal to the people,[103] while he denounced Alexander the Great for cutting himself off from the people by declaring he was of some divine origin.[104]

What Napoleon did admire, though, was the military genius of both Caesar and Alexander, and it was the battlefield which would decide Napoleon's fate. Despite growing authoritarian tendencies, increasing burdens on the broader population, and Napoleon alienating himself from those groups which had made his rise to absolute power possible, the existence and continuation of the imperial regime seemed secure as long as the military forces continued to succeed. With the most powerful army of Europe loyal to and gloriously led from victory to victory by its commander-in-chief one can hardly imagine a scenario in which any political force in France could have posed a threat to the imperial order and the Emperor's personal power. But when Napoleon's nimbus of military brilliance was irretrievably shattered in the fatal Russian campaign of 1812, and strategic initiative switched to the Allied armies, this marked the beginning of the end of the Empire.

In a combination of personal (military) hubris and stubbornness to accept peace with the Allies only on his terms, Napoleon missed the opportunity to safeguard the political system of the Empire and his own position, which was still within the realms of possibility. The failed peace talks at the Congress of Châtillon provoked a declaration of the allied powers released on March 25, 1814[105] preparing the French nation for the deposition of Napoleon; but in the end—an irony of history—it was a French political body whose members owed their titles and fortunes to Napoleon that declared he had forfeited his throne: the Senate.[106] Under the aegis of Talleyrand, who had become the head of inner-French opposition since his replacement in 1807 and was actively supported by Tsar Alexander of Russia, the Senate released a corresponding decree on April 3, 1814:[107] it was not because Napoleon had seized power unlawfully, but because of the way he irresponsibly exercised his prerogatives that he had lost his claim to rule. The evidence for the degeneration of his reign was a long list of constitutional breaches, among them the illegal imposition of taxes, declaring and waging war without authorization by the legislative body, the qualification of constitutional powers, the destruction of the independent judiciary and the suspension of the freedom of the press. Perhaps more powerful than any legal argument, however, was the allegation that the Emperor had become estranged from the nation's fundamental wishes and "destroyed" the former "treaty" between himself and the French people.[108] This argumentation focused on the "reasonableness" of political actions and their unison with the "will of the people", and was thus a powerful evocation of the principle of popular sovereignty. When even the military leaders refused to obey orders to recapture Paris on April 4, Napoleon's regime was at an end; the Emperor's authority and so too the basis of the imperial system was irretrievably undermined. Two days later, on April 6, 1814, Napoleon I formally renounced the throne for himself and his heirs.[109]

However, neither his downfall in 1814, nor the unsuccessful episode of the "Hundred Days" in 1815 did any lasting harm to the "Napoleonic legend". On the contrary: it was this political failure which fuelled the memory of Napoleon Bonaparte, transforming it into a myth. Napoleon himself made every effort to nurture the "historical myth" of Bonaparte in his exile on Elba and later on Saint Helena, where he found plenty of time to reflect upon his world-historical role as well as to idealize his political achievements and rule. He was in no doubt that the more time passed, the brighter his legacy would shine: "It is a fact that my destiny is the inverse of other men's. Ordinarily, a man is lowered by his downfall; my downfall raises me to infinite heights. Every day strips me of my tyrant's skin, of my murderousness and ferocity."[110] The most pervasive picture which he managed to convey through his memoirs and writings in exile was that of the spearhead of progress and liberal ideas:

> Liberal opinions will rule the universe. They will become the faith, the religion, the morality of all nations; and in spite of all that may be advanced to the contrary, this memorable aim will be inseparably connected with my name; for after all it cannot be denied that I kindled the torch and consecrated the principle, and now persecution renders me the Messiah. Friends and enemies, all must acknowledge me to be the first soldier, the grand representative of the age. Thus I shall forever remain the leading star.[111]

Part of this picture was the vision of a peacefully united "Europe of the fatherlands", entrusted with progressive institutions.[112] At the same time, Napoleon endeavored to play down his personal ambitions and to portray himself as a leader who had only taken up and defended the cause of the people. He took pains to minimize the dictatorial elements of his regime and portray them as a necessary evil which would have immediately ended with the establishment of a durable peace order in Europe. After that, he declared at one stage, "I would have proclaimed the immutability of boundaries, all future wars, purely defensive; all new aggrandisement, anti-national; I would have associated my son with the empire; my dictatorship would have terminated, and his constitutional reign commenced".[113] The picture which he frequently drew of himself was that of the nation's saviour, needed and anticipated by the people. The description in his memoirs of the events surrounding his seizure of power in 1799 impressively reflects this self-depiction, Napoleon describing France as a country in a shameful state and with a crackle of expectation charging the air.[114] Despite his own fate, Napoleon was convinced that the need for a popular "tutelary genius", a leader taking the peoples' fears and desires seriously, would persist. He also ventured to remark that in the future "the sovereign, who, in the first great conflict, shall sincerely embrace the cause of the people, will find himself at the head of all Europe, and may attempt whatever he pleases".[115]

In his last years, Napoleon not only made projections about times to come, but also looked back in history to that person with whom he had been compared most: Caesar. At the end of his exile on Saint Helena, Napoleon dictated his *Précis des guerres de César*, which was posthumously published in 1836. Though mainly a military history of Caesar's campaigns, it offers a political assessment and a telling insight into Napoleon's understanding of his own rule. Napoleon rejects the idea that Caesar had been striving for the royal crown as pure defamation by his enemies: Caesar would not have attempted to take such a step without the support of the Senate and people as the legitimate institutions of Roman constitutional life, nor would he have overthrown established political traditions just for the sake of a blunt title. Napoleon's *Précis* concludes:

> Caesar did not want to be king, because he could not want to; he could not want to because after him, for six hundred years, none of his successors wanted to. It would have been a strange policy to replace the curule chair of the world's conquerors with the rotten throne despised by those who had been conquered.[116]

This was clearly a dig at the restored Bourbon monarchy and traditional beliefs in what made political authority legitimate. According to Napoleon, Caesar's authority had been legitimate not because he had inherited or been bestowed a particular title, but "because it was necessary and protective, because it maintained all of Rome's vested interests, because it was the result of the opinion and the will of the people".[117] This observation reflected Napoleon's view on his own rule as well: a rule adapted to the needs of the time, aware of tradition but correspondent to the existent moment of crisis as well, and based on the will of the people. While Caesar's regime had been a response to the devastating civil war, the Napoleonic order thus appeared as the "Caesaristic" answer to the political and social crisis originating from the end of the *Ancien Régime* and the vicissitudes of the Revolutionary age. Napoleon's nephew and heir Louis-Napoléon Bonaparte later summed it up in a nutshell: "The Emperor was the mediator between two enemy centuries; he killed the *Ancien Régime* by restoring all that was good in that *Régime*: he killed the revolutionary spirit by having the benefits of the revolution triumph everywhere."[118]

But while Napoleon reasoned about Roman Caesarism in exile and did his part to create his own myth, intensive public debate about his own regime and his place in history was already well underway and had been so for some time—actually since the memorable events of Brumaire, which sparked a controversy unprecedented in history between supporters and opponents.

2.3.2 Contemporary Perceptions of the Napoleonic Regime

One may surmise that Napoleon Bonaparte dominated the imagination of the nineteenth century more than any other historical figure had dominated a century before or after him.[119] The pre-eminent role Napoleon assumed even in the minds of his contemporaries is well illustrated by George Ponsonby (1755–1817), who—as leader of the Whig opposition—declared in the House of Commons on May 25, 1810:

> Is he not one of those extraordinary men whom providence creates to bring about those great and extraordinary revolutions, which in two or three thousand years are produced; and totally change the moral and political state of the world? Is he not unparalleled in the history of the world, both as a military man, and a general statesman? I say he is the greatest man that has ever appeared on the face of the earth. I speak not of his moral character; I speak of the strength of his faculties and of the energies of his mind.[120]

Almost concomitant with Napoleon's rise to power and especially since the Brumaire coup, every diagnosis of his personality and rule had been caught up in the fierce quarrels between supporters and opponents of the Corsican. Nevertheless, the focal point of interpretation, which was to remain central to the debates on "Bonapartism" and "(modern) Caesarism", was consistently the relation of the leader to the Revolution. It was against the background of the pervasive "revolutionary experience" that Napoleon's regime was either praised or damned and that all constitutional as well as historic-philosophical parallels received their momentum. In this context, Julius Caesar was not the only model that commended itself to those with a penchant for heroic parallels. Other persons whose character and deeds were compared with Napoleon's were Alexander,[121] Charlemagne,[122] and Cromwell,[123] who were actively instrumentalized in Bonapartist propaganda as well, but also figures historically less distant such as Frederick II of Prussia.[124] But no other analogy has proved more historically seductive than the one linking Napoleon Bonaparte's political achievements with those of Caesar, and it was the name of the former which would stick to the Corsican more than any other.[125] That the "great parallel" persisted was an expression of a deep desire to define one's own position in the ever more dynamic process of political, social and cultural change. In such an environment historical analogies helped to provide orientation and stability at the same time.

A common trait of contemporary reception was not only to compare Napoleon with previous historic leaders, but also to evaluate him according to whether he completed and perfected or rather terminated and overcame the Revolution. In this regard, one particular challenge was to make sense of and come to terms with the puzzling parallelism of liberty and authoritarianism, equality and distinction, democracy and dictatorship, pragmatism and charisma that Napoleon and his political regime embodied. The confusingly numerous facets of Napoleon, difficult to accommodate, were later eloquently expressed in an official history of the Peninsular War commissioned by the Spanish King: "a man who was at once passionate for glory, and a tyrant, a royalist, a republican and an emperor, who indiscriminately donned the turban of the Moslems, the cap of the Jacobins, the crown of Charlemagne and the diadem of the Caesars".[126] A similar picture was painted in the *European Magazine* of 1814:

> Such a medley of contradictions, and, at the same time, such an individual consistence, were never united in the same character. A Royalist, a Republican, and an Emperor—a Mahometan—a Catholic and a patron of the Synagogue—a Subaltern and a Sovereign—a Traitor and a Tyrant—a Christian and an Infidel— he was, through all his vicissitudes, the same stern, impatient, inflexible, original, the same mysterious, incomprehensible *self*—the man *without a model and without a shadow* imitative of his obscure substance.[127]

It is symptomatic of descriptions of Napoleon at the time that the same person who was among the loudest voices to denounce the Corsican might in the same breath still acknowledge his extraordinary merits, as François-René de Chateaubriand (1768–1848) summarized in his *Mémoires*: "My admiration for Bonaparte has always been great and sincere, even when I was attacking Napoleon with the greatest ardour."[128] Similarly, ardent admiration among contemporaries could swiftly switch toward passionate rejection, or vice versa.

German debate in the early nineteenth century is particular proof of the double-edged and ever-changing nature of Napoleon's reception in Europe. It was in Germany that in the wake of the Revolution expectations of "change" and the launch into modernity became mixed up with fears of anarchy and foreign tutelage and hegemony, and that universalist hopes formulated by philosophers and writers clashed with national(ist) reaction. These contradictions are represented *in persona* by Joseph von Görres (1776–1848), one of the few German revolutionary thinkers to have actually been involved in politics. Member of a delegation of the Rhenish provinces sent to Paris in 1799 to prepare the formal union of the Cisrhenian Republic with France, Görres arrived in Paris briefly after Napoleon had assumed power. This personal experience left a lasting impression, as his tract *Resultate meiner Sendung nach Paris im Brumaire des achten Jahres*, published on his return in 1800, reveals: unlike many of his contemporaries, Görres did not consider Napoleon to be the safeguard to a return to order, but shared the opinion of those who saw "the achievement of the Revolution swallowed up by the ambition of a single man".[129] To him, the coup of 18 Brumaire seemed to be the natural consequence of the events which preceded it, and marked both the end and failure of the Revolution. Henceforth Görres considered the national characters of France and Germany to be basically irreconcilable, promoting the idea that Germany's moral superiority empowered her to replace France as a beacon to other nations.

At the turn of the century, however, overall German public opinion towards the new political regime in France was not as negative as Görres would have us believe. The meteoric ascent of the young artillery officer was generally accompanied by positive comments and remarks from the provinces east of the Rhine, even though induced by different points of view. Some observers saw in Napoleon a dam to restrain the frightening tide of the Revolution, others greeted the new leader as catalyst for the "Europeanization" of the—now finally "rationalized"—Revolution. Among the latter was the German historian Karl Ludwig von Woltmann (1770–1817), who in 1804 declared Napoleon the only person "who grasped the revolution in its essence and could consequently never become its partisan [*Schwärmer*]". Therefore, he managed "to halt the revolution at that moment when everything that it had promised seemed to be fading away".[130] Hegel, too, welcomed Napoleon: not only because—as he later famously elaborated—he saw symmetries between Alexander, Caesar and Napoleon as "world-historical individuals" (*weltgeschichtliche Individuen*), who played a crucial role in introducing world-impacting concepts and fostered the emergence of the universal from the particular through its negation,[131] but also out of more pragmatic political interests and hopes. In his early work on the German Federal Constitution, written between 1800 and 1802, Hegel expressed the hope that the developments in France would bring about a new Theseus for Germany as well, providing for the unity of the German Empire.[132]

While Hegel and others continued to understand the Napoleonic rule in the categories of "constitutional monarchy", there were others who emphasized the novel character of the political system created by the Corsican. The writer Friedrich Buchholz (1768–1843), for example, apostrophized in 1805 the synthesis of democracy and dictatorship, symbolized by Napoleon. For Buchholz, the 18 Brumaire solved the problem "of reconciling the unity of the powers (the monarchy) with the fundamental principle of equality as addressed in the First Constitution [1791]". It was due to Napoleon—for Buchholz the incorporation of the "new Leviathan"—that government had finally become "an integral whole". Buchholz emphasized the need for strong leadership with utter conviction and defended the belief that "a government cannot be good without being strong at the same time, and that there is no greater misfortune for a great people than weakness on the part of the highest power". Neither Napoleon's actual authority, nor even the way he had seized power had anything reprehensible about it, since calling Napoleon a "usurper" would make no sense at all: "He has usurped nothing more than what [. . .] always has been and will be usurped."[133]

In 1806/1807, Johann Gottfried Seume (1763–1810) described Napoleon as a new phenomenon, too, but without any of the positive tones and associations expressed by Buchholz. For him, there was an irreconcilable difference between the Revolution, which had to be credited with bringing "principles of reason" into "constitutional law", and Napoleon, whose arbitrariness would always betray his task of becoming a "fixed star of reason". The French Emperor would content himself with "being a comet that threatens devastation". If those dearly bought principles of reason were to be annihilated, every part of the world would deserve its own "sublimated Bonaparte".[134] Thus, Seume was among the first to characterize Napoleon as the archetype of the post-Revolutionary age; an age, which—if it did not manage to internalize the very principles of the Revolution—would have to suffer the rule of despotism and destruction.[135] At the same time, Seume's critical remarks reflect the fact that anti-Napoleonic rhetoric was becoming all the louder in Germany the more French imperialism stretched into German lands. The project of the Confederation of the Rhine, which was so auspiciously praised by Bonapartist propaganda as the beginning of a liberal age in Germany, did not reverse public opinion, but rather accelerated it due to obvious discrepancies between political promises and practice. In Germany, at least, Napoleon visibly lost the battle for the *vox populi*. Gradually, he turned from an icon of order and liberty into a symbol of foreign rule, and the more time passed the more aggressive the attacks became. The sheer output of anti-Napoleonic literature and pamphlets of the time bears witness to this.[136]

Napoleon's defeat in 1814/1815 marked the day of reckoning of the German national camp with the (remaining) Bonapartists, yet also boosted the critical assessment of his rule and the attempts to understand his regime as a new "constitutional phenomenon" of the (post-)revolutionary age. A typical example of such attempts was the historian Heinrich Luden (1780–1847), for whom Napoleon was the executor of Rousseau's political thought. "Rousseau had demanded unity, indivisibility, inalienability of sovereignty, Bonaparte achieved it", Luden declared in his journal *Nemesis. Zeitschrift für Politik und Geschichte* in 1814, where he summarized the core ideology of the Bonapartists as follows:

> The centre is everything to them; [...] everything has to emanate out from and not somehow converge in it. Everything must be done for the people, absolutely nothing by the people itself; the Regent does not govern through his own will, but the general will. He represents the people; how is another representative alongside him even conceivable? No one has an authority over others except him [...] Any autonomy of any limb of the body politic is nonsensical; it goes against unity and indivisibility.[137]

Bonapartist government, it seemed, boiled down to "unrestricted monarchy", but it was in fact more than that: "oligarchic despotism like in China", with the *apparatchiks* of the regime being the "true bearer and explicator of the general will".[138] By using the comparison of "oriental despotism", Luden was referring to a well-known *topos* in Western political thought, but at the same time emphasizing the novelty of the Bonapartist system for Europe.

With the fall of the Napoleonic regime and the end of strict censorship, efforts were made in France as well to critically evaluate the Napoleonic system, and attempts to reason a new "regime type" intensified. Benjamin Constant (1767–1830), perhaps the most distinguished liberal writer of the early nineteenth century, made a start in 1813/1814, putting forward the first elaborate theory of "Bonapartism" and "Caesarism"—without explicitly naming it as such—in his *De l'esprit de conquête et de l'usurpation dans leurs rapports avec la civilisation européenne* whilst making a case for "constitutional monarchy".[139]

Constant's analysis of what he called "usurpation" wavered between taking recourse to established concepts and terminologies on the one hand and stressing the innovative and hence dangerous nature of the phenomenon on the other. What Constant set out to express was the fact that while a constitutional monarchy such as England had developed into a stronghold of freedom, a "republic" like France had degenerated into a state of terror and arbitrariness. To this aim, Constant contrasted "usurpation" with "(hereditary) monarchy".[140]

He argued that while the two appeared to be similar entities, since both rested on one man, closer scrutiny would reveal fateful differences: "monarchy" was characterized by intermediary powers, tradition and the monarch not being perceived as an actual person by his subjects, but as an "abstract being" coagulating "a whole race of kings, a tradition of several centuries". "Usurpation", on the other hand, was "a force that nothing modifies or softens. It is necessarily stamped with the individuality of the usurper, and such individuality, because it is opposed to all pre-existing interests, must be in a state of permanent defiance and hostility".[141] Part of this sprang from a burden that would not plague hereditary monarchy: while a monarch mounting the throne of his ancestors had no need to "make his reputation", being the "only one of his kind" and not "compared with anyone else", a usurper was:

> exposed to all the comparisons that regrets, jealousy or hopes may suggest. He is obliged to justify his elevation. He has contracted the tacit obligation to crown such great fortune with great results. He must fear disappointing the expectations which he has so powerfully aroused. The most reasonable and best motivated inaction becomes a danger to him.[142]

The drawbacks of a usurper's position would concur with the vices of his character, since such vices were always implicit in usurpation. Usurpation by its sheer nature demanded "treachery, violence and perjury", such acts imported into and established in the regime. "A monarch ascends nobly to his throne", whereas "a usurper slithers onto it through mud and blood, and when he takes his place on it, his stained robe bears marks of the career he has followed".[143] Such structural aspects would also help to explain why the usurper must be at the center of things, the focus of attention, whether he wants to or not, whereas a king could take a backseat and delegate power without endangering his position. It was characteristic for the system of usurpation that the initial act of seizing power—with the active support of the army—was transformed into "incessant warfare", allowing the usurper to mobilize and discipline the military forces in his support, to "dazzle people's minds and, for lack of the prestige of antiquity, to win that of conquest".[144] But since conquest and thus military success must be substituted for authority, one single defeat could signal the regime's end.[145]

Constant not only distinguished usurpation from monarchy, but also highlighted the differences between usurpation and conventional forms of "despotism". "Consolidated despotism" would indeed "banish all forms of liberties", but was at least transparent in its destruction of liberty. Usurpation, on the other hand, was deeply corrupting, because it:

> needs these forms [of liberties] in order to justify the overturning of what it replaces, but in appropriating them it profanes them. Because the existence of public spirit is a danger for it, while the appearance of one is a necessity, usurpation strikes the people with one hand to stifle their true opinion, and subsequently strikes them again with the other to force them to simulate the appropriate opinion.[146]

Thus, while the despot "prohibits discussion and exacts only obedience, the usurper insists on a mock trial as a prelude to public approval". This "counterfeiting of liberty" would combine "all the evils of anarchy with all those of slavery. There is no limit to the tyranny that seeks to exact the signs of consent." Where despotism "stifles freedom of the press, usurpation parodies it". In a nutshell, "despotism rules by means of silence, and leaves man the right to be silent". Usurpation, however, "condemns him to speak, it pursues him into the most intimate sanctuary of his thoughts, and, by forcing him to lie to his own conscience, deprives the oppressed of his last remaining consolation".[147]

As in so many contemporary works, the evocation of ancient Caesarism was not lacking in Constant's writing either:

> In thinking of the famous usurpers who are celebrated over the centuries, only one thing seems wonderful to me, and that is the admiration that people have for them, Caesar and Octavius, called Augustus, are models of this type: they began by proscribing all that was eminent in Rome; they continued by degrading everything that remained noble; they ended by bequeathing to the world Vitellius, Domitian, Heliogabalus and finally the Goths and the Vandals.[148]

Nevertheless, Constant did not deduce an immediate parallel between ancient usurpers and Napoleon, nor a prospect of inevitable nemesis. In Constant's eyes, Napoleon was certainly a usurper, but one who embodied all that was worst in despotism as well, namely "arbitrary power"[149] and the reduction of all political bodies to instruments of personal will. At the same time, Constant expressed confidence that this amalgamation of usurpation with despotism would be a fleeting phenomenon: "As usurpation cannot be maintained through despotism, since in our days despotism itself cannot last, usurpation has no chance of enduring."[150] This view sprang from his conviction that the moral and economic conditions of modern civilization would eventually make despotism "impossible".[151] In returning to the differences between the ancient and the modern world, he argued that unlike the former, in which there had been little sense of "individual liberty", modern societies had incorporated this sense, thereby providing people with a new hub of resistance against despotic—and usurpatory—government.[152] In another passage of his work Constant declared that "each century awaits a man to represent it", but that the "more advanced a civilization, the more difficult it is to represent it". He firmly believed that a situation "when a civilized nation is invaded by barbarians, or when an ignorant mass penetrates to its heart and takes over its destiny", thus the breeding ground for a usurper, was less and less likely due to the achievements of the Enlightenment.[153]

One weak point in Constant's theory, however, was his definition of political legitimacy, and more particularly his consideration of the democratic element, which had been a crucial component of Napoleon's rule and conflicted somewhat with the concept of "arbitrary rule". Constant therefore added a corresponding chapter in the fourth edition of his work, in which he acknowledged two types of legitimacy: "one positive, which derives from free election, the other tacit, which rests upon heredity;"[154] He conceded that "of the two kinds of legitimacy which I admit, the one which derives from election is more seductive in theory, but it has the inconvenience that it can be counterfeited", as it was both by Cromwell and by Napoleon.[155] Constant's allegation that Napoleon's authority had not been actually established by national will in the same way as that of Washington or William of Orange and was thus genuinely usurpatory and illegitimate prompts him to restate the reproaches against the regime of the Corsican: unlike the conquerors before him he had chosen barbarism, he had "sought to bring back the night" and to "transform into greedy and bloodthirsty nomads a mild and polite people"; his sole resource had been "uninterrupted war", because "had he been pacific, he would never have lasted for twelve years"; but his regime had to fall "by the inevitable effect of the wars which it requires", perhaps not this time, but some other time, since "it is only too natural that a gambler, who every day takes a new risk, should some day meet with the one which must ruin him".[156]

Constant's study was probably the most comprehensive and theoretically most profound analysis of "Bonapartism" at the time, which was to structure the upcoming debate on "Caesarism" throughout the rest of the nineteenth century. More expressly than most other contemporary observers, Constant sought to understand the Napoleonic regime not so much as an outcome of Napoleon's personal flaws and passions, but as a phenomenon reflecting more general historical developments.[157]

What made Constant's analysis particularly perceptive was that he did not portray arbitrary power and usurpation as the product of a ruthless will to oppress only, but demonstrated that both could be the outcome of apparently reasonable measures and considerations, short-sighted Machiavellianism, social change and ideological fallacies. Similarly, the true horror of despotic government, as he described it, did not always lie in excess, cruelty and terror, but in the corruption of liberty, daily acceptance of compromise, the slow erosion of human solidarity and decency, and the sharing of guilt and complicity by the whole body politic.

Though written with a critical punch, Constant managed to paint a more complex picture of the Corsican than the majority of anti-Napoleonic liberal pamphleteers at the time, who considered him an evil outlaw, whose leadership had not been used to fulfill the Revolution, but to pervert it by "selfish Cunning, oath-trampling Usurpation, remorseless Tyranny, and thirst of War and Rapine".[158] At the same time, Constant provided an analysis distinct from the ones put forward by conservatives such as de Maistre and Louis-Gabriel-Ambroise de Bonald (1754–1840). Following Burke's lead, they attempted to prove that there would be a slide from revolutionary government based on popular sovereignty into military domination by a single commander, with the one usurping power setting up a far more absolute and repressive regime than had existed before the Revolution. While Constant shared the "negative consensus" that prevailed among liberals and conservatives alike in rejecting the theory of an unlimited sovereignty of the people, he abstained from accepting the absolute inevitability of this slide and dissociated himself completely from the conclusions drawn by the conservatives.

In contrast to them, Constant saw the restoration of a traditional monarchical order "willed by God" neither as a likely nor as a reasonable alternative for the post-Napoleonic age. He believed it was necessary to learn a lesson from the Napoleonic experience and to establish—following Constant's principle that "no authority upon earth is unlimited, neither that of the people, nor that of the men who declare themselves their representatives, nor that of kings, by whatever title they reign"[159]—a representative political system characterized by strict separation of powers, whose main concern was the safeguarding of individual liberties and rights.

Given his optimistic take on history, expecting enduring political progress from enlightened philosophy and civilization no less than commercial society, Constant in 1814 considered Napoleon's regime to be just one—though disagreeable—historic episode. This view may help to explain Constant's striking willingness to assist Napoleon in revising the Constitution of the Empire during the Hundred Days: the same man, whom he had so ardently attacked in the previous years.[160]

Constant had been able to pin down the characteristic traits of "Bonapartism"; but he had failed to recognize this type of regime as the lasting signature of the post-revolutionary age. His assessment that "usurpation" would have no prospects, neither in political theory nor practice, was soon proven to be a grave misjudgement.

2.4 Conclusions

The "Great Revolutions", especially the French Revolution, as a point of entry for utopian visions of political and social renewal had shattered the traditional bedrock of political life and legitimacy. Revolutionary activism went beyond the mottos of enlightened philosophy: "Sapere Aude!" and "Have courage to use your own understanding!"[161] Increasingly, it was now also about "Creare Aude!" and "Have courage to create your own world!"

But as appealing as the perspective might have appeared to design one's own "Elysium on earth", equally as sobering was the public awakening in the French Revolution, when the shady side of seemingly "infinite liberty" became glaringly obvious in the face of instability, disorder and economic chaos. The more obvious the "crisis" became, the louder demands for a "domestication" or termination of the Revolution were. The chances for a figure with "heroic" appeal were excellent: traditional monarchy might have been sacrificed on the altar of "popular sovereignty", but not so faith in strong leadership. Moreover, revolutionary deicide had created a gap which was likely to be filled by a charismatic character, epitomizing stability while not sacrificing the prospect of progress.

It is no wonder that at the sight of the "revolutionary crisis" the republican model faced growing scepticism, too, and that the "great parallel" with antiquity assumed a negative aftertaste. More than before, ancient republicanism was now invoked as a warning, as something to be feared, not emulated, and major currents of political thought across the ideological spectrum attempted to make sense of contemporary events via the example of the Ancient world and Rome in particular as "paradigmatic" in a negative sense. Recurring elements of the "negative great parallel" included the masses as the new barbarians, civil war, and popular usurpatory militarism as the dominant type of state. This was also the position of Edmund Burke, who asserted that because the new republican regime could not rest upon a basis of traditional authority, it would be so unstable as to produce a military dictatorship. A single man would rule by a power unchecked because any limitation would be regarded as incompatible with the revolutionary principles of popular sovereignty. This, in effect, would lead to a regime oriented to dominion and conquest. French royalist writers took a slightly different view. De Maistre, for example, made an analogy anticipating the later use of "Caesarism" as the term for plebiscitary dictatorship when he emphasized that Providence would always deny the people the possibility to designate their own rulers. The Roman plebs had enslaved itself by revolting against the aristocracy; similarly, in 1789 the French people, already in possession of all necessary liberties, had taken up arms against their legitimate rulers. As a consequence, the nation had been enslaved and exploited.

However, while a "new Caesar" might be perceived as a *bête noire*, one could also see him as "saviour", or at least born of necessity. In the early years of the Revolution there was no real "candidate" for this role: while the Marquis de La Fayette was unwilling, Robespierre was unable to fulfill it. The quest continued, and the rise of the victorious general Napoleon Bonaparte finally provided a concrete face for the debate which until then had been rather abstract.

Backed by his military victories abroad, Napoleon took effective advantage of the historical chance being offered at 18 Brumaire. A set of conditions made the coup of 18 Brumaire possible: the breakdown of traditional authority and a civilian political consensus; the emergence of the armed forces as the one body actually holding power; the actual or alleged need to prevent chaos; an attitude of acquiescence among the population, particularly since Frenchmen saw in Napoleon what they hoped to see.

The new Consular Constitution effectively deactivated parliament and the representative system altogether. "Popular will" was now expressed by a new instrument, which would evolve into a permanent *signum* of "Bonapartism": plebiscites. However, this plebiscitary element was less about achieving a means for political opinions to be articulated, than about the affirmation of the leader's authority and policies.

Napoleon actively advanced his authority and power, well aware that his successful policies—domestic as well as foreign—generated the popular support he required. The backing Napoleon enjoyed in the population found clear expression in the plebiscite on lifelong Consulate: while the result of the plebiscite legitimizing the 18 Brumaire had needed to be "burnished" by manipulation in order to guarantee a glowing result, in 1802 a majority of the electorate stood behind Napoleon even without governmental fraud. Public enthusiasm in France for the Corsican was perhaps never higher than around the Peace of Amiens: the First Consul had achieved peace and international preponderance through military victory, economic stabilization, as well as the repatriation of most *émigrés*. All this occurred without jeopardizing civil equality, the abolition of seigneurialism, or the transfer of the *biens nationaux*. Indeed, "Bonaparte seemed to be sustaining the most tangible interests created by the Revolution while soothing its most aggrieved victims."[162] Napoleon's coronation in 1804 marked the climax, but somehow also termination of the *système Napoléon*, not least since the—relatively—disappointing results of the plebiscite on the establishment of hereditary Empire demonstrated the frontiers and fragility of the "plebiscitary model". Tellingly, the plebiscite of 1804 was the last until the collapse of the regime in 1814, and marked the beginning of an increasingly authoritarian style of reign.

Napoleon was cautious to keep up appearances of being "the nation's tribune" and "Emperor of the French" rather than "Emperor of France", but at the same time made efforts to draw on alternative sources of legitimacy, most notably rationality and tradition. However, the long-term institutionalization of his position remained a difficult endeavor. Ultimately, Napoleon's rule depended on the category of "success", military and otherwise. Famously, Napoleon is said to have voiced himself that whereas established monarchs could suffer a dozen defeats and still be accepted as rulers by their peoples, he could survive only through continuous victories and was dependent on being perceived as "fortune's son".[163] Whether these utterances are authentic or not,[164] they certainly reflect a characteristic feature of his rule, which never entirely escaped a basic fragility. In the end, it was perhaps not military defeat as such which put an end to his reign. Yet the burden of continuous warfare and the accompanying economic consequences undermined Napoleon's domestic basis of power, eventually allowing the same political elite in the Senate, which owed Napoleon status and power, to declare him forfeit his throne in April 1814.

However, it is one of the trademarks of Napoleon that legend and myth did not end with his defeat, but were rather grounded on his failure. In exile Napoleon worked hard to create his own legacy: he emphasized what would have been possible if hostile Europe had allowed him to put his visions into practice, and played down the authoritarian elements of his regime arguing that these were only due to the exceptional circumstances of the time, with the reign of liberty and happiness already envisaged for the time after the wars. Despite actual historical evidence, the image of the nation's "saviour", needed and anticipated by a desperate people, was preserved—an image, which allowed favorable analogies with Caesar to be drawn: like Napoleon, Caesar's sole concern had been the wishes and anxieties of the people; he had not been striving for the royal crown, but only served as the crowned representative of the body politic; and akin to Napoleon later on, he was hindered by his contemporaries in achieving even greater feats.

While the Napoleonic propaganda machine did its best to present the Corsican as an "exceptional phenomenon" of history, even among observers of the time the idea grew and developed that he was "singular", if only in a negative respect. "That he has done much evil, there is little doubt—that he has been the origin of much good, there is just as little", the contradictory "Caracter [*sic!*] of Buonaparte" was summarized in 1814.[165] In public perception, the "great parallel" to other figures of world history and Caesar in particular was frequently referred to as well, with the main question being Napoleon's relation to the epoch-making event of the Revolution: was he the heir and executor of the French Revolution, "the personified Revolution in one of its stages", as Karl Wilhelm Koppe (1777–1837) argued in 1815,[166] or liquidator of revolutionary ideals? This question was—and continues to be—one which is difficult to answer.

After Brumaire, Napoleon himself had coined the famous formula *Ni bonnet rouge, ni talon rouge, je suis national,*[167] a version of "national populism" *avant la lettre*. Reversely, one could argue that Napoleon carried on both pre-revolutionary and revolutionary traditions. The construction of a hereditary monarchy as well as the (re-)establishment of nobility evoked reminiscences to the *Ancien Régime*. At the same time, links to the Revolution were clearly apparent as well, including even such to Jacobin rule. Bureaucratic gigantism and state paternalism, centralization, a powerful executive branch seeking to legitimize its authority through the incitement of patriotic fervour and thus inclined towards war—all these had been characteristic features of the French Jacobin State as well. What the Italian writer Guglielmo Ferrero later determined as perhaps the most important "nexus" to the Jacobin "heritage" was that Napoleon's reign had "saved France and the work of the Revolution, by definitely organizing, on the lines traced out by the Convention, the new universal secular protection of the Jacobin State in place of that formerly exercised by the Church".[168] The fact that Napoleon could be seen as the embodiment of secularization by some observers, while others—including a majority of the French clergy at the beginning of the nineteenth century—hailed him as the providential saviour of the Church and compared him to Cyrus or Moses underlines still further the ambivalence embodied by the Corsican.

Along with contemporary debate about what Napoleon ultimately represented, the questions as to the "novelty" of his regime gained importance as well. This also drove the discourse on categories of political legitimacy and illegitimacy, which had been prepared by the reinterpretation of classical "tyranny" in the eighteenth century. Here and there, Napoleon's regime was seen not only as being "special", but also as an archetype of the post-Revolutionary age, in which democracy and dictatorship were conflated in a particular way. But Napoleon's fall also raised expectations that his rule might have been only a temporary phenomenon.

This opinion was also shared by Benjamin Constant. In 1814, he provided the first more detailed "theory" of what was soon to be termed "Bonapartism" or "Napoleonism". Constant characterized Napoleon's rule as "usurpation"[169] based on and converged with despotism, and in his eyes, the regime was illegitimate not only since "the usurper sits with fear on an illegitimate throne, as on a solitary pyramid",[170] but also because it derived from a seizure of power and demanded constant warfare. Despite all his merits in understanding "Napoleon" as an essentially "systemic" phenomenon and challenge, and demarcating Napoleon's regime from classical forms of illegitimate rule, Constant was fundamentally wrong with respect to the potential which "Bonapartism" might unfold in the long run.

Constant neglected that it had been "liberals" such as himself who had helped to provide convincing arguments for the abandonment of popular democracy and the move towards a strong state authority even before Brumaire. For a long time, liberal thinkers had challenged the republican model; for them, the great mistake of the Revolution and its ideologues was to try to recapitulate Graeco-Roman antiquity and to impose on modern "public opinion" what was no longer suitable for it. "In the present era liberty means everything that protects citizens' independence of the government", Madame de Staël aptly summarized liberal positions. Thinkers like Rousseau had lost sight of the fact that "public opinion will be based upon the love of tranquillity, the desire to acquire wealth, and the need to preserve it; that people will always be more concerned with administrative concepts than political questions because they bear more directly upon private life."[171]

But was it not actually this wish for "tranquillity", on which Napoleon's rule had rested, the guarantee of stability and the protection of vested rights, in particular for the middle classes—in exchange for restricted political liberty and participation? Indeed, contrary to Constant's optimistic conception of civilization, "Bonapartism" was anything but a phase-out model of history.

3

"Bonapartism" as Hazard and Promise

3.1 Political Legitimacy in Post-Napoleonic Europe

At first glance, the general political situation in Europe seemed to be quite clear in 1814/1815: with Napoleon's military defeat, the Revolution had finally been overpowered, its ideological foundations shattered, and the victorious anti-Napoleonic forces could feel free to turn the clocks back. Practically all over Europe the practice and language of "Revolution" was compromised, and among conservatives and liberals alike the concept of "popular sovereignty" served to denote—and indeed demonize—all the burdens, crises and sacrifices Europe had suffered in the previous quarter of a century. It was hard to find active advocates of radical political, social or economic change; instead, the main discourse of the time was about durable peace, reconstruction, or at most reform.

Despite the fact that the partisans of the Revolution were on the defensive, however, hardly anywhere on the continent did restoration policies have the character of pure reaction or a return to pre-revolutionary conditions. For the most part, the old—or, as in the case of France, "new old"—monarchical elite of Europe was aware that trying to undo the fundamental changes in practically all areas of public life that had been taking place during the previous decades was a dangerous if not impossible endeavor.[1] There was widespread agreement that albeit in different forms and to differing extents, all European states had to face up to the legacies of the Revolution, no matter how much the traditional elites might loathe this heritage. A particular challenge was to find a way of reconciling post-revolutionary societies' expectations of both a constitutional state and the preservation of the political as well as legal innovations generated since 1789 with monarchical claims for personal government and sovereignty characteristic of the previous centuries. This challenge gave rise to the concept of "monarchical constitutionalism", which might justifiably also be characterized as "constitutional monarchism";[2] first of all in France, where the need to come to terms with the Revolution was most immediate. The new monarchical constitutional order made the monarch the dominant political power and declared him the sole holder of the *pouvoir constituant*, yet was based at the same time on a written constitution providing for civil liberties and allowing citizens to partake in the political, and above all legislative, process. The restoration of the Bourbons in 1814 on the basis of the *Charte constitutionnelle*[3] thus became, as the Revolution itself had been, an act of European importance; an act which might now serve as a key to coming to terms with the revolutionary epoch permanently.

Constitutional monarchism became a nineteenth-century model on a European scale, and constitutional systems following the example of the *Charte* were set up, e.g., in the United Netherlands (1815), Congress Poland (1815), the Southern German states of Bavaria (1818), Baden (1818) and Württemberg (1819), or later Spain (1834) and Greece (1844).[4] A key element of the *Charte* and its successors was the—at least formal—repossession of constituent power and hence sovereignty by the monarch. Seen from this angle, the traditional legitimacy of the *Ancien Régime* in terms of the doctrine of divine right seemed to have been reinstated, and the constitutional guarantes a mere means to disguise this radical break with the revolutionary past. Such a view, however, is misleading and ignores the Janus-like nature of constitutional monarchism, which was the institutionalized acknowledgment that the way in which monarchical rule could be legitimized had fundamentally changed.

In France, where the ties between the former dynasty and French society were of a highly fragile nature, the monarchy had to be given new foundations. Accordingly, Louis' guarantee to uphold the achievements of the Revolution in the *Charte* was a political necessity: concessions had to be, and were made.[5] In so doing, the main source of legitimacy essentially shifted from "tradition" to "law" and thus became "rationalized", despite the fact that the political rhetoric of the Restoration continued to play on the *topoi* "custom" and "divine right".

This ambivalence did not go unnoticed, especially among those who had hoped for a complete departure from the "revolutionary spirit" after Napoleon's fall. One such person was Joseph de Maistre, who in a letter from St. Petersburg, dated July 18, 1814, referred to the contradictions of the Restoration by emphasizing that it would be entirely wrong to believe that Louis XVIII had returned to the throne of his ancestors. Rather, he had only jumped in Napoleon's seat and continued the Revolution by other means.[6] Since 1814 marked a "royal Revolution", but a revolution nevertheless, the Bourbon Restoration was a project far from perfect in the eyes of de Maistre and of other reactionaries and conservatives: the granting of comprehensive legal guarantees, the constitutional restriction of monarchical power, but above all acknowledging the social order created during the revolutionary and Napoleonic age, were just too far removed from their anti-revolutionary ideology. The restoration of the monarchy, which de Maistre had intended to become the exact "opposite of the Revolution",[7] had now turned into a political compromise.

Post-Napoleonic constitutional monarchism left rulers with different playing cards, giving political legitimacy a new character. It was no longer possible to found rule exclusively upon the idea of an "authority of the past" that had been distinctive for the pre-modern age and served as a regulator for political life. Rather, political institutions were now forced to reassert their legitimacy by continuous action, activity and innovation. Monarchs, favored by their legal abstraction into "constitutional bodies", were increasingly judged from a rational perspective, in which former awe for the office holder was now replaced by pragmatic respect. Within an increasingly "functional" understanding of monarchy,[8] the main factor of legitimacy of the rulers was their ability to meet public expectations. In former days, indeed, monarchs might tell and write about freedom or constitutional government, and yet go on governing like a despot; but in the nineteenth century "the royal amateurs would now be taken at their word, and their pleasant speculations turned into anxious realities".[9]

The framework within which monarchical power could be exercised after the revolutionary experiences was aptly characterized by Talleyrand in his final report on the Congress of Vienna, addressed to Louis XVIII and written immediately after Napoleon's Hundred Days.[10] The "principle of legitimacy", Talleyrand pointed out there, was endangered most by those of its supporters who confused "source" and "exercise" of state power and would therefore mistake "legitimate" for "absolute" authority.[11] He stressed that it was of vital importance that the exercise of power was adjusted to the *Zeitgeist*. Fighting the spirit of the time was doomed to failure: the nature of legitimacy had changed, and "divine right" was no longer a reliable basis for monarchical rule.[12] At the present stage of history, only rule that guaranteed the happiness and peace of its subjects would be legitimate. The virtues and positive traits of the sovereign monarch alone would not suffice. It was stable institutions which had to be set up as reliable cornerstones of trust. In Talleyrand's eyes, yet more was needed to ensure their durability:

> It would be pointless for institutions to guarantee people happiness. Even if they did, they could not inspire confidence without establishing that form of government that contemporary general opinion considers the only one capable of reaching this goal.[13]

Yet which form of government would indeed correspond best with public opinion and be thus truly "legitimate" and most apt to achieve the aim of guaranteeing the "luck of the peoples" was anything but self-evident, remaining a matter of fierce debate even during the Restoration period. It was in the context of debates on forms of political legitimacy and how to organize political—and particularly monarchical—power that politico-theoretical reflections on the classification and assessment of the Napoleonic experience continued and advanced after 1814/1815. At the end of the day, "Napoleonism" shared a fundamental similarity with constitutional monarchism notwithstanding obvious differences between the two: while they were diametrically opposed in terms of defining the ultimate holder of "sovereignty" and "constituent power", they equally represented attempts to reconcile the legacy of the Revolution with monocratic rule.

In *De l'esprit de conquête et de l'usurpation* of 1814,[14] Constant suggested that despotism was an antiquated form of domination. He argued that what had been created in the Revolutionary and Napoleonic age were regimes that penetrated and controlled society far more than ever before, their power to mobilize citizens deriving from revolutionary and democratic energies unleashed in this form for the first time. While "usurpation" used existing "despotic" governmental structures, it did so by creating an unprecedented form of oppression made possible by demagoguery, propaganda, and mass conscription. In other words, Constant theorized a regime type which aligned itself with a series of "negative models" of government in Western political thought,[15] but which at the same time was distinctively new.

Constant was not alone in his judgement that the concepts of tyranny and despotism were inadequate to define—and indeed criticize—the system of government created in the wake of the eighteenth century's Great Revolutions. Among the authors arguing in the same vein after 1814/1815 was François Guizot (1787–1874), who embedded his reflections on the Napoleonic age in a broader theory of political sovereignty and legitimacy. Of the two main anti-Napoleonic schools of thought in the Restoration, namely royalism and liberalism, Guizot was the main representative of the latter together with Constant. His position, however, differed from Constant's in several respects.

When Guizot sought to revive the use of history in political argument during the Restoration, he actually neutralized the democratic position of other thinkers such as Sieyès by adopting a theory of legitimacy theoretically diverse and at the same time politically pluralistic. While assuming that two different criteria for legitimacy could be applied, either conformity to reason and justice, or else the acceptance over time of a regime by the people, Guizot's theory of legitimacy actually rested on the postulation that any unchecked power was illegitimate.

The cornerstones of Guizot's theory were set in his famous lectures on the *History of Civilisation in Europe* (1828) and the *History of Civilisation in France* (1828–1830), in which he revamped the concept of legitimacy in such a way as to maintain it as the standard for a pluralist theory of justice, reason, and right in politics.[16] At the same time, he declared legitimacy based on birth and inheritance, i.e. essentially the claims of the Bourbon legitimists and ultras, to simply one element of "legitimate sovereignty". For Guizot, political legitimacy was indispensable to the progress of European civilization; but as a matter of historical fact, no *one* system had ever dominated Europe, all of them had some—though limited—right to recognition in the present. In addition, Guizot also afforded a definition of legitimacy in terms of "reason". In his view, legitimacy had noting to do with absolute power and was incompatible with the personal will of any individual or group. This, in turn, also demarcated political illegitimacy:

> [...] the merest common sense will acknowledge that the sovereignty of right completely and permanently can appertain to no one; that all attribution of the sovereignty of right to any human power whatsoever, is radically false and dangerous. Hence arises the necessity for the limitation of all powers, whatever their names or forms may be; hence the radical illegitimacy of all absolute power, whether its origin be from conquest, inheritance, or election.[17]

Guizot essentially identified four types of "illegitimate"—since "absolute"—power held by men: "feudal despotism", "religious despotism", "monarchical despotism" and "democratic despotism". He made a clear distinction between feudal despotism on the one hand, and religious and monarchical on the other. While theocratic and monarchical despotism had more than once obtained the consent of the population subjected to it, feudal despotism had always been repulsive and odious. This was since feudal despotism was altogether different: "it was the power of the individual over the individual; the dominion of the personal and capricious will of a man. This is, perhaps, the only tyranny of [*sic!*] which, to his eternal honour, man will never willingly accept."[18] This left "democratic despotism" as the fourth type of illegitimate power.

Guizot argued that the worst form of democracy was one based on the delegation of supreme power by the people to a representative. In his *History of Representative Government in Europe* (1820–1822), Guizot had openly denounced the theory of representative government and, more particularly, the idea that an agent could represent the people having abdicated their power to the full extent of their inherent sovereignty. Guizot found that this concept, which he identified both with the Convention and with Napoleon,[19] was, "obviously, pure and unmixed despotism, rigorously deduced from the principle that wills are to be represented in government". The declaration that "the elect of the sovereign is itself sovereign" had to lead almost necessarily to the "destruction of all responsibility in power, and of all rights belonging to the citizens".[20]

What called for explanation, though, was how Napoleon had managed to compel overwhelming allegiance despite his "illegitimacy", as Guizot had himself defined it. The answer to this question lay in the double nature of "great men", among whom Guizot did not hesitate to count Napoleon in the same breath with Charlemagne. Starting from the premise that great men were not "merely a burden and a useless wonder to mankind" and a "sterile scourge, or at very best, [. . .] a burdensome luxury", but played a fundamental role in the development of (Western) civilization, in his *History of Civilisation in France* Guizot pointed out that "the activity of a great man is of two kinds". Correspondingly, two stages could be distinguished in his career, thus outlining what was to become a common theme in the nineteenth century. In a first stage, he would understand the necessities of his time better than other people, "its real, present exigencies; what, in the age he lives in, society needs, to enable it to subsist and attain its natural development". By understanding these necessities better than any other person of his time and knowing better than any other how to wield the powers of society, and direct them skillfully towards the realization of this end, his power and glory would proceed: "it is in virtue of this, that as soon as he appears he is understood, accepted, followed; that all give their willing aid to the work which he is performing for the benefit of all."[21] This was the source of his legitimacy.

After this initial stage, however, with the "real wants" of his time satisfied to some degree, the great man would refuse to stop: "The ideas and the will of the great man proceed further. [. . .] He aspires to extend his activity and influence indefinitely, and to possess the future as he has possessed the present. Here egoism and illusion commence." For a while people would continue to follow, believe and obey him on the face of what he had already achieved. Sooner or later, however, they would discover that they were being forced in a direction in which they have no desire to move. This in turn would force the great man to use ever more arbitrary means: "he now seeks to employ the public force in the service of his individual ideas and desires; he is attempting things which he alone wishes or understands." Disquietude and uneasiness were the consequences: "for a time he is still followed, but sluggishly and reluctantly; next he is censured and complained of; finally he is abandoned and falls; and all which he alone had planned and desired, all the merely personal and arbitrary part of his work, perishes with him."[22]

Applied to Napoleon, Guizot emphasized that when Napoleon had seized power in France, the imperious want of the French nation had been the safeguarding of national independence against foreign aspirations and civil life at home. "To put her, in a word, into the possession of independence and order, the only pledges of a long future, this was the desire, the general thought of the country." This Napoleon had understood and achieved. Yet when this was accomplished, he proposed a thousand other projects, which he aimed to push through by all available means—ultimately with dramatic consequences for his reign:

> Potent in combinations, and of an ardent imagination, egoistical and thoughtful, machinator and poet, he, as it were, poured out his activity in arbitrary and gigantic projects, children of his own,—solitary, foreign to the real wants of our time, and of our France. She followed him for some time, and at great cost, in this path which she had not selected; a day came when she would follow no further, and the emperor found himself alone, and the empire vanished, and all things returned to their proper condition, to their natural tendency.[23]

For Guizot, who propagated a constitutional redefinition of political legitimacy, Napoleon exemplified a form of democratic illegitimacy that derived from an absolutist application of the theory of popular sovereignty. This did not imply, however, that illegitimate forms of government were all in vain right by definition. On the contrary, all forms of government would have their moments of historical necessity, including the "system of Bonaparte", which—as Guizot declared in 1818—had been "a violent method of getting out of the Revolution, as the Revolution had been a violent method of getting out of the *Ancien Régime*". But while ascribing historical use and need to the Napoleonic regime, Guizot shared Constant's characterization of the system being just a temporary phenomenon: "the system of Bonaparte could have never been anything else but an ephemeral system".[24] In his view, the regime had merely fulfilled its civilizing purpose—no more, no less.

For Guizot, this was even truer after the Revolution of 1830 and the establishment of the July Monarchy, in which he played a decisive part, and which in his eyes was lastingly to guarantee the true postulations of 1789: a liberal-constitutional monarchy, rejecting both excessive monarchical claims to sovereignty and power and the doctrine of unlimited popular sovereignty. Abiding by the doctrine of parliamentary sovereignty, the new regime rested on a revised, more liberal version of the Constitutional Charter, while continuing to adhere to a strictly limited franchise. For any kind of "plebiscitary leader" there was neither room nor need therein.[25]

The fact that key figures of French intellectual life such as Constant, Madame de Staël and Guizot collaborated in designing a new negative regime type during the Restoration that was personified by Napoleon does not imply, however, that their critical view of the Napoleonic regime was unchallenged. Despite the unfavorable political circumstances during both the Restoration and the July Monarchy, Bonapartist ideas actually continued to receive considerable support not only in parts of the broader population, but also among many contemporary writers and scholars. Stendhal's *Vie de Napoléon* (1817–1818) and his *Mémoires sur Napoléon* (1836–1837) are prominent literary examples of a favorable, indeed venerating assessment of Napoleon and his form of government.[26]

In his *Vie de Napoléon*, written as a direct refutation of Madame de Staël's portrait of Napoleon in her *Considérations*, Stendhal (1783–1842) defended the "military despotism" that was installed by the coup of 18 Brumaire as the best alternative. Without it, "France had, in 1800, the events of 1814 or the Terror".[27] In the conclusion of his work, Stendhal described Napoleon as "the human being most admired for his talents since Caesar", and drew analogies also to other historical figures such as Alexander and Frederic the Great, "people alongside whom he will be placed and whose glory will shine every day".[28] His *Mémoires sur Napoléon*, written around twenty years later, argued in a very similar vein. Therein, he defended not only Napoleon's political, legal and social achievements, but also his regime *per se*, and stressed the great parallel which by then had already become somewhat commonplace: "I experienced a kind of religious feeling", Stendhal remarked, "when writing the first sentence of Napoleon's story. It is, indeed, about the greatest man who has appeared in the world since Caesar [...], the most amazing man who has appeared since Alexander [...]"[29]

The identification of Napoleon with Caesar and other great characters of world history was a common feature of the "Napoleonic myth" and "cult" in France, which gained in strength the bigger the gap to the historical events and the susceptibility to glorification and idealization became. But appreciation, if not adoration, of Napoleon and his "system" was not confined to France. It could also be found beyond its borders, including Germany, where after 1814 a remarkable change in public attitude towards Napoleon, which had been almost unanimously hostile during the *Befreiungskriege* ("Wars of Liberation"), started to take place.[30] This was particularly due to the bitter disappointment felt among broad parts of the population, but especially among the educated middle-classes (*Bildungsbürgertum*), who felt their hopes both for national unification and comprehensive political and social reforms had been betrayed by ever harsher reactionary policies in the newly founded German Confederation.[31] Even the constitutionalization processes, which had so promisingly picked up pace after the enactment of the French *Charte* in 1814 and culminated in the proclamation of new constitutions in Southern Germany (Bavaria, Baden and Württemberg), soon abated. Above all, Austria and Prussia, the two most powerful and dominant German states, remained without any formal constitution and turned towards increasingly repressive measures in order to keep the national and liberal forces under control. The enactment of the Karlsbad Decrees in 1819[32] and of the *Wiener Schlussakte* in 1820[33] in the Confederation, burned the bridges for political cooperation between rulers and the liberal *Bürgertum*. For the latter it became clear that the ruling classes were not going to make any serious efforts for reform and change voluntarily. In view of the "Metternich system", it was no wonder that the wish for a radical political solution was on the increase, even though it was almost impossible to formulate such views publicly due to strict censorship, as was popular desire for "great men" as Napoleon had represented one. In the early 1820s, Johann Georg Rist (1775–1847), a writer and Danish official from Holstein, wrote to the German publisher Friedrich Christoph Perthes (1772–1843):

> Even if the world generally seems to be no less evil than it used to be, it still lacks
> one thing entirely, it lacks great, significant personalities, standing out from the

crowd, representatives of a nobler and stronger humanity, those in whom the individual can eagerly mirror himself and take pleasure.[34]

On another occasion, Rist sagaciously highlighted the factors that helped the former "Scourge of Germany" become a heroic figure:

> Who has ever hurt the Germans more than Napoleon, and yet the people's instinct again seeks out precisely this man among the ruins under which he lies buried, and even now counts him among the heroes; because he was taken out of their midst and had brought forth a mythical time of upheavals and acts of violence, which in our sober times seem almost unbelievable.[35]

Quite similarly, another friend of Perthes pointed out that "the transformation of sentiment towards Napoleon verges on the unbelievable", and Perthes, being an ardent patriot who had distinguished himself during the period of Napoleon's supremacy by his steady resistance to French pretensions, had to acknowledge in his response that: "Napoleon will still become the idol of the period. Already many are longing for such a despot to appear anew. It would not be impossible for their longing to be satisfied; for out of [public] sentiments like those predominating today, dragons arise."[36]

It comes therefore as no surprise that the Revolution of 1830 further intensified these tendencies. The French July Revolution proved the apparent political tranquility in Germany and elsewhere to be fallacious, with revolutionary uprisings taking place in various parts of Europe (Belgium, Poland and Italy), including several German states like Brunswick, Hesse and Saxony. Metternich's hopes for achieving stabilization by means of "political paralysis" had been dashed, but a policy change did not ensue. Instead, the German Confederation introduced even harsher reactionary measures in the wake of 1830, both with regard to fundamental rights and the scope of constitutional government: whilst the *Zehn Artikel* ("Ten Articles") of July 5, 1832 were a means to suppress the liberal movement by further limitations of civil liberties,[37] the *Sechs Artikel* ("Six Articles") of June 28, 1832 sought to interpret existing constitutions more rigidly than ever before and to enchain the parliamentary opposition.[38] These reactionary measures were later specified in the *Sechzig Artikel* ("Sixty Articles") of June 12, 1834.[39]

In view of the Revolution, which in Germany only brought further repression and continued political stagnation, the longing for a personified "liberator" grew even faster. Under the impression of the events, even Perthes became convinced that "France is in need of a great despot and Europe in need of a great man".[40] The Napoleon cult became a projectory for suppressed hopes and expectations in German society. This was particularly true for the new liberal-democratic movement of the Young Germany (*Junges Deutschland*) in its anti-legitimist self-understanding. For them, worshipping Napoleon was a means to keep liberal ideals alive. Not quite unusual was also the conviction that only some sort of "national-democratic dictatorship" could sweep away the Metternich system.[41]

Perhaps the most prominent supporter of Napoleon—or rather of the ideal of him—among the Young Germans was Heinrich Heine (1797–1856), who had described the French Emperor effusively as early as 1828:

every inch a god! [. . .] His name even now sounds to us like a word of the early world, and as antique and heroic as those of Alexander and Caesar. It has already become a rallying word among the peoples, and when the Orient and the Occident meet, they fraternise on that single name.[42]

Heine's literary occupation with Napoleon Bonaparte did not confine itself to elevating the man and his glory, but advocated a broader viewpoint and agenda. On the death of Napoleon's only son, the Duke of Reichstadt and former King of Rome, in July 1832, Heine underlined that faith in Napoleon and his political program was not bound to any blood line:

[. . .] for those Bonapartists who believe in an Imperial resurrection in the flesh, all is at an end. Napoleon is for them only a name, like that of Alexander of Macedon, or Charlemagne, whose direct heirs died early in like manner. But for the Bonapartists, who believe in a resurrection of the spirit, there now blooms the best hope. For them, Bonapartism is not a transferral of power by begetting and primogeniture; no, their Bonapartism is now free from all animal admixture; it is for them the idea of an autocracy [*Alleinherrschaft*] of the highest power, applied to the best condition of the people, and he who shall have this power, and will so apply it, him they will call Napoleon II. As Caesar gave his name to absolute rule [*bloße Herrschergewalt*], so the name of Napoleon will be bestowed on a new Caesardom [*Cäsarthum*], to whom he alone has the right who possesses the highest ability and the strongest will.[43]

This passage in Heine's work is remarkable as it is one of the early instances that "Bonapartism" is actively used as a politico-theoretical term, depicting a specific, though "depersonalized" political program, ideology and category of rule. Bonapartism and Napoleonism had occasionally been used before, but more casually to describe attachment to or support for Napoleon's policy and his dynasty. In this context, for example, James Mackintosh (1765–1832) had talked of "Napoleonism, which is now become so general, chiefly, perhaps, as a sort of anti-Bourbonism" in 1814,[44] and Thomas Jefferson (1743–1826) of the "remains of Bonaparteism [*sic!*]" in 1815.[45] But it was only in the 1830s that Bonapartism began to assume the character of a political concept,[46] and it is revealing that the use of this politicized "-ism" by Heine comes at a time when the person referred to and his immediate descendants are no longer alive.

Noteworthy is not only the conceptual change reflected in Heine's writings, but also the conciseness with which he pictures "Bonapartism" and relates it to "Caesarism" (literally "Caesardom", *Cäsarthum*), both terms which were soon to become frequently used and a common part of intellectual discourse.[47] For Heine, the democratic element was certainly a crucial one in his understanding of Bonapartism. Yet he did not see Bonapartism as an ideal form of government *by* the people, but much more so *for* the people: "The best democracy", Heine later wrote in his book on Shakespeare (1838), "will always be that where one person stands as incarnation of the popular will at the head of the state, like God at the head of the world's government, for under that incarnate will of the people, as under the majesty of God, blooms the safest human equality, the truest democracy".[48] Heine did not confuse democracy with egalitarianism either; he understood it in terms of "equal opportunity", merits and accomplishments being the main criteria of social status and advancement. It was exactly these elements which made the political system of Napoleon Bonaparte so splendid and appealing; a ruler, whom Heine characterized as a type of "Saint-Simonian emperor":

> for as he [Napoleon; MJP] reached the highest power by his intellectual superiority, so he contributed only to the advancement of men of capacity, and aimed at the physical and moral well-being of the more numerous and poorer classes. He reigned less to benefit the third estate, the middle class, the *Juste-milieu*, than the men whose means consisted of hearts and hands alone; and even his army was a hierarchy whose grades of honour were gained solely by intrinsic value and capacity.[49]

Bonapartism was not about social levelling down, but allowing the "rule of the best", i.e. those with the greatest merits; an attitude, which Heine would continue to consistently defend in the forthcoming decades. Such views made him dislike a great social (world) revolution, which he saw approaching and feared. As early as 1842, Heine saw "communism" and "rule of the proletariat" looming dangerously on the horizon: "Communism is the secret name of the terrible antagonist which sets proletarian rule in all its consequences in opposition to the bourgeois regime of today. It will be a terrible conflict."[50] In an almost prophetical tone, he saw "the demons of overthrowing unbridled", an upheaval which would finally culminate in "the European, the world Revolution, the gigantic battle of the disinherited with the aristocracy of possession":

> in that free will be no question of nationality or of religion: there will be but one fatherland, the earth, and but one religion, that of happiness on [this] earth. [...] Perhaps there will be only one flock and one shepherd, a free shepherd with an iron crook and one great herd of men all shorn and all bleating alike. Wild and gloomy times come roaring on, and the prophet who would write a new Apocalypse would have to imagine new beasts, and those so terrible that the old symbols of St. John as compared to them will seem like soft doves and amorettos. [...] The future has an odour as of Russian leather, blood, blasphemy, and much beating with the knout. I advise our descendants to come into the world with thick dorsal skins.[51]

Heine saw Bonapartism as a potential preventer or terminator of chaos and civil war, particularly communism.[52] He was clearly ahead of his time in his understanding of the historical role a "new Caesar" could play in a time of social revolution.[53] This was not only because the "red menace" was not yet all too obvious in 1842, but also because the "European Restoration" was still sufficiently functional, above all the Metternich system in the German Confederation. But in the not too distant future the Revolution of 1848 would radically change the general framework.

During the *Vormärz* period, Heine was not alone in reasoning about the state of political affairs, the potential nature of a future Revolution, and the role of Caesar figures therein. Also among those German contemporaries who did not share or even vehemently opposed Heine's enthusiasm for Napoleon and Bonapartism, debates on these issues gathered momentum long before 1848. This was especially since the events of 1830 had proven that the Revolution was anything but over. While the answer to the question which direction future developments would—and even more so should—take varied, the common denominator of the "anti-Caesaristic discourse" was that a new Caesar was neither desirable nor inevitable. In 1832, for example, the conservative Karl Ernst Jarcke (1801–1852) considered the merger of absolutism and Revolution, which had been perfected by Napoleon and "by virtue of which state authority can at any moment dispose of the full extent of all capacities of each individual in the entire country", as a virulent danger of his time.[54] But while the identity of absolutism and Revolution was a risk inherent in every modern polity, there was still reasonable hope that established institutions might avert the worst. Among these institutions was not least the church, which the historian Johann Friedrich Böhmer (1795–1863), another catholic-conservative author, called the best guarantee against revolutionary and Caesaristic aspirations in 1847: "We are heading for a new Caesarism. Thanks be to God that at least the old Church has never bowed before Caesarism and has always been victorious in its opposition to it."[55] This was one of the very earliest documented appearances of the term "Caesarism", even though the usage was more casual than theoretical. Its political meaning, however, was already distinctive.[56]

Other contemporaries considered traditional hereditary monarchy as a viable means to thwart Bonapartism and Caesaristic ambitions. Among them was the aforementioned Friedrich Christoph Perthes (1772–1843), who elaborated on the clash of desires for freedom and mastery in 1834:

> Despite its liberalism, the whole world longs to be ruled. Such longing is also ancient, as ancient as mankind itself; but since the rule of powerful individuals must always be despotic, we must thank God that in order to protect human freedom, history has created monarchs, that is fictions of powerful individuals, and endowed them with the power to render the truly mighty individuals harmless.[57]

While Perthes thus declared monarchy a bastion against the rule of "grand individuals", whose aspirations necessarily ended in tyranny, he suggested at the same time that the cutting line between monarchy and Bonapartism could not be be easily drawn, and that even traditional rulers had to be endowed with certain "Caesaristic" traits. This seemed all the more true in times of accelerating change.

For many German liberals, it was this obvious change in European societies which served as a source of optimism that "rule of the one" in general and forms of dictatorship in particular would steadily lose in importance. A good example of this mindset, which followed the beaten track of Constant, is the 1837 entry "Dictator, Dictatur" in Carl von Rotteck's and Carl Theodor Georg Philipp Welcker's *Staats-Lexikon oder Encyklopädie der Staatswissenschaften*,[58] perhaps the most notable and influential piece of German nineteenth-century liberal writing.

Drafted by Wilhelm Schulz-Bodner (1797–1860), the entry acknowledged dictatorial rule by one individual as a historical—and, indeed, almost natural—phenomenon, which had become particularly important in the recent past:

Over the centuries, the constitution of the Roman Empire had transformed from a kind of kingdom into a free state [*Freistaat*] and finally into imperial rule. Recently, we saw essentially the same cycle of events in France compressed within a few decades, and finally Napoleon played the dictatorial role of Caesar and Augustus. And as everywhere similar causes produce similar effects, as the distress of pressing conditions can make unconditional trust in and reckless devotion to the will and leadership of an individual into well-recognised needs and a duty of self-preservation for an entire people, thus the phenomenon repeats in the most recent American wars for independence, so that individual generals—Bolivar among them—knew for a time how to unite an unlimited and undisputed power in their person during the struggle for freedom and in the interest of that struggle. Even in the struggle for independence of the North American Free States, budding freedom was at the point of seeking support in dictatorship.

Thus, Schulz-Bodner acknowledged the close relationship between democratic revolutions and dictatorship, which were not necessarily mutually exclusive. However, his article abstained from elaborating further on the nature of this relationship, and provided an optimistic outlook for the future:

Notwithstanding these most recent experiences, it can be asserted that in the recent cultural history of the civilized peoples, all the driving forces aim at increasing the individual's self-regard [*Selbstgefühl*] and making room for a greater number of developing talents by expanding the external conditions for general educational cultivation. But this self-regard is not keen to submit blindly to the unlimited will of an individual, and every developing talent, limited and conditional, will stand on the side of acknowledged effectiveness.

According to Schulz-Bodner, modern civilization was, in effect, unfavorable both to the emergence and the upkeep of dictatorial rule:

It is rather the defining feature of our times that the relevance of the individual is swiftly disappearing in relation to that of the masses; that the creators of a people's fate are no longer individuals but rather the people themselves.[59]

Schulz-Bodner's faith in the formative power of the masses, which would eventually make great individuals obsolete, did not mirror the *Zeitgeist*. It stood in sharp contrast to growing fears of a radical "social revolution" and widespread contemporary appreciation of "great men", be it in popular hero and specifically Napoleon worshipping, or in theoretical works, which in the tradition of Hegel argued the eminent role of "world historical figures" and "heroes".[60] The most pointed contribution in this respect was a British, namely Thomas Carlyle's (1795–1881) *On Heroes, Hero-Worship, and the Heroic in History* (1840), in which he elaborated on the importance of heroic leadership. In Carlyle's view, which had already been voiced in *The French Revolution: A History* (1837), chaotic events demanded dynamic "heroes" to control the competing forces erupting within society. Only they could master events and direct spiritual energies, i.e. the hopes and aspirations of the people, effectively.

Carlyle compared a wide range of different types of heroes—"divinity", like Odin, "prophet", like Mohammed, "poet", like Dante and Shakespeare, "priest", like Luther and Knox, and "man of letters", like Johnson, Rousseau and Burns—, but considered the "heroic leader" embodied by Cromwell and Napoleon as the most important:

> he to whose will our wills are to be subordinated, and loyally surrender themselves, and find their welfare in doing so, may be reckoned the most important of Great Men. He is practically the summary for us of *all* the various figures of Heroism; Priest, Teacher, whatsoever of earthly or of spiritual dignity we can fancy to reside in a man, embodies itself here, to *command* over us, to furnish us with constant practical teaching, to tell us for the day and hour what we are to *do*.[61]

Blind confidence in the power of democratization, as expressed in the *Staats-Lexikon*, not only ignored the prevailing appeal of a "saviour", but also neglected the potential dialectic of democracy and despotism. Not all liberals of the time, however, shared this naivety, among them Alexis de Tocqueville (1805–1859). He specified those forms of total domination posing a potential threat to modern democracies, which he considered to be "the" form of government for the future, and thus made an important contribution to theorizing modern Bonapartism and Caesarism sociologically without actually using the terms.[62]

Tocqueville, who as a young man had attended Guizot's lectures on the history of European civilization, went beyond the Restoration consensus that democracy was by its very nature illegitimate. Instead, Tocqueville acknowledged that Bonapartist dictatorship as one form of illegitimate government could be the outcome of attempts to achieve democracy, but he refused to concede that it was inevitable, as thinkers like Constant and Guizot had argued before him. Although he felt no less antipathy than they had done for the Reign of Terror and the Empire, Tocqueville came to different conclusions about the possibility of combining democracy with liberty and popular sovereignty with the guarantee of individual rights. In his view, only in a democracy modern men could learn to respect rights, and only by participating in government would they be able to identify with it.

While Tocqueville admitted that democracy—explicitly in its American form—had substantial merits, it was at the same time, by its very nature, subject to a number of potential dangers. In two of the last chapters of his classic account of the democratic system of the United States, *De la démocratie en Amérique*, Tocqueville held forth about the type of despotism democratic nations had to fear and the possible means to safeguard liberty in an egalitarian society.[63] During his stay overseas, Tocqueville had become convinced that "a democratic social state similar to that of the Americans could offer singular opportunities for the establishment of despotism", a danger also clearly evident in Europe, where "[at the time of my return] most of our princes had already made use of the ideas, sentiments and needs that arose from that social state, in order to expand the circle of their power."[64]

Given the specific character of modern (Western) society, which in Tocqueville's eyes was unprecedented in history,[65] he had come to the conclusion that modern despotism, too, was distinct from everything that had been encountered before:

[…] the type of oppression by which democratic peoples are threatened will resemble nothing of what preceded it in the world; our contemporaries cannot find the image of it in their memories. I seek in vain myself for an expression that exactly reproduces the idea that I am forming of it and includes it; the thing that I want to speak about is new, and men have not yet created the expression which must portray it; the old words of despotism and of tyranny do not work.[66]

Drawing a comparison with antiquity, Tocqueville argued that despotism in a modern egalitarian society would differ from and far exceed the degree of control ever achieved when Roman Caesarism was at its height. The emperors may have possessed "an immense power without counterbalance" which they often happened to abuse "in order arbitrarily to take away a citizen's property on his life". However, while their tyranny "weighed prodigiously on a few", it "did not extend to a great number; it was tied to a few great principal matters and neglected the rest; it was violent and limited".[67] Else despotism if it came to be established among modern democratic nations, where it would be "milder", though, but more extensive, degrading men without actually tormenting them.[68] Similar to Constant in his *De l'esprit de conquête et de l'usurpation* of 1814,[69] Tocqueville saw the danger of modern despotism by virtue of the fact that it allowed rulers to penetrate more habitually and more deeply into the private lives and minds of individuals than those of antiquity had ever been able to do.

Government in a modern democratic society could—and to a certain extent indeed had to—rely on a centralized administration to make its will prevail throughout its realm, hence potentially regulating both private and social life. The inner mechanisms of a democratic society *per se* were favorable to the genesis of a paternalistic, nevertheless menacing, "guardian":

I see an innumerable crowd of similar and equal men who spin around restlessly, in order to gain small and vulgar pleasures with which they fill their souls. Each one of them, withdrawn apart, is like a stranger to the destiny of all the others; […] Above those men arises an immense and tutelary power that alone takes charge of assuring their enjoyment and of looking after their fate. It is absolute, detailed, regular, far-sighted and mild. It would resemble paternal power if, like it, it had as a goal to prepare men for manhood; but on the contrary it seeks only to fix them irrevocably in childhood; it likes the citizens to enjoy themselves, provided that they think only about enjoying themselves.[70]

Having seized each individual citizen and fashioned him according to its own desire, the sovereign power now extended across the whole of society: "it covers the surface of society with a net of small, complicated, minute, and uniform rules, which the most original minds and the most vigorous souls cannot break through to go beyond the crowd; it does not break wills, but it softens them, bends them and directs them."[71] But why would people in a democratic society accept such tutelage? For Tocqueville, the answer lay in "two hostile passions" by which people would be incessantly tormented: the desire to remain free versus the need to be led. Unable to destroy either the one or the other, they worked hard to satisfy both at the same time:

They imagine a unique, tutelary, omnipotent power, but elected by the citizens. They combine centralization and sovereignty of the people. That gives them some relief. They console themselves about being in tutelage by thinking that they have chosen their tutors themselves.

Many contemporaries would all too easily accommodate this compromise between "administrative despotism and sovereignty of the people", thinking that they have "guaranteed the liberty of individuals when it is to the national power that they deliver that liberty".[72] All things considered, Tocqueville came to the conclusion that despotism was "particularly to be feared in democratic ages":

> I believe that it is easier to establish an absolute and despotic government among a [democratic] people where conditions are equal than among another, and I think that, if such a government were once established among such a people, not only would it oppress men, but in the long run it would rob from each of them some of the principal attributes of humanity.[73]

However, he did not feel this implied that an egalitarian democratic society was doomed to failure, or that the central power directing a democratic people had to be debilitated: "It is not a matter of making it weak or indolent, but only of preventing it from abusing its agility and strength."[74] Since the political world was changing, merely new remedies had to be sought for new evils:

> To fix for the social power extensive, but visible and immobile limits; to give to individuals certain rights and to guarantee to them the uncontested enjoyment of these rights; to preserve for the individual the little of independence, of strength and of originality that remain to him; to raise him up beside society and sustain him in the face of it: such seems to me to be the first goal of the legislator in the age we are entering.[75]

Convinced that both liberty and equality were within the realms of possibility, Tocqueville vehemently opposed two "equally fatal ideas" among his contemporaries: on the one hand those who "see in equality only the anarchical tendencies that it engenders", being afraid of their free will and themselves; on the other those who:

> alongside the road that, starting at equality, leads to anarchy, have finally found the path that seems to lead men invincibly toward servitude; they bend their soul in advance to this necessary servitude; and despairing of remaining free, they already adore at the bottom of their heart the master who must soon come.[76]

What Tocqueville achieved with his *De la démocratie en Amérique* was thus not only to provide a key work of democratic theory and one of the founding moments of political science, but also an empirically based study on the precariousness of democracy and the character of despotic rule under the conditions of modern societies. He consciously analyzed a new phenomenon, for which classical terminologies no longer seemed appropriate. At the same time, however, Tocqueville abstained from using the terms Bonapartism or Napoleonism, which might have challenged the universality of the tendencies he observed. The new despotism he saw looming—a specific "total(itarian) democracy" with a sovereign dictator at its head—was neither the result of a perversion of progress, as many liberals might argue, nor the outcome of decline, as conservatives might claim, but a latent possibility of modern civilization. To Tocqueville, the future was anything but predestined. Since "the world that is rising is still half caught in the ruins of the world that is falling, and amid the immense confusion presented by human affairs", no one could say which institutions and ancient mores would eventually remain and which would ultimately disappear:

> This new society, which I have sought to portray and which I want to judge, has only just been born. Time has not yet set its form; the great revolution that created it is still going on, and in what is happening today, it is nearly impossible to discern what must pass away with the revolution itself, and what must remain after it.[77]

1848 spectacularly furnished proof for Tocqueville's conviction that the Revolution was still going on. It was in the context of the European revolutionary upheavals that the discourse of "Bonapartism", "Napoleonism" and "Caesarism" reached a height and that the chances in the political arena for ambitious individuals to seize power and take the role of "Caesaristic" leaders increased. This was in contrast to the post-1814 period: while debates on the Napoleonic regime, illegitimate forms of rule, and the need or danger of a heroic saviour had been vivid, such figures had been of marginal importance in European politics. Above all, this was due to the European great power's paradigm of stability under the umbrella of the Congress System, which did not leave much room for political change.

Even the Revolution of 1830 had not considerably altered the general framework and itself was lacking in radicality, resulting in perhaps more "liberal", nevertheless still monarchical political systems just as before. France and Belgium are two revealing examples in this respect: in both countries the preference for reform rather than radical change or even a republican experiment was motivated by the political classes' fear of foreign intervention, but also by the widespread belief that a constitutional monarchy would best suit their own—that is predominantly bourgeois—interest and needs. This was not without popular, indeed populist, attributes, with Louis-Philippe in France a case in point with his emphasis on the popular origins of his reign, his self-characterization as "King of the French" rather than "King of France", and his attempts to invoke a national spirit. Still, his reign could hardly be compared to that of Napoleon before him, manifest among other things in the denial of plebiscitary means for legitimizing the regime change of 1830 and the persistence of hereditary monarchy.[78] It was only in 1848 that time seemed to be ripe for a "new Caesar" in the European context and in France in particular.

3.2 Conclusions

Napoleon's fall in 1814/1815 marked the military victory of the anti-revolutionary powers after almost a quarter-century of continued wars and turmoil in Europe, yet anything but a return to "business as usual". This was true for both political theory and the sphere of actual politics.

The Revolution and the Napoleonic Age had created precedents which even Europe's monarchs could not avoid. A *modus vivendi* had to be found with the legacy of the previous decades in order to secure stability and order. The revolutionary paradigms of and calls for "change", "political participation" and "constitutional government" had been all too powerful and pervasive to be neglected. Perhaps the most explicit attempt to reconcile the pre-revolutionary with the revolutionary heritage was the model of monarchical constitutionalism, first put into practice by the French *Charte constitutionnelle* of 1814, which was to become a successful "export model": a regime type claiming sovereignty and constituent power exclusively for the hereditary monarch perceived in traditional terms, i.e. the core of legitimist thought, but at the same time making concessions to representative forms of government and offering the nation possibilities for political participation, even if only limited ones. Louis XVIII in France and other fellow rulers in Europe thereby nourished the hope to have conserved the true nucleus of monarchical government and preserved it for the future. In point of fact, however, monarchical constitutionalism amounted to an institutionalized avowal of the crisis into which traditional monarchies had slipped.

The doctrine of the "divine rights of kings" might still serve its purpose for monarchical propaganda, but was no longer a sound and unchallenged basis for the justification of rule. Faith in a divinely-ordained political system and hereditary rights of the ruling dynasty alone were not a reliable guarantee for the preservation of the monarchy. What became a growingly important factor in acknowledging an authority— the *Legitimitätsglaube* ("belief in legitimacy"), as Weber would later define it[79]—were good governance and the ability to meet public expectations. Whether they wanted or not, monarchs were increasingly driven by external circumstances and turned from subjects into constitutional "objects", playing a powerful, albeit functional role, which was ultimately dependent on popular opinion.

Acknowledging that after the Revolution even monarchical rule could not have the same character as before paved the way for a broader debate on the nature and organization of government, the relation between Revolution and counter-Revolution, democracy and dictatorship. For many observers in the post-Napoleonic age the old discourses carried associations which they felt were inadequate to convey the new reality that had burst forth around them. They realized that a chasm had opened up between the language they had inherited from the eighteenth century and the current situation they found themselves in, resulting in an intensified search for new terminological coordinates. Since "legitimacy" was not something to be taken for granted, the most fundamental question now was which form of government could claim to be "legitimate" and why, by implication defining "illegitimate" or "degenerate" rule. These debates provided new impulses for dealing with the Napoleonic experience as well, eventually resulting in the birth of Bonapartism and Napoleonism as political concepts, later to be followed by Caesarism.

Most authors in the post-1814 age, particularly during the French Restoration period, considered Napoleon Bonaparte's regime to be the opposite of legitimate rule. Such rule was widely considered to be embodied by a constitutional monarchy averting political extremes,[80] even though there were clear differences of opinion concerning the exact delimitation of regal and parliamentary powers between royalism and liberalism. An advocate of constitutional monarchy among contemporary French liberals was not only Constant, but also Guizot, who declared political legitimacy to be *the* key issue of the progress of Western civilization. Starting from the premise that any form of unchecked power was reprehensible, Guizot denied sovereignty to any of the major claimants: the monarchy, the Church, the aristocracy or the people. He also denied that any of these groups could delegate absolute power to an individual or assembly. Therefore he also branded the "democratic despotism" represented by the Napoleonic regime as one form of political illegitimacy. Guizot acknowledged that while Napoleon might have been an illegitimate ruler, he had nevertheless been a popular one, enjoying significant support. This, however, was not necessarily a contradiction, especially because Guizot distinguished the earlier, brighter phase in Napoleon's career from the later, darker one; a dichotomy which in his view was significant of all great men, who suffered from an almost natural hubris: great men pushed important matters and were hence important for the progress of civilization, Guizot argued in picking up a key element of Hegel's philosophy of history,[81] but they lacked the ability to hold their ambitions after initial success and conducted themselves more and more tyrannically over time. Their fall was thus predestined. However, what made Napoleon's rule illegitimate at the end of the day was not so much his individual conduct, but the very foundations of his rule: usurpation of power and a misguided notion of the popular will. For Guizot, as for other contemporaries, Napoleon was the necessary outcome of the Revolution and one possible result of desires to achieve unlimited popular sovereignty, which made them most reluctant to democratic aspirations of any kind. This became obvious in the July Monarchy with its limited concessions to the sovereignty of the people and perpetuation of the restrictive franchise of the Restoration.

While the concepts of Bonapartism (and Napoleonism, respectively), plebiscitary dictatorship and Caesarism were taking shape in the political thought of the time, not all observers shared the critical attitude towards Napoleon and his regime, nor the belief that the eschewal of "political extremes" was the best available alternative. This was not only true for France, where Stendhal and others actively promoted the legend of Napoleon and portrayed the emperor's "military despotism" as without any alternative, but also other parts of Europe. Germany, too, was an elucidating example in this respect.

The German case demonstrates the direct link between unaccomplished political and national expectations and a radical change of attitude towards Napoleon within a short period of time. While Napoleon had served as the personification of evil and object of collective hatred during the Wars of Liberation, this negative image changed to the opposite the more averse to reform and the more oppressive the Metternich system became. To have a "heroic leader" and "liberator" of the kind Napoleon had allegedly been for France was the wish of a growing number of people also in Germany. This was the case to an even greater extent after 1830, a period which—rather than in an expected liberalization boost—only resulted in even further repression, with the sustained political-institutional stagnation being all the more evident and dramatic since it was in sharp contrast to the ever faster social change taking place during the first half of the nineteenth century.

Against this backdrop, especially the movement of the Young Germans argued for a radical break with the existing monarchical order, considering a kind of "national dictatorship" as one conceivable alternative. It was around this time and under the active involvement of Heinrich Heine that Bonapartism and Napoleonism respectively started to get used as politico-theoretical concepts, of a political "supra-program", obviously borrowing from the name giver, though, but no longer immediately bound to his person or actions. This was facilitated by the fact that in the meanwhile both Napoleon and his only legitimate son had died, thus helping to "transcend" the terms and uncouple them from dynastic considerations. In Heine's understanding, Bonapartism represented the ideal of a polity *for* rather than *by* the people, the top and amalgamating element of which was a glorious leader to which the whole people could look up to. Such a leader would be the guarantor that a new state order would essentially be a meritocracy and not degenerate to a "rule of the equals", but remain a "rule of the best". For Heine, this was all the more important given the dangers of a new and even more radical social (world) Revolution that he saw looming on the horizon.

Not all German contemporaries shared Heine's enthusiasm for Bonapartism. But even many critics, including conservatives, did realize that the appeal of Bonapartist and Caesaristic-type government grew out of the unresolved conflict between love of liberty on the one hand, and the craving for mastery on the other. Tellingly, it was in this context that the issue was raised as to whether traditional monarchies, too, should incorporate Caesaristic traits, and princes turn from rulers to leaders to ward off potential Bonapartist usurpers. In contrast, for many liberals in Germany and elsewhere, the attraction of Bonapartism as well as of personalized leadership would wane sooner or later anyway due to the growing maturity of Western societies and ever more democratic political systems. However, the naive idea that the problem would sort itself out was not shared by every liberal, least so by Alexis de Tocqueville.

In his celebrated *De la démocratie en Amérique*, Tocqueville offered new explanatory approaches to the hidden dialectics of democracy and despotism, and elaborated on the particular importance of such dialectics for the modern age. Unlike earlier forms of despotism, the probable "administrative despotism" in modern democratic societies would do without too much violence and open arbitrariness. It would hence look mild, but under this smoke screen actually have a comprehensive, indeed almost total and highly corrupting character. Like others, Tocqueville identified the reason why people would bow to "complete tutelage" in common desires for leadership and guidance. Such desires were no less, if not even more, present in modern than in traditional societies.

Overall, Tocqueville's work fits well into what can be considered a characteristic feature of political discourse in the "European Restoration" period after 1814; namely an increasingly prevalent understanding that Bonapartism and Napoleonism were detached from their eponym and needed to be considered first and foremost as a structural problem of the modern age. These terms—together with the nascent Caesarism, which even more distinctively marked the turning away from a concrete person of contemporary history[82]—developed into a watchword for a new form of government distinguished by the duopoly "strong leadership" and "popular foundation" in an environment of crisis, while leaving broad scope for its actual form; a form of rule which—depending on the viewpoint of the observer—could be seen as a means to break out of fossilized and set political structures, a guarantee for stability or preventer of radical (social or political) upheaval, but also as a result of errant doctrines of revolutionary thought or permanent challenge and danger for modern societies. For all of these interpretations, 1848/1849 was to provide illustrative material.

4

From Bonapartism to Caesarism: The
Mid-Century and Louis-Napoléon

4.1 The Revolution of 1848 and the Dawn of Caesarism

The growing political-institutional and constitutional ossification after 1814/1815 was contrasted by the changes that had been taking place in European societies throughout the first half of the nineteenth century. Political awareness had grown and was becoming increasingly popularized even where censorship tried to keep an ever more varied and active press scene under control, helping to make liberalism, nationalism, constitutionalism and—to a slighter degree—also socialism the prevalent ideas of public life. At the socio-economic level, (proto-)industrialization provided fertile soil not only for the redistribution of power and influence in society, but also for revolutionary unrest. This was manifest in the middle classes' tangible discontent that their growing economic and societal role was not matched by their political influence. Fast population growth during the first half of the nineteenth century contrasted with stagnating productivity, and the fact that agriculture was in a state of crisis increased discontent among the growing group of landless peasants and the emerging industrial proletariat. The "social question" thus helped to provide a new revolutionary basis that socialist ideas could impinge on.

Clearly, conflict was in the air, as even the Revolution of 1830 had demonstrated. The situation heated up from the mid-1840s onwards, with a series of economic downturns and crop failures in Europe, particularly those in 1846, triggering rising prices and starvation. Neither trade nor manufacturing were spared this socio-economic crisis and were hit hard by falling demand. The crisis resulted in popular protests, revolts and cases of "machine breaking", harbingers of the "European Revolutions" that were to take place in 1848. Widespread discontent with the existing conditions culminated in political uprisings against the Spanish Bourbons in Sicily and against the Habsburg Empire in Lombardy as early as January 1848. The initial spark for the Europe-wide revolutionary wave, however, was once again France, where the February Revolution ended the July Monarchy and led to the Second Republic.

In the 1840s, France represented a transition society: economy was still driven by agriculture; at the same time, however, there were already signs of a shift towards an "industrial economy". This ongoing transition was not without a distinct element of crisis and went hand in hand with economic difficulties, which from 1845 onward "combined the features of a traditional subsistence crisis with those of over-production/ under-consumption and loss of confidence in financial markets more typical of an industrial society, as well as the fears and aspirations which informed political activity".[1] The situation was not eased by the pro-business "laissez-faire" policy advocated by the July Monarchy, favoring the interests of the *grands notables*, who made up the elite of the regime. Notables and the government alike were fully committed to maintaining both the social and the political *status quo*, thus hampering every initiative for substantial reform.[2] While this resistance to change might have been tolerated before, it now became a real obstacle when economic problems grew stronger in the second half of the 1840s.

Nevertheless, the sudden fall of the July Monarchy in early 1848 had hardly been foreseeable, not least because the opposition in the country—from Bourbon legitimists on the right to republicans on the left—had presented itself as generally weak and divided since 1830. What actually sparked the February Revolution in France was the suppression of the *campagne des banquets* by the Guizot government, whose authoritarian style had alienated it from the liberal wing of the Orléanists gathered behind Adolphe Thiers (1797–1877). As in July 1830, the French regime change of 1848, too, occurred at breath-taking speed: no more than three days, namely February 22–24, were effectively needed to end the monarchy of Louis-Philippe. Similar to the situation eighteen years earlier, a combination of ineffective crisis management on the part of the government and military ineptitude allowed public protest to turn into an insurrection and finally revolution.

February 26, 1848 saw the creation of the Second Republic by a small group of republicans, who had managed to assume power when governmental authority collapsed. In view of the militant crowds in Paris vociferously demanding political and social improvements, one of the first legislative acts of the new republic was the granting of universal male suffrage on March 2, increasing the number of voters almost forty-fold to around 10 million.[3] This, however, did not help to improve the economic situation, which remained desperate, nor did it significantly contribute to a lessening of political unrest. The enfranchisement of the entire male population did favor the formation of radical leftist political societies and clubs in the urban areas that sought to instrumentalize the now "politicised masses". One widespread postulation that was actively propagated by means of "political education" in newspapers, workers' associations and cafés stressed the need for "social change" which would have to follow the construction of the republic. For many contemporaries this demand perhaps more than everything else revealed that the Revolution in 1848 was different from both the ones in 1789 and 1830. Among them was also Tocqueville, who emphasized the new "socialistic character" of the Revolution and provided a vivid picture of the political atmosphere and sentiments at the time in his posthumously published *Souvenirs* (*Recollections*).[4] Seeing the lower classes in control of political power in Paris, a mixture of uncertainty and dread about what would eventually come was predominant among the property-owning classes; a situation which, according to Tocqueville, "was only to be compared to that which the civilized cities of the Roman Empire must have experienced when they suddenly found themselves in the power of the Goths and Vandals".[5]

Fear of a redistribution of property, but also of anarchy, helped to strengthen the ranks among "anti-socialists", who won the majority in the National Constituent Assembly elected on April 23.[6] This, in turn, caused great dissatisfaction amongst urban radicals, resulting in even more political agitation and turmoil. On May 15, an armed mob attempted, but eventually failed, to overwhelm the Assembly. This strengthened both government and parliament in their determination to take harsh counter-measures, eventually culminating in the civil-war-like June Days Uprisings (June 23–26, 1848). Their crushing, followed by intense political repression, marked the end of the hopes of a *République démocratique et sociale* and the defeat of the radical left. Still, even though the new constitution approved by the Constituent Assembly on November 4 lacked the guarantee of "social rights" and "welfare institutions" socialists had so adamantly fought for, it did not only stick to the ideal of a liberal democratic republic with a unicameral parliament, but also retained universal male suffrage.[7] This ensured the continuation of political disquietude and sustained the anxiety especially among conservatives. All the bigger were the hopes that at least the new president, to whom the executive power was delegated and who was to be elected for four years by direct ballot, might serve as an institution granting predictability and stability both in political and social respect.

The new constitutional system of the Second Republic heightened the dilemma which had already been present in the First French Constitution of 1791 with both the legislative and the executive branch potentially asserting claims to represent the national will. In 1848, this was a quandary *a fortiori*, with the president being elected on a broader popular basis than the chamber and thus embodying "national sovereignty" at least to no lesser degree than parliament, no matter whether the president *de jure* remained subordinated to the legislative or not. Left-wing republicans like François Paul Jules Grévy (1807–1891) therefore had proposed to confer the chief authority to the president of the ministerial council, elected and removable by the Assembly, rather than a strong popular presidency. In the latter, he saw the inevitable risk of restoring a monarchy or even worse, as he outlined in the National Assembly on 6 October 1848, recalling the events of 1799.[8]

All initiatives for a true parliamentarization of the French political system, however, failed. Not least, because a strong presidency was also institutionalized expression of an overriding appetite for a "firm hand" after the rough-and-tumble of the previous months. In this respect, the situation in 1848 bore clear resemblances to 1799, and it was again a Bonaparte who was ready to take advantage of the situation: Louis-Napoléon (1808–1873), the nephew of the Emperor.

At the beginning of the Revolution it was not at all clear that the by then already 40-year-old son of Louis Bonaparte (1778–1846), former King of Holland, would play a decisive political role. Two bumbling attempts to seize power in 1836 and 1840 had been a farce, and in early 1848 not one of the influential newspapers in France supported Louis-Napoléon. However, even the success in the by-elections held on June 4, in which Louis was elected as a representative in no less than five departments, proved that he was a force to be reckoned with. He benefitted from the widespread Napoleon cult in the population, which had been fostered throughout the decades since the fall of the Empire in popular culture: through war veterans, heroic tales, mugs and pipes depicting the Emperor, lithographs, songs and plays. In the crisis of 1848, the legend of Napoleon I took on political momentum to the benefit of Louis-Napoléon, favored by the widening of the electorate.[9] The motives for the support of Louis and the hopes attached to him could be quite the opposite, as had already been the case with his uncle. While some considered him to be the master and halting force of the Revolution, others saw Louis as the personification of the very same Revolution. Paradoxically enough, after February 1848 cries of *Vive Napoléon, à bas la République!* and *Vive Napoléon, vive la République!* could be heard at the same time around France.[10]

What contributed to Louis' popularity was that during exile he had commended himself to the *Zeitgeist* with his writings, and during his imprisonment from 1840 to 1846 he had shown a clear awareness of the ever more burning social question. Louis' writings following his first publication, the *Rêveries politiques* of 1832, included *Des Idées Napoléoniennes* (1839), *L'analyse de la question des sucres* (1842) and *Extinction du paupérisme* (1844).[11] Thus, he had actually been able to prepare a comprehensive political program, which made him distinct not only from most politicians at the time, but also Napoleon I. Louis consciously devoted much of his writing to the social and economic challenges resulting from the effects of the Industrial Revolution and rapid population growth. This was not without political calculation. Louis envisaged himself following in the tradition of his uncle, though, but not as a cheap copy of Napoleon I, rather as someone with his own distinct personality and aware of the needs of the time. In this vain, Louis had made clear in his *Idées Napoléoniennes*, which would sell half a million copies by 1848,[12] that:

> the Napoleonic idea is hardly one of war, but rather a social, industrial, commercial, humanitarian idea. If to some it always appears surrounded by the thunder of combats, that is because it was in fact for too long veiled by cannon smoke and battle dust. But now the clouds have dispersed, and we can spy, through the glory of arms, a greater and more enduring civil glory.[13]

However, Louis not only presented the "Napoleonic Idea" as a political vision and a peace project in times of political trouble in rather abstract terms, but he also made suggestions on how existing social and economic problems might be tackled. In his 1844 pamphlet on the *Extinction of Pauperism*, a melange of romanticism, authoritarianism and Saint-Simonianism, Louis-Napoléon advocated active state intervention in the economy.[14] Therein, taxation was portrayed as the main means by which the state could promote industrialization and the emancipation of the workers at the same time. Louis did not acknowledge any fundamental difference between the interests of industry and those of the working classes. What was crucial, in his view, was the effective organization of labor. In this respect, he pushed for militarily organized "agricultural colonies" (*colonies agricoles*) to be set up.

That reflected Louis-Napoléon's conviction that in modern societies it was virtually impossible to rule without the masses. Rather than "self-determination", however, the masses required "guidance":

> Today, the reign of castes is over: one can govern only with the masses; they must therefore be organized so that they can formulate their wishes, and be disciplined

so that they can be guided and enlightened about their own interests. To govern is no longer to dominate the people by force and violence; it is to lead them to a better future, by appealing to their reason and to their heart.[15]

The Napoleonic legend together with Louis-Napoléon's reputation as a political and social reformer ultimately paved the way for his overwhelming triumph in the presidential elections on December 10/11, 1848. With 5.5 million votes (74.2 percent), Louis-Napoléon outclassed his rival Louis-Eugène Cavaignac (1802–1857), who—as the suppressor of the June Days uprising and current *Président du Conseil des ministres* with far-reaching executive powers represented an alternative "republican dictatorship"—received less than 1.5 million votes (19.5 percent).[16] "France has appointed Louis Bonaparte President of the Republic because it is tired of parties",[17] Pierre-Joseph Proudhon (1809–1865) noted on the impressive support shown for Louis-Napoléon not only in the countryside, the basis of Bonaparte's electoral strength, but also in the cities.[18] The elections could be interpreted as an expression of widespread Bonapartist sentiment and a vote for a man heralding a better future, but also as a vote against the republican and parliamentary establishment. Louis was willing to capitalize on popular mood for his own benefit, exploiting the presidential powers entrusted to him by popular vote and the widespread idea of him as the "man of providence". In the following months and years, Louis systematically strengthened his political position, thus preparing the *coup d'état* that was to take place in December 1851.

While Louis-Napoléon was engaged in satisfying his personal ambitions and in putting his political program into practice, the events of the 1848 Revolutions in France and elsewhere were reflected in various politico-theoretical studies. One of the most pressing questions was how the rising power of the lower and working classes so forcefully demonstrated during the Revolutions could best be dealt with, and which style of government would be best suited to address the new "social challenge". Not surprisingly, very different answers were provided.

For the German economist and social thinker Lorenz von Stein (1815–1890), "industry" was the characteristic feature of his era, providing a new dimension for the traditional relationship between a proprietary and ruling class on the one hand, and the unpropertied and ruled on the other. It was in this vain that he had addressed the *Socialismus und Communismus des heutigen Frankreichs* as early as 1842.[19] Under the impact of the Revolution of 1848, he refined and expanded his analysis, leading to his three-volume opus *Geschichte der socialen Bewegung in Frankreich von 1789 bis auf unsere Tage* in 1850.[20] Stein argued that the attempts of the non-ruling class were quite naturally directed "to change their social position by means of the state so that they are no longer dependent, that is, to make their members participants in the capital of the nation". However:

If it [...] can be neither denied nor prevented that this merely working class gains its place in state power [*Staatsgewalt*], then it will quite unavoidably and quite tirelessly put forward the question everywhere within that power of whether and in what way it is possible to make the position of this class (which is necessarily dependent upon the nature of mere labor) independent and materially free, using the state power and especially the state administration. It will make the answer to this question the task of the entirety of state life, it will consider all who obstruct work toward this answer its enemy to be persecuted.[21]

Thus, "the task and the power of the state power in relation to the dependency of the simply working, unpropertied class is the real social question of our times", the resolution of which was "the greatest task of history".[22] Unlike socialism and communism, the social question was not one dealing with "purely abstract, unworkable ideas", but actually addressing "real conditions".[23]

What Stein argued for was a "kingship of social reform" (*Königthum der socialen Reform*).[24] Due to its independence from the ruling class, only the monarchy—conceptualized as a constitutional monarchy occupying the role of a *pouvoir neutre*—was in a position to devote itself to the welfare of the underprivileged who did not have the means themselves to make progress; rather, they were in the dilemma of becoming ever more dependent on those who had these means. If the monarchy would wisely use its power for the benefit of the lower classes, it could be certain to win overwhelming approval and allegiance. By identifying "the throne with the idea of liberty [*Freiheit*]", the monarchy would provide the former with "the most secure support human affairs can find", and "wear a double crown, insofar as it finds its true divine purpose in its people!"[25]

Consequently, social policies was the most promising strategy to gain legitimacy for the monarchy and to thwart political "extremism". By expanding the *Rechtsstaat* ("state of law") to a welfare state, not only social revolution would be effectively thwarted; also dictatorship would be evaded, characterized by "absence of any constitution" and "exclusive rule of state power".[26] This had been the case under Napoleon I. Nevertheless, his regime, too, was—as every other form of government—only a product of "social development":

> Napoleon was not born a despot; he became one. [...] It was not choice, not Napoleon's character that made him a despot; it was the undeniable need of society. This society [...] needed a man who had the courage to put his personality in place of a constitution [...] It is an incontrovertible certainty that without his despotism, Napoleon would not have had the support of all the people, nor would he have served his country as well as he did. Society made him an absolute ruler.[27]

The fact that Napoleon's dictatorship, similar to that of Oliver Cromwell, had developed "organically out of the life of the people" made it significantly different from those dictatorships that "arise in the blink of an eye, and are only occasioned by either administrative or military expediency", and which were thus being destined to be shortlived:

> These [i.e. dictatorships *à la* Napoleon; MJP] are permanent because they are generated by a particular condition of society; the principle which dominates this class of dictatorships appears to be that the disintegration preceding a new social order makes dictatorship of the singular individual [*Einzelnen*] desirable, and that

the initial period of the new social order is always the true beginning of a dictatorship, which we might call the "social".[28]

At the end of the third and last volume of his study, Stein also tackled the new presidency of Louis-Napoléon. He abstained from speculating on what would eventually happen, and was reluctant to give a personal assessment of the new president. What seemed obvious to Stein, however, was that the key factor which had secured Bonaparte's electoral victory in 1848 was the French nation's wish for a surrogate monarch; a man who, "standing outside of all parties, could provide assurance against the future rule of parties in the country by his very name and singular personality. This man, who should be a king, without the name, power and dignity of a king, was Louis Napoleon". But no matter how commendable "the elevation of the state above the rule of political parties" might be *per se*: Stein saw the constitution of the new political system as suffering from a fundamental malady, which was not so much the fact that it had created a head of state which "had slightly too much power for a president, definitely too little anyways for a monarch". Rather, the main problem was the "contradiction [...] between the legal validity of universal suffrage with the present form of French society". The constitution conflicted with the order of society insofar as "the lower class of society had a political right which it did not fulfill due to its social status".[29] Further struggles between proprietaries and non-proprietaries were thus predestined. Out of self-interest, Louis had already made his decision in favor of the former.[30] Stein cited the harsh repression of socialists after Louis' assuming office as unambiguous evidence for the president's partiality. But while the eventual outcome of the fight just about to start was open, it was clear to Stein that it was "from now on no simple fight between labor and capital, but the fight of the social democracy [*sociale Demokratie*] with the industrial reaction".[31]

No less—if not even more—than on Lorenz von Stein, the revolutionary upheavals of 1848 made a deep impression on the Spanish politician, diplomat and theorist Juan Donoso Cortés, marqués de Valdegamas (1809–1853).[32] While Stein considered a moderate "social monarchy" the best alternative to deal with the revolutionary potential of modern industrial society, Donoso Cortés arrived at very different conclusions. For him, dictatorship had become the only reasonable political alternative in the present state of Europe.

Before the Revolution, Donoso Cortés had in fact been a spokesman of the Spanish liberal-conservatives (*moderados*). Like them, he had been a proponent of doctrinary liberalism *à la* Guizot and Pierre Royer-Collard. 1848, however, demonstrated the weakness of a class rooted in the Revolution, while at the same believing in their finitude, not only in France, but also Spain and other European countries. In this respect, Donoso Cortés was in agreement with the diagnosis of many other observers at the time that the social and political order was now severely unstable. While offering very different remedies, most of his fellow contemporaries shared the belief that a new and durable stability could be found, and that liberty would survive or could be restored in one way or another. But not so Donoso Cortés: for him, the ideals of liberty and freedom were essentially dead. This was the key message of Donoso Cortés' philosophy of history so decidedly pessimistic and apocalyptic, which he developed in his post-1848 theoretical contributions and which made him a defender of dictatorial rule on the basis of pragmatic rather than ideological reasoning.[33]

In a much-noticed speech in the Spanish *Cortes* on January 4, 1849,[34] Donoso Cortés used the opportunity for a general analysis of the Revolutions which had so mightily shattered the political foundations of Europe. He criticized the "lamentable lightness with which the deep causes of the revolution have been discussed", the seed of which he saw "in the populace's overexcited desires caused by the publicists that exploit and benefit from them".[35] For Donoso Cortés there was no doubt that "The world [...] walks with the quickest steps towards the constitution of the most gigantic and desolate despotism that there has ever been in the memory of mankind", and that everything was prepared "for a gigantic, colossal, universal, immense tyrant".[36] This was the ultimate consequence of centuries of decline in the Western World since the days of Jesus Christ; noticeable, among other things, in state power having become ever more extensive and penetrating. The actual reason for this political downfall was the demise of Christianity, as Donoso Cortés argued: "[...] it was necessary [...] that the thermometer of political repression went up because the thermometer of religion continued to fall."[37] The only means which could possibly prevent disaster was not the granting of more rights and liberties, more guarantees, or new constitutions: "the catastrophe [...] will [only] be avoided if everyone tries, as far as our forces suffice, to provoke a salubrious, religious reaction." However, he deemed it most unlikely that such "religious restoration" could succeed: "I have seen [...] and known many individuals that abandoned faith and have come back to it: unfortunately, I have never seen a people who have come back to their faith after having lost it."[38]

The only thing that remained was to offer the biggest possible resistance against the revolutionary powers. This was especially since the question from time immemorial whether preventing revolution by resistance or concession was the better alternative had been unmistakably answered in favor of the former in 1848: "In France, the monarchy did not defend itself and was defeated by the republic [...]; [but] the republic, that barely had any force to move, defeated socialism because it offered resistance."[39] In the present time of decay and crisis, Donoso Cortés concluded, the remaining choice was no longer between liberty and freedom on the one hand and dictatorship on the other, in which case there would hardly be disagreement about which one to choose:

> [...] it is a matter of choosing between the dictatorship of insurrection and the dictatorship of the government. In this case, I choose the dictatorship of the government as less burdening and less contentious. It is a matter of choosing between the dictatorship that comes from below, and the dictatorship that comes from above. I choose the one that comes from above because it comes from cleaner and more serene regions. It is a matter of choosing, in the end, between the dictatorship of the dagger and the dictatorship of the sword: I choose the dictatorship of the sword because it is the noblest one.[40]

In other words, an "orderly" governmental dictatorship was preferable to an anarchical dictatorship of the mob. This dictatorship had to go beyond the forms of a temporary "legal dictatorship" as practised in the previous months in Spain by General Ramón María Narváez (1800–1868), which seemed no longer sufficient to combat the poisonous delusions and doctrines instilled into the European nations by the abusive means of freedom of expression and liberty of the press.

While one might still discern some hopes Donoso Cortés nourished in early 1849, this was less the case one year later. In another parliamentary speech on January 30, 1850[41] he arrived at an even more pessimistic assessment than before, painting a disillusioning picture of contemporary Europe. He bewailed that while the revolutionary movement had been defeated in most parts of the continent, the reprieve gained had not been used properly to address the sole issue of true relevance: the re-establishment of Christianity. Outlining a powerful political theology, Donoso Cortés saw "affirmative civilization", mainly characterized as "progressive and catholic", in the state of transcending to a negative and revolutionary period. Three negations fundamentally challenging the three divine affirmations that 1) there was an omnipresent God, 2) that this God ruled heaven and earth, and 3) that this God ruled godly and human affairs alike featured this period. The first negation, put forward by deists, claimed that "God exists, God rules; but God is so high above that he cannot govern human things", which in the political sphere would correspond to "the king exists, the king rules; but he does not govern".[42] The second negation was the pantheist's denying God's personal existence, correlating to political republicanism:

> power exists; but power is not [bound to a] person, nor does it rule or govern; power is everything that lives, everything that exists, everything that moves; thus, it is the crowd, and it follows that there can be no other means of government than universal suffrage, no other form of government than the republic.[43]

The third negation, finally, to go beyond which in terms of radicalism was impossible, was the atheist's assertion that: "God does not rule or govern, nor is he a person, nor is he the crowd; he does not exist." In political terms, this was the justification for non-governance and anarchy.[44] The whole of Europe was just about to enter the second of these negations, and on its way to the third: a course of events, which Donoso Cortés saw no legitimate hope to be able to change anytime soon.

Against the backdrop of his critical attitude that became increasingly fatalistic in the last years of his life, Donoso Cortés' judgement of Louis-Napoléon and his regime remained slightly ambivalent, too. He was to appreciate Louis' coup in late 1851, which he actively supported in his function as Spanish ambassador in Paris and from which he seemed to hope some positive impulses for a religious restoration he saw European civilization in such dire need. However, his hopes pinned on the politician who he once compared with Augustus, a nephew of Caesar as Louis was a nephew of Napoleon I, soon waned, and were perhaps more due to amicable sentiments for the man whose groomsman Donoso Cortés' should eventually become.[45] His reports from Paris reflect growing concern about the feasibility of Louis' daring political experiment, and the personal abilities of the Emperor. After all, the damage already done by the diabolic forces of liberalism and socialism as well as pantheism and atheism, polemically attacked in Donoso Cortés' perhaps best known work *Ensayo sobre el catolicismo, el liberalismo y el socialismo considerados en sus principios fundamentales* (1851),[46] seemed all too advanced to be remedied.

Donoso Cortés' political thought, which made him one of the nineteenth-century masterminds of conservative authoritarianism, was to find many recipients in Europe and beyond. Quite a few of them, however, shared the Spaniard's gloomy attitude that in the world's disastrous state its destiny could no longer be influenced by human action, but was rather subject to God's final judgement. Among those who did not call the directing force and power of political action into question as Donoso Cortés did was his perhaps most direct disciple: François-Auguste Romieu (1800–1855), a Frenchman, whose overall legacy as a politico-theoretical writer can be described as modest, but who is commonly seen as the first to introduce into intellectual discourses the term "Caesarism" in its modern meaning, describing a genuinely new and clearly defined political concept.[47] Romieu also made headway in theory construction, specifically by turning the concept of Caesarism into a central element of anti-revolutionary as well as pro-Bonapartist propaganda and by using it in a deliberately polemical way.

Romieu rose to the post of prefect during the July Monarchy and was later to be appointed general director of the French libraries (1853). As with so many other contemporaries, the Revolution of 1848 had made deep impact on Romieu, the written result of which was the publication of *L'ère des Césars* in 1850, arguing for "Caesarism" (*césarisme*) as the only form of government suitable under the present circumstances.[48] In line with Donoso Cortés, Romieu's overarching argument was essentially that in the interest of the nation, power had to prevail over debate. In times without legitimacy and faith, without social and individual morale, only authority and force could guarantee the minimum of order essential for survival: "Men have two kinds of respect: for what is holy and for what is strong. The holy no longer exists in this century; the strong is eternal, and it alone can restore the holy."[49] As for his Spanish paragon, the concentration of all state powers was thus not only a means to avert anarchy and civil war, but also the prerequisite for keeping the chance of restoring religion alive.

Romieu's intellectual energies were directed against the noxious socialist aberrations,[50] but no less so against liberalism. For him, socialism and the rise of the new "inner barbarians"[51] had been made possible only by the spread of liberal ideas, shattering the moral foundations of Europe. Under the banner of "reason" and "progress" as the alleged guiding forces of man, the liberal doctrine had poisoned the mind of France and all other European nations, fostering nothing else but unending discord, uncertainty and chaos.[52] In the political and constitutional arena, the liberal principle had found its clearest expression in the growing fashion for parliamentary government; a form of government not only noxious in that it deprived a body politic of resolute leadership in favor of a cacophony of conflicting opinions producing only blarney and vacillation, but also unnatural:

> I have never seen anyone attempt to trust an assembly with the management of a ship, and I know why: the ship and the assembly would sink two leagues from the port. In that case, the danger of the institution would be immediate [...]. But in politics, foolishness is only evident after months or years. One soon forgets the

cause. Likewise, it has not occurred to anyone to put a regiment under the command of a committee. [...] When men are directly concerned, they only advance by a unified, single will, so certain are they that they cannot do better or faster. And in this serious matter of conducting the state, men manage, with an incomprehensible incongruity, to reject this natural rule, which is as enduring as humanity!![53]

In outlining the disastrous state of the present world, in which tradition was openly abandoned or ridiculed and everything prepared for chaos and ruin, Romieu stressed analogies to ancient times: he compared the Roman Empire being threatened by the barbarian invasions with the current dangers represented by bourgeoisie and proletariat alike, and considered contemporary European civilization "situated in conditions almost similar to those that characterized the time when the Caesars appeared". Along the lines of this great parallel, Romieu therefore also compared Julius Caesar with Napoleon Bonaparte, that modern Caesar, whose strong arm had restored order in France after the "revolutionary orgies" and put into motion again "the eternal workings of all human society, faith, justice and authority".[54]

Which political alternative did these historical examples suggest for the present crisis? While going back in history and restoring the past was impossible, to place one's hope on monarchical legitimism was no alternative either. Not because the idea of legitimism was bad *per se*, but because traditional monarchical legitimacy had become inanimate and could not be effectively revitalized.[55] The return to the forms of a constitutional monarchy as during the era of Louis-Philippe was doomed to failure as well. The simplistic formula of the constitutional monarchists that France was "monarchical by its instincts and liberal by its ideas"[56] would disregard existing realities. To restore constitutional monarchy would mean nothing else but the tranquil installation of all elements of a future revolution.[57]

More than everything else, however, the dramatic loss of faith, spiritual convictions and honor made any restorative endeavor moribund right from the beginning: "Morality, belief, respect, everything is destroyed. [...] And one would like to build on such ground! It will suffice to pitch a tent."[58] Romieu therefore concluded that the only system of government that could guarantee stability and establish a new, promising order of things with some durability was "Caesarism": "Studying the past and present simultaneously has made me believe that there is a point of extreme civilization among people, when the obligatory outcome is CAESARISM." For Romieu, Caesarism was not to be confused with "kingship", "Empire", "despotism" or "tyranny", but had a very particular and—so far—quite unknown meaning.[59] Caesarism, proposed as the "general form of the very near future", differed from monarchy in one crucial aspect: "[the monarchy; MJP] is founded and endures on the condition of beliefs.—The other survives by itself." In actual fact, Caesarism had the tendency to move towards a monarchical system without ever actually achieving it; it was a wild-goose chase of base dynastic aspirations on unprepared ground.[60] Rather than some kind of monarchy, Caesarism should be thought of as a modern rule of force replacing the principle of discussion as well as heredity. Since in the foreseeable future no ruler would be able to establish a permanent dynasty, the characteristic feature of the "age of the Caesars" was both naked power and vicissitude: "[...] I cannot imagine not so much another end, as another outcome of our troubles than a succession of masters suddenly springing up, who last only as long as their fortune, and who are powerless to found, but quick to dominate. This is what I call THE CAESARS."[61]

Romieu acknowledged that some might find his open defense of power rude. However: "I wanted, in these times of sophisticated arguments, to utter a dirty word of truth, one that many think."[62] The danger in which not only France, but European civilization as a whole, found itself, demanded ruthless candour. Civil war was in the air, as any reasonably minded-person could sense: "Blind are those who do not assist with the preparations! Deaf those who do not hear the rustle of the masses, tempted by the great orgy!" Dramatic times, however, required and justified drastic solutions: "It is cruel to live in such times; but we cannot choose our epoch, and God only grants us the freedom to witness it."[63]

Even in his *L'ère des Césars*, Romieu portrayed the proletarian populace as *the* looming danger which France would have to face in 1852 at the latest, when the presidency of Louis-Napoléon was supposed to come to an end.[64] He became more explicit in his pamphlet *Le Spectre rouge de 1852*, written in the run up to the expected elections of 1852 and addressing more directly than his former work the particular French situation, in which Romieu portrayed the year as the moment of fate for France and Caesarism as the only means to fight the "red menace":

> The red menace of 1852, which no one wanted to see and which I mention again, appeared to a stupefied society. Every day and every hour its threatening proportions increase; it seems that a great act of nature must be concluded, and that every creature has an instinct for it.[65]

The present situation was described as desolate, while the future held out no hope and heralded worse things than just civil war:

> It is no longer only civil war that awaits us; it is the Jacquerie. The work of depravity was carried out steadily, in the midst of this mild peace that June's repression had half-heartedly imposed on the destroyers. They understood that their battlefield was the Constitution; they have retreated there, and have begun to undermine it, with unavoidable effects.[66]

Not despite, but because of the constitutional-parliamentary form of government that spent time with endless jabber called "politics", France was on the brink of disaster. To believe that this danger could be banned within and by the means of the present representative political system was tomfoolery: "[...] to want, when faced with a universal outbreak, to oppose arguments and legislative processes shows a lack of understanding of the powerlessness of elected assemblies in the presence of great human upheaval."[67]

More than anything else it was the ruling elite itself that had to be blamed for the loss of the venerable principles that had guided former generations, namely religious faith, fidelity and honor. With their *philosophisme* they had prepared the ground for the "blood spectacle" which was soon to come:[68]

We have simply listened too much, learned too much, retained too much. We know what we have left: an inconceivable disorder of ideas, a confused confrontation of opinions, the absolute death of the heart, scornful laughter at beliefs, merry and derisive laughter at the old word *virtue*.[69]

Blind idolatry of "progress", "reason" and "natural law" since the Revolution of 1789 had obfuscated the people and perverted society, which allowed for one conclusion only: "That society must die."[70] The bourgeoisie was neither entitled nor able to fight the inevitable battle to come: "The conflict will be between the furious madness of the masses and the vigorous discipline of the army. Your books, your speeches, your Constitutions, your principles must vanish into the smoke of this great fight. The duel is between ORDER and CHAOS." In brief, the remaining alternative was to choose between "the reign of the torch and the reign of the sword".[71] Romieu saw a rigorous military dictatorship under the lead of a new Caesar as indispensable not only in stabilizing France and restoring order, but also to put the dissolute masses once and for all in their historical place: "I will not regret having lived in these sorry times if I can finally see the CROWD chastised and condemned. It is a cruel and stupid beast, which I have always abhorred."[72]

Romieu was noncommittal on who the leader against the red menace might eventually be; but whoever it was, his role would be simple:

To take, with a firm hand, the most absolute dictatorship, and to replace all the texts that have governed us for sixty years. [...] Simply by blowing on the house of cards of 1789, and then announcing, THE STATE IS ME, one could give France the only government that is uniquely French, and the only that France could love, despite the rhetoricians who have turned it around for their advantage—in other words, a strong, brilliant, glorious government, like those of Louis XIV and Napoleon.[73]

At the end of the day, Romieu concluded, a new era of authority would start which might not be perfect, but would have achieved to bring an end to the aberrations of philosophy and ban the red menace:

[...] at the end of these great disasters, which I believe can be short, a strong power will take hold to usher in a new era of authority. It will pass through many hands, which will engage in armed combat. But at least sophistry will no longer be in play, with its terrible consequences. It is better to see the people fight for Caesar than for National Workshops.[74]

Romieu's key message, like that of Donoso Cortés earlier,[75] was as simple as it was plausible, especially since it gave the impression of being largely "de-ideologized": European civilization in its contemporary post-revolutionary state was facing a crisis which asked for dictatorial rule. The crisis, however, was so fundamental, and the existing problems were so overwhelming, that a "commissarial" form of dictatorship was no longer adequate. Only a "sovereign" dictatorship could deal with the challenges of the time. In his suggestions, though, Romieu concretized and went beyond the ideas of Donoso Cortés: emphatically, the Frenchman demanded Caesarism be raised to a new, lasting and independent form of political rule. According to Romieu, Caesarism was the only possible response to the social question, for which he saw no other realistic solution after bourgeois liberalism had set the stage for the insurrection of the populace: by abandoning traditional values, by teaching the masses dissatisfaction through the abusive means of rampant freedom of expression and liberty of the press, and by fuelling their greed.

Romieu's writings had a clear Bonapartist drift, and helped to prepare the intellectual ground for the *coup d'état* of Louis-Napoléon in December 1851, not least due to wide dissemination in the country. Together with other advocates of Bonapartism like Jean Gilbert Victor Fialin, duc de Persigny (1808–1872) and Adolphe Granier de Cassagnac (1806–1880),[76] who essentially shared the concept of rule outlined by Romieu, the latter thus appears as one of the intellectual pioneers of the Second Empire.

Yet it is remarkable that while Napoleon I is portrayed as a great leader who performed deeds similar to those of the ancient Caesars and as a harbinger of Caesarism throughout Romieu's work, Louis-Napoléon is assigned a much more humble role. This was partly since Romieu did not want his writings to appear as propaganda, but as an objective analysis of his time. But it might also be taken as an indication that Romieu himself had personal doubts about whether Louis-Napoléon represented the kind of Caesar he yearned after. His recourse to antiquity and the great parallel fairly obscured what was effectively "new" about the imminent *césarisme à la* Louis-Napoléon, namely the ascendency of social politics. This, however, was perhaps less due to a neglect of Louis-Napoléon's political positioning since the 1830s by Romieu, than the expression of distinct differences of opinion. At several instances, Romieu did voice his concerns that the contemporary political system in France was not plagued by a lack of "social awareness" and corresponding legislation, but, on the contrary, had already become much too "social".[77]

Nonetheless, even if the conclusions as to what concrete measures had to be taken might not have been identical, both Louis-Napoléon and Romieu shared the conviction that the social question was *the* central challenge of the time that could best be mastered within the realms of a new political order. And in different respects, both rendered great service to the "making" of Caesarism: while Romieu's writings introduced Caesarism as a clear-cut notion into French and European politico-theoretical discourses, it was Louis-Napoléon's *coup d'état* and the establishment of the Second Empire which made for the swift dissemination and definite assertion of the term as a political concept and typology throughout the continent and beyond.

4.2 The Coup of 1851 and the Birth of the Second Empire

The elections of the National Assembly in May 1849 proved to be highly politicized, with a clear right-left division emerging. Even though the conservative *Parti de l'ordre* gained a comfortable majority of 53 percent of the popular vote , the success of the far left, with about 25 percent of popular votes being cast for the "Mountain" (*La Montagne*, also known as *démocrate-socialistes* or *démoc-socs*), the platform of the radical republicans and socialists, as opposed to only 11 percent for moderate republicans, alarmed conservatives and centrists alike.[78] In May 1850—following weak by-election results in March—the rightist majority in the Assembly adopted restrictive legislative measures, including a new electoral law disenfranchising the poorest.[79]

Meanwhile, Louis-Napoléon steered a course of his own: measures were taken against the media and organizations considered left-wing or to oppose government policies. By the means of growing state repression, which made it difficult to distribute the republican and socialist message through newspapers, publications or pamphlets and organize political activities by legal means, the left was incrementally squeezed out of the public sphere and forced underground. At the same time, however, Louis-Napoléon carefully distanced himself not only from legislative efforts to drastically infringe upon universal suffrage, but also from the majoritarian Party of the Order, primarily composed of Orléanists and Legitimists. He thus dashed the expectations of Adolphe Thiers and others that the President would be weak and easy to manipulate. Rather than a puppet in the parliament's hand, Louis-Napoléon proved himself a cunning politician, not only breaking away from the control of parliament, but also willing to risk open conflict by filling important posts with friends and declared allies and transforming the government into an extra-parliamentary body. Even so, continuing tensions as well as animosities between Orléanists, Legitimists and moderate republicans hampered joint and decisive action in the right camp and left Louis-Napoléon in an increasingly strong position, notwithstanding the fact that the constitution ruled out a second presidential term. Unable to agree on another candidate, the conservative factions' fear of a radical-socialist electoral victory in 1852 and the "red menace", which Romieu and others so dramatically summoned, made the incumbent president look almost without alternative and increased the willingness among the population to accept even drastic measures to safeguard political and social order.

Louis-Napoléon for his part was determined not to hand over the reins of power, doing his best to orchestrate Bonapartist propaganda in order to increase popular support and come across as a "man of the people". In June 1851, he declared during a public event in Dijon:

> France neither wishes to return to the *Ancien Régime*, whatever form may disguise it, nor to try out fatal and impracticable utopias. It is because I am the most natural adversary of both that France has placed its trust in me.[80]

In his speech, he skillfully combined the assurance of stability with what might best be described with the later term "populism", that is accusing the political establishment of betraying the people and neglecting their wellbeing by thwarting beneficial legislation and initiatives. While Louis-Napoléon was preparing the nation for constitutional change, he was nevertheless still nourishing hopes that the political elite represented in parliament might be brought back to "reason" in view of the loud "popular voice".[81]

However, the president's hopes for a constitutional change, which would have allowed him to be re-elected, foundered in July 1851. Although the initiative for a revision of the Constitution gained a majority of the representative in the assembly, it fell short of the three-quarter majority required by law. Therewith the course for a *coup d'état* was set, even more so after presidential initiatives to restore universal suffrage and a request to reconsider constitutional reform were turned down by the National Assembly. Preparations for a coup were meticulously being made from summer 1851 onwards, with the installation of loyal Bonapartists in military and administrative key positions being a central element of the planning. Tellingly, the coup bore the name "Operation Rubicon", alluding to Julius Caesar's famous crossing of the eponymous river in 49 BC that started the Great Roman Civil War and ultimately led to the establishment of the Empire. It was scheduled to take place on December 2, the anniversary of the coronation of Napoleon in 1804 and the battle of Austerlitz in 1805.[82]

That very day, the army occupied strategic points in Paris, and preventive arrests removed both top republicans and potential leaders of the monarchical opposition. In public addresses to the nation and the army, Louis-Napoléon declared the National Assembly dissolved and elaborated on the motives for his action. He described the coup as necessary to safeguard the state endangered by the Assembly, which had become a platform for political complots and anti-national activity.[83] Louis-Napoléon asked for the support of the nation to accomplish the "great mission"[84] he envisaged. Stressing the "legitimate needs of the people" and proclaiming "the people" the "only sovereign I recognize in France", Louis-Napoléon held out the prospect of re-establishing universal suffrage, but also outlined key elements of a new constitution. Above all, there would be "a responsible leader appointed for ten years". Moreover, unlike the unicameral system, which was blamed for the recent trouble and disorder, a tripartite legislation was proposed. Louis-Napoléon left no doubt as to the historical model he had in mind for the new political system: "This system, created by the First Consul at the beginning of the century, has already given France respite and prosperity, and it still guarantees them."[85]

The coup did not remain without reaction from oppositional forces and triggered revolts in Paris and other places across France. The insurgents, however, were soon defeated by the army, which stood loyal to the President. All in all, the coup was welcomed positively or at least received indifferently by the majority of the population. Even among the workers there were only a few who were prepared to risk a repetition of the June uprisings of 1848. This was hardly surprising since they would have been defending a conservative assembly against a president who staged himself not only as the defender of popular sovereignty, but also promised to restore universal male suffrage and benefitted from the legend of the Emperor whose name he bore.[86]

Not only how Louis-Napoléon assumed power and its justification that the age of the Revolution needed to be closed and stability restored were akin to the eighteenth Brumaire; also in legitimizing the regime change the nephew traced the path his uncle had chosen fifty-two years earlier, namely by opting for public approval in order to give the coup the appearance of being democratically wished. A plebiscite was scheduled to take place on December 20/21, 1851, in which the nation was asked to vote on whether it wished to maintain the authority of Louis-Napoléon and delegate to him the powers of establishing a new constitution, following the five principles outlined already in the public address of December 2: a head of state in office for ten years, ministers exclusively dependent on the executive body, and a legislation consisting of three distinct bodies.[87] Clearly, it was the acclamation of the nation, not its decision, that both Napoleons sought, and arguably they would not have been willing to accept a negative vote. Unlike 1799, however, no electoral fraud was needed in 1851 to guarantee an overwhelming majority of around 7.5 million "yes" to only 650,000 "no" votes.[88] Even areas which in the parliamentary elections of 1849 had voted "red" now showed strong Bonapartist sentiments,[89] the expression of a strong identification of Louis-Napoléon with the "doer" necessary in the present situation, or the much needed "saviour" of the nation.

Backed by the strong popular support, the new French Constitution was drafted within three weeks under the direction of Eugène Rouher (1814–1884) and proclaimed on January 14, 1852.[90] It established the institutional structures for the Second Empire, but without yet actually declaring it. In the preamble-like proclamation accompanying the constitutional document, Louis-Napoléon re-emphasized that the model followed were the Constitutions of the Consulate and Empire.[91] Louis-Napoléon claimed that "everything that has been organized since the Revolution and that still exists was made by Napoleon", enumerating, among other things, national unity, administrative and social reforms, the reorganization of education, and the *Code Napoléon*. "[…] the framework of our social edifice", Louis-Napoléon concluded, "is the work of the Emperor, and it has survived his downfall and three revolutions". Why then, it was asked rhetorically, should the political institutions of the Empire not get the same chance of durability?[92] These institutions were deemed most fit for a "country of centralization", the roots of which dated back centuries in history. Despite its focus on the executive's authority, accountability was declared a key component of the new political order. Accountability, however, required the *chef* to be free and unrestricted in his actions. Moreover, the principle of accountability would not characterize the relationship between the executive and legislative, but only apply to that between the leader and the sovereign people.[93]

It was along the lines of these guiding ideas that the 58 articles of the Constitution gave legal form to the second Napoleonic regime, which had clear traits of a hereditary monarchy right from the beginning. While guaranteeing "the great principles proclaimed in 1789, […] which are the basis of the public law of the French" (Art. 1), the Constitution provided for a head of state to be elected for ten years (Art. 2), with the right to nominate his own successor (Art. 17). The "President of the Republic", as he was still called, was entrusted with comprehensive executive and legislative powers. This included his role as head of the armed forces and freedom of action in all aspects of foreign affairs as well as the right to enact personal ordinances and other legal acts (Art. 6), the right to declare a state of emergency (Art. 12) and the prerogative to initiate and sanction laws, which was his alone (Art. 8 and 10). Ministers were responsible to the head of state alone. In many respects, the President's prerogatives were patterned on the regulations of the Bourbon *Charte constitutionnelle* of 1814, frequently even verbatim, thus demonstrating parallels between constitutional monarchism and the Napoleonic system.[94] At the same time, however, the provision of Article 5 that the

President was responsible directly to the people, to who he could always appeal in form of plebiscites, gave the office of the "President King" and the constitutional system as a whole a very distinct character. In contrast to the authoritative President, the three bodies involved in legislation lacked powers and independence. This was particularly true for the *Conseil d'État* (Art. 47–53), whose main task was the preparation of laws, and for the *Sénat* (Art. 19–33), envisaged as "guardian of the basic covenant and public liberties" (Art. 25). Both of them were more or less directly controlled by the President, who had essentially a free hand in nominating its 40 to 50 (Council of State) and 80 to 150 members (Senate) respectively. Only the elected *Corps législatif*, composed of 275 deputies (Art. 34–46), could claim some autonomy, limited by the President's privilege to nominate the chamber's president and vice-presidents (Art. 43) and his right to convoke, adjourn or dissolve the *Corps législatif* (Art. 46).

From within parliament, effective resistance against a further strengthening of Louis-Napoléon's personal position and the restoration of the Empire in particular was thus not to be expected. Pro-Empire demonstrations and public acclamations of the Prince-President—partly organized by the prefects, but partly also expressions of true popular sentiment—convinced Louis-Napoléon that the Empire was not only desirable, but the nation's will. It was in this vein that in a speech at Bordeaux on October 9, 1852 he publicly announced his commitment to an imperial restoration.[95] At the same occasion, he emphasized the objectives of the Empire, reciting the mantra outlined in his previous political writings that the "Napoleonic Idea" was not one of war, but essentially peace, national reconciliation and progress.[96]

Only one month later, imperial dignity was established by the same means as under the rule of Napoleon Bonaparte, namely a formal revision of the existing Constitution through the procedure of a *sénatus-consulte*. The constitutional change of November 7, by which a hereditary Empire was established and Louis-Napoléon made Napoleon III,[97] was subjected to another plebiscite taking place on November 21 and 22. The approval rate was even more impressive than it had been eleven months earlier, with 7.824.189 official *oui* votes outnumbering the 253.145 *non* votes by more than thirty times.[98] Thus, the Second Empire had now become political fact. Endowed with plebiscitary legitimation and strengthened by further constitutional modification on December 25, 1852 that sought to reinforce the power of the Emperor while encroaching on that of parliament,[99] Napoleon III could now proceed to put his political visions into practice, which in the two decades to come were to keep not only France, but the whole of Europe in suspense.[100]

4.3 The Reception of the Coup and Napoleon's Rule

Louis-Napoléon's coup in 1851 and the establishment of the Second Empire was eagerly received throughout Europe. The regime change and its possible consequences loomed large not only because of France's importance, but also because the country had once again become *the* "laboratory" of dealing with a distinctly revolutionary situation. Given many obvious parallels, the events of 1851 rekindled memories of Napoleon Bonaparte's seizure of power, which had eventually resulted in dramatic consequences for France and the European political order. A central question therefore was in how far the situation of 1851 could be compared to that of 1799, and to what extent the two Napoleons were similar or different in their personalities and political ideas. Louis-Napoléon's advent to power also raised anew the question as to whether Bonapartism and Caesarism were indeed a universal, or only a specifically French phenomenon. People arguing in the latter vein could fall back, among others, on Chateaubriand, who in his *Mémoires d'outre-tombe* emphasized the peculiar national character of the French that had been perfectly matched by Napoleon (I):

> [...] the French are instinctively attracted by power; they have no love for liberty; equality alone is their idol. Now, equality and despotism are secretly connected. In those two respects, Napoleon took his origin from a source in the hearts of the French, militarily inclined towards power, democratically enamored of the levelling process. Mounting the throne, he seated the people there, too; a proletarian king, he humiliated kings and nobles in his ante-chambers; he equalized social ranks not by lowering them, but by elevating them: levelling down would have pleased plebeian envy more, levelling up was more flattering to its pride. French vanity was inflated, too, by the superiority Bonaparte gave us over the rest of Europe.[101]

In what follows, attention will first be paid to some of the reactions to Louis-Napoléon's seizing power and its assessment among French intellectuals. Subsequently, the reception of the events and the new political regime abroad will be taken into closer examination, with a focus on Germany.

4.3.1 French Voices

In France itself, the reception of Louis-Napoléon's seizure of power was of a dichotomous nature: in the majority, one could find positive assessments or even openly propagandistic pieces, part of which were certainly steered by the regime, but part of which were also the expression of true relief and satisfaction in educated circles about the end of political uncertainty; in the clear minority remained works by declared opposition members, most of whom had been forced into exile or underground, that were all the more critical and pejorative in their tone and as such faced tight state restrictions. Since the first group of pro-Napoleonic writings largely aligned themselves with and repeated earlier arguments for a "Caesaristic" or Bonapartist regime present in authors like Romieu and the works of Louis-Napoléon himself, some examples in the second group of anti-Napoleonic utterances should now be examined.

The best known—and perhaps most influential—French intellectual who raised his voice against Louis-Napoléon was Victor Hugo (1802–1885). Even in the run-up to the coup, Hugo—an elected Member of Parliament—was a decided critic of Louis-Napoléon and an eloquent defender of the republican cause. As early as in July 1851, in a debate taking place in the *Assemblée nationale legislative*,[102] Hugo coined the famous *Napoléon le Petit*, which was to become the title of Hugo's most outspoken account of Napoleon and Bonapartism one year later and turned into a common denominator of the "would-be Napoleon" in opposition circles. As one of the figureheads of the republican opposition, Victor Hugo actively resisted Louis-Napoléon's coup in December 1851 and had to leave the country, relocating first to Brussels, then Jersey and finally Guernsey, where he was to live until 1870. It was in exile that between mid-June and mid-July 1852 *Napoléon le Petit* was drafted.[103] The manuscript that went to print quickly and was soon smuggled into France was a virulent pamphlet, in which Hugo elaborated on the methods used to achieve the coup. At the same time, it was a ferocious personal attack on Louis-Napoléon.

Under Louis-Napoléon, for whom to describe Hugo falls back on the concepts "dictatorship" and "despotism" rather than Caesarism, the words independence, enfranchisement, progress, popular and national pride, and greatness could no longer be pronounced. He would treat France like a conquered country: "He effaces the republican inscriptions; he cuts down the trees of liberty, and makes firewood of them."[104] Political went hand in hand with moral degradation, for which Bonaparte had to be blamed as well. Hugo accused him of having done more than kill people: "he has caused men's minds to dwindle, he has withered the heart of the citizen. [...] an indescribable gangrene of material prosperity threatens to cause public honesty to degenerate into rottenness."[105] True, Louis-Napoléon could refer to the majority of Frenchmen having cast their vote in his favor. But *who* had voted? Frightened citizens and ignorant peasants, according to Hugo. And what was the choice offered to them by Bonaparte? No real one:

Choose between beauty and the beast; the beast is communism; the beauty is my dictatorship. Choose! There is no medium! Society prostrate, your house burned, your barn pillaged, your cow stolen, your fields confiscated, your wife outraged, your children murdered, your wine drunk by others, yourself devoured alive by the great gaping-jaws yonder, or me as your emperor! Choose! Me or Croque-mitaine!

This, in turn, also highlighted *what* people had actually been "voting" for on December 20, 1851:

Dictatorship, autocracy, slavery, the republic a despotism, France a pashalik, chains on all wrists, a seal on every mouth, silence, degradation, fear, the spy the soul of all things! They have given to a man [...] omnipotence and omniscience! They have made that man the supreme, the only legislator, the alpha of the law, the omega of power! They have decreed that he is Minos, that he is Numa, that he is Solon, that he is Lycurgus! They have incarnated in him the people, the nation, the state, the law![106]

For Hugo, there were axioms in probity, honesty and justice as there were axioms in geometry. Accordingly, moral truth was no more at the mercy of a vote than algebraic truth, a conviction he condensed in the sentence:

[...] cause seven million five hundred thousand voters to declare that two and two make five, that the straight line is the longest way, that the whole is less than a part;

cause eight millions, ten millions, a hundred millions of voters so to declare, and you will not have advanced a single step.[107]

Hugo's widely read work was witty and intellectually stimulating, providing inspiration to the regime's opponents and setting the tone for future republican historians of the Empire. However, it remained an invective against Louis-Napoléon rather than a politico-theoretical treatise trying to develop a more complex understanding of the coup and Bonapartism. This was also the view of the *Westminster Review*, which in its October issue of 1852 bluntly stated: "Of explanation we have little in this volume. The poet revels in images; the orator in apostrophes and epigrams; the philosopher is nowhere to be found. Page after page of splendid writing; not a page of careful thinking. It is a cry, a protest, an appeal."[108] In a similar vein, Karl Marx (1818–1883) later criticized Hugo's description of the events of 1851 "like a bolt from the blue", as "the violent act of a single individual" only, whereby Hugo—against his very intentions—made Louis-Napoléon "great instead of little by ascribing to him a personal power of initiative unparalleled in world history".[109]

The verdict to be first and foremost a personal diatribe against France's new leader holds true for other works, too, including Victor Schoelcher's (1804–1893) *Histoire des crimes du 2 décembre* (1852), whose title speaks volumes.[110] Contemporaries acknowledged that the work "wants the splendid rhetoric and scarcasm [*sic*!] of 'Napoleon le Petit'; but it compensates the deficiency by presenting a circumstantial, animated, detailed history of the *coup d'état*".[111] Narrative in its approach, the pamphlet—in spite of the palpable indignation of the author—is indeed written with slightly more impartiality than Hugo's. Nevertheless, Schoelcher, too, essentially describes the "crime of December 2" as a personal one of Louis-Napoléon, while absolving the French people, who—looking upon Bonaparte as the armed solution of their difficulties—had been duped by his artful restoration of universal suffrage and promises of amelioration.

All in all, an objective and impartial assessment of Louis-Napoléon could hardly be expected in mid-century France with its sharp ideological divisions, even less so among his political adversaries. Quite remarkable is therefore Pierre-Joseph Proudhon's *La Révolution sociale démontrée par le coup d'état du 2 décembre* (1852), which saw four editions in just two months.[112] Appearing at the same time as Hugo's and Schoelcher's pamphlets, the work of Proudhon as the mastermind of French socialism at the time is special: his was not written in exile, but while serving a three-year sentence for anti-governmental activities and *offense au Président de la République* in particular (June 1849 to June 1852); his book could only be published in France after Proudhon had intervened against its initial ban with a personal letter to Louis-Napoléon; and his did not lapse into a furious attack against the Emperor-to-be and offering a predominantly "individualized" analysis of the coup. Rather, Proudhon's book accepted the coup as another step towards the final triumph of socialism, and was less of a critique than an appeal to Louis-Napoléon to work for the revolution and embrace a progressive political program.

For Proudhon, "Louis Napoleon is, like his uncle, a revolutionary dictator, but with the difference that the first Consul had closed the first phase of the revolution, while the President opened the second". To denounce the president as a counter-revolutionary was declared absurd: "not only does Louis Napoleon bear, on his forehead and his shoulder, the stigmata of revolution; he is the agent of a new era, he expresses a superior expression of the Revolution".[113] The coup of December 2, 1851 was "the signal of an advancing march in the revolutionary way", its significance "the democratic and social Revolution".[114] Whether Louis-Napoléon actually wanted to be in the forefront of the revolutionary movement and whether he would be able to master this challenge in the end was a different issue. Nevertheless, the "idea" he and his coup represented was genuinely revolutionary.

The regime change of 1851 was—according to Proudhon—the natural consequence of three years of reaction with permanent preaching against socialism, and the need for a restoration of authority, the absorption of individual liberty in the state. The December 2 coop had only been possible because Napoleon had internalized the one secret that explained all previous revolutions in France: the problem of the proletariat, *l'idée sociale*. The perception of him as the representative of the social idea together with the defense of universal suffrage had granted public support and made his success possible.

These views were coupled with his theory of non-government or "anarchy", which this coup illustrated anew, given that it "highlights the contradiction of governmentalism and the economy, of state and society, in today's France".[115] Under the present state of affairs, Proudhon concluded, "Caesarism" was no true alternative to "anarchism" or "socialism" any longer, as Romieu and others had suggested. The (geo-)political and even more so societal conditions *vis-à-vis* Roman Caesarism were too different. For Proudhon there was no doubt whatsoever: "we are in total socialism".[116] The decisive question was just how socialism would be continued and finalized in the future.

Proudhon's work did try to provide a "structural" understanding of Louis-Napoléon and his regime by emphasizing the peculiar characteristics of mid-century industrial society. A French contemporary one might have expected to choose a similar approach or even to provide a full-fledged theory of Bonapartism in post-revolutionary societies was Alexis de Tocqueville. He had not only submitted a pioneering assessment of Bonapartism as one possible form of modern-day illegitimate rule in his *Democracy in America* (1835–1840), but also recognized at an early stage the genuinely "socialist" character of the 1848 Revolution, distinguishing it from previous revolutionary upheavals. Yet Tocqueville did not present a monographic study on the subject. This does not imply a lack of concern with Louis-Napoléon's seizing power and Bonapartism in general, however. On the contrary, the experience of the 1851 coup was a crucial stimulus for starting his study of the old regime and the French Revolution (*L'Ancien Régime et la Révolution*, 1856),[117] to be followed by a second volume on the French Revolution as such and to be completed by a third analyzing the regime of Napoleon Bonaparte and its effect on government and political culture in France. But his early death in 1859 frustrated these plans. Nevertheless, it might be worthwhile to extract Tocqueville's attitude towards Louis-Napoléon and the Second Empire from the assessments he made in his *Souvenirs* and in his correspondence.[118]

Tocqueville's utterances in the late 1840s and 1850s reveal that he was aware of the equivocal aspects which made the "Napoleonic system" appealing to many: its combination of revolutionary and conservative qualities, the promise of stability alongside progress, peace alongside national *grandeur*. None of these aspects, however, seemed tempting to Tocqueville, since the price the nation had to pay for the new political system was the loss of liberty. Indeed, as regards personal liberty, Tocqueville deemed the situation worse under the nephew than under the uncle, and he had even less sympathy for the former than the latter. In view of what Tocqueville held in high esteem throughout his life, namely steadfast attachment to the principles of regulated liberty and a dedicated respect for legality, Louis-Napoléon's coup was illegitimacy and illegality in essence. To Tocqueville—among 230 parliamentarians voting for the immediate deposition and impeachment of the usurper on December 2—the legitimization *a posteriori* of the coup by plebiscite seemed a farce as well, as he made clear in a letter to the editor of the London *Times*:

> [...] never was a more odious mockery offered to a nation. The people is called upon to express its opinion, yet not only is public discussion suppressed, but even the knowledge of the facts. The people is asked its opinion, but the first measure taken to obtain it is to establish military terrorism throughout the country, and to threaten with deprivation every public agent who does not approve in writing what has been done.

All in all, the condition France faced after Louis-Napoléon's act of violence could only be described as miserable:

> Force overturning law, trampling on the liberty of the press and of the person, deriding the popular will, in whose name the Government pretends to act—France torn from the alliance of free nations to be yoked to the despotic Monarchies of the Continent—such is the result of the coup d'état.[119]

What seemed a characteristic feature to Tocqueville was the decisive role of the army in the December coup. In this respect, he saw a clear difference even to Bonaparte's 18 Brumaire, as he explained in a conversation with Nassau William Senior (1790–1864) on December 22, 1851. For Tocqueville, Louis-Napoléon's coup was unique since this was "the first time that the army has seized France, bound and gagged her, and laid her at the feet of her ruler". In contrast, every previous revolution had been made by a political party, including the 18 Brumaire: it had ended, but not begun in "military tyranny", since there had been widespread support among the educated classes for the removal of the Directory. 1799 had thus been "almost as much a civil as a military revolution", while Louis-Napoléon was a much more isolated figure whose real support lay in the army. For a real parallel one would have to go back 1,800 years in history.[120] However, Tocqueville saw "militarism" not only as a crucial element of the regime's coming into being, but the very heart of the whole system, which would inevitably result in expansionist and belligerent endeavors.[121]

Despite the distaste of Louis-Napoléon and his regime, whose establishment Tocqueville considered a national humiliation and disaster, he did not exclusively cast the blame for the misery on the second Bonaparte, as Hugo, Schoelcher and others did. In his view, society played an important part. As early as in 1849 Tocqueville remarked that the current situation would "result from the crude and unintelligent aspiration of the popular masses for a constitution of any power whatsoever and from the discouragement of the enlightened classes, who hardly know any longer what to wish for".[122] December 2, 1851 as well as the Second Empire then only continued and accelerated the corruption of the French *mores*. The longer the new regime was in power, the more disenchanted Tocqueville became, convinced that France had lost her aspirations for noble ideals, moral principles and great deeds. Instead, citizens had become subjects dreaming only of petty affairs and material comforts. This, Tocqueville argued, included the learned elite of the country. Yet the best men of his time would learn to accommodate themselves to the empire and even learn to acquire a "taste for servitude".[123]

In September 1858, Tocqueville wrote to Arthur de Gobineau (1816–1882) about the intellectual climate in France: "People believe strongly in nothing, they love nothing, they hate nothing, and they hope for nothing [...]"[124] However, until the very end of his life, Tocqueville did not abandon himself to fatalism or even acquire a taste for the "government of the sabre" and the "baton". Rather, he held the hope that things could take a turn for the better, that "a better upbringing could redress the evil that a bad upbringing has accomplished".[125]

Severity and objects of criticism varied considerably among French intellectuals in opposition to Louis-Napoléon, but arguments for the coup and the Napoleonic system by supporters were not uniform either. This holds true for the domestic reactions in France and the tremendous reaction the meteoric rise of Louis-Napoléon provoked abroad. Taking a look beyond the French borders will provide an additional outside perspective on the perception of Louis-Napoléon and provide an idea how the debate about Caesarism was developing in a mid-century environment of "national awakening" and "nation building". An example of particular interest in this respect is—once more— the German-speaking world.

4.3.2 Perception Abroad: German Reactions

It is striking that the examination of the December coup and the engagement with Caesarism on a European level ensued particularly swiftly and thoroughly among German intellectuals of the time. Several factors, both domestic and foreign, favored an intensified perception in the German-speaking world. On the one hand, it was the geographic proximity of France—a nation gradually assuming the role of the *Erbfeind* ("Hereditary Enemy") in German public opinion since the *Befreiungskriege* ("Wars of Liberation")—which made for the immediacy of French political developments in Germany. Closely linked to that was the unresolved national question and the realization of Germany's continued inferiority as long as it was not able to confront *La Grande Nation* united and strong. Such fears seemed anything but unreasonable if Louis-Napoléon should pursue a foreign policy as expansive as his uncle. At the same time, however, Louis-Napoléon's agenda of a militarization and centralization of rule and society also commanded some admiration, commending itself as a possible model for developing and strengthening the German nation.

Another factor that made for the intensity of the debate on French politics and Caesaristic forms of government was that the Revolution of 1848/1849 had marked a particularly dramatic caesura for the German-speaking world, given the massive political concussions that all German states—including Austria—had undergone, and which had brought some of them to the brink of downfall. These verberations at the end of the 1840s appeared all the more spectacular bearing in mind the decades of political quiescence and attempted depoliticization since the Congress of Vienna under the reactionary Metternich System, a period also known as *Biedermeier*. The Revolution itself had ended in somewhat of a draw without a clear political decision that would have offered a map for future developments. Conscious of the immediate revolutionary danger, German rulers had made concessions to the liberal and democratic movement, manifest in granting wide-ranging constitutional and legal guarantees. Many of these concessions, however, were revoked as soon as revolutionary energy had abated or the insurgent movements had been crushed with military power, which was often followed by clear neo-absolutist policies. A true democratization and constitutionalization of the political systems hence failed, but a restoration of the *status quo ante* proved to be impossible as well. Consequently, political uncertainty was perpetuated beyond 1848/1849.

Against this backdrop and in view of obvious social and economic transformation processes, the question as to the compatibility of progress and stability, democracy and despotism gained new dynamic in Germany with the rise of Louis-Napoléon. It speaks for the *Zeitgeist* and the similarity of political concerns in mid-century France and Germany that Romieu's works on *L'ère des Césars* (1850) and *Le Spectre rouge de 1852* (1851) were almost immediately translated into German.[126] It was above all due to the translation of Romieu's books that "Caesarism" finally entered German political language (*Cäsarismus*).[127]

After the coup of Louis-Napoléon, this concept swiftly gained currency and soon became a fixed component in German political thought, the widening usage going hand in hand with increasing theorization, but also differentiation of the concept. The sheer multitude of opinions expressed in an intellectual environment turning not only growingly "public", but also complex, makes it difficult to locate clearly discernible "schools of interpretations". Even at the individual level, a clear distinction of positions for and against Caesarism and Bonapartism sometimes proved problematic, since both could be expressed by one and the same person, depending on the context in or the intention with which the phenomenon was assessed. In view of these challenges, the following is not intended to offer a systematic reception history, but rather an attempt to demonstrate the wide range of interpretations the coup of Napoleon III and (French) "Caesarism" experienced in the German-speaking area during the 1850s and 1860s.[128]

One of the earliest and most elaborate attempts to evaluate the coup of 1851 in depth was Constantin Frantz's (1817–1891) *Louis Napoleon* (1852), the result of a trip he had made to France in order to get first-hand experience of the political situation and to study the comparatively new phenomena of socialism and communism *in situ*.[129] The text not only reflects Frantz's strong aversion to parliamentary democracy, but also offers one of the clearest justifications of the recent coup carried out by Louis-Napoléon as both republican and democratic.

In the introduction, Frantz made clear that his ambition was not to provide a biographical study of the French leader. Rather, his aim was to assess the underlying principles of which Louis-Napoléon was not only a bearer, but which even carried him.[130] This was the principle of *Napoleonismus*,[131] its characteristic feature being the ambivalent parallelism of monarchical and republican elements:

> [...] a body politic that is neither a true republic nor a true monarchy: one-man rule, which as such is similar to a monarchy, but because it is not founded on its own right but rather emerges from the will of the people, makes the whole just appear to resemble a monarchy.[132]

Frantz argued that the Revolution had created irremovable precedents in France, and perhaps the most important *sine qua non* in France was acknowledging the principle that "public power must emanate from the people". However, Frantz discounted the belief of "democrats" that a representative body (*Volksvertretung*) or parliamentary government would be best suited to determine "ends and means of this power".[133] In a post-revolutionary society as centralized and atomized as the French, he claimed, parliamentarism could only produce "organized demagogy".[134] The only feasible answer to the political challenge of a people "which destroyed the entire substance of its previous political life [*Staatsleben*] and has been without a shared perspective on the state ever since, but is nevertheless in need of public order", was the following:

> This people puts one man at the peak, who represents the collective will of the people in his very being, and this man provides a constitution which is ratified by the people. This man does not rule on the strength of his legitimacy, or any other moral legitimacy, but rather in the name of a physical necessity, since he rests upon the majority and there is the necessity for the minority to submit itself.[135]

This was the very essence of Napoleonism. According to Frantz, the "substantial form" of such a system, whose superiority to the alternatives arose from its ability to integrate popular sovereignty, the popular will and reason—thus crucial elements of republicanism—in a single ruler, was necessarily "dictatorship" (*Dictatur*): not an "exceptional dictatorship" (*exceptionelle Dictatur*), as seen in other historical moments, but a "dictatorship in principal" (*prinzipielle Diktatur*), "exactly because the French Republic is a very singular body politic such as has never been seen before".[136] More consciously than most other political thinkers of the nineteenth century, Frantz hence pre-empted and argued for Schmitt's later distinction between sovereign and commissarial dictatorship.

For Frantz, Napoleonism was not only distinctively republican, dictatorial and permanent, but essentially based on democratic principles, too: "The state power must have the majority of the people behind it, [...] only then does the collective will, united in the leader, have the power of a physical necessity." For that reason, suffrage had to be universal, since "universal suffrage is the official expression of equality, and because equality is the only clear political vision of the French people".[137]

All in all, Napoleonism was more than just an alternative to parliamentarism, it was its inversion:

[...] according to the parliamentary system, the people choose to be represented, but here they choose to be governed; there, the so-called executive power is subordinate and serves parliaments, here, it is superordinate and controlling; There the state power rests in the parliament, here it rests in the leader [*Chef*].[138]

As much as Napoleonism was a counter model to parliamentarism, it was the negation of the "principle of discussion" and "dialectics".[139] Human nature was first and foremost manifested in "will" (*Wille*), only a derived and secondary activity of which was "thinking" (*Denken*). Never in history had states and empires been instituted by doctrines, and never had doctrinaires blessed mankind, but men with true strength of will. In fighting the wrong philosophy of thinking and discussion, eventually a single man would take the lead, having a sabre in his hand: "Sic jubeo, sic mando, stat pro ratione voluntas."[140] That man was Napoleon (I). It had been his historical achievement, "to seal the crater of the Revolution with the throne of the Caesars".[141] The "Napoleonic principle" was now to be perpetuated by Louis-Napoléon, who was predestined to take over the role of his uncle not because of his family relations, but because he had dared to be the living proof of his uncle's principle.[142] He had demonstrated the indispensable will to power in earlier attempts to usurp and even more so in the successful coup of 1851. In assuming power, however, he had not acted against the *volonté générale*. On the contrary, he had been elected president to undertake a coup. The crucial task that remained to be achieved in France was to crack "egoism" (*Eigenwille*) and help turn it into an "ethical will": "If the people elect a leader to whom they deliver up their own self-will in order to obey this leader, and if in turn this leader forgoes his own self-will in order to serve the people, then a moral bond develops between both parts."[143] Even though Napoleonism was not without its risks, as Frantz had to acknowledge, it was the inevitable principle of contemporary France: the "left path", via parliamentarism, would lead to communism; the alternative to the right, via legitimism and restoration, to another abyss of Revolution.[144] Therefore the middle path embodied by the Napoleonic principle was the only one that could reasonably be chosen: "Resting on the debris of factions, it is the only system that is not directed toward party building, but rather to the organization of the state."[145]

Making a strong plea for "Napoleonism", Frantz clearly recognized the interconnectedness of dictatorship and *volonté générale*. This, together with the incisiveness and cogency of his analysis, elevated Frantz's study above the average assessments by German conservatives at the time. Quite a few of them wavered between uncritical expressions of appreciation that Louis-Napoléon had terminated the danger of revolution on the one hand, and strict rejection of everything that could be subsumed under Caesarism or Bonapartism, respectively, on the other.[146] In this vein, the Prussian statesman and general Joseph Maria von Radowitz (1797–1853) declared "modern Caesarism" to be "a mere rule of violence"[147] and the most obnoxious form the reaction to the Revolutions of 1848 had taken, the other two represented by the *altständische* model (estates-based corporatism) and the *Patrimonialstaat* (patrimonial state).[148] However, though Radowitz declared that every other party in France could claim more legitimacy than Louis-Napoléon, whose basis was "really nothing more than the most impure, most reprehensible, personal ambition of a human being", he still desired the usurper's triumph. Caesarism was, after all, a lesser evil than a victory of the Reds, the only likely alternative. Full of disillusionment, Radowitz remarked on the present state of affairs: "justice, reason, moral law have lost their right."[149]

Radowitz, as most other contemporary observers in the conservative camp, eventually approved of the coup of 1851 for at least preventing even worse. At the same time, there was widespread agreement that Bonapartism and Caesarism was a genuinely French phenomenon that was both unfeasible and even less desirable for Germany. Many declared liberals and democrats shared this opinion.

In the 1850s and 1860s, there were still a few liberal-minded figures with Napoleonic sentiments in the German states; but altogether, German "Bonapartism" (in the classical sense of the word) was already a descending branch when Napoleon III assumed power. This was above all due to the growing nationalistic *Zeitgeist*, in the context of which Louis-Napoléon was perceived not so much as a symbol of political change and an alternative "Caesaristic" system, but as Emperor of the French and thus potential enemy of Germany. The range of critical encounters with French Napoleonism encompassed abstract-philosophical contributions, such as Karl Christian Planck's (1819–1880) *Deutschland und der Napoleonismus* (1860),[150] and down-to-earth pamphlets alike. Many of the authors opposing the regime of Napoleon III made an effort to contrast more generally "Romanism" with "Germanism", a distinction that was anything but unfamiliar in contemporary scholarship.[151] Among them was Gustav Diezel (1817–1858), whose publications of the 1850s attracted considerable attention and a wide readership.

In his works, notably *Deutschland und die abendländische Civilisation* (1852) and *Frankreich, seine Elemente und ihre Entwicklung* (1853),[152] Diezel critically addressed French post-revolutionary politics and the challenges Europe and Germany faced in an age of Napoleonic Caesarism (*Kaiserthum*). He detected a distinction between two different forms of democracy.[153] The first form was French and neo-Roman, rooted in the principle of equality and compatible with both the ancient ideal of Empire and the French *Ancien Régime*. Eventually, this kind of Romanic democracy had to take the form of "absolutism of the people, that ancient Roman lust to rule",[154] which found its most explicit expression in the regimes of the two Bonapartes. The path leading to the establishment of a Caesaristic regime under Napoleon I, in Diezel's eyes a representative of "absolute Romandom",[155] appears as a repetition of classical Rome's transition from "republic" to "empire", marked by violent battles over property distribution. This was the necessary outcome of France's long-term history of centralization, despotism and lack of any true sense of liberty (*Freiheit*). The similarity of the events in 1848 and 1851/1852 led Diezel to conclude *a fortiori* that a Roman-Caesaristic type of dictatorship was the only possible form of government in modern-day France, a nation declared unfit for "a freer constitution and for any kind of self-government".[156]

Diezel contrasted Romanic democracy, associated with Rome, Caesarism and the principle of equality, with "true" (*wahr*) and "reasonable" (*vernünftig*) democracy, termed "Germanic". *Germanische Demokratie* was grounded on property, free labor, and—above all—individual liberty (*individuelle Freiheit*). According to Diezel, Germanic liberty and democracy in the modern world found its clearest expressions in the constitutional systems of Britain and the United States. On the basis of such presumed antithesis, Diezel arrived at what he deemed a "universal dialectic".[157] Indeed, Britain and the United States might be seen to have assumed the role of institutionalized expressions of Germanic liberty and democracy. The nation, however, to which these principles were the most natural and intrinsic for Diezel was the German one. The pressing challenge was thus to revive the Germanic spirit in Germany by eradicating all Romanic and Caesaristic elements which had been injected into the system not only by the French and by political thought in the tradition of Jean-Jacques Rousseau, but also by the Habsburgs and the papacy. Only by wiping out the neo-Roman elements in the body politic could a powerful German national state be successfully built, which would be a prerequisite for the durable defense of liberty and security in Germany against both French Caesarism and Russian absolutism. France, whose historical fate was "foreordained by its culture [*Bildung*] and emergence, by the nature of its national spirit", and whose development had been inevitable, lacked every prospect of national development. Not so Germany, which faced a potentially bright future: for Diezel, it was at the discretion of Germans to decide upon their own destiny and "to arrive at a form appropriate to the national character, guaranteeing the free movement of the individual".[158] This was not only in the interest of Germany, but of Europe as a whole, since "the further development of civilization on the Continent depends upon the constitution of the German nation".[159]

Disqualifying Caesarism as a "French peculiarity" and the expression of distinct "Romanism" prevailed beyond the German-speaking world proper. One noteworthy example is the German-American liberal thinker Francis (originally Franz) Lieber (1800–1872), who in his work *On Civil Liberty and Self-Government* (1853) sharply distinguished between republicanism and democracy, allowing him to praise American republicanism and self-government while describing the affinities between absolutism and democracy as a French particularity.[160] Even more explicitly than Diezel, Lieber made an attempt to understand both the first and second Napoleonic Empire in ancient Roman rather than in modern terms, thus reviving the grand parallel which had been so prominent at the turn of the century. In particular, he analyzed the question of legitimacy from the point of view of the ancient Roman *lex regia*, arguing that post-revolutionary French politics and Caesarism were in the end nothing less than the outcome of the transmutation of that ancient Roman legal fiction as manifest in the social contract theories of Hobbes and Rousseau. For him, the imperial regimes established by the two Napoleons were simply modern repetitions of the ancient practice of transferring *maiestas* from the *populus romanus* to the emperors. Lieber concluded that the "transition from an uninstitutional popular absolutism to the imperatorial sovereignty" was not only "easy and natural", but indeed nothing essentially new.[161]

Underlining the neo-Roman character of contemporary Caesarism and Bonapartism or their parallels to the ancient world, which was fairly common in intellectual encounters at the time, did not remain unchallenged. Even more than in the context of the late eighteenth century, the prerequisites as well as the social and political framework of "ancient" and "modern" Caesarism struck contemporaries as being very different in the mid-nineteenth century. Perhaps the most distinguished intellectual authority arguing against equalizing modern Caesarism with the ancient rule of the Caesars was Theodor Mommsen (1817–1903), one of the greatest classicist of the nineteenth century and later honored with the Nobel Prize in Literature 1902 for his work on Roman History.

The third volume of Mommsen's *Römische Geschichte* (1856) ended with a most positive, if not glorifying, depiction of Julius Caesar, whom Mommsen described as a "perfect statesman" with a world-historical mission, namely the transformation of the *Imperium Romanum*.[162] While Mommsen was thus clearly in the tradition of Hegel's idea of "great men in history", he emphasized that Caesar could not easily be compared with figures like Alexander or Napoleon. What made him distinct was that despite his military genius, he had remained first and foremost a statesman: unlike them, he had started and pursued his career as a politician (*Demagog*) like Pericles and Gaius Gracchus, aiming—whenever possible—to reach his objectives without force of arms. The one person he could most likely be compared with was Cromwell, someone who managed to climb from being leader of the opposition to head of the army and then "democratic king" (*Demokratenkönig*), and who "in his development, as in his objectives and successes, perhaps among all statesmen most resembled Caesar".[163]

Despite the qualifications made, Mommsen's positive depiction of the historical Caesar could be interpreted as an appraisal of modern Caesarism and Bonapartism, and of the regime of Napoleon III in particular. In the second edition of his *Römische Geschichte* Mommsen therefore felt compelled to object especially against the practice of "reinterpreting judgement about Caesar into judgement about so-called Caesarianism [*sic!*]". Rather, Mommsen considered the "history of Caesar and Roman Caesardom" as "a more bitter criticism of modern autocracy than a human hand is able to write".[164]

> If [. . .] in Caesar's own soul the hopeful dream of a union between free national development and absolute rule still prevails, then the rule of the very gifted emperors of the Julian dynasty has taught in a dreadful way how feasible it is to carry fire and water in the same vessel.

For Mommsen, Julius Caesar's dictatorial form of rule was legitimate only because it had been the necessary outcome of the particular conditions of the time. In other contexts, however, Caesari(ani)sm lacked such historical legitimacy and was "simultaneously a hideous face and a usurpation".[165]

In a review of Adolphe Thiers' work *L'histoire du consulat et de l'Empire* one year later (1858), Mommsen drew a clear distinction between the rule of Caesar and Napoleon Bonaparte, dismissing the latter's: "The mysterious connection between nation and ruler, as it existed between Caesar and the Romans, between Cromwell and the English nation, never transpired between Napoleon and the French."[166] Napoleon might have been a great ruler, Mommsen admitted; but in essence, he had always remained an autocrat: "He did not become an autocrat, he was one."[167]

On the person and regime of the Emperor's nephew, Napoleon III, Mommsen seems to have had a less clear attitude. A certain personal admiration for the second Bonaparte on the French throne shines through at least in private correspondence.[168] All in all, however, Mommsen kept critical distance to the "Caesarism" of Louis-

Napoléon. This was not least since he, as so many fellow countrymen, remained biased towards French politics for national-political reasons. Against the background of both his scholarly and national reservations, Theodor Mommsen declined the invitation to collaborate in writing a history of Julius Caesar with Napoleon III, who was smart enough to identify the German classicist as a potential intellectual ally of much international weight for creating his own "legend". Ultimately, Napoleon III realized his publication project—following in the footsteps of his uncle's *Précis des guerres de César*—with the support of French classical and military scholars. Yet the result in the form of a two-volume *Histoire de Jules César* (1865/1866), which was translated almost instantly into a number of European languages, turned out to be a very conventional piece.[169] It did not include anything particularly novel concerning either the ancient Caesar or modern Caesarism, even though the preface contained the unambiguous remark that the very aim of this book was to demonstrate that figures like Caesar, Charlemagne and Napoleon were destined by providence to lead the way for the peoples of the world.[170] Accordingly damning was Mommsen's criticism, who found not only fault with the "miserable script", which gave "quite the impression of being a brief sketch of Roman history for upper secondary students", but also declared his expectations belied of "seeing Caesarism defended by a practitioner".[171]

Mommsen was not the only one who disapproved of Napoleon III's attempt to underpin his regime with ancient analogies. An unknown reviewer of Napoleon's work in the *Allgemeine Zeitung des Judenthums* expressed not only his discomfort about the latent anti-Semitism in the introduction, but also called to mind that "circumstances, situations, personalities and events never repeat themselves in history".[172] Roman Caesarism had been built on the ruins of a republic which had prospered for centuries and managed to make Rome the center of the world; a republic, which had crossed its zenith and was no longer suitable for the time. Napoleon Bonaparte, on the other hand, had appeared on the scene of history:

> when an absolutism riddled with feudal institutions had been overthrown and the short-lived republic had not yet gained the time and strength to arrange the debris and the agitated elements into an organism, to shape and establish itself; he did not appear when the French Republic had defeated and subjugated the peoples, so that he would only have faced subjected and degenerate peoples, but rather he himself strove to subjugate the nations and failed in this attempt; even less is Napoleon III facing a weakened, spent humanity. Napoleon I and III may have seen the need for a momentary dictatorship within French conditions: in all other respects, there is no coincidence with Caesar or Augustus.[173]

While these remarks are indicative of a positivist assessment of the general state of modern civilization being so very different from the ancient one, the author was noncommittal as to whether and how long the project of "Caesarism" might be continued in France, the only country in which it could possibly thrive. He left no doubts, however, as to what he considered characteristic of the system of Caesarism, a term considered better applicable to Napoleon III than Napoleon I, whose system of government was rather termed Bonapartism;[174] namely the covered "perpetuation" of dictatorial rule:

Caesarism [...] is autocracy with the semblance of liberal institutions. It is not despotism, which declares the people and all their material and intellectual possessions its unconditional property, to be disposed of as it likes; it is not absolutism, which permits the state to be governed according to law, but places the legislative and executive power solely and unreservedly in the person of the monarch. Caesarism recognises popular sovereignty and conveys this in the complete equality of all members of the state; it recognises institutions which are conceded a say in legislation and administration [*sic!*]. But it transfers the unconditional plenitude of power to Caesar, to whom people and institutions are completely subordinate, so that they must bow to the will of Caesar.

Caesarism was essentially grounded "partly on the fatigue of the people, on the lack of energy of the spirit, but also on the power of the sword, on the devotion of the army".[175]

In its lack of enthusiasm towards Caesarism and the straightened vision of the phenomenon as relevant only for France, but not Germany and Europe, the reviewer in the *Allgemeine Zeitung des Judenthums* complied with mainstream liberal as well as conservative political writing. An exception in both respects was the statesman, historian and jurist Philipp Anton von Segesser (1817–1888). Tellingly, Segesser was Swiss and Catholic, thus not caught up in German national categories and more open to the idea of political universalism. As such, he not only defended and argued for the Caesarism of Napoleon III in France, as Constantin Frantz had so eloquently done in his *Louis Napoleon* of 1852, but advocated both Napoleonic France and the system of Bonapartism as *the* cornerstones of a new European order.

Segesser's political thought was based on the postulation that the substratum of politics had always been and would always remain religion. Europe as the Christian *Kulturkreis par excellence* was portrayed as being divided into three distinct zones: an orthodox, mainly Slavic; a Protestant, mainly Germanic; and a Catholic, mainly Romanic. Segesser envisaged a peaceful coexistence of these three political-confessional regions, but was at the same time convinced that the Romanic-Catholic group was predestined to gain predominance in the not too distant future. What made him confident more than anything else were the achievements of Napoleon III, for whom Segesser was full of praise in his various *Studien und Glossen zur Tagesgeschichte* throughout the Second Empire and even beyond its fall in 1870.[176]

According to Segesser, the "new Caesar" in Paris had founded the one system of government which corresponded to the *Zeitgeist* more than any other. In its combination of democracy and authority it was "fundamentally the most perfect thing that the European spirit has managed to achieve in the realm of constitutional law in our century".[177] Segesser was not unaware of the fact that the regime of Napoleon III had been erected by a *coup d'état* and that Caesarism could not be understood without the revolutionary energy surrounding it. Louis-Napoléon's actual achievement, however, was that he had succeeded in restraining the Revolution and instrumentalizing it for his own purposes by means of social reform policies and a relentless pursuit of order. He had hence become the spearhead, organizer and master of a disciplined Revolution. In two respects, Segesser described Bonapartism as innovative and epoch-making for European civilization: firstly, as a counter-movement to nineteenth-century individualism; secondly, as the renovator of monarchy and the monarchical principle in a new form. Dismissing legitimism and the doctrine of divine right as unviable, Segesser contrasted the "old monarchy" with the much-praised Napoleonic "democratic monarchy",[178] matching the *Zeitgeist* and the needs of peoples better than any other alternative, and offering a means to push back Republicanism in Europe. Raised by the popular voice, relying on the legacy of the First Empire and justified by the restoration of the religious principle, Napoleon III appeared as the true and best "modern European". Segesser acknowledged that the actual practice of the Second Empire was not without its faults and was even partly immoral. However, there was no doubt in his mind that it was French Caesarism which "alone embodies the politics of the future [. . .]" and "alone promises a political future for Catholicism".[179]

It was out of religious considerations that Segesser cultivated a universalistic approach to and grasp of modern Caesarism. Another group which developed a "universal" understanding by their very scholarly interest were authors dealing with the "soci(et)al dimension" of modern body politics and Caesarism/Bonapartism in particular. This dimension had never been entirely separated from the "political" in the narrow sense of the word and had been present in the debate about Caesarism from the late eighteenth century onwards. It gained in importance, however, with the rise of socialism and communism, but was not at all confined to socialist authors only. Tocqueville had been an early analyst of Caesarism from a clear "social" and "sociological" perspective, and German liberals in the mid-century followed his lead. One of them was Theodor Mundt (1808–1861).

Even in his *Pariser Kaiser-Skizzen* (1857), containing personal reflections on a recent stay in the French capital, Mundt—a moderate member of the "Young Germany"—displayed a clear and acute view on the cultural, social and political conditions in France at the time. Among other things, the work contained a detailed and astute analysis of the "Napoleonic Ideas", and Mundt came to conclude that the historical appearance of "Napoleon III was "certainly not to be assessed according to an old and traditional type of despotism in history".[180] The one characteristic feature of the Second Empire, "the common thread running through all those situations", was termed "imperialism" (*Imperialismus*) by Mundt.[181] Yet he had some doubt whether imperialism in its "exclusive focus on violence" would be as apt as a constitutional monarchy to perform the tricky task of "turning the ideas of the Revolution into legitimate facts".[182]

Mundt's evident interest in the societal transformations taking place in the Empire continued and intensified in his book *Paris und Louis Napoleon*, published in 1858. There, not without some admiration for the Emperor as a person, Mundt considered "Napoleonism" (*Napoleonismus*) as an adequate expression of a new social reality. It was a synthesis of democracy and absolutism, obtaining its historical justification and power from two sources, namely the destruction of the feudal system on the one hand and the promotion of industry as the corner stone of the modern state on the other. Napoleonism was "at the start of an epoch that, with respect to its historical development, is only industrial and military", with industrialism as its very *signum* and soul.[183]

In referring to the "reduction" of state to army, and society to industry in the system of Napoleonism, Mundt's analysis corresponded with two characteristic features of the Second Empire: 1) the militarization of the political system both as a means for domestic politics and prerequisite for an ambitious foreign policy conceived in global dimensions; and 2) the industrialization of France, which was expedited and gained momentum since Louis-Napoléon's seizure of power. Closely linked to the industrialization policy were efforts to address the social question, which Louis-Napoléon had designated as fundamental as early as in his writings of the 1830s and 1840s. While it is true that Napoleon III never made any serious effort to put his most radical social ideas—as expressed, e.g., in *Extinction of Pauperism*[184]—into political practice, his social policies adhered to the general principles developed in his programmatic writings, namely that it was the task of the state to actively promote economic development in a way which would also benefit the working classes. This was also in acknowledging that he himself had described the legitimacy of his regime resting to a good part on the economic and social development of the country.

Considering the social policies and the obvious advances Napoleon III made to the working class, Mundt—as others—was inclined to describe "Napoleonism" as "governmental socialism".[185] If it continued along the same path, the government of Napoleon III could only finally arrive at socialism as its destination.[186] For the aforementioned Gustav Diezel it was clear as early as 1852 that "with Louis Napoleon, the single, undivided, equal people has ascended the throne. Its program in the interior will be essentially socialism, i.e., the use of state power to attract and pacify the hitherto depressed classes", even though "far more the rural population than the educated and more free-thinking urban workers". Accordingly, no one had less reason for complaint about the Napoleonic regime than socialists and communists. Bonaparte was *their* man and had proved to be "a skilful worker in perfecting Communism", not least in that he "has made the power of the state even more absolute and more ingeniously and comprehensively centralized".[187]

And indeed, notwithstanding the fact that social-revolutionary intellectuals belonged to the most ardent opponents of the Napoleonic regime and would hardly agree in general on what Diezel had put forward, even authors of the radical left acknowledged that Bonapartism might be a significant stage on the way to socialism. After all, this was not only the opinion of Proudhon in *La Révolution sociale démontrée par le coup d'état du 2 décembre*, but also of Karl Marx, who with his *Der 18te Brumaire des Louis Napoleon* (1852) provided perhaps the most famous politico-theoretical answer to the *coup d'état* of 1851 and the Napoleonic system.[188]

Written between December 1851 and March 1852 during his exile in London, Marx's *Eighteenth Brumaire*, in which he demonstrated wide knowledge of contemporary history and the socio-economic situation in France as well as his sense of sarcasm, combined sociological analysis and revolutionary prophecy. At first sight, Marx does not seem to take Bonapartism all too seriously when famously citing the coup of Napoleon III as an example how history repeats itself as a "miserable farce" after it had initially—namely under Napoleon I—occurred as a tragedy: "The eighteenth Brumaire of the idiot for the eighteenth Brumaire of the genius!"[189] This, however, did not make the phenomenon less remarkable and instructive for Marx, whose aim—as he later declared in the preface to the second edition of 1869—was to "demonstrate how the class struggle in France created circumstances and relationships that made it possible for a grotesque mediocrity to play a hero's part".[190] It was also in the 1869 preface that Marx rejected the Napoleonic regime being characterized by "the school-taught phrase of so-called Caesarism", which suggested a deceptive parallel to the ancient world:

> In this superficial historical analogy the main point is forgotten, namely, that in ancient Rome the class struggle took place only within a privileged minority, between the free rich and the free poor, while the great productive mass of the population, the slaves, formed the purely passive pedestal for these combatants. People forget Sismondi's significant saying: The Roman proletariat lived at the expense of society, while modern society lives at the expense of the proletariat. With so complete a difference between the material, economic conditions of the ancient and the modern class struggles, the political figures produced by them can likewise have no more in common with one another than the Archbishop of Canterbury has with the High Priest Samuel.[191]

In his political philosophy, Marx made out two groups that constituted the political power base for Louis-Napoléon: the *Lumpenproletariat* and, to an even greater extent, the most numerous class of French society, i.e. the small-holding peasants (*Parzellenbauern*). Their support was due both to material and ideological moments. The *Lumpenproletariat* had been co-opted with the promise of social and political reforms. The peasantry, on the other hand, was not only a traditional stronghold of the Napoleonic cult, but owing to their mode of production also unable to develop an independent class consciousness and hence dependent on a strong authority, in the mid-century embodied by Louis-Napoléon:

> Just as the Bourbons were the dynasty of big landed property and just as the Orleans were the dynasty of money, so the Bonapartes are the dynasty of the peasants, that is, the mass of the French people. Not the Bonaparte who submitted to the bourgeois parliament, but the Bonaparte who dispersed the bourgeois parliament is the chosen man of the peasantry.[192]

With their support—though essentially advancing the interests of the finance aristocracy—Louis-Napoléon had managed to place himself above the two main classes of society, proletariat and bourgeoisie. In this position, he had managed to take the French (political) nation by surprise:

> The Constitution, the National Assembly, the dynastic parties, the blue and the red republicans [...], the thunder from the platform, the sheet lightning of the daily press, the entire literature, the political names and the intellectual reputations, the civil law and the penal code, *liberté, egalité, fraternité* [...]—all has vanished like a phantasmagoria before the spell of a man whom even his enemies do not make out to be a magician.[193]

Outward characteristics of Bonapartism were military penetration of society and quasi unrestricted executive power for the government. However, while the immediate and palpable result of Louis-Napoléon's coup was "the victory of Bonaparte over parliament, of the executive power over the legislative power, of force without words over the force of words", Marx was in no doubt that "the overthrow of the parliamentary republic contains within itself the germ of the triumph of the proletarian revolution".[194] At the end of the day, Bonapartism paved the way for the rule of the proletariat: the erratic policies of Louis-Napoléon, who was driven by the contradictory demands of his situation, made "some tolerant of revolution, others desirous of revolution, and produces actual anarchy in the name of order, while at the same time stripping its halo from the entire state machine, profanes it and makes it at once loathsome and ridiculous".[195] Together with the leveling and centralizing effect of Bonapartism, this would eventually guarantee the victory of the proletariat over the bourgeoisie as a prerequisite for a classless society.

However, it was especially, though not exclusively, with respect to his 1852 assessment of Bonapartism as merely the immediate and inevitable prelude to a proletarian revolution—a view shared by other socialist thinkers—that Marx was rebutted. He, as many other contemporary critics, overestimated the regime's reliance on deceit, corruption, coercion and force of arms, while underestimating its ability to create and preserve popular allegiance over a period of ultimately almost twenty years.

4.4 Legitimization Strategies of the Second Empire

To gain popular support and assume power in the wake of the 1848 Revolution had been a remarkable triumph for Louis-Napoléon, as had been the erection of the Second Empire. It had become possible due to a wide spectrum of fears, hopes and expectations in the French population: partly paranoid panic of the red menace and the wish for a protection of vested rights and the preservation of the existing social, legal and property order among members of the middle classes; hopes for a melioration of their standard of living and working conditions in the lower and working classes; increasing annoyance with the parliamentary-representative system being stuck in ideological fragmentation; corresponding desire for identifiable leadership, effective government and political calculability.

Gaining power was a crucial first step, consolidating it a no less important second one. Repression was one potential alternative for the regime, however a very dangerous one. What was decisive for the endurance of the Napoleonic regime was its ability to fulfill the high expectations of different groups of society and to generate necessary legitimacy through its policies. In this regard, Louis-Napoléon was in a more difficult situation than his uncle had been half a century before him. The latter was considered a "national hero" and "decision maker" long before the 18 Brumaire, whereas the former still had to prove his qualities as a leader; and while there was certainly frustration over the republican system in 1851, popular support had been even lower for the corrupt Directorate in 1799. There was hence urgency for Louis-Napoléon to prove himself and his regime as the best alternative for the future

France, and Napoleonic propaganda did its best to demonstrate that this was indeed the case.

Exemplary for the regime's self-conception and self-staging as "unifier" and "benefactor" of the whole nation is a public speech of Jean Gilbert Victor Fialin duc de Persigny, one of the key theorists of Bonapartism and holding high government positions in the Second Empire, which he gave in Saint-Étienne on August 26, 1863 *Sur les principes politiques de l'Empire.*[196] As to the character of the Empire, Persigny described it as the only reasonable substitute for the other three political alternatives which had torn France apart in the previous decades: Reaction and Restoration; rule of the bourgeoisie and the *juste milieu*, as under the July Monarchy; and Republicanism. Unlike these three, which had eventually led to a series of revolutionary regime changes, the Second Empire did not represent the interest of one particular group, but of society in its entirety and was thus in the position to overcome the rifts traversing the nation:

> For the men of the upper class party, more inclined to worship royal traditions, the Empire, lacking its old legitimacy, at least offered a sort of monarchical unity; to those of the middle-class party, it guaranteed a sort of liberty moderated by the order necessary for the prosperity of commerce and industry; and those of the working class party saw in it the brilliant triumph of democracy. The new party of the Government, although composed of seemingly heterogeneous elements, therefore had the great advantage of representing the three opinions, three parties, three classes.[197]

Persigny portrayed the "three Frances" not only as being merged in the Empire, but the latter also as a fortunate realization of the classical principle of the separation of powers outlined by Montesquieu and Machiavelli (!) as well as Locke.[198] The most important achievement of the Second Empire to Persigny, however, was the re-establishment of "order" both in the political and social field:

> [...] by restoring the fundamental principles of authority and freedom to our institutions, the Emperor has restored order to the State, just as he, in creating the Government party independently of class antagonism, restored order to society. To ensure the destiny of the Empire, nothing more is needed.[199]

His outlook for the future was correspondingly optimistic:

> A day will come when, under the reign of a prince called Napoleon IV or Napoleon V, our grandchildren will say with pride about each of us: He belonged to the party that was faithful and devoted to the country, that, by founding the Empire, put an end to our revolutions and guaranteed the greatness, the prosperity and the freedom of France![200]

Yet any propagandistic utterance could only be as convincing as the actual political achievements of the regime against which it could be measured.

Given that expectations with regard to Louis-Napoléon were so different right from the beginning and that most diverse interests needed to be satisfied, delivering policies that would gratify the nation as a whole was a most challenging task. To increase the chances of success, several policies and legitimization strategies had to be pursued at the same time. A particularly important element was the combination of forced economic development with social reformism so prominently stated in Louis-Napoléon's political writings. In the event of the envisaged "industrialization with social conscience" succeeding, a crucial contribution to domestic pacification could be made.

4.4.1 Economic and Social Reformism

Napoleon's economic policy was ambitious and altogether successful. It was targeted at improving infrastructure, especially transport infrastructure, which—compared to Britain—left a lot to be desired at the beginning of the 1850s. In less than twenty years the rail network expanded from 4,000 kilometres at the beginning to 20,000 kilometres at the end of Napoleon's rule. Railway construction served as a leading sector for the expansion of the steel and heavy industry as well, and helped to increase the trade volume by an estimated 101 percent over the period 1851–1863 and no less than 248 percent between 1851 and 1882. Parallel to the development of the rail network and the improvement of the road system and the waterways, the extension of modern means of communications—in particular the electric telegraph—and the postal service was driven forward, too.[201]

A prerequisite for the dynamic development of the infrastructure was the modernization of the French banking system. Particularly important in this respect was the creation of the *Société Générale du Crédit Mobilier* and the *Crédit Foncier de France* in 1852, both of which were also intended to expand French investments outside Europe. The *Crédit Mobilier*, becoming one of the leading financial institutions of the world during the nineteenth century, was founded to give loans to the owners of movable property. By mobilizing savings of middle class French investors, the declared object of the investment bank was to promote industrial enterprises of all kinds, especially the construction of railways in France and abroad. In contrast, the *Banque Foncière de Paris*, which soon became amalgamated with similar institutions at Nevers and Marseilles under the title *Crédit Foncier de France*, was a mortgage bank lending money on the security of real or immovable property.[202]

Clearly, the promotion of economic development by Napoleon III was not solely intended to strengthen France's power-political standing in Europe, but to no lesser degree as a means to create public confidence in the regime at home. And indeed, due to the political stability and its pro-business policies, the Second Empire soon earned a significant degree of respect and creditworthiness. This, in turn, was most favorable for accelerated economic growth.[203] The credit status which the regime had gained after only a couple of years was demonstrated when during the Crimean War the government decided to issue a state bond publicly rather than via the banking system. The undertaking, which can be seen as an "economic plebiscite" over the regime,[204] was a full success for the Emperor: with 468 rather than the expected 250 million francs the government loan was easily oversubscribed.[205]

In his efforts to boost the French economy, Napoleon III never lost sight of the social question, aware of the fact that universal suffrage made the regime dependent on the support of the rising working classes. Thanks to the *de facto* expropriation of the House of Orléans in early 1852, Louis-Napoléon had gained financial leeway for socio-political projects. Among other things, these assets were used to support mutual societies (*sociétés de secours mutuels*), by which workers made provisions for health-care and old-age collectively. In addition, these societies—precursors of modern social security systems—also sponsored the construction of working class housing in the industrial centers.[206] In general, Napoleon's social and welfare policies aimed at expanding—with state support—the activities of (workers' and other) associations, which had been created by private initiatives. This also allowed for a close control of their activities by the authorities, under whose influence the number of associations rose from 2,400 to 3,400, their membership figures from 271,000 to 426,000 between 1852 and 1856 alone. By the end of the Second Empire (1869), around 800,000 full and around 100,000 honorary members were organized in 6,000 associations.[207]

With a look to the working class, Napoleon also pushed for a liberalization of foreign trade, perhaps the most eminent outcome of which was the signing of a commercial treaty with the United Kingdom in January 1860. Napoleon III not only expected sustainable economic growth from such liberalization efforts, but also a considerably raised standard of living for the working classes.[208] In doing so, however, a serious conflict of interests and objectives became obvious in the regime's home policy. Substantial parts of the business classes and the bourgeoisie felt uncared for and their vital economic interests being sacrificed, resulting in a growing estrangement of Napoleon III and the upper middle classes, whose confidence in the regime had been shattered.[209] The reform of foreign trade became a major factor in the rise of opposition to the Napoleonic order, and the gradual liberalization of the political system in the 1860s has not least to be seen as an attempt of the Emperor to compensate decreasing support for his economic policy among the elites by making concessions to political participation.

4.4.2 Charisma and Plebiscitary Mass Democracy

Like his uncle before him, Louis-Napoléon capitalized not only on a distinctive political and social crisis for his seizing power, but also on widespread hopes of salvation by a "national saviour". This charismatic element remained characteristic of the regime throughout its existence. From the beginning, it was linked with the prospect of economic and social development on the one hand, and the promise of (re-)establishing (plebiscitary) democracy and universal suffrage on the other. While the plebiscitary element had been promoted and successfully practiced even under Napoleon Bonaparte, a new element of Louis-Napoléon's rule was that the second parliamentary chamber (*Corps législatif*) was periodically re-elected by universal male suffrage in direct ballot. Unlike Napoleon I, his nephew had to make sure he won not only the plebiscites as expressions of "democratic legitimacy", but also the parliamentary elections. Since he did not wish to merely "reign" like a constitutional monarch, but actually "rule", Louis-Napoléon became an active political player, whose policies together with the whole regime were up for approbation in every single election. This put the Second Empire in a more delicate position than its predecessor and implied permanent activism on the part of the government.

Given the vital need for electoral success, "electoral steering" became a fixed element of constitutional practice in the Second Empire. The most effective instrument to produce the desired outcomes was the system of "official candidacy" (*candidature officielle*). Before every election, essentially in each constituency one suitable person loyal to the regime was picked as the official government candidate and supported by the public administration. Those candidates profited from simplified administrative procedures and active support for their canvassing, and they were also empowered to hold out the prospect of various kinds of material "gratuities" for their voters. The system, however, did not confine itself to promoting government representatives, but also included massive discrimination of unsolicited candidates, no matter which political leaning. The hindrance repertoire included prohibiting electoral rallies as well as threatening printers publishing advertising material for "unofficials" with an employment ban. As a result, Napoleon III was able to secure a largely obedient parliamentary majority for most of his rule.[210]

The practice of the official candidates both complemented and perfected the plebiscitary system: the exertion of direct influence on the electorate degraded parliament to a mere executive body of the government and rendered every independent role in the political process void. If successfully applied, the Emperor never had cause to resort to his constitutional right of an *appel au peuple*[211] to overrule parliament and affirm his political pre-eminence, since a rupture between government and parliament could not possibly develop. The apparent conformity between the executive and legislative branch was intended to underline national unity and the effectiveness of the system. And indeed: after the two successful plebiscites of 1851 and 1852, Napoleon III had no need to fall back on this political instrument during the next eighteen years of the Empire.

Considering the manipulation of the political system by the regime, one might be inclined to denounce the Caesarism of Napoleon III as mere pseudo-constitutionalism, and its elements of civic political participation as pure *ersatz*-democracy. Indeed, the anti-democratic elements of the regime have long been underlined from various ideological perspectives. Contemporary critics so different in their political views as Victor Hugo and Karl Marx were in unison when vehemently attacking Louis-Napoléon's government as despotic and arbitrary. Others were perhaps less harsh in their choice of words, but nevertheless stressed that the Second Empire was an aberrance of "true democracy". One of them was the French republican philosopher Jules Barni (1818–1878). In his work *La morale dans la démocratie* (1868) he argued that "democracy" was often used to palliate absolute power:

> A specific political constitution that declares people sovereign and even invokes universal suffrage is often labelled as democracy, but it promptly transfers absolute power to a ruler—elected or hereditary (little matter)—who, concentrating all power in his hands, is in fact the absolute master of citizens' liberty, property, and even life.

This had been the case with Roman Caesarism under the reign of Tiberius, Caligula and Nero, all of whom had claimed democracy for them; but not only then. A similar phenomenon could be detected now: "the new Caesarism, established in France on 18 Brumaire, did not fail to present itself as the crowning achievement of democracy, and this particular claim found too many advocates." However, no matter how often it was claimed, "this is hardly democracy; this is only a lie. Democracy, I have said and will repeat, is not *equality in servitude*, but *freedom in equality*."[212]

Indeed, the fact that Napoleon III tried to give his Caesaristic regime the appearance of being more of a democracy than it was can hardly be denied. Therefore it comes as no surprise that a majority of later political historians stressed the anti-democratic nature of "Bonapartism" or emphasized its deviation from the republican norm.[213] According to this view, Bonapartism appears to be merely concerned with power politics, with any reference to democracy as simply instrumental. This undemocratic image seems even more justified when post-Second Empire Bonapartism is taken into account, which was to demonstrate distinct political authoritarianism and social conservatism.

To disqualify the Bonapartist regime between 1851 and 1870 in these terms, however, does not do it historical justice. To assume that "democracy" was just a chimera understates Louis-Napoléon's commitment to mass democracy. To start with, there are two facts which cannot be denied: Firstly, that it was under the Second Republic that significant restrictions to universal male suffrage had been introduced in 1850, and that it was Napoleon who restored it immediately after his coup in 1851. Secondly, that Napoleon III remained firmly dedicated to universal suffrage during the Second Empire, never making any attempts to infringe upon this fundamental principle, and that despite the existing system of the "official candidates", electoral fraud in the proper sense of the word was never an issue.

It was only under these framework conditions that the electoral system could develop its own "democratizing" dynamics in the second half of the Second Empire's existence, which in turn helped to propel the liberalization of the regime as a whole. Favored by growing resentment towards bureaucratic formalism and by increased self-confidence of local dignitaries, prefectural control over local politics and the electoral system were increasingly challenged during the 1860s. It was not by coincidence that political emancipation efforts on the local level, but also allowing for an incremental democratization,[214] went hand in hand with growing opposition tendencies among the middle-class elites on a national level. Since the aforementioned free trade agreement with Great Britain in 1860, which had been signed against the declared will of the financial capital, frustration with the regime's policies had continuously grown bigger. Middle-class opposition represented a considerable challenge to the regime's authority and complicated domestic politics, since it soon became clear to the government that in the long run it was impossible to turn a blind eye to the bourgeois elites' interests. Their influence was too considerable not only in the economic, but also in the political sphere. Growing opposition and the interlinked erosion of the regime's system of "electoral steering" during the 1860s demonstrated that there was a real danger of the electorate emancipating itself from official control, and of a permanent hotspot developing.

To counter such dangers, the regime allowed for several reforms and extended liberties to be incrementally introduced from the early 1860s onwards, which marked the evolution of the empire towards a more liberal form. Following the general amnesty of August 16, 1859, which was meant to demonstrate the Emperor's will to exercise leniency even with his enemies, important political concessions were made in late 1860, when the Chambers were granted the right to vote an address in answer to the Emperor's annual speech from the throne as a means to air their opinions and grievances on the acts of the government. Further decrees and *sénatus-consulte* increased the power of the assemblies and the *Corps législatif* in particular, progressively retrieving them from the marginalized role they had been given in the Constitution of 1852. Among other things, granting the chambers the right to make parliamentary debates public through the media and the right of voting on the budget by sections (1861) as well as the legislative's power to direct questions to the government, gained in 1867, were important steps in this respect. Despite a trend towards parliamentarization, however, an encompassing revision of the constitution and the political system remained a desideratum. The opposition—strengthened by the successful attempt in the elections of 1863 to bring together (moderate) legitimist, liberal and republican opponents of the regime in a *Union libérale*, the head of which was Adolphe Thiers— thus continued to voice ever more urgently its demand for "necessary liberties".

The result of the elections of May 1869, which took place in an environment of strikes and manifestations of public unrest in the urban centers, eventually tipped the scales in favor of more sweeping constitutional reform. In spite of the established system of official candidates and a renewed warning against the *spectre rouge*, the elections inflicted a serious defeat upon the Empire. Nationwide, the regime won only 57 percent of the popular vote (4.44 million votes), while in Paris the opposition parties managed to gain around 75 percent of the votes. With 3.96 million Frenchmen declaring themselves anti-government in 1869, the opposition had increased its share of the votes by more than two thirds as compared to 1863 (1.95 million) and actually more than quintupled it as against 1857 (with only 0.67 million).[215]

For the Emperor, these results confirmed the need to make more concessions to liberal opinion in order to secure a broader political basis and isolate the irreconcilable republican left. This was most likely to be achieved by restoring the political influence of the social elites. At the same time, however, Napoleon III did not want to risk a radical regime change going beyond a reform of existing institutions and was intent on safeguarding as much of his political leadership as possible. The liberal Bonapartist Pierre-Charles Chesnelong (1820–1894) pointedly referred to the tightrope the regime had to walk between "conservative" and "liberal" interests, paradigms of "order" and "change", when declaring that "in spite of its faults, the Empire is still the pivot of order in France and in Europe. We need to know how to maintain it in resisting it, in developing within it [...] the spirit of purified conservatism represented by a sincere and prudent liberalism".[216]

The constitutional changes resulting from the *sénatus-consulte* of September 8, 1869 reflected the oscillation between concessions and defense of the *status quo*.[217] The powers of the *Corps législatif* were increased, e.g. with respect to the right of interpellation (Art. 7), control of the budget (Art. 9) and customs treaties (Art. 10). The ministers remained exclusively "dependent" on the Emperor, but the new clause that *Ils sont responsables* could be read as a rapprochement to the principle of a more extensive parliamentary accountability (Art. 2). Even more importantly, the Second Chamber gained the right to initiate legislation (Art. 1), which had previously been a prerogative of the Emperor.

In return, however, Napoleon III retained considerable executive powers, including quasi unrestricted control over the entire state administration, foreign policy and the armed forces. No concessions were made with regard to the Emperor's right to declare war and to appoint the members of the Senate—and hence influence the majorities in the First Chamber—at his discretion. Most notably, Napoleon III was eager to keep his prerogative of appealing directly to the people without consulting parliament.

Rather than renouncing the instrument of plebiscite, which had cemented his power in 1851 and 1852, the Emperor was determined to use it again: formally to let the French people approve the constitutional changes, but essentially to reaffirm his personal legitimacy and that of his regime. To ask for a national "vote of confidence" was not without risk. The preparations of the plebiscite, which was scheduled for May 8, 1870, were accordingly diligent. In a public proclamation to the French people on April 23, 1870, Napoleon III emphasized that it was indispensable that any new "constitutional pact" be approved by the nation. He explained that he deemed it necessary to develop the imperial order further into a more liberal form in order to equip France with continued stability and progress. The Emperor promised that a positive vote would not only sanction the reforms introduced since 1860, but consolidate the whole political system durably, and facilitate a later transition of power to his successor. He therefore empathically asked the voters for another act of personal faith.[218]

To insinuate that a "nay" would nurture the threat of revolution was a central element of the official campaign, which appealed to social fears reinforced by a carefully engendered "red menace". A diffuse fear of social revolution not only haunted the liberal elites, who worked for more political participation and the limitation of the Emperor's personal power, but were above all worried about the preservation of the social order; in the provinces, too, resentment of "Paris" and horror of political radicalism as well as anticlericalism were rekindled. Seen from this angle, the plebiscite became much more than a simple "yes" or "no" on constitutional issues.

This ultimately made for the overwhelming approval the plebiscite found, with the number of "yes" votes (7.35 million) outnumbering the "no" (1.39 million) by almost five.[219] Louis-Napoléon's personal authority had—once more—been confirmed, and so that of his political regime. On May 21, 1870, Napoleon III commented on the result of the plebiscite correspondingly: "The enemies of our institutions have made the question into one between Revolution and Empire. The country has chosen for the system that guarantees order and freedom. Today, the foundations of the Empire have been strengthened."[220] Indeed, the plebiscite of 1870 could only be seen as a success for the Emperor: the approval of the plebiscite by the French people made the liberal concessions made during the 1860s—underlined by the appointment of the former republican Émile Ollivier (1825–1913) as head of a new cabinet on January 2, 1870— practically irreversible. At the same time, however, Napoleon III got his categorical "no" for far-reaching structural change and the introduction of parliamentary government sanctioned, too. Somewhat paradoxically, political polarization in the run-up to the plebiscite had also thinned out the opposition to the regime, leaving radical republicans as virtually the only serious adversaries of the regime.

In the summer of 1870 there thus appeared to be no real threat to the Second Empire, and Roger Price notes: "The establishment of a Liberal Empire, with a strong executive power held in check by rejuvenated parliamentary institutions, seemed to herald a long period of political stability [...]"[221] It looked as if the regime had successfully mastered the crisis which it had drifted into during the 1860s, and had actually accomplished the daring and difficult transition from its usurpatory origins to institutional stability. Yet this stability was deceptive. What would destroy the regime was not political opposition from within, but military defeat, the shipwreck of another feature of its existence: imperialism.

4.4.3 Imperialism and Bellicism

Even before his ascent to actual power, Louis-Napoléon had not grown tired of emphasizing that the "Napoleonic idea" was in essence an idea of peace, not war, and still as President of the Republic he continued to stress that the most important political objective of French policies and his government was the creation and preservation of (domestic) peace. Yet Louis-Napoléon's definition of "Napoleonism" as a "peace project" did not imply that the Second Empire was to become a peaceful period in French history. This was neither the case with regard to the regime's establishment by a domestic coup that was essentially military, nor even less so in terms of foreign policy. Quite the contrary: from its very beginning in 1851/1852, military interventionism and expansionism were characteristic features of Napoleon's rule. In its eighteen years of existence, the Second Empire not only participated in the Crimean War (1853–1856) and took sides for the Kingdom of Piedmont-Sardinia in the Second War of Italian Independence against the Austrian Empire (1859), but also intervened militarily in Mexico in the 1860s (1861–1867) and ultimately declared war on Prussia-Germany in 1870, which was to bring about the downfall of Napoleon III.

Indeed, the fact that the Second Empire waged a series of wars made it distinct from both the short-lived republic and the two monarchies preceding it, while parallels with the imperial past of the First Empire are evident. One might therefore suppose that the regime of Louis-Napoléon was after all—as that of his uncle earlier—only concerned with glorifying force and exercising military power, which in turn might prove the centerpiece of Constant's theory of usurpatory rule: usurpers had to conduct war in order to justify their rule and create legitimacy, while traditional monarchs could trust on dynastic legitimacy even without military success and glory.[222] Conversely, this implied that military defeat was fatal for usurpatory regimes, while it was not necessarily the case for monarchies. But how convincing is the argument that usurpatory rule is ultimately dependent on perpetuated military success when applied to Napoleon III?

There seems to be some empirical evidence which endorses a greater systemic resistance of "traditional monarchies" towards military failure. The experiences of the first half of the nineteenth century proved that losing a war did not jeopardize the reign of a historical monarch: the continued military failure of the Habsburg Emperor Franz II (later Emperor Franz I of Austria) in the first four coalition wars against revolutionary and later Napoleonic France and even his total defeat in the Franco-Austrian war of 1809 cost him territory and forced him to renounce the dignity of the Holy Roman Emperor, though, but never endangered his monarchical power *per se*. Similarly, Friedrich Wilhelm III of Prussia managed to keep his throne even after the disastrous defeat of Jena and Auerstedt in 1806, and neither did the Russian Tsardom under Nicholas I and Alexander II forfeit its autocratic powers due to the loss of the Crimean War. Not so Napoleon I, who lost his Empire in the context of military defeat both in 1814 and 1815.

However, even in the case of Napoleon Bonaparte the role of military failure is less clear than it might appear at first sight. Constant's theory of the dependency of usurpers on victory in war does not quite explain the double downfall of Napoleon I. Even the French Senate, which had initiated his dethronement in April 1814, did not charge him with having illegitimately assumed power and being a usurper, but justified the Emperor's deposition along the lines of historical models blaming monarchs to have abused their power and become tyrants.[223] Undoubtedly, Napoleon's falling military star from the failed Russian Campaign onwards did not help to boost popular belief in his leadership capacities. Yet it is daring to say that it was primarily military setbacks which cost him the support of the French nation. Rather, military setbacks—and more so Napoleon's refusal to accept the peace conditions offered by the coalition—prepared the ground for domestic opposition to argue for the end of his regime, and made the public, so heavily burdened by conscriptions and confiscations as well as the economic side effects of a dragged out large scale war, accept it without resistance.

For his nephew Napoleon III, the verdict on the role of failed imperialism and military success is not unambiguous either. As for the motives of the Second Empire's "active" foreign policy, which—depending on the point of view—one might be inclined to call ambitious and grand, or aggressive and belligerent, various readings have been put forward. Certainly the most flattering is the one which considers Napoleon III to be the visionary of a united "Europe of the nations", and French foreign policy during his rule essentially as the attempt to put the Emperor's idealism into political practice. Seen from this perspective, Napoleon III appears to have taken up his uncle's exile writings—containing the vision of a common Europe united in peace—as a foreign political program; a program, for which war and expansionism was just a necessary and temporary means to a noble end.

Others have interpreted the "imperialism" of the Second Empire not so much as the expression of idealism than of conventional power politics, which was characteristic for other states and political systems at the time, too. Prominently, Napoleon's later opponent Otto von Bismarck (1815–1898) also characterized the regime in this vein. In a memorandum written for minister Otto Theodor von Manteuffel (1805–1882), dated June 2, 1857, Bismarck negated that the Emperor of the French and his legitimation differed considerably from other contemporary European rulers.[224]

However, there have also been voices stressing that the Empire's military imperialism needs to be explained systemically, that is as the result of the Napoleonic regime's specific character. Even early observers suggested that Louis-Napoléon would not only seize power with the support of the army, but that military elements and expansionism would also be a determining element of the new regime's policies. Among them was Auguste Romieu, in whose writings "Caesarism" and "imperialism"/"militarism" appear closely interlinked. He characterized Caesarism as "rule of the sabre", but also associated "fame" and "glory" with the new political order he sketched. After the 1851 coup, Tocqueville and Jules Barni, among others, identified (Louis-Napoléon's) "Caesarism" with militarism, too, though in a clearly derogatory tone. In his *La morale dans la démocratie* (1868), Barni repeatedly stressed his conviction that "despotism naturally leads to war", and that "Caesarism and militarism are two inseparable scourges".[225] To Barni, the French Empire under the two Napoleons was *the* modern paragon of despotism and Caesarism; a "regime of military monarchy", as he formulated it in a speech at the *Congrès international de la paix* in Geneva 1867, "which sacrifices the liberties of all for the power of a military leader, measures the power of the state by the number of its soldiers and seeks continually to expand the mass of men it can bend to its laws".[226]

Undeniably, the army continued to play a central role throughout the Second Empire's existence, and the regime displayed a considerably greater readiness to wage war than its predecessors had. This was certainly in part due to personal ambitions for military fame on the part of Napoleon III, who did not want to be second to his uncle, even though he lacked the latter's military genius. More than that, the prospect of being perceived as a "war hero" by the nation must have been appealing to Napoleon III. This was especially true in a period in which bellicism—going hand in hand with increasing nationalistic tendencies—played an ever greater role in domestic politics. Aiming for foreign political and military success to increase legitimacy was a hazardous endeavor, nevertheless an enticing one which seemed to have been tailor-made for Napoleon III, whom many contemporaries had started to characterize as an adventurer as early as after his failed attempts to seize power through military coups in 1836 and 1840, respectively. But can the increased willingness of the Second Empire to wage war be explained by Napoleon III's need to prove his and his regime's legitimacy?

The answer might rather be "no" than "yes". The series of wars France waged after 1851/1852 may primarily be accounted for by the greater room for maneuver French diplomacy gained in the ongoing disintegration of the European Concert that had been (re-)established at the Congress of Vienna.[227] That room—one might concede—was actively and decisively exhausted by Napoleon III; it was an opportunity, however, which would most likely have been seized also by a regime less "Caesaristic" than the Napoleonic one.

A determining element and objective of French foreign policy common to all political regimes from the First Empire onwards had been the revision of the Peace Treaties of Paris (1814/1815) and the retrieval of an "appropriate" political role for France within the European great powers; that was a role at least on a par with the continental powers Austria and Russia. Even the Restoration and the July Monarchy had clearly pursued these objectives. Regarding the former, France's readmission into the European Concert and the extension of the Quadruple to a Quintuple Alliance in 1818 was as important a milestone of revisionist policies as the French intervention in Spain 1823, which was essentially an attempt by the French government to regain influence on the Iberian Peninsula and strengthen its position among the other European powers. During the July Monarchy, revisionist aspirations came to the forefront during the Rhine Crisis in 1840, when the French Government under Adolphe Thiers openly—though unsuccessfully—made demands for the territories on the left bank of the Rhine, repeating old claims for the Rhine to be the natural frontier of France. But while farther-reaching ambitions of the French governments under Louis XVIII, Charles X and Louis-Philippe continued to be dashed by the united front of the former allied powers, growing antagonisms and animosities between Britain, Russia, Austria and Prussia finally opened new perspectives for France in the 1850s. These were then promptly exploited by Napoleon III.

In the Crimean War (1853–1856)—the first instance since the Congress of Vienna in which members of the former anti-French Quadruple Alliance, which had dominated European foreign policy ever since, were in open conflict with each other—France strengthened its role as a continental power at the expense of Russia and ended its (relative) diplomatic isolation. Three years later, Napoleon's intervention in Italy weakened France's second "historical" rival on the continent, Austria. Throughout the 1850s and 1860s, the Second Empire steered a foreign political course that was anything but "exceptional" in that it continued traditional French interests. This also holds true for the policy towards Germany.

While Napoleon III had initially considered Prussia to be a "natural" ally against Austria, this attitude changed after 1866. Prussia's swift and full victory in the Austro-Prussian War thwarted not only French ambitions to assume the role of a mediator between the two conflicting parties and thus increase its influence in Germany, but also demonstrated that Prussia had irrevocably turned from a regional to a European power keen to repulse any foreign attempt to intervene in inner-German affairs. This could only be perceived as a defeat by Napoleon III, for whom future chances to pursue French national interests in Germany by diplomatic means receded into the distance, not even to mention the old dream of the Rhine border. French policies of the following years were therefore eager to compensate for what was seen as a humiliation. In that, however, the government did not position itself against public opinion. On the contrary: public opinion and the media perhaps even more than the state authorities were intent on getting their revenge. It was not least the anti-German *vox populi* calling for action to be taken against the nation's eastern neighbor that induced Napoleon III to take a firm position in the "July Crisis" of 1870 and eventually made him declare war on Prussia on July 19, 1870 after the Ems Dispatch.[228] Napoleon III had thus been coerced—or at least strongly encouraged—by public opinion in his decision making.

Which conclusions can thus be drawn regarding the role of imperialism and militarism for the Second Empire and its "Caesar"? It seems clear that the increased "activism" of France during the 1850s and 1860s cannot necessarily be ascribed to the specific regime type. Rather, as Roger Price puts it, "Napoleon's vision of the unrealised greatness of France was a widely shared feature of the general political culture", even though perhaps one "reinforced in his case [...] by his Bonapartist inheritance".[229] The Emperor's European endeavors do not reveal a break with traditional French foreign policy, and his extra-European "adventures"—most noteworthy the Mexican expedition—were in line with the colonial ambitions of other European powers.

For the regime itself, the accumulation of additional political legitimacy through foreign political and military success was definitely appealing and useful. However, it was not a *conditio sine qua non* for its existence, particularly because the Napoleonic system could rely on important domestic achievements—politically, socially and economically—through which it had proved its value for the nation. To state that imperialism and bellicism were not "regime-immanent", however, does not say anything about the susceptibility of the Second Empire to military defeat. In this regard, in fact, it appears that the highly personalized and centralized Napoleonic system was quite vulnerable. This was confirmed in the Franco-Prussian War.

For the understanding of the concurrence of military defeat and regime change in 1870, different explanatory approaches can be cited. First, "rational choice reasoning" on the part of the French nation. As far back as 1859, during the French military intervention in Italy, a governmental report on general public opinion noted that war would remain popular "for as long as taxes are not increased and the cost of exoneration from military service remains the same, and for as long as trade and agriculture are not affected profoundly"; in other words, as long as the population was not expected to make "heavy sacrifices",[230] which did become the case in 1870. In contrast to the earlier wars since Napoleon's coup in 1851, the sacrifices in 1870 were not only disproportionally heavier, but for the first time the war was also waged on French soil. The way the French were personally affected was more immediate than before, potentially lowering the masses' preparedness to back the regime's war efforts. While this dimension was not specific to the Napoleonic system—even though Napoleon I had faced a similar situation in 1814—, the other two essentially were.

On the one hand, a "structural" dimension can be mentioned. The army was the primary representative of Napoleonism and the symbol of the nation's glorious past. It was *the* central institution of both the coup of 1851 and the regime. Hence, the repercussions of military failure would be dramatic, since the Second Empire would lose its most important instrument of power. This was true on a symbolic as well as a practical level, since the army was the guarantor for the preservation of public peace and a bulwark against any revolutionary upheaval in the country; an eventuality wherefore detailed operational plans had been prepared. Perhaps even more important than the "structural" was the "power-sociological" dimension: while the Napoleonic system rested on and gained its stability from the Emperor, it also fell with him. This was what happened in 1870, favored by the fact that the heir apparent was too young to have acquired any personal popularity of his own, and that the regime had existed for too short a period of time for any sustainable traditional legitimacy to develop.

Napoleon's elevated political role made him the responsible for the military catastrophe in 1870; all the more so, because throughout his rule Napoleon had been determined to reserve the spheres of military and foreign policy for himself. In July 1870, albeit under pressure for tough action from the public and from parliament, the ultimate decision to go to war rested with the Emperor. Napoleon III not only made the choice between war and peace, but even decided to assume personal command of the French armies. While he hoped that military glory would be his in the event of victory, as in the Italian campaign of 1859, it was discredit the Emperor eventually earned after the lost Battle of Sedan. The defeat was a personal one and shattered his claim to lead the nation. In the eyes of the French, Napoleon III was responsible for the disaster not only on a political, but also on a military level. The whole Napoleonic regime appeared delegitimized more than that of Napoleon Bonaparte ever had been, who—at least till Waterloo—bore the nimbus of the military genius, whose failure could appear as being due to unfavorable circumstances and the sheer superiority of the allied powers.

The speed with which the Second Empire evaporated only a few months after the successful May plebiscite was illustrative of the shaky ground on which it was ultimately built. *Ex post facto*, the plebiscite had even accelerated the downfall of the Empire: the overwhelming approval had suggested unfettered support for Napoleon III and his policies, and had made the Emperor and his advisors believe that a successful military campaign might further strengthen the Bonapartist regime *vis-à-vis* its opponents. While there might have been a slight chance for the Emperor to remedy the situation and save his throne by his personal presence in Paris, the fact that Napoleon III was taken prisoner by the Prussians at Sedan on September 2, 1870 rendered this last hope void. Acephalous and apathetic, the regime was unable to exert any influence on events in the capital, the outstanding importance of which for French politics was once more illustrated: while in many parts of France support for the regime was still discernible, Parisian deputies usurped the power in the capital without much resistance. Just two days after the Emperor's capture, the Third Republic was proclaimed on 4 September 1870. While the new republic was not acclaimed with great enthusiasm, it did mark a new form of government less discredited than the previous one, which in the eyes of many Frenchmen had demonstrated its inability and thus forfeited its legitimacy.

4.5 Conclusions

Which concluding assessment can be given of the regime of Louis-Napoléon and the state of the more general debate on Caesarism in the mid-nineteenth century?

It can be shown that after 1848 the term "Caesarism" gained more and more acceptance in European political discourse as a denominator for a new form of government somewhere between "democracy" and "dictatorship", though other concepts, most notably Napoleonism and Bonapartism, continued to be used parallel to it. Around 1850, the debate on "modern Caesarism" and Bonapartism proved even more complex and heterogeneous than at the beginning of the century. The wide range of people from different political camps acquiring a taste for the regime of Louis-Napoléon attests to the "flexibility" of the Caesarism concept: not only did conservatives like Donoso Cortés, Romieu, Frantz or Segesser welcome Napoleonic Caesarism, mainly for confronting the red menace, containing revolutionary fervor, reaffirming private property and generally restoring "order"; liberal and socialist thinkers, too, were not immune to at least some admiration, however different and sometimes equivocal the motivations might have been, as the stances of Mundt or even Proudhon have revealed.

Also in terms of the segments of the population which Napoleon managed to appeal to, heterogeneity—and partly contradictoriness—is characteristic: while fear of socialism and radical political rhetoric drove the middle classes away from the republicans to Louis-Napoléon, the rural population showed strong loyalty to "their Emperor" as the one protecting them from a return to the *Ancien Régime* on the one hand, the exploiting bourgeoisie and radical socialism attempting to topple the existing property order on the other. Considerable parts of the working class, in turn, considered Napoleon to be the politician who took their claims for social reform seriously and was willing to make it part of the political agenda. Quite naturally, this "broadness" also implied that strongly divergent expectations needed to be fulfilled in the regime's policies.

Given its evident "historical complexity", the concrete institutional form of Bonapartism was far from static, making it difficult if not impossible to isolate any clear "essence" even within the French context: not only was the First Empire considerably different from the Second, but there were also notable political variations within the latter, of which the authoritarian early years contrasting with the later liberal years was only one. Acknowledging "differences" in an environment of dynamic social, economic and political change also put the "great parallel" with antiquity into perspective. Comparing antiquity with the present still played a role in the mid-century, but lost in importance, with most of the works dealing with the Bonapartist regime— or more generally Caesarism—declaring it to be a qualitatively new form of rule. This was yet another sign of the mutations that language (and practice) of Caesarism had already undergone and would continue to undergo in its curious evolution.

Despite increasing differentiation of the concept, by the mid-century also a couple of themes had crystallized which remained fairly constant in later discussions on Caesarism: firstly, the matter of Caesarism's legitimacy; secondly, its relationship to the "masses". In light of the ever more burning social question, the second point was gaining in importance and dynamism at the time, as the Second Empire had demonstrated *in situ*, heralding a fundamental change of political paradigm. Louis-Napoléon's interventionist economic and employment policy, his Keynesianism *avant la lettre*, the forceful promotion of infrastructure and heavy industry projects, but above all the attempt to include the proletariat in the "political nation" marked the transition from legal to social statism, from *Rechtsstaat* ("state of law") to *Sozialstaat* ("welfare state"), and a change of emphasis from constitution to administration.

Yet in other respects the Second Empire brought more lucidity, namely with regard to the immanent strengths, but also shortcomings, of a regime type characterized as "democratic dictatorship" or "plebiscitary monarchy". Perhaps plainer than its predecessor half a century earlier, the Second Empire highlighted both. One obvious advantage was the clear identifiability of rule and responsibility with one person, which was a crucial advantage for seizing power, particularly in moments of crisis when a *bellum omnium contra omnes* was looming ahead due to the fragmentation and ideologization of the political sphere. Rather than a civil war, Caesarism offered the prospect of coherent and rapid decision making, guaranteed by the elimination—or at least marginalization—of intermediary bodies. In addition, ideological "flexibility" enabled Louis-Napoléon to mix conservative, liberal and social(ist) elements at his discretion and provided for a potentially broad basis in society, whilst the regime's form being *sui generis* allowed to appeal to multiple sources of legitimacy: besides the characteristic charismatic element, the regime did its best to strengthen a traditional element by establishing a dynastic hereditary monarchy and was also able to rely on a rational element ("good politics"). Each of the three plebiscites held under Louis-Napoléon can be seen as representing one of the three legitimatory pillars on which the system rested: charisma (1851), tradition (1852) and rationality (1870).

The regime's ability to appeal to different sources of legitimacy, however, could not hide the fact that the regime's authority was of a particular character and permanently endangered, since it depended on fickle public opinion that had to be fought for on a daily basis. Coercion, propaganda, demagogy, sensationalism, electoral steering and corruption were as much part of the means used to meet this vital need as were the regime's practical policies, especially in the economic and social field. Louis-Napoléon was well aware that his ability to gain and defend his power ultimately depended on sedulous flattery towards the populace. Nevertheless, Louis-Napoléon needs to be given credit that unlike most other important politicians of the nineteenth century, including his uncle Napoleon Bonaparte, he never talked contemptuously about the populace, but always in the mood of the starry-eyed and philanthropic idealist he seemed to have remained throughout his life. Even so, gratitude on the part of the masses was limited, as the abrupt end of Napoleon's rule in 1870 demonstrated.

The deposition of the Emperor on September 4, 1870 turned out to be a *de facto* plebiscite unveiling the flipside of any plebiscitary political system. The fact that less than four months after the formal May plebiscite—which had ended with a superb success for the regime—the nation came to a totally different "resolution" proved the Emperor's cousin Jérôme Napoléon Bonaparte (1805–1870) right, who in September 1869 had remarked on plebiscitary government: "If the people says yes, it is an illusion; if it says no, it is a revolution."[231] Doomed to fulfill the political and material expectations of the electorate on a permanent basis, the nation's solidarity was at risk to dwindle overnight as soon as any serious setback arose. In the end, Louis-Napoléon himself was one of the first victims to suffer the "political mobilization" which he had so effectively— and quasi irreversibly—pushed by opening up politics to the masses.

Nonetheless, Caesarism kept its appeal to contemporaries: not only for ambitious individuals the perspective of becoming a "new Caesar" was all too appealing to lose attraction only because of deficits which might have become visible; from a "systemic" perspective, too, there were still a number of good arguments which could be put forward in favor of this regime type. Germany in particular turned out to be—or rather remained—fertile ground for the concept of Caesarism, albeit during the time of Louis-Napoléon German thinkers and politicians did not tire of branding the "Romanic" system of plebiscitary dictatorship and Bonapartism. Criticism of Bonapartism, however, did not imply that Caesarism was similarly condemned: the trick was to distinguish between them. In the following chapter, "Germanic" concepts of Caesarism in the second half of the nineteenth century are turned to, which are intrinsically linked with the one statesman commonly referred to as the key "architect" of the German nation state: Otto von Bismarck.

"Germanic Caesarism" and the *Bismarckreich*

5.1 From *Ideal-* to *Realpolitik*: Debates on a German Caesar

The *topos* of France as the *Erbfeind* ("hereditary enemy") of the German nation—which had gathered momentum after 1848 and found its reciprocal, though perhaps less distinct, equivalent on the other side of the Rhine—suggests an insurmountable antipathy between Germany and France in the 1850s and 1860s. The Franco-Prussian War of 1870/1871 can be seen as an acknowledgment and further aggravation of that antipathy, reinforcing the impression that Germans had been in unanimous opposition against France for a considerable time. Yet even if a pronounced antagonism between France and Germany during this period is acknowledged, the question remains whether this translates into an antagonism of the respective political systems and an incompatibility of French and German political thought.

In actual fact, the reception of the Second Napoleonic Empire in Germany exemplified in the previous chapter proves that a majority of contemporary German observers either had certain reservations against the regime or ruled out any "model role" of France for Germany. More than anything else, however, this needs to be seen in the context of political rivalry between two divergent versions of nationalism: on the one hand that of France, a time-honored nation undergoing an "imperial renaissance" and thus seen as a distinct threat by its Eastern neighbor; on the other hand that of Germany, a nation still divided but aware of its potential power and keen to make up for the lack of a nation state, and for the same reason—and the prospect of another continental rival—feared and opposed by France. At the intellectual level, this conflict translated into the highly ideologized dualism between Romanism and Germanism used by both partisans of a *Kleindeutsche Lösung* ("Lesser German Solution") and a *Großdeutsche Lösung* ("Greater German Solution"); a dualism, however, in the context of which any French system of government would have suffered from prejudice.

Close inspection reveals that the impression of a united German front against concepts of Bonapartism and Caesarism *per se* is deceptive, since the unanimous rejection of French power-political and territorial claims did not translate into unanimous rejection of Caesarism as a "political life-form". Even though French Bonapartism was often stigmatized as being "un-German", many German political thinkers recognized the political viability and potential inherent in the idea of a "modern dictatorship". Among such thinkers were contemporaries with neo-absolutist sentiments, for whom Caesarism was quite simply a new variation of and synonymous with autocratic rule having the potential to crush progressive forces of whatever kind. Yet many liberals and democrats, too, developed varying degrees of sympathy for some sort of a "German(ic) Caesar".

An interesting case is the earlier-quoted Gustav Diezel, in whose works the dilemma of rebuffing "Romanic" tyranny and a positive appreciation of authoritarian forms of rule becomes particularly apparent. The same man, who in his "universal dialectic" of regime types declares dictatorship and popular absolutism a perverted Romanic form of government, is full of praise for a figure like Oliver Cromwell, "that organizer of democracy, that triumphant commander, that tamer of monarchy". Diezel harshly attacks those who would not find any fault with that "a few hundred sovereign representatives barter away the freedom, the honour, the present and future of their people", but at the same time found it obnoxious that "a man, not born on the throne, should take it upon himself to raise his people to greatness and world-historical importance". For Diezel, it is exactly this latter kind of leader he aspires for Germany: "If only Germany had found a Cromwell instead of dishonorable parliamentary prattlers, then it would not have descended to a 36-fold potentiated Ireland!"[1]

While Diezel focused primarily on the role of the actual leader, other commentators had more the structural dimension—and potential *fortes*—of Caesaristic government in mind, which often coincided with less explicit reservations against the Bonapartist system in France. One such observer was the Prussian officer and historian Heinrich Blankenburg (1820–1897), who eighteen years after Diezel's *Deutschland und die abendländische Civilisation* (1852) analyzed *Verfassung und innere Politik des zweiten Kaiserreichs* (1870). Blankenburg acknowledged that (parliamentary) constitutionalism offered certain advantages, above all that of being a barrier "against ambitious evolutions of the sovereign, against the artificial diversion of interests to the outside, against the masses' excesses of chauvinism".[2] However, in the long run it proved an unworkable system, mainly for France, but for other nations, too, including Germany. Since Bonapartism did offer a remedy for France, Blankenburg reasoned that "it is therefore by no means impossible that the idea of Napoleon III has a future", and that throughout Europe the time might be ripe for a new constitutional alternative challenging "constitutionalism" as the dominant paradigm.[3] Nonetheless, this did not imply transplanting existing French constitutional forms to other nations and the Second Empire—which he characterized as a "democratic-imperialistic system"[4]—becoming a new "universalist" regime type. On the contrary, the form of government Blankenburg had in mind was quite different: "In keeping with the spirit of our time, it would be such [a form of state] in which the national moment [. . .] claims a special status."[5]

As these two examples demonstrate—the one from the very beginning, the other from the very end of the French Second Empire—, there was continuing if not intensifying openness towards a political regime guaranteeing strong leadership without sacrificing "progressive" elements altogether. At least on detours, many German liberals and democrats were developing a taste for Caesarism, and incorporated it into their political thinking. This might have been due to the strong presence and persuasiveness of Hegelian dialectics, which had become a prominent feature among the German intelligentsia at the time: for whoever had absorbed the paradigms of dialectics, the prevailing antitheses between monarchism and republicanism, conservatism and liberalism, was asking to be "remedied" by a synthesis of a monarchical governing authority approved by and bound to the people.[6]

Even in May 1848, at the height of the Revolution, the German philosopher and Hegel disciple Johann Karl Friedrich Rosenkranz (1805–1879) had declared in an article for the *Hartungsche Zeitung* that it was the task of the Prussian government to "move forward between the revolution, which is firmly intent on proceeding towards a republic, and the reaction, which only wants to shape constitutionalism aristocratically, towards a democratic monarchy as our true future".[7] While Rosenkranz did not outline the design of such a democratic monarchy, others were slightly more decided. Concepts promoting some sort of "social monarchy" were prominently advocated by Lorenz von Stein, but also by the German-Swiss thinker Friedrich Rohmer (1814–1856), a somewhat "nonconformist" political theorist, who is hard to pin down ideologically and now largely forgotten.

In his pamphlet *Die Monarchie und der vierte Stand* (1848),[8] Rohmer argued the case for an organic symbiosis and partnership of crown and fourth estate representing the mass of the population, which were mutually dependent on each other. For the populace, it was indispensable to have a guardian defending their interests, represented by the crown. In return, it was in the vital interest of the crown to accept this role.[9] Rohmer dared to predict that in Germany only that power could assume hegemony and hope for the Imperial dignity whose monarch clearly grasped this need. The kind of monarchical authority Rohmer envisaged was a powerful and independent one:

> The people long for real monarchs. It does not want portraits of princes, but real ones. It desires that the supreme power be strong and active, not weak [...] In this difficult time everyone really longs for a focal point, to which the wavering can cling and the ambitious can adhere.

In acting accordingly strongly and decidedly, yet still on the grounds of constitutionality and the rule of law, the monarchy in Germany was destined to achieve what Republicanism in France had failed to: "to finally secure the lot of the lower classes, to finally realize freedom for all."[10]

The simultaneousness and comparability of Rohmer's considerations and those of French political thinkers at the time, including Louis-Napoléon himself, proves that there might not necessarily have been intellectual dependence of the one on the other, but that in any case similar answers to pressing contemporary challenges were found in different national contexts. In the German context, Rohmer outlined the core structure of what in his eyes might become a "Germanic Caesarism": the replacement of the concept of *Bürgerkönig* ("Citizen King") by *Volkskönig* ("People's King"), the merger of liberal-democratic and conservative-authoritarian elements, and the cult of a leader both charismatic and determined.

While people like Rohmer might advocate a new and powerful regime type, they continued to base their argument on unconditional adherence to a notion of the *Rechtsstaat* ("state of law") that originated in an understanding of politics as essentially based on ethical and moral premises. This made them considerably different from the one "pragmatic" school of thought that gained more and more support in mid-nineteenth century Germany: that of *Realpolitik*. Brought about primarily, though not exclusively, by disappointment regarding the non-achievement of national unity in the previous decades and continuing power-political limitation, *Realpolitik* was a potent reaction to and reflected a considerable break with the image of Germany as the land of the poets and thinkers cultivated since the eighteenth century.

In 1853, August Ludwig von Rochau (1810–1873), commonly accepted as the one having put the term in circulation, explained the principle of *Realpolitik* as follows:

> The discussion of the question: who should rule, whether it be law, wisdom, virtue, whether an individual, a few or many, this question belongs to the realm of philosophical speculation; above all, practical politics has only to do with the simple fact that power alone can rule. To rule is to exercise power, and power can only be exercised by the one who possesses it. This direct correlation of power and domination constitutes the fundamental truth of all politics and the key to history.[11]

In that they declared the exercise of power—no matter in which form—the essence of any form of rule and as such the core around which political debates had to revolve, adherents of *Realpolitik* had an ambivalent attitude towards the Bonapartist regime. While accepting Napoleon III as the greatest obstacle standing in the way of Germany's (re-)invigoration, the "spirit of power" embodied by the French Emperor did attract attention and respect. Rochau himself is a good example of this two-headed attitude of mind. Though a declared enemy of the Second Empire, he extrapolated clear historical lessons from Napoleon's coup of 1852:

> These events contain one of the greatest political lessons that history has ever provided. What follows from this above all, and with a clarity never seen, is the irredeemable emptiness of constitutions, which attempt to decouple public law from public power, which confront unarmed law with armed force. The politics of facts overthrow powers and create powers; constitutional politics [*constituirende Verfassungspolitik*] essentially has to do nothing more than recognize the existing powers, and give them the benediction of the written law.[12]

For Rochau, the Napoleonic coup in France exemplified what was considered a universal key feature of *Realpolitik*, namely that power shapes and enforces (constitutional) law, not *vice versa*.

Immanent in the concept of *Realpolitik*, which became the subject heading for a reorientation of German liberal politics during the second half of the nineteenth century towards a decidedly national form (*Nationalliberalismus*, "National liberalism"), was a palpable peril. From declaring power to be the soul of politics it only took one further step to accept any political force that pushed for a desired outcome, no matter how arbitrary and objectionable the means used to this effect might be. In other words: it was permissible to become a defender of pure Machiavellianism.

In 1858, the Westphalian writer and politician Karl Bollmann (1833–1891) published his *Vertheidigung des Macchiavellismus*, in which he turned against liberal doctrines and analyzed the first and second regimes of *napoleonischen Cäsarismus*,[13] their social foundations and the role of the masses. All of this was from the viewpoint of the lessons which might be learned and the opportunities which might reasonably ensue in any project for a united and strong German nation.

For Bollmann, a characteristic feature of good political leadership was to take the fullest possible advantage of a given situation and to mobilize all available national resources to achieve the political goals. In this regard, he had some admiration for the French Emperor: "Napoleon III understood how to search out the right moment for his plans in the most elegant manner, placing them in direct connection with the entire European political situation [*europäische Weltlage*]. In this, he is considered markedly superior to his model, Napoleon I." He also applauded Napoleon's "remarkable virtuosity [...], in cultivating the most perfect Caesarism in the interior".[14]

According to Bollmann, some of the most effective instruments to win the approval of the masses was to safeguard material prosperity, but also to instrumentalize the press, which had become a "real power". In revealing his contempt for the populace, Bollmann had no doubt that whatever the masses heard over and over again they were ultimately willing to accept, considering their incapability of forming an opinion on their own.[15] However, at the end of the day domestic policies were subject to the success of foreign politics, above all the preservation of independence. A foreign political "awakening" of Germany seemed hence vital in Bollmann's view.

The conditions for such an awakening were actually quite favorable. On the one hand, the Crimean War had changed the geopolitical situation considerably and proved the Congress System was dead. On the other, a new *geistige* ("spiritual") era was about to dawn, moving on from the previous one. This was, Bollmann reasoned, *the* historical moment for a true national leader to seize the mantle. This leader had to abstain from erroneous political modesty, be readily prepared for anything and to make use of all available means in (foreign) politics, including—where necessary—forgery and dishonesty: "Germany needs [...] an armed reformer who, even if he had to march through the red sea of a general war, will lead us to the promised land of national unity and independence."[16] In Bollmann's work, it was not only German unification which assumed a clear *ersatz*-religious dimension, but also the leader he envisaged for the nation, whom he portrayed as some kind of modern, secular Messiah. The last lines of the text in particular bespoke hopes of mundane salvation, covered in metaphoric language:

> When will You appear, King of the future? When will You cut through the thorny hedge of internal patriotic splinter and kiss the sweet mouth and the closed eyes of the sleeping beauty of national happiness to her joyous awakening? [...] O come, come soon! and all the gates will open to You and all the Germans will cheer for You and follow You to battle and victory! Come, King and Master![17]

Yet Bollmann's open canvassing for "pure Machiavellianism" and charging his political ideas with a messianic spirit remained an outsider position even among the staunchest representatives of the national-*realpolitisch* camp. This, however, did not preclude that a considerable number of his German contemporaries of all political backgrounds were open to the idea of some—at least temporary—political dictatorship. Such thoughts had been harbored for a long time by people in opposition or even open enmity to the existing monarchical regime, like Heinrich Heine and other representatives of the Young Germany (*Junges Deutschland*) during the *Vormärz*, or later Gustav Diezel; people who dreamed of a "Germanic hero" or "Caesar" overthrowing the established order that was perceived as hampering both German unity and reform. In the late 1850s and 1860s, especially under the impact of the acute constitutional conflict between crown and parliament (*Preußischer Verfassungskonflikt*), also voices more benevolent of and closer to the government reasoned whether a dictatorial or "extraordinary" style of government might not be a suitable answer to the political needs of the country. Among such voices was the historian Maximilian Duncker (1811–1886), a political advisor of the liberally-minded Prussian Crown Prince and later short-time Emperor Friedrich III (1831–1888), who thus had access to the innermost circle of the monarchy. In a memorandum sent to the Crown Prince in November 1861, he advocated a "liberal dictatorship" as a way both to concentrate national resources and win over the support of German liberals.[18] Later, in a letter to the then Minister of the Interior Graf Maximilian von Schwerin-Putzar (1804–1872) of February 1862, Duncker maintained that "the German question is a question of power, indeed, the question of Germany's power", and that he—for the sake of German national policy—was willing to accept a "military dictatorship" since to merely dissolve the renitent parliament "will only restore democracy to a greater extent".[19]

Even firm defenders of liberal values like the Karlsruhe historian Hermann Baumgarten (1825–1893) suggested that German and particularly Prussian politics needed to strike new paths, oriented more towards action than discussion. "Why is everything here so excessive?", Baumgarten asked in a letter to Heinrich von Sybel (1817–1895), dated March 21, 1861 and written during his time in Berlin, providing the answer in the same breath: "Because countless people are talking and writing about everything, and everyone is tired when it comes to actually doing something. Here, in handling business, nothing is monarchical, everything disintegrates into republicanism. [...] The mass [*Masse*] of equal [*gleichmäßiger*] intelligence makes any rapid, radical action here impossible." He thus yearned for "a great genius or a mighty tyrant" who was capable of quick and decisive action, without actually seeing who this might be.[20] Five years later, he seemed to have a slightly clearer opinion, when he argued against liberal doctrinarism and for ideological "openness" in his essay *Der deutsche Liberalismus. Eine Selbstkritik* (1866), supporting the Prussian government's policies and a stronger governmental orientation of German liberalism.[21] Yet it was not so much Bismarck, whom Baumgarten saw as a potential point of reference, but the Italian statesman and architect of the *Risorgimento*, Camillo Cavour (1810–1861). Spotlighting Cavour rather than Napoleon III or Bismarck was in line with a broader trend in the 1860s to invoke *Cavourismus* as a potential model for Germany:[22] on the one hand, it avoided mentioning the widely disliked "French system" of Bonapartism; on the other, it circumvented any appearance of being a mere footman of Bismarck's regime. At the same time, the parallels between the Italian and German nation building projects were obvious enough to be perceived as such by the public.

With this in mind, Baumgarten wrote that "the only great, brilliant victory of liberalism known to our century was won in Italy". This, however, had only been possible because it had been "the many" who obediently followed and supported "the one". It was a fact that the truly decisive impulses did not emanate from the Italian people, nor from any Italian Party, but from Cavour. Baumgarten reasoned that for nations to accomplish great deeds, great men were indispensable. In modern democratic societies this was particularly the case: "[...] democracy needs a head. Only aristocracies can allow the masses of the chosen to practice a collective activity."[23]

On the whole, it can hence be demonstrated that the readiness in Germany—especially, though not exclusively, in Prussia—to perceive some form of Caesaristic government as "necessary" was considerable in the 1850s and 1860s even among many liberals. More than anything else, this was due to the as yet unresolved "national question" (*nationale Frage*). Yet which concrete approach did the ruling dynasty and leading (Northern) German politicians adopt towards a "Caesaristic" or (semi-) dictatorial form of government?

5.2 Bonapartism and the Ruling Class

Trying to assess the attitude of the Prussian ruling class towards Caesarism and Bonapartism in the mid-nineteenth century essentially means dealing with a distinctively "conservative" group of people in the traditional sense of the word, devoted to monarchical legitimacy.[24] Therefore the answer to how the regimes of the two Napoleons were perceived seems obvious: blunt rejection. And indeed, many examples can be quoted in which the Napoleonic regimes and their leaders were dismissed and openly attacked by high representatives of the Prussian state. The most significant person testifying the repudiation of "Napoleon(ism)" is certainly King Friedrich Wilhelm IV (1795–1861) himself, a key figure of both nineteenth-century German Romanticism and conservatism. His invectives especially against Napoleon I are legion, whom he defamed at many instances in a highly polemical way.

Friedrich Wilhelm IV felt strong personal antipathy towards Napoleon Bonaparte, whom he had met as a boy at Tilsit in 1807 after Prussia's devastating military defeat by the French; this antipathy transformed into hostility against the whole dynasty and everything smacking of "Bonapartism". His aversion, however, was also clearly ideological, reflecting the inviolable principles of that strand of conservative thinking as whose main protagonist Friedrich Wilhelm was considered throughout the *Vormärz* period: the *Altkonservativen* ("Old Conservatives"), or *Hochkonservativen* ("High Conservatives"), respectively.

Strongly influenced by the Swiss jurist Karl Ludwig von Haller's *Restauration der Staats-Wissenschaft* (1816–1825),[25] but also—though to a lesser degree—by Friedrich Karl von Savigny's (1779–1861) "Historical School of Law," the "Old" or "High Conservatives" were fervent defenders of a patrimonial and *ständisch*-corporatist monarchy divinely ordained. They advocated an "organic" and "historically grown", thus effectively decentralized, body politic based on divine kingship and limited political rights of the traditional *Landstände*, while repudiating contract and natural law theories and especially the universalistic principles of the Enlightenment and the Revolution, including rationalism and popular sovereignty. Rather, this kind of "universalism", considered a form of historical relativism, was contrasted with the concept of Christian universalism. The High Conservatives, whose main representatives included the brothers Ludwig Friedrich Leopold (1790–1861) and Ernst Ludwig von Gerlach (1795–1877), Karl Ernst Jarcke (1801–1852), Friedrich Julius Stahl (1802–1861), Marcus von Niebuhr (1817–1860) and Hermann Wagener (1815–1889), passionately pursued what might best be characterized as an ideologically infused *Prinzipienpolitik*. Political and moral "principles" occupied a central role in their thinking, as epitomized in the title of Stahl's famous work *Das Monarchische Princip* (1845),[26] in which he made a plea for monarchical legitimacy and authority, contrasting the ruinous "parliamentarian principle" with the "monarchical principle", which he called "the foundation of German state law and German statecraft".[27] Yet Stahl's theoretically grounded and conclusive work, termed a "quantum leap" in conservative thought,[28] also demonstrates that the High Conservatives were not simply old-fashioned reactionaries or anti-intellectual "deniers of modernity". They clearly had a sound grasp of contemporary developments and made use of modern forms of publicity to argue their agenda, which included founding the (in-)famous *Neue Preußische Zeitung*—known as *Kreuzzeitung* due to its emblem, an Iron Cross—in 1848. These characteristic features set them apart from both the backward-looking, aristocratic "Junker conservatism" (*Junkerkonservatismus*), and the more pragmatically oriented conservatism prevalent in the Prussian bureaucratic apparatus (*Beamtenkonservatismus*).

In the eyes of the High Conservatives, Napoleon(ism) was the incarnations of the damnable principles of the Revolution, "that monster", as the then Crown Prince Friedrich Wilhelm described it in 1832, "which first saw the light of the world forty years ago, and which, were I apocalyptically inclined, I would immediately compare to the Beast *par excellence*".[29] The Revolution was *the* nightmare of the High Conservatives, against which their project of a conservative-legitimist monarchical order was directed. Therefore not surprisingly, the outbreak of the Revolution in 1848 not only in France and neighboring European states, but also Prussia, came as a shock to them. The meteoric rise of yet another Bonaparte from a derided "want-to-be Napoleon", via President to Emperor within a few years seemed to confirm the worst fears and prejudices of the High Conservatives *vis-à-vis* "Bonapartism", against which they polemicized all the more actively. At the forefront of rejection were the two Gerlach brothers, whose *ständisch*-patrimonial and Christian-Germanic background made them view Bonapartism as the synthesis of two equally false principles against which they had been fighting throughout their lives: popular sovereignty and absolutism.

Shortly after Louis-Napoléon's successful coup in Paris 1851, Ludwig Friedrich Leopold von Gerlach—general adjutant to the King and one of his closest political advisors and friends—expressed his concern about the events in France in a letter to Otto von Bismarck, with whom he regularly corresponded: "I do not ignore the good side of the coup d'état, but I am armed with the history of the old Bonaparte so as not to be misled by it." Gerlach was certain that Bonapartism merely replaced the "absurdity of constitutionalism" with a "deceitful and nonsensical sovereignty of the people, an even more nonsensical and impossible division of power and a dreadful centralization (*viribus unitis*), in other words, absolute despotism".[30]

A few days later (December 26, 1851), in a private note, Gerlach remarked about the "resurrected Bonapartism" in a similar fashion:

> People believe that the victory of the President over the Reds and Constitutionalists will liberate them from the fear of 1852, that disastrous, notorious year. One forgets that he, just as his uncle, is himself the concentrated revolution and *heros necessarius* of it, partly because of their relationship, partly because of his revolutionary origins founded upon perjury and breach of faith, but especially because, without any right and without any higher calling, he has the revolutionized and atomized France at his feet.[31]

From late 1851 onwards, Gerlach did not tire of warning about the "despicable figure of Bonapartism", which had recently risen up,[32] the "dangerous and great power of Bonapartism, this child of the vile marriage of absolutism and liberalism",[33] and of Napoleon III, who represented as much the "incarnated Revolution" as his uncle had done before him—regardless of whether they had intended to or not.[34] In equal terms, Leopold's younger brother Ernst Ludwig von Gerlach, co-founder of the *Kreuzzeitung* and whip of the conservative party in the upper house of parliament, wrote in February 1853 that it "is good that we have eluded the Charybdis of revolution [. . .], but now we are falling into the Scylla of Bonapartism".[35]

However, while the developments in the wake of the 1848 Revolution sharpened High Conservatives' awareness of Bonapartism as a problem and fortified their opposition to the phenomenon, the revolutionary trauma in turn increased the preparedness of certain conservative Prussian politicians to rule in a way perceived as "Napoleonic". What may look like a paradox at first sight turns out not to be so on closer examination.

After March 1848, Friedrich Wilhelm IV, who had always cherished the hope of a renewal—or rather "reinvention"—of corporatist-*ständische* institutions, now presided over nothing less than Prussia's transition to modern constitutionalism. Although in December 1848 he and his government managed to seize control of the revolutionary movement and to unilaterally impose their constitutional draft—which followed the model of "constitutional monarchism", preserving the dominant status of the crown, and became even more conservative due to revisions undertaken in 1850—, this was hardly of great comfort: from now on, the King had to live with a Constitution which he could not realistically revoke in its entirety. Whether they wanted it or not, king, government and the conservative party had to find a *modus vivendi* with the Constitution. Forced to adapt to the new constitutional age, however, they in fact soon recognized that the Constitution might be to their advantage and used for counter-revolutionary purposes.

For Friedrich Wilhelm IV, this meant doing everything in his power to relativize the Constitution from within, that is by using the monarchical prerogatives with which he had been entrusted. Even though the King never succeeded in neutralizing the hated Constitution towards which he was unable to develop an impartial relationship, his efforts to strengthen monarchical authority opened the door for "Bonapartist appetites"[36] in the government. This development did not go unnoticed by Leopold von Gerlach, who identified Bonapartism as a problem not only in France, but throughout Europe and even in Prussia. "What I find truly disheartening", Gerlach confessed in a letter to Bismarck in 1855, "is the widespread Bonapartism and the indifference and foolishness, with which one sees this greatest of all dangers approaching".[37] Two years later he expressed his conviction that "most statesmen, not just here, but in other countries as well, are in truth [Bonapartists]", citing the British Prime Minister Lord Palmerston (1784–1865) and the Austrian politicians Alexander von Bach (1813–1893) and Karl Ferdinand von Buol-Schauenstein (1797–1865) as examples.[38] In the Prussian context, Gerlach and his fellow High Conservatives pinpointed Otto Theodor von Manteuffel (1805–1882), minister of the interior from 1848 to 1850 and prime minister from 1850 to 1858, to be a notorious Bonapartist.[39] Manteuffel—nicknamed *Fra Diavolo* ("Brother Devil") by his conservative opponents, bearing the same name as the Neapolitan guerrilla leader Michele Pezza (1771–1806)—appeared as the personification of bumbledom, absolutism and Bonapartism alike:[40] "What are we left with if we get rid of the constitution?", Gerlach asked in November 1852: "the Manteuffels".[41] In view of such a prospect, he was in no doubt that constitutionalism was the lesser of two evils: "[…] I do not want to defend constitutionalism, […] but I prefer it to absolutism."[42]

What made Manteuffel and his political style look so "Bonapartist" to the High Conservatives? He was among those who were impressed by the Napoleonic coup of December 2, 1851: not so much by the "Napoleonic idea", which might be behind the seizure of power, but by the immediate political effects of the coup. The re-establishment of order and the—seeming—unrestricted nature of Napoleonic leadership in France were appealing to a Prussian conservative politician sympathetic to the idea of an authoritarian-bureaucratic system of government. His actual policies in the 1850s could indeed give some cause for concern among High Conservatives, with Manteuffel manipulating public opinion by means of a newly created Central Press Office, and establishing a network of informers and spies to control and monitor real and alleged opposition forces, including the *Kreuzzeitung* party.

Yet taken as a whole, it seems that Manteuffel's style of government, though reflecting certain Bonapartist elements, was not so "Bonapartist" as to place it anywhere near that of the two Napoleons. Differences to the French model are tangible, for example, in Manteuffel's rejection of a "Caesaristic" plebiscitary system and in his lifelong reluctance to make political concessions to the masses and to the working class in particular. Manteuffel was not unaware of the social question in modern-day society, and was most likely influenced in his views by the writer Wilhelm Heinrich Riehl (1823–1897). In his work *Die bürgerliche Gesellschaft* (1851), Riehl asserted that it was no longer three, but four groups that constituted contemporary (German) society: aristocracy and peasantry as the "powers of social persistence", the *Bürgertum* and the proletariat as the "powers of social movement".[43] Manteuffel shared Riehl's conviction that it was time monarchical government acknowledged these divisions and that it was fatal to build its legitimacy and power on solely one group. The government should instead stand above class conflicts and assume the role of a "mediator". These ideas, however, did not translate into any serious attempt to integrate the lower classes into the political process and boost social policies, as Napoleon III was doing. On the contrary: Riehl's and Manteuffel's idea of how a stable monarchy could best be achieved was to isolate the revolutionary underclass by forming a counter-coalition of the other three groups in society.

The fact that notwithstanding such obvious differences to Napoleon III Manteuffel was branded a "Bonapartist" by the Gerlach circle, albeit the Minister-President compared himself rather to a person like Frederick II, shows how varied—even confused—the perception of Bonapartism could actually be at the time. The term could serve as a descriptor of a concrete regime type resembling those of the two Napoleons, but also as a denominator for one specific component of these regimes, e.g. the authoritarian one, or simply as a political combat and defamation term. As the utterances of Leopold von Gerlach prove, one and the same person could use the concept of Bonapartism both selectively and inconsistently: one time with an emphasis on its revolutionary character, another time stressing its autocratic components, but sometimes also underlining that Bonapartism was not the same as absolutism, nor the same as Caesarism. In June 1857, Gerlach declared in this vein that:

> Bonapartism is not absolutism, not even Caesarism [...] Caesarism is the presumption of an *imperium* in a rightful republic and justifies itself by a state of emergency; for a Bonaparte, however, whether he likes it or not, it is the Revolution, which is to say the sovereignty of the people, that is the internal and also, with each conflict or need, the external legal title.[44]

Contrary to the general trend in politico-theoretical discourse, Gerlach was inclined to make a clear distinction between Bonapartism and Caesarism, understanding the latter to be a justified and legitimate form of (crisis) government, in line with the classical Roman understanding of (temporary) dictatorship. Bonapartism, in turn, was characterized by its illegitimacy and viciousness, resulting from its revolutionary origins.[45]

Against these very criteria, the verdict that Manteuffel was a Bonapartist made only limited sense, since it could hardly be claimed that the Prussian Minister-President was a product of the Revolution or pursued a revolutionary agenda. Someone who seemed to represent Bonapartist principles better and whose political initiatives could more easily be compared with those of the two Napoleons was another advisor of Friedrich Wilhelm IV after 1848, namely Karl Ludwig Friedrich von Hinckeldey (1805–1856). A career bureaucrat as Manteuffel, Hinckeldey became police president in Berlin in 1848, and the King's principal confidant in security matters. In his position, he not only created a modern police force and perfected surveillance of political opponents as well as censorship of the media, but also pushed for a modernization of Berlin, including ambitious construction projects and administrative as well as social service reforms. Hinckeldey envisaged "positive state action" becoming a key instrument in mobilizing popular support for the monarchical cause. David E. Barclay goes as far as to claim that "with his mixture of rough authoritarianism, populism, and welfare paternalism, with his emphasis on the extension of state power and his simultaneous support for modern forms of economic activity", Hinckeldey represented "an early form of Prussian crypto-Bonapartism".[46] Yet Hinckeldey's scope of action and influence remained limited both in spatial and temporal respect, given that his main field of activity continued to be Berlin, where he died in 1856. Always in the shadow of his King and of other politicians, he never managed to unfold his political ideas at a supra-regional level and did not even come close to gaining the status of a "national leader".

Even though High Conservatives spared no effort in stigmatizing their political adversaries in the ruling class as Bonapartists, this was for the most part a concern within the segmented conservative party: Hinckeldey was—and indeed could—not be seen and remembered in such terms by a broader public for his inferior political position alone; Manteuffel for his actual style of government, which resembled neo-absolutism rather than Bonapartism. Yet the situation looks different regarding that man who—endowed with a clear sense of power—became Prussia's Minister-President in 1862; a statesman who more than any other has monopolized the role of key figure of German nineteenth-century history and defied any clear categorizations of being reactionary or revolutionary, authoritarian or democratic: Otto von Bismarck.

5.3 Otto von Bismarck: a German Bonaparte?

The life and political achievements of Bismarck, who has entered history books as the architect of German unification as much as one of the most skilled (or at least most vulpine) diplomats in world history and an ambitious political reformer at home, have been retold so often that there is no need to go into details here. We can confine ourselves to the one question which is central in the context of this inquiry and which in itself is complex enough: in how far was Bismarck seen as a "German Bonaparte" and "German Caesar" by contemporaries, or considered himself as such, and in how far can Bismarck's leadership style and policies be legitimately described as "Bonapartist" or "Caesaristic"? The most obvious way to address this issue is by investigating the extent to which Bismarck can be compared to the two Napoleons, and to Napoleon III in particular.[47]

One can justifiably object that a search for parallels or differences between these statesmen and their regimes can only be a superficial endeavor, simply because they are hardly comparable characters and found themselves in fundamentally different social and political roles: unlike either Bonaparte, Bismarck was a member of the traditional aristocratic elite; and unlike them, Bismarck never acquired or even aspired to the position of formal head of state or monarch, but ultimately remained dependent on his sovereign, which was not the people, but the Prussian King.[48] Still, the fact that Bismarck could never assume the role of a "leader" or "ruler" in the same way as Napoleon I or Napoleon III should not be overemphasized. Collating Bismarck with the French Emperor(s) can be justified for two reasons: firstly, it can be argued pragmatically that despite his formal constitutional subordination to the King, Bismarck actually occupied a pseudo-monarchical and quasi-independent role that provided him with substantial room for maneuver, at least under the rule of Wilhelm I (1861–1888); secondly, comparing Bismarck Germany and Napoleonic France in terms of Bonapartism and

Caesarism is not the contradiction it might first seem to be if these concepts are considered first and foremost as a style of government and technique of rule, potentially functional in varying systemic contexts, rather than a clearly defined "ideal type". While a case can thus be made for the comparability of Bismarck Germany and Napoleonic France *per se*, this does not, however, establish whether they were indeed comparable. In order to come closer to an answer, getting a better grasp of Bismarck's (early) political concepts in general and his attitude towards French Bonapartism in particular might be useful.

5.3.1 Conservative Dissonances: *Recht* vs. *Macht*

In his early political life, Bismarck gained the reputation of a politician with a gift for stinging rhetoric, defending the interests of the landed nobility within the conservative camp and standing loyal to the Gerlach circle and its political beliefs. But while Leopold von Gerlach and his brother Ludwig helped to launch Bismarck's political career in 1847, when he became a representative to the newly created Prussian legislature (*Vereinigter Landtag*), existing differences to the *Kreuzzeitung* party and the political theory of a Friedrich Julius Stahl were discernible even at this early stage. These differences were manifest in Bismarck giving priority to considerations of power and interest over principle, which ultimately also included the position of his political friends and his own.[49] The pragmatism and opportunism with which Bismarck approached and practised politics became even more pronounced after he was appointed Prussia's envoy to the Diet of the German Confederation in Frankfurt in 1851, a post he held for the next eight years until January 1859.

These attitudes became especially apparent in Bismarck's unbiased, not to say friendly, stance towards France under the rule of Napoleon III; a stance, which put him in opposition not only to general public opinion in Germany, but also—and more importantly—to the High Conservatives in the government. Bismarck's openness towards a Franco-Prussian rapprochement was dictated by power-political reasoning: he was convinced that in order to counteract Austria's influence in Germany, it was necessary for Prussia not only to gain the support of other German states, but also to keep the possibilities for alternative alliances alive, including those with Russia and France. Friendship—or at least a working relationship—with both Russia and France seemed necessary for Bismarck to threaten Austria, but also to prevent France and its Emperor from allying themselves with Russia. Even though the Crimean War saw Russia and France as opponents, this was of no relief for Bismarck. The fact that Prussia remained isolated throughout the Crimean War and was almost not invited to the peace talks in Paris further increased Bismarck's fear of Prussia losing her role as a European power, and confirmed his opinion that an undogmatic and flexible foreign policy was essential to counteract this development. He outlined his foreign political concept in the so-called *Prachtschrift* (or *Prachtbericht*) of April 26, 1856, addressed to Manteuffel, in which improving relations with Napoleonic France was of crucial importance.[50] This, together with the two journeys Bismarck made to Paris in 1855 and 1857 respectively, put him in open conflict with the High Conservatives, for whom France and Napoleon III had always been and remained the natural enemies of Prussia and Germany as a whole. What displeased the High Conservatives in particular was the fact that Bismarck did not seem to find any real fault with the Napoleonic political system, which posed the danger of his being discredited not only as a mere (foreign-political) opportunist, but also (ideological) Bonapartist.

As their correspondence demonstrates, Leopold von Gerlach felt more and more compelled to make his former protégé aware of the dangers of Bonapartism, the harmfulness of which Bismarck did not seem to be able to clearly recognize. In 1857, when the exchange of letters on the issue reached a peak, Gerlach failed to understand how "a man with your mind can sacrifice the principle to a single man, such as this L [ouis] N [apoleon]".[51] Bismarck's reply a couple of days later denied any particular personal sympathy for the French Emperor, but also made a strong case against legitimism playing a central role in foreign policy and for his argument that Prussia would have to deal with France, no matter under which government it might currently be.[52]

In response, Gerlach felt obliged to remind Bismarck that the "revolutionary spirit", the fight against which he considered to be both his own and still also Bismarck's life task, should not and could not be decoupled from the present regime in France under Napoleon III: "My political principle is and remains the fight against the Revolution. You will not be able to convince Bonaparte that he is not on the side of the Revolution. He does not want to be anywhere else, since this side has its clear advantages for him."[53] Two weeks later, Gerlach assured Bismarck that—knowing his views in domestic policy—he did not consider him a Bonapartist, an allegation against which Bismarck had felt compelled to defend himself.[54] However, Gerlach considered it all the more inexplicable "how you look at our foreign politics", Bismarck's concept of which lacked "head and tail, principle and goal of politics". He also found it strange that Bismarck could overlook the fact that Napoleon III "was subject to the consequences of his position of absolutism founded on popular sovereignty (l'élu de 7 millions), which he feels as much as the old [Napoleon I; MJP]". Making overtures to France and cooperating with Napoleon would ultimately mean strengthening the revolutionary spirit in Europe with Prussian support.[55]

In reaction to this, Bismarck not only re-emphasized his position that modern foreign policy had to be guided by need rather than principle, but also pointed out that he was unable to share Gerlach's and the High Conservatives' assessment of Napoleon III and their unfettered appraisal of the anti-revolutionary axiom. Pre-empting—in part verbatim—what he was to outline only three days later in the aforementioned memorandum to Manteuffel regarding the suggested "normalization" of Franco-Prussian foreign relations,[56] Bismarck posed the provocative question: "How many existences are there in today's political world that are not rooted in revolutionary soil?" One did not even have to cite Spain, Portugal, Brazil, the various republics in the Americas, Belgium, Holland, Switzerland, Greece, Sweden or England as examples. Even the German princes would not be able to claim any fully legitimate title to rule in their respective territories in a traditional sense of the word. Since the omnipresence of the revolutionary legacy in the modern world was a fact, the present Napoleon-phobia appeared unreasonable to Bismarck.[57] What was crucial was not whether a regime might be of revolutionary origin, but in how far a regime attempted to leave the

Revolution and its missionary zeal behind. And in this respect, the Bonapartes appeared in a much better light than the three last Bourbon kings in the eighteenth century: "The House of Bourbon has done more for the Revolution than any Bonaparte [...] Bonapartism is not the father of the Revolution; just like every absolutism, it is a fertile field for sowing it." Both Napoleons had been heirs of the Revolution, not their propagators, and both had been inclined "to gain for themselves firmer foundations than those of the Revolution". This was particularly true of Napoleon III, who was more than aware of the flaws of the Bonapartist system of government, which he realized and complained about. However, Bismarck reasoned that "for France, the present form of government is nothing arbitrary, something that L. Napoleon could establish or change", and most likely "the only method by which France can be ruled for a long time to come". He thus insinuated that neither Napoleon III nor Bonapartism *per se* were a hazard; on the contrary, they were the best available guarantee for the containment of revolutionary energies.[58]

Which conclusions can be drawn from the correspondence between Gerlach and Bismarck with regard to the latter's political mindscape? On the one hand, the differences between the two are symptomatic of a growing gap within the ranks of Prussian conservatives, with the older generation of High Conservatives becoming increasingly isolated both intellectually and politically. Bismarck in particular embodied a shift from High Conservative *Prinzipienpolitik* to a *Realpolitik* based on pragmatic—*Altkonservative* might call it "amoral"—calculations of state interest on the governmental level, which reflected a more general trend in German political debates. The legitimist camp with a romanticized idea of *Rechtsautoritarismus* ("legal authoritarianism") as its guiding principle was more and more on the defensive against those making a case for an interest-guided *Machtautoritarismus* ("power authoritarianism"), like Bismarck, who with growing self-confidence criticized the Gerlach circle for ignoring existing realities and for being anachronistic. Bismarck's key message was that it would be not only unwise, but actually irresponsible to bind one's own policies to one single "subjective" principle and thus limit the available options right from the beginning; or, as Bismarck famously put it in his last known letter to Gerlach of May 2, 1860: "You cannot play chess if you are prohibited from using 16 out of 64 squares from the outset."[59] Against an argument as simple and convincing as this, the High Conservatives could only fight rearguard battles. This was particularly true after 1861, when King Friedrich Wilhelm IV as their political and Leopold von Gerlach as their intellectual figurehead died.

In the first instance, Bismarck's *Realpolitik* emerged from geopolitical reasoning and was seen as an instrument applicable in foreign relations. However, the foreign political pragmatism shown towards France and her ruler was also to be extended to other areas, such as ideology and domestic politics. With the same "openness", with which France was seen as a political state actor, one could actually perceive French Bonapartism: it might be a regime of revolutionary origin and far from perfect, but why should that matter if it was the best available alternative for the moment? Tentative steps in the direction of an "ideological relativism" were even discernible in May 1860, when Bismarck openly declared—certainly not raising his aging mentor's spirits—that the differences between "right [*Recht*] and Revolution, Christianity and unbelief, God and Devil" were not quite obvious to him. By then, at the latest, there could be no further doubt that Bismarck was right in claiming that "I am a child of other times than you are, [...] one just as truthful to his as you are to yours".[60]

Throughout his first fifteen years as an active politician, Bismarck repeatedly stressed that he deemed not only the former Bourbon kings, but also the constitutional monarchy of Louis-Philippe far more abhorrent than the Napoleonic regimes. From this one could infer some sympathy at least within the French context, but one would search in vain for any clear personal positioning towards Bonapartism as a potential (domestic) form of rule, or even an open appreciation of the same. If there had been any sympathies, it was not to be expected that Bismarck would have made them public and risked widening the gulf between him and his conservative fellow party members and the King, on whom his career ultimately depended. But there was actually also no immediate need to declare himself on this issue as long as he acted as a foreign politician with limited, albeit considerable, power of decision, and not a national political leader; a position, into which he grew after his appointment to Minister-President in September 1862. From that moment on, Bismarck's policies and actions became the best indicator of the degree to which his style of government is comparable to that of the two Bonapartes in France, and whether it can justifiably be called "Bonapartist".

5.3.2 Bismarck and Napoleon III: Their Two Regimes Compared

In trying to get a better understanding of Otto von Bismarck's leadership techniques after 1862—first as Prussian Minister-President (1862–1890, with a short interruption in 1873), later as Federal Chancellor of the North German Confederation (1867–1871) and then Chancellor of the German Empire (1871–1890)—several explanatory approaches have been taken. Among those most frequently used are "negative integration", "amalgamation policy" and "social imperialism", each with their own distinct strengths and weaknesses.[61]

The idea of "negative integration" essentially implies that Bismarck Prussia and Germany shared a uniting fear of a minority within their own body politic (most notably socialists and Catholics) and a foreign enemy (Austria and even more so France), artificially created and skillfully exploited by the government. "Amalgamation policy" (often referred to as *Sammlungspolitik*), in turn, suggests that Bismarck's power basis was the coalition he had managed to form between the two most powerful interest groups in German society, namely the traditional elite of the land-owning nobility and the upcoming industrial and financial (bourgeois) elite, against other social classes and the proletariat in particular. Both approaches thus share the similarity of essentially being conflict-oriented, establishing an "in group" on the one hand, an "out group" on the other, with the differences mainly to be found in the driving motivations of the "in group": fear in the case of negative integration, the preservation of the socio-economic *status quo* in the case of amalgamation policy. Unlike these two explanatory approaches, "social imperialism"—intrinsically linked with the German social historian Hans-Ulrich Wehler—suggests itself as a more generally applicable one. It makes the claim that in order to stabilize an existing political and social order, domestic tensions are diverted outwards to the "imperial space", thus offering a potential explanation and basis of comparison for different forms of nineteenth-century European imperialisms.[62] However, the one approach that has been consistently applied over time more than any other to characterize Bismarck's policies is that of Bonapartism and—slightly less frequently—Caesarism.

Unlike the above-named characterizations of Bismarckian politics, which gained importance only after the Second World War, Bonapartism and Caesarism had even been used by many of Bismarck's contemporaries, be it politicians or political thinkers. In one way or another, they saw—or at least sensed—an intrinsic affinity in style between the policies and political principles of Napoleon (I and III) and Bismarck, like Friedrich Engels, who in a letter to Karl Marx portrayed the Bismarck regime as a "Bonapartist semi-dictatorship" in 1866.[63] Four years earlier—when Bismarck had just been appointed Minister-President of Prussia—the Italian member of parliament Giuseppe Lazzaro (1825–1910) had denounced Bismarck as a Bonapartist in a pamphlet that was also to become the first explicit politico-theoretical encounter with Caesarism (*Cesarismo*) in Italy: Lazzaro contended that like Napoleon III, Bismarck, too, was an autocrat masquerading as the people's benefactor and paying sham homage to "progressive ideas" (*idee progressiste*).[64]

Analogies between the Bonapartes and Bismarck have been emphasized ever since. Yet quantity does not say anything about the qualitative value of the Bonaparte analogy. And indeed, while Bonapartism and Caesarism is employed as one of the most common "systemic descriptions" of Bismarck, it is perhaps also the most vague and tentative explanatory approach to characterize his leadership style from the 1860s to 1890. It has been argued that "Bonapartism" and "Caesarism" lack any precision and are used rather abstractly,[65] and some scholars have placed doubt whether these concepts can be used to describe Bismarckian politics in any useful way at all,[66] the latter view having become predominant in contemporary research.[67] These scholarly assessments correspond with the view of those nineteenth-century observers denouncing the idea of Bismarck being a "second Napoleon", among them the German liberal Ludwig Bamberger (1823–1899).[68]

While there has been some fierce arguing for and against "Bismarckianism" being "Bonapartism" or "Caesarism", it is astonishing that the one thing which would seem quite natural to start with plays a relatively limited role: a critical-analytical comparison of Bismarck and Napoleon III and their respective regimes; that is, a comparison which would go beyond formal (dis-)similarities and help to produce more sophisticated answers that are neither stuck in *a priori* efforts to making abstract generalizations, nor emphasizing (national and biographical) idiosyncrasies. To do this in any exhaustive manner would certainly require a monograph of its own. Still, this does not preclude making an effort to highlight at least some of the (structural) differences and parallels between the two regimes.

A systematic comparison of different regimes has to take into account at least three levels, which are unquestionably interconnected with each other, but not to be confused: 1) the "structural" level, describing the socio-economic, broader political and cultural framework within which regimes come into being and function; 2) the level of the "formal constitution", prescribing the institutional roles and rules of the regimes; finally 3) the level of the "real" or "material constitution", which—broadly understood—

reflects the practical functioning of regimes as well as the strategies and policies applied for their legitimization. Let us first turn to the "structural embeddedness" of Bismarck's regime and that of Napoleon III, respectively.

In this regard, obvious similarities can be discerned. Napoleon III and Bismarck alike faced the task of exercising political power in a rapidly industrializing state, characterized by an ever-decreasing share of the population working in the primary sector of the economy and in agriculture in particular. In the long-run, this was to become a considerable challenge for two regimes receiving much of their support from the rural population. Moreover, both France under Napoleon III and Prussia under Bismarck can be characterized as post-revolutionary societies: not only in the sense that they necessarily had to deal with the underlying political and intellectual legacy of the eighteenth century's "Great Revolutions", but also in that the Revolution of 1848 had been a formative element of immediate relevance for the genesis and, indeed, legitimacy of both regimes. The success of the 1848 Revolution in France certainly set a somewhat dissimilar stage for Napoleon III than the failure—to a large part—of the 1848/1849 Revolutions in Germany for Bismarck, but the policies of both men essentially represented a continuation of the Revolution by other means, intrinsically mingling revolutionary with anti-revolutionary and modern with conservative elements. Characteristically, both in France and Germany the experience of Revolution together with the tangible impact of industrialization brought about a latent "red scare" and fear of a democratic-Jacobin republic. This gave rise, among other things, to the middle classes and traditional elites (at least in part) closing ranks, and eventually favoring reform over radical change.

Yet despite such parallels, a number of contentions have been voiced against the structural comparability of the (Second) French Empire and the *Bismarckreich*. These include, for example, the fact that while nineteenth-century France had been a nation state for many centuries, the nation-building process in Germany came to a conclusion only after the War of 1870/1871. In addition, substantial dissimilarities can be discerned between French and German society in the second half of the nineteenth century, and an accordingly different "social basis" of the Prussian-German monarchy compared to the French. It can indeed be maintained that post-1848 Prussian-German society was different from the French, which had undergone no less than three revolutionary *caesura* (1789, 1830 and 1848) that had tapered social differences and strengthened the role of the bourgeoisie and the "fourth estate" alike. Unlike France, the industrialization process in Prussia took off within a still largely feudal-conservative *Obrigkeitsstaat* ("state of authority"), in which the agrarian aristocracy had managed to preserve much—though not all—of its former political power. Bismarck's social challenge was thus not so much the "domestication" of the "revolutionary masses", as it was for Napoleon III in France, but harmonizing the conflicting political, social and economic interests of the *Bürgertum* with the existing *Junker* system. Bismarck's solution to this challenge was eventually to foster the re-feudalization of politics and society, especially after 1878/1879; something which was in distinct contrast to Napoleon's program of establishing a post-revolutionary order inclining towards egalitarianism. The clash of bourgeois-liberal and conservative interests became obvious even during the first "practical test" of Bismarck's leadership, the Prussian

Verfassungskonflikt ("constitutional conflict") between 1859 and 1866, which will be looked at more closely in the later comparison of French and German constitutional practices. Initially, however, the "formal constitution" of Napoleonic France and Bismarckian Germany is to be examined.

One obvious difference between the constitutional frameworks within which Napoleon III and Bismarck operated was the absence of a formal "constitutional breach" in the case of the latter. While Napoleon tailored the legal-institutional order to suit his needs in the wake of the *coup d'état* of December 2, 1851, Bismarck continued to rule within a given constitutional system after becoming Minister-President of Prussia in 1862. Yet this difference is qualified in view of the year 1871, which provided Bismarck with a unique opportunity to put his personal mark on the constitution of the newly-created German Empire. Moreover, one could assume that even the Prussian constitution guaranteed Bismarck a powerful-enough position and sufficient room to maneuver politically for whatever Caesaristic ambitions he might have had. With the "revolutionary" character of the legal-institutional order *per se* hence being of only limited analytical value, let us focus on the positions occupied by Bismarck and Napoleon III in their respective constitutional systems and their role in the law-making process in particular.

Essentially, the constitutional orders of the French Second Empire as well as that of the Kingdom of Prussia and later the German Empire can be categorized as "monarchical-constitutional": a monarchy (understood in its Greek original meaning as "rule of the one", without necessarily implying any hereditary character) with a ruler disposing of encompassing powers, which at the same time are limited—at least formally—by a written constitution and a parliamentary body. Yet this common typology is not particularly helpful, considering that "monarchical constitutionalism" thus broadly interpreted was the almost universal model of nineteenth-century constitutionalism in Europe.

If a slightly more specific definition of "monarchical constitutionalism" is applied, however, which assigns this classification only to regimes with monarchical legitimacy being the primary source of legitimacy and monarchical sovereignty the underlying concept of sovereignty, an obvious difference is discernible. Such characteristics of what might be called more accurately "constitutional monarchism"[69] apply to both the Kingdom of Prussia and also—through to a lesser degree—the later German Empire: revolutionary constitutionalism with its language of popular sovereignty was repudiated, as was the idea of a separation of powers *sensu stricto*, in which each of the constitutional actors dispose of a legitimacy of their own. Rather, the monarch was claimed to be the bearer of all sovereignty and state authority (*plenitudo potestatis*), and only the execution of the same was left in part to certain constitutional institutions.[70] In other words, while the only holder of *ius* is the monarch, the other powers in the political system are subordinate and only have delegated power (*exercitium*), making such a system appear as a "constitutionalized" form of enlightened absolutism. This concept, which found its politico-theoretical expression in the later formula of the "monarchical principle", had made it into the *Wiener Schlussakte* of 1820 as the basic political norm of the German Confederation,[71] and was to become the core of German constitutional law and practice until the First World War.

In France, the situation was quite different: the *Charte constitutionnelle* of 1814 had provided Europe with the most influential model of constitutional monarchism, but in France itself the restored Bourbon monarchy's anti-revolutionary experiment of a constitutional order based on monarchical legitimacy and sovereignty failed even with the July Revolution of 1830, and definitively with the February Revolution of 1848. The Constitution of 1852—as the earlier constitutions of 1799, 1802 and 1804—was solidly grounded in revolutionary rhetoric and acknowledged the principle of popular sovereignty (cf. Art. 1). Following this logic, Napoleon III, like his uncle before him, was the product of and thus dependent on the will of the people. In constitutional terms, he was merely a *pouvoir constitué*, not the *pouvoir constituant*.

Irrespective of whether one characterizes the constitutional systems within which Napoleon III and Bismarck operated in equal measure as "monarchical-constitutional" or not, it can be stated that at least in legal terms neither system was a dictatorship or autocracy—attributes that have been used for Napoleonic France in particular.[72] Both in France and Germany, the executive body was restrained by constitutional provisions, and legislative power to be exercised only in collaboration with parliament. Thus, a dualistic element was apparent, although monarchical power was undoubtedly the predominant factor in law-making. In the French Imperial Constitution of 1852,[73] only the Emperor—supported by the State Council (*Conseil d'Etat*)—had the right of initiative (cf. Art. 8 and 50); he was endowed with an absolute veto (cf. Art. 10). Moreover, foreign and military policy was effectively his exclusive competence, and he had the authority to issue regulations and decrees in his own right (cf. Art. 6). Ministers were dependent on and answerable to the Emperor alone (cf. Art. 13). Similar prerogatives of the crown can be found in the Prussian Constitution of 1850[74] absolute veto (cf. Art. 62), discretionary power to issue decrees and determining the members of government (cf. Art. 45), the absence of ministerial responsibility towards parliament (cf. Art. 44 and 45), as well as almost full control of foreign policy (cf. Art. 48). Despite these similarities, however, the competences of the Prussian bicameral parliament were all in all more encompassing than that of its counterpart in France. This was particularly due to its disposing of a full right of legislative initiative (cf. Art. 64), which was also perpetuated in the Imperial Constitution of 1871[75] (cf. Art. 23 of the *Verfassung-Urkunde für das Deutsche Reich*)—a privilege granted to the French chambers only at the very end of Napoleon III's turn to the *empire libéral* (cf. Art. 12 of the French Constitution of 1870).[76]

Yet more importantly for the overall weaker systemic position of Bismarck *vis-à-vis* Napoleon III than the more comprehensive rights of the Prussian-German parliament was another, more obvious factor mentioned in the introduction to this chapter: their respective constitutional status. While in France Napoleon III assumed the undisputed role of monarchical head of state, Bismarck's rule in Prussia and later the German Empire continued to be dependent on king and emperor, respectively. It is true that the Imperial Constitution of 1871 in particular, bearing his personal hallmarks, put Bismarck as *Reichskanzler* ("Chancellor of the Empire") in a predominant position. Parliament had no means to legally force his abdication at any moment, he was at the same time chancellor and foreign minister with essentially free rein in foreign and military policy, and he did not have to worry about the federal element of the constitution either, given that he was Minister-President of Prussia—the most powerful of the federal states—in personal union. Nevertheless, the structural constellation of Napoleon's and Bismarck's rule was fundamentally different. Bismarck was not a self-made ruler, he had been appointed by the King of Prussia—and was eventually to be dismissed by the German Emperor. Despite his impressive plenitude of power, "disposability" was a characteristic feature of Bismarck's position throughout his career.

These observations lead to the question of how the legal-normative restrictions of Napoleon III and Bismarck respectively played out in constitutional practice of the regimes, and whether Bismarck was perhaps able to compensate for his inferior systemic role in everyday politics. This refers to the third and last element of our comparison. For a more focused comparative assessment of constitutional practices and the way power was exercised by Napoleon III and Bismarck, respectively, let us focus on four particular features of their regimes: I. anti-parliamentarism and authoritarianism; II. democratic-plebiscitary legitimacy; III. imperialism; and IV. social policies.

The rule of both Napoleon III and Bismarck was characterized by their anti-parliamentary impetus already immanent in the respective constitutional systems outlined above. The dominance of the executive was to be guaranteed by a far-reaching marginalization of and control over representative bodies in everyday politics, yet without going so far as to eliminate these bodies altogether and thus moving towards a dictatorship proper. Overall, it seems that Napoleon III was more successful in containing parliament than Bismarck, at least until 1869. Not only did the French Constitution of 1852 provide Napoleon with more legal instruments—especially the exclusive right of initiative—to steer parliament than the Prussian and later German Imperial Constitution did for Bismarck; also the system of "influencing", not to say rigging, elections in order to resolve any potential conflict with parliament *a priori* was more perfected in France, manifest in a system of "official candidates" that guaranteed stable majorities in the chambers. Accordingly, Bismarck had to face the political realities of an unruly parliament opposing (parts of) government policies for much of his time in political leadership. Unlike Napoleon III in France, Bismarck remained in "indirect dependency"[77] from parliament throughout his career, characterizing the inner dualism between *Reichstag* and government in the German Empire, and he had the difficult task of creating and managing changing parliamentary majorities. Relying on a system of dependencies and complaisances, Napoleon III maneuvered between the political fractions and aimed at positioning himself above them. In contrast, Bismarck's striving for parliamentary support continued to be dependent on tactical and temporary alliances with one political party or another. Against this background, the executive branch never managed to gain as much autonomy as in Napoleonic France, which has also to do with the latter's form of a unitary state: while the rule of Napoleon III largely relied on a centralized and hierarchically organized state administration, Bismarck's power mainly depended on his skillful yet at the same time restless playing off various parties and institutions against each other, and holding the balance between different federalist and unitary tendencies especially after the foundation of the German Empire.[78]

Bearing these challenges in mind, Bismarck's successful thwarting—essentially until 1890—of parliamentary aspirations to have an effective say in shaping policies is all the more remarkable and underlines his reputation as a virtuoso, or rather technician, of power. The Prussian *Verfassungskonflikt* ("constitutional conflict"), which was also the first political litmus test after his appointment as Prussian Minister-President, is symptomatic in this regard. At the center of the conflict between King Wilhelm I (1797–1888) on the one hand and the Prussian *Abgeordnetenhaus* ("House of Representatives") dominated by liberals on the other was the fight over the reform and reorganization of the Prussian armed forces; particularly the financial means required for the envisaged extension of the standing regular army, which the chamber was reluctant to approve. At the peak of the conflict in March 1862, Wilhelm I appointed a new conservative government and dissolved the *Abgeordnetenhaus* that had only been elected in January, but saw himself confronted with yet a new liberal majority after the elections in May. With further attempts to end the deadlock between crown and parliament failing in September, the King—already considering abdication in favor of Crown Prince Friedrich Wilhelm (1831–1888), the later short-term Emperor Friedrich III—finally appointed Bismarck, at that time ambassador in Paris, as Prussian Minister-President (September 22) and shortly thereafter also foreign minister. Even at the first audience with Wilhelm I, the new Minister-President left no doubt about his stance in the constitutional conflict, which to him put the idea of monarchical government fundamentally at stake and hence required resolute action:

> I succeeded in convincing him [the King; MJP] that it was not about conservative or liberal in this or that hue, but about royal government [*Regiment*] or parliamentary rule, and that the latter was necessarily, and also by means of a period of dictatorship, to be averted.[79]

Bismarck made it known in no uncertain terms that in order to frustrate abhorrent parliamentarism, all necessary action was justified, including a *coup d'état* and temporary dictatorship. Even though he abstained from the *ultima ratio* of unilaterally overthrowing the existing constitutional order in 1862, as Louis-Napoléon had done in December 1851, Bismarckian politics never excluded the option of a "Brumaire". From the beginning, threatening to commit a coup was effectively used as a means of crisis management and tool of power politics on the home front,[80] and in more than one respect Bismarck's methods of government were unconstitutional in strictly legal terms, and close to an undeclared state of exception. In the context of the Prussian constitutional conflict, Bismarck's *Machtautoritarismus* ("power authoritarianism") was played out in the form of his four-years (1862–1866) of governing against the will and intentions of the majority in parliament, without a lawfully adopted budget and under restriction of civil liberties and freedom of the press in particular, yet backed by the Prussian bureaucracy and with the army as a subtle "last resort". Bismarck's "solution" to the constitutional conflict was the so-called *Lückentheorie* ("Gap Theory"), which essentially claimed that the crown in its role as sovereign power had the legal authority to take decisions whenever the constitution did not provide any explicit provision. Its intellectual originator was Friedrich Julius Stahl, whose works made him one of the most influential legal and constitutional scholars of the nineteenth century. In *Das Monarchische Princip* (1845) and later *Die Revolution und die constitutionelle Monarchie* (1848), he had developed a coherent theory of what both Stahl and later observers[81] considered the distinguishing feature of German constitutional law: the "monarchical principle". Above all, the principle claimed "the prince has the right and power to reign by himself".[82] In the event of diverging interpretations of the constitution or a constitutional conflict, "preserving the prestige of the monarch must, according to the monarchical principle, be the overriding principle".[83] For Stahl, the monarch had the ultimate say in interpreting the law, as he was the father of the constitution both in the figurative and literal sense. Consequently, a legitimate right of initiative could be derived for the monarchical power in all politically contentious issues, which Bismarck applied to the concrete case of the state budget: given that the (Prussian) Constitution did not stipulate explicitly how to proceed in the event of king and both chambers failing to agree on a budget (cf. Art. 62 of the 1850 Constitution), Bismarck as representative of the crown saw himself entitled—if not obliged—to take unilateral action in order to guarantee the proper functioning of the state.

Eventually, the constitutional conflict was formally settled after the Second Schleswig War of 1864 and Prussia's victory in the German War of 1866—foreign-political successes securing Prussian hegemony in Germany and boosting Bismarck's public repute at the same time. "Corrupted" by these successes,[84] which opened up the prospect of a German nation state, the Prussian *Abgeordnetenhaus* approved Bismarck's *Indemnitätsvorlage* ("Indemnity Bill") on September 3, 1866 with a large majority of 230 to 75 votes: the *Indemnitätsvorlage* retroactively confirmed the constitutionality of all budgets between 1862 and 1865 and hence also legalized the government's actions in the previous years.[85] To a certain degree—even though differences are clearly evident—, this was the Prussian version of the Napoleonic plebiscite, in that accomplished political facts were legitimized *a posteriori*. Parliament yielded to the policies and authoritarian style of Bismarck, who was granted an additional triumph insofar as the decision on the Indemnity Bill led to a durable split within the liberal camp, with the new National Liberal Party (*Nationalliberale Partei*) breaking away from the German Progress Party (*Deutsche Fortschrittspartei*) and henceforth largely supporting Bismarck's political program. As during the Prussian constitutional conflict, Bismarck also managed later in the German Empire to effectively thwart parliamentary control of the army as a central power factor, to which a large part of the government budget was devoted. In the continuing struggle about military expenses, Bismarck prevailed over parliamentary claims for annual budgetary procedures and got a multiannual financial framework (*Septennat*) approved in 1874, which was successfully renewed in 1880 and 1887, in the latter case after the dissolution of the intractable *Reichstag* and new elections bringing about the desired parliamentary majority for the government. Accepting the *Septennat*—as previously the *Indemnitätsvorlage*—did not formally infringe on the budgetary rights of the *Reichstag*, yet symbolized its self-disempowerment and reinforced the *de facto* primacy of the executive over the legislative. Any genuine parliamentarization of the political system was and continued to be a chimera in Bismarckian Germany.

It can thus be stated that like in Napoleonic France, anti-parliamentarism and authoritarianism—though certainly different in their concrete expression—were idiosyncratic for Bismarck's system of government, too. Under Napoleon III, anti-parliamentarism was complemented by a distinctive democratic and populist element, the most important component of which was universal suffrage. This raises the question of the significance of this element in Bismarck's policies.

Even during the *Verfassungskonflikt*, Bismarck—in clear contradiction to traditional conservative positions—was playing with the idea of universal (male) suffrage, and had entered into talks about this issue with Ferdinand Lasalle (1825–1864), president of the General German Workers' Association (*Allgemeiner Deutscher Arbeiter-Verein*), the first mass party of the organized labor movement in Germany.[86] Considering this option was certainly not due to any ideological proximity Bismarck had to the principle of equality or to altruistic motivations, but sprang from well-reasoned *Realpolitik*: Bismarck calculated that given its still limited size and importance at the time, it would not be so much the working class that would benefit most from opening up the existing franchise system, but rather the rural population in its structural-conservative and pro-monarchical stance. Thus, a powerful counterweight to the politically aspiring (liberal) bourgeoisie was potentially at hand.

The same reasoning with regard to universal suffrage prevailed in the French Second Empire. In 1863 it was Napoleon III himself who communicated to Bismarck his personal experiences with the expansion of suffrage, outlining that it was considerably easier to steer the masses through *suffrage universel* than controlling the bourgeoisie who were profiting greatly from census suffrage. Napoleon III thus considered it a great mistake of the Prussian Government to have called new elections for the *Abgeordnetenhaus* in 1862 without revising the electoral law.[87] Despite his pursuing a different agenda essentially aimed at stabilizing the Prussian state with its pre-industrial oligarchy, Bismarck shared Napoleon's views on the potential of a democratic franchise, which promised a congenial way of linking power and masses. In 1866 he elaborated in a similar vein that "direct elections" and "universal suffrage" were apt to re-establish "the contact of the supreme power with the healthy elements that make up the core and mass of the people"[88]—not the "anarchical revolutionized masses of the modern cities".[89] Thus, Bismarck purposefully enforced general, equal, direct and secret (male) suffrage, initially for the North German Confederation, later also for the Imperial Constitution; a suffrage which demonstrated not only a striking resemblance to the demands of the Revolution of 1848 and was one of the most progressive in Europe at the time, but also stood in stark contrast to the existing electoral law in the individual German states, including Prussia, where the three-class franchise system (*Dreiklassenwahlrecht*) was to remain in force until the end of the monarchy.

The latent proximity of universal suffrage to authoritarian and more particularly Caesaristic government did not go unnoticed by contemporary observers, among them the liberal politician Karl Twesten (1820–1870), who during a meeting of the *Reichstag* of the North German Confederation declared on March 30, 1867: "On the one hand, the military force, stronger and more extensive than ever, subsumed in warmongering hands, and beside it, the general equal, direct suffrage; these are the means [...] through which the Caesarian dictatorship is built in France."[90] Napoleon III, in turn, understandably expressed his delight about France's neighbor east of the Rhine adopting what he considered *the* fundament of France's contemporary constitution and the basis for his imperial power.[91]

One may feel inclined to challenge the accuracy of this assessment, and the comparability of the "democratic moment" in the policies of Napoleon III and Bismarck, respectively: for the latter, that moment had an even more instrumental character than for Napoleon III, and was characterized almost exclusively by a conservative-preserving impetus. The corresponding hopes placed by Bismarck in universal suffrage were soon defeated by reality. Ever increasing voter turnouts at the elections to the *Reichstag*, rising from 51 percent at the first elections to 77.5 percent in 1887 and reaching as much as 85 percent in 1912,[92] marked the growing politicization of the masses though, but not necessarily in the sense of Bismarck, who was increasingly concerned about the way the right to vote was being used by the electorate.[93] In hindsight, Bismarck was forced to acknowledge that his conservative party was not in a position to become a national majority party—something which had already become apparent in the need to forge alliances and make compromises with other parties while in power, the most explicit example being the *Kartellparteien* ("cartel parties") in the last years of his chancellorship.

Against this background alone, it would be misleading to talk about a "plebiscitary regime" *strictu sensu* with regard to Bismarck. Unlike the two Bonapartes, Bismarck never sought—and indeed never had to seek—direct confirmation of his position and his leadership skills by popular vote, even if the elections to the *Reichstag* especially in 1878 and 1887 might have had the character of a plebiscite for and against the "iron chancellor". Nevertheless, Bismarckian politics was of a distinctive "popular", not to say "populist", nature, relying from beginning to end on a number of methods to rally public support and to play off carefully influenced public opinion against political and particularly parliamentary opponents.

It is not only with regard to universal suffrage that Bismarck made instrumental use of what can be termed "Caesaristic methods" for his project of a Prussian-conservative order, but also in connection with the one historical accomplishment with which his name continues to be associated more than any other: the creation of the German Empire. Caesaristic-plebiscitary motives played a crucial role in the making of the *Kaiserreich* 1870/1871,[94] and even if he eventually repudiated the existing idea of an emperor being proclaimed by his soldiers,[95] Bismarck was well aware of the potential immanent in the *Reich* becoming the symbol of Germany's unification during the Franco-Prussian War and eventually the *signum* of a common, amalgamating and after all obliging victory. Accordingly, Bismarck acknowledged the "title of Kaiser" as a "publicity element for unity and centralization" in his memoirs,[96] possibly realizing that the *Kaisergedanke* ("imperial idea") could assume a similar integrative capacity for the German *Reich* as the Napoleon cult had done for France and the French Second Empire in particular. Yet at the same time, establishing an empire was never an end in itself for Bismarck, rather another tool for stabilizing the existing political order with a clear anti-revolutionary function. Bismarck welcomed the empire exclusively on the premise that it was founded by and derived its political legitimacy from the German princes; the *Reich*, in his words, was to be "a mere history-based symbol of the independence of the German princes", in no way an expression of popular sovereignty "in the manner of the Empire formed by universal suffrage".[97] In line with these principles—and in acknowledging the political obstacles that would have complicated ambitions for a more unitary nation state anyway—, the German Imperial Constitution of 1871 abstained from fashioning the Empire along the lines of the Napoleonic *empire français*, with the emperor representing a unitary-national institution relying on plebiscitary legitimacy. Instead, the *Bismarcksche Reichsverfassung* established a monarchical confederation headed by the King of Prussia, who had the title of German Emperor (*Deutscher Kaiser*), but was a mere *primus inter pares* among the German sovereigns. The title of "German Emperor" in itself was emblematic for Bismarck's conceptualizing the *Reich* and the envisaged power-political status of the emperor in particular: "Emperor of Germany", an alternative that was much closer to the heart of Wilhelm I, would have insinuated a hegemonic claim to power over Germany in its entirety, which contradicted not only political realities, but would have also been an insult to the other German princes and was hence successfully repudiated by Bismarck. Conversly "Emperor of the Germans"—in analogy to *empereur des français* carried by both Napoleon I and Napoleon III—would have paid tribute to the principle of popular sovereignty, which was totally unacceptable to Bismarck and hence not even taken into consideration.

Even in the wider sense of an expansive and aggressive foreign policy, "imperialism" was an instrument that was used by Bismarck only with particular caution. It is certainly true that he did not shy away from using force to achieve his goal of a unified Germany led by a powerful Prussia, as he so famously proclaimed in his "Blood and Iron" speech of September 30, 1862.[98] Being prepared to resort to war if required for the project of German unification and the expansion of its continental power corresponded with Bismarck's frequently being portrayed in uniform and spiked helmet—a martial depiction that does not exactly evoke imaginations of a "peace chancellor", but rather "soldier politician", as which Napoleon I and to some extent also Napoleon III wished to be perceived. However, from the beginning Bismarck vehemently denied accusations by contemporaries that "Iron and Blood" was to be taken as a public announcement of a dictatorship in the making, searching legitimacy through foreign-political activism. And indeed: especially after the *Reichsgründung*, Bismarck can neither be blamed for having pursued an overly aggressive or interventionist stance in foreign policy, nor having been particularly keen to stabilize the domestic regime through victories abroad.

Often it was Bismarck who within the government assumed the role of admonisher for a restrained foreign policy, for example after the victory in 1866, when he successfully insisted *vis-à-vis* the King on abstaining from unnecessary humiliation of the enemy and the incorporation of Saxony into the Prussian state, and managed to push through a moderate and quick peace allowing Austria as well as its German allies to save face. After 1871, Bismarck's foreign policy was directed towards a prosperous development of Germany by ensuring peace and political stability in Europe. Until the very end of his chancellorship, he remained a fierce proponent of a European balance of power and the Congress System, which saw a significant—and final—achievement in the form of the Congress of Berlin in 1878. Moreover, it was only very late and not out of conviction, but driven by growing public pressure animated by the *Zeitgeist* that Bismarck had

Germany join the colonial expansion of the other European powers; and it is revealing that it was the dispute between Bismarck and the young emperor Wilhelm II about the future foreign policy of the *Reich*, with the latter urging for a more ambitious and confrontational *Weltpolitik*, that heralded Bismarck's resignation in 1890.[99]

Overall, "imperialism"—understood as the advocacy of an empire and a policy of extending a country's power and influence through use of military force and colonization—has only limited analytical value for explaining the Bismarckian system of government, and in any case less than it has for explaining the rule of Napoleon III. This is despite the fact that in the latter's case "imperialism" has been demonstrated as not necessarily being regime-immanent.[100] A larger similarity between the two regimes seems to have existed regarding the last element of their respective constitutional practice that is taken into comparative analysis: social policies.

Like Napoleon III in France, Bismarck monitored and promoted the advancing industrialization of the country with an active economic policy, not least with a view to help raise the power-political status of Germany in Europe. Yet the march into the modern industrial world brought not only massive economic but also social changes, requiring adequate political answers. At the latest after the foundation of the Empire, the working class became a (political) factor in Germany, too, which the government could not ignore. In trying to find answers to the pending social question, which was mainly a "worker question", Bismarck applied a seemingly ambivalent double strategy of repression and embracement. While repression was not particularly surprising given Bismarck's background and political socialization, his far-reaching concessions to the "fourth estate" were not necessarily to be expected. Bismarck's readiness to abandon ideology had already been demonstrated in the 1860s by his contacts with Ferdinand Lassalle (1825–1864)—a leading figure of German socialism—and his promoting universal suffrage, provoking harsh criticism from conservatives and liberals alike that Bismarck was a "revolutionary". This was later followed by comprehensive social (security) legislation: Bismarck not only initiated statutory accident insurance, but also sickness and disability insurances as well as a pension scheme to reduce the risks of poverty in old-age. He was thus the trailblazer for a modern welfare system in Germany and a pioneer of social state interventionism in Europe.

However, as in other areas, Bismarck's social policies—which went beyond the socio-political initiatives of Napoleon III in France, including the support of "mutual societies" (*sociétés de secours mutuels*)—can be chiefly explained by his target-oriented understanding of politics requiring flexibility and, at times, randomness in choosing the most appropriate means to reach an objective. With regard to Napoleon III, one can assume the presence of some altruistic desire to help improve the situation of the working class apart from all political motivations. In the case of Bismarck, considerations of *Realpolitik* seem to have prevailed almost exclusively. The ultimate ambition was nevertheless the same for both: monopolizing the working class by the state and assuring its long-term loyalty in order to remove it from the influence of the organized labor movement, which in the German context was formed in the 1860s after its first beginnings during the Revolution of 1848. Accordingly, the socialist *Arbeiterbewegung* ("workers' movement"), discredited as *innerer Reichsfeind* ("interior enemy of the

Reich"), was unrelentingly antagonized by Bismarck through various instruments, with the *Sozialistengesetz* ("Socialist Law") of 1878 being one of the legislative cornerstones. Adopted by the *Reichstag* after two failed attempts to assassinate Emperor Wilhelm I, which had been instrumentalized by Bismarck, and fierce parliamentary debates, the *Gesetz gegen die gemeingefährlichen Bestrebungen der Sozialdemokratie* of October 21, 1878[101] aimed to lastingly cripple the Socialist Workers Party—the later Social Democratic Party—that was blamed for revolutionary agitation and subversive activities. The law banned socialist and social democratic (sub-)organizations, including trade unions, throughout the Reich and outlawed their activities such as public meetings and publications, thus amounting to a full-scale party ban. Extended four times (1880, 1884, 1886 and 1888) and slightly modified over time, it was to remain in force until Bismarck's leaving the political stage in 1890.

Bismarck bluntly expressed his hopes that isolating and cutting off the roots of the organized labor movement, while at the same time implementing a version of top-down "state socialism", was apt "to generate a conservative attitude in the great mass of the propertyless".[102] Or, as he put it elsewhere: "My thought was to win over, or should I say bribe, the working classes into regarding the state as a social institution that exists on their behalf and cares for their well-being."[103] In the end, Bismarck thus worked as well towards a *soziales Volkskönigtum* ("social popular monarchy") that Lassalle had been reasoning about[104]—though with fundamentally different motivations and intentions.

The actual success of Bismarck's social policy was certainly modest: parliament watered down his state-socialist plans and refused to take harsher repressive measures against the organized labor movement, and Bismarck failed in durably alienating the working class from the social democratic party by accustoming them to the *Obrigkeitsstaat* ("state of authority") he envisaged. Nevertheless, his attempts at "collective bribery" through (social) benefits, though perhaps morally reprehensible, demonstrated Bismarck's astute understanding of the fundamental role played by the "masses"—which in the industrial age was increasingly represented by the working class—in modern politics even for a traditional hereditary monarchy. In this regard, if in no other, parallels to Napoleon III cannot be denied.

This leads us to a concluding assessment of Bismarck and the foundations as well as style of his government, bringing us back to the initial question of whether he can be considered a "German Caesar" or "German Bonaparte".

5.4 Conclusions

In mid-nineteenth-century Germany, lively debate revolved around the need for a "modern Caesar" favored by the unresolved national, but also the increasingly pressing social question. In view of existing challenges and the need to provide fresh authority for the existing monarchical system in the wake of the revolutionary crisis of 1848, willingness to pursue "new" and "unorthodox" forms of governance was growing among politicians of the time, too. This was promptly perceived and denounced as a turn towards "Bonapartism" by traditional conservative circles. Therefore it comes as no surprise that the one politician who is seen as the father of German unification, and who more than anyone else determined politics in Germany throughout the 1860s, 1870s and 1880s with policies and a style of government considerably diverging from classical conservatism, was described as a German version and proponent of Bonapartism or Caesarism even by contemporaries.

Analogies between Bismarck and Napoleon III in particular suggested themselves at the time, and the famous painting of 1878 by Wilhelm Camphausen (1818–1885) depicting the two together—dressed in uniform and sharing a bench after the Battle of Sedan—was thus also to be taken as a reference to assumed ideological-political proximity. Famously, Marx and Engels were among those observers who deemed both statesmen typical representatives of a new "real type" of modern political rule that could be observed in the nineteenth century: "The period of revolutions from below was concluded for now; there followed a period of revolutions from above"—a period that turned the "gravediggers of the Revolution of 1848" to "executors of its will".[105] Generations of authors have continued to consider intrinsic analogies between the two Bonapartes—especially Napoleon III—and Bismarck as a given fact. In their minds, Bismarck had essentially copied Napoleon III, "whose government was sustained by the masses and opposed by a portion of the educated middle class; Napoleon had introduced universal suffrage to get rid of the Second Republic and had been successful in that. Bismarck was confident that he would be able to achieve the same success".[106]

Yet no less is the number of those especially in more recent scholarship that have cautioned against any fundamental comparability of the two or emphasize that Bismarck's form of rule was similar to that of Napoleon III only insofar as it was tailored for a "Caesaristic statesman".[107] And indeed, both ways of thinking can be reasonably argued. Depending on the point of focus, similarities or dissimilarities prevail. In particular the fundamentally different constitutional role of Napoleon III and Bismarck, but also other factors such as the dissimilar socio-economic situation in post-1848 France and Germany with the distribution of powers between social groups and the resulting room for political maneuver being unalike, cautions against depicting Bismarck as a "German Bonaparte". At the same time, however, there are striking resemblances, from their being both products of and managers of crisis, to their innovatively combining repressive and progressive policies as well as multiple sources of legitimacy. And assuming that each and every historical phenomenon is somehow *sui generis* and distinct from other phenomena, the common features shared between Napoleon III and Bismarck seem all the more noteworthy.

So what conclusion can be drawn? Was Bismarck a Bonapartist or a (new) Caesar? No, he was neither of the two, for the social and political framework in itself stood in the way of any such aspirations that might have existed. But did Bismarck utilize a "Bonapartist" or "Caesaristic" toolset? Yes, he did, and quite actively so. This underlines the need to distinguish between "system" and "method of government", and approach Caesarism chiefly under the latter. At the end of the day, Bismarck was and continued to be an "absolutist public servant in the age of mass politics".[108] He fulfilled this role congenially. While his policies were "conservative" and aimed at strengthening the Prussian-German monarchical state, he far-sightedly realized that in order to do so, disentanglement from some traditional conservative positions and the application of revolutionary and Bonapartist means was inevitable. Affinity with and conscious imitation of Bonapartist techniques of rule cannot be denied: a militant domestic policy, alternating between conservative and revolutionary paradigms, disdain for traditional forms of political legitimacy, active social and welfare policies, populism and instrumentalization of the masses, to mention but a few. A static defense of the *status quo* seemed unwise, indeed dangerous, in view of the dynamic changes of the framework conditions for political and social processes to take place. "Revolution" and "counter-Revolution" were no longer to be seen as dichotomies: "There are times when you have to govern liberally, and times when you have to govern dictatorially, everything changes, there is no eternity here."[109] Modern politics was about paying tribute to the *Zeitgeist*, which meant above all that if in the second half of the nineteenth century—with the advent of mass societies and the mediatization of politics—trends towards parliamentarism had to be halted and monocratic rule to be perpetuated, "personalized power" and the "masses" had to converge and enter into a relationship of mutual benefit.

Towards the end of the nineteenth century, this challenge of linking populace and "Caesar"—in the specific case of Wilhelmine Germany, *Demokratie und Kaisertum*[110]—proved increasingly appealing, but also difficult, throughout Europe.

6

Mass Democracy and "Scientification":
Caesarism at the Turn of the Century

6.1 Discourses on a "New Caesar" in the Late Nineteenth Century

As has been demonstrated in the previous two chapters, debate on the risks of, but also potential need for, a "new Caesar" had reached a new peak around the mid-nineteenth century. In the wake of the revolutionary events of 1848 it had mainly been the seizure of power by Louis-Napoléon and the founding of the Second Empire in France which served both as a focal point of discussion in Europe and as a central stockpile of arguments for and against an elusive phenomenon still widely referred to as Bonapartism; a phenomenon that due to continuing industrialization and the concomitant "social question", which was above all a question of how to deal with the mounting working class, was gaining in momentum and direction considerably different from that of the early nineteenth century. The role of the Second Empire mirroring contemporary theoretical and political debate alike is also manifest in that French developments and the regime of Napoleon III served as *the*—mostly negative— reference point and benchmark for assessing the risks and chances of a "German Caesar" and later the actual policies of Bismarck. It is therefore not surprising that the downfall of Napoleon III and his "Caesarian democracy"—as which the German writer and historian Karl Hillebrand (1829–1884) characterized the Second French Empire *a posteriori* in 1873[1]—had substantial repercussions on Caesarism discourses far beyond the borders of France.

For the period after 1870/1871, two interrelated trends are discernible:

1. The end of the Napoleonic regime and the ensuing calmer waters the country entered—at least in terms of foreign policy—not only limited dealings with French (political) affairs in journalism and writing abroad, but also resulted in the terms "Bonapartism" and "Napoleonism" losing their immediate relevance and historical presence. This allowed the term "Caesarism" to unfold, become more commonly used and assume the role of the key concept to describe regimes between democracy and dictatorship such as those of the two Napoleons.
2. Favored by its severance from day-to-day (French) politics, Caesarism—with its additional advantage of not smacking of a specific national location—gradually became a matter of the evolving (social) sciences, which helped to further depoliticize

the concept. Even previously there had been sporadic attempts to approach what was termed Bonapartism or Caesarism impartially and to develop more universal political theories around it, but for the most part the debates of the previous decades had been distinctly embedded in tangible political and ideological disputes. Growing efforts to turn Caesarism into a scientific and more universal concept, attributing it a place in what was to be called "political sociology", did not lack ideological moments and also reflected specific historical circumstances. Yet increasingly, these moments and circumstances were present in a "filtered" rather than open manner.

Notwithstanding these processes of change, however, discourse on Caesarism remained entangled with broader concerns about organizing political rule and managing society: deficits of existing political systems and how to remedy them, appropriate forms of representation, and—as an overarching theme—political legitimacy. Since the American and especially French Revolutions, challenging traditional forms of political power and redefining sovereignty, the question of legitimacy had become central to political discussion. It developed into something even more fundamental with the "masses" assuming ever-more political power from the mid-nineteenth century onwards. The "will of the people"—one of the key drives of the Revolution—demanded acknowledgement. Yet in what concrete form that will should be acknowledged was left open, as was the issue of whether a "democracy" had to be understood as "rule of representatives", or if it could also be interpreted as "rule of the masses".[2] With the latter view gaining prominence as the nineteenth century progressed, Caesarism, too, became ever more "involved with the new importance given to the masses as a political force in the post-revolutionary age".[3]

But what did "the masses" actually epitomize? Was it a mature and responsible demos, or rather a pliable crowd susceptible to demagogues? If the latter was the case, how were the masses to be kept under control—or unleashed? And what was the fate of not only representation and popular sovereignty, but also liberty and freedom in an environment supposedly receptive to demagogic leaders? Finally, what sort of legitimacy was fitting for an age in which traditional forms appeared to be becoming less and less conclusive and reliable?[4]

These were all questions of a pertinent and essentially universal nature. Accordingly, the problem—or promise, depending on the point of view—of mass democracy was a key priority in the mind of many political thinkers and practitioners throughout Europe at the time. This chapter sets out to highlight the European, if not global, dimension of late nineteenth- and early twentieth-century debate on mass democracy, in which the concept of Caesarism played a pivotal role. At the same time, it is to be demonstrated that with the "currency" of the Caesarism term growing in the second half of the nineteenth century, the complexity of its usage and trajectory increased as well. If "everybody is now talking of Caesarism", as Ludwig Bamberger remarked as early as in 1866,[5] they were doing so in a broader sense than ever before. This makes it even more difficult than for the first half of the nineteenth century to provide anything like a comprehensive overview of the surrounding debates, and little more than a sketchy "panorama" of general trends will have to suffice; notably by focusing on five cases: Great Britain, the USA, Italy, France and Germany.

6.1.1 Great Britain, the USA and Italy

The spread of the debate on Caesarism saw its most practical manifestation through the canonization of the term in an increasing number of lexica and dictionaries of the time. The "how" and "when", however, allows one to draw inferences about the actual importance and character of the discourse in different national contexts. It is worth noting, for example, that while in other countries the term had long since been established in reference works, one cannot find any explicit entries for "Caesarism"—or "Bonapartism" and "Napoleonism"—in the Encyclopaedia Britannica throughout the entire nineteenth and early twentieth century. This may have to do with the fact that the British continued to deem Caesarism to be a mainly continental—and perhaps even more specifically, French—phenomenon, triggered by conditions peculiar to the continent. While a feeling of British political distinctiveness had grown during the French Revolution, such a feeling became even more distinct after the mid-nineteenth century, with Britain experiencing no equivalent to the 1848 revolutions in Europe. Nonetheless, it would be misleading to assume that Caesarism did not play any role for or in political discourse, especially since in view of the challenges posed by a mass society, the future of the political system was being discussed as avidly as in other parts of Europe. The main difference was rather the way Caesarism was taken up, which in Britain almost exclusively served the purpose of a "negative foil".

In line with this critical stance, the Oxford English Dictionary, for example, records the ire of a contributor to the Westminster Review complaining in 1858 of the "clumsy eulogies of Caesarism as incarnate in the dynasty of Bonaparte".[6] Caesarism was becoming an issue in the context of debate on reforming the English Constitution and franchise in particular, which had already seen a first extension through the Great Reform Act of 1832. More importantly in quantitative terms, however, were the Acts of Parliament in 1867, 1884 and 1885, accompanied by fierce debate on how the "masses" should best be dealt with and contained under the specificities of the British political system. An 1866 reviewer of the new edition of John Earl Russell's *Essay on the History of the English Government and Constitution* (1865),[7] for instance, captured the shortcomings of parliamentary rule when he wrote of the dangers of a weak government being elected by some "ignorant multitude", referring to the United States:

> America during the last five years has only repeated to the world the lesson that had already been taught in France, that, if you will have democracy, you must have something like Caesarism to control it. The feeble and pliable Executive of England is wholly unsuited to such an electoral body. A Government that yields and must yield to the slightest wish of the House of Commons, is only possible so long as that House of Commons is the organ of an educated minority. Such an instrument of Government has never yet in the history of the world been worked by a Legislature chosen by the lower class.[8]

Across party lines, it was taken for granted that the masses were not just uneducated, but irrational and thus potentially dangerous. Caesarism, in this context, was seen to fatally rest on and even actively promote the ignorance of the illiterate masses, or "collective mediocrity", to use a notion by John Stuart Mill.[9] It was with this push that in the mid-1860s Walter Bagehot (1826–1877) made one of the most significant—and at the same time most sarcastic—contributions to British debates on Caesarism in the nineteenth century. In his succinct article *Caesarism as it now exists*, first published in March 1865,[10] Bagehot pondered on the French Second Empire in order to draw lessons for his British readership. He saw clear parallels between Julius Caesar, who for Bagehot was "the first instance of a democratic despot", and the regimes of the two Bonapartes in France. Caesar had overthrown an aristocracy "by the help of the people, of the unorganized people. He said to the numerical majority of Roman citizens, 'I am your advocate and your leader: make me supreme, and I will govern for your good and in your name.'"—which was exactly the underlying principle of the French Empire, too. For Bagehot, it was Louis-Napoléon—a "Benthamite despot"—who had perfected Caesar's style of rule: "He is for the 'greatest happiness of the greatest number'. He says, 'I am where I am, because I know better than anyone else what is good for the French people, and they know that I know better.' He is not the Lord's anointed; he is the people's agent."[11] Bagehot acknowledged the achievements of the Second Empire, characterizing it as the "best finished democracy which the world has ever seen. What the many at the moment desire is embodied with a readiness, an efficiency, and a completeness which has no parallel".[12] Nevertheless, all potential advantages of democratic despotism were overshadowed by a fundamental constructional flaw: it stopped "the effectual inculcation of important thought upon the mass of mankind".[13] This was a systemic must, since "a democratic despotism is like a theocracy: it assumes its own correctness"; but as a result, leaves the masses totally unschooled, not least in political matters, hence corrupting the future: "France, as it is, may be happier because of the Empire, but France in the future will be more ignorant because of the Empire."[14] A second fundamental flaw identified by Bagehot was that "an enormous concentration of power in an industrial system ensures an accumulation of pecuniary temptation", making the Empire endure "the daily presence of an efficient immortality". Yet another problem was the institutionalization of the regime, since its existence depended "on the permanent occupation of the Tuileries by an extraordinary man. The democratic despot—the representative despot—must have the sagacity to divine the people's will, and the sagacity to execute it. What is the likelihood that this will be hereditary?"[15] Together, these were traits which did not make Caesarism a model worth striving for.

Five years later, with the Second Empire in its final throes, Bagehot returned to the topic, offering not only a concise definition of "Caesarism", but also an explanation for its utter failure in France. In *The Collapse of Caesarism*, he defined "that peculiar system of which Louis Napoleon [...] is the great exponent" as follows:

> [Caesarism] tries to win directly from a plebiscite, i.e., the vote of the people, a power for the throne to override the popular will as expressed in regular representative assemblies, and to place in the monarch an indefinite "responsibility" to the nation, by virtue of which he may hold in severe check the intellectual criticism of the more educated classes and even the votes of the people's own delegates. That is what we really mean by Caesarism,—the abuse of the confidence reposed by the most ignorant in a great name to hold at bay the reasoned arguments

of men who both know the popular wish and also are sufficiently educated to discuss the best means of gratifying those wishes. A virtually irresponsible power obtained by one man from the vague preference of the masses for a particular name—that is Caesarism [...][16]

It was in the very nature of such a system that "all intermediate links of moral responsibility and cooperation" between throne and people were absent, given that the plebiscitary moment so characteristic of Caesarism entrusted the Emperor with an authority reducing all intermediate powers to comparative insignificance whenever they collided with his own. Consequently, virtually everything depended on the plebiscitary leader and his abilities.[17] Disposing of "indefinite power but not indefinite capacity", the "Caesarist system"—whose physical basis Bagehot considered to be the army—was left with no reliable "check on recklessness or incapacity at the head". The only controlling mechanisms were "the wishes of the masses of people, and that is often the source of the greatest weakness": a Caesar who was supported against the aristocracy and the educated classes by the ignorant masses was "compelled to limit his measures by their ignorant likes and dislikes". Bagehot concluded, therefore, that Napoleon had failed "not only through that loneliness of power which has given him not natural allies among the educated people", but also "in consequence of his abject dependence on that ignorant conservatism of the peasantry to which he has looked for the popularity of his regime".[18]

In the British context, publications taking up Caesarism with a comparable sharpness of mind and as explicitly as Bagehot's remained the exception. The concept, however, continued to be ever-present, weaving its way into the predominant discourse on the potential risks of mass democracy, and how best to immunize the British political system against them. Among those who explicitly warned of mass democracy was the jurist and historian Henry James Sumner Maine (1822–1888), seen as one of the forefathers of modern legal anthropology and sociology of law. In a volume of essays published in 1885 entitled *Popular Government*, generating much comment at the time, Maine portrayed democracy—to him an "extreme form of popular government"[19]—as by no means more stable or necessarily more progressive than any other form of government. Quite the contrary: "as a matter of fact, Popular Government, since its reintroduction into the world, has proved itself to be extremely fragile."[20] Of all forms of government, democracy was by far the most difficult. The greatest and most permanent of all the difficulties of democracy lay in the constitution of human nature: to Maine, it was a given fact that all government and rule was about exertion of will, "but in what sense can a multitude exercise volition?" Maine blamed modern enthusiasts of democracy for making one fundamental blunder, namely "mix[ing] up the theory, that the Demos is capable of volition, with the fact, that it is capable of adopting the opinions of one man or of a limited number of men, and of founding directions to its instruments upon them".[21] He was thus referring to the malleability of the masses and their being merely an instrument of the political leader: "There is no doubt that, in popular governments resting on a wide suffrage, [...] the leader, whether or not he be cunning, or eloquent, or well provided with commonplaces, will be the Wire-puller."[22]

Much of the debate on the consequences of the masses becoming a political force of increasing importance and the concomitant chances for populist leaders to seize their opportunities revolved around the question in how far British politics itself—and its premier system in particular—had become a version of Caesarism. Among other publications, this was a key concern of the 1909 *The Crisis of Liberalism: New Issues of Democracy* by John Atkinson Hobson (1858–1940), an English economist and popular critic of imperialism.[23] In the recent history of his country, Hobson saw clear and alarming tendencies in this direction, with "a Cabinet autocracy qualified in certain electoral conditions by the power of some enclave or 'cave' in a party" looming. The current state of affairs might "easily lead to Caesarism, where a magnetic party leader either succeeded in capturing the imagination of the populace or in engineering a supremacy among competing politicians". In order to avert this danger, reforms of the existing electoral institutions aimed at "reversing the tendency towards increased Cabinet control" were therefore deemed indispensable. According to Hobson, this was to be achieved by establishing "a real and firm check upon abuse of power", including "the House of Commons [. . .] be made more accurately representative, and representative government [. . .] be supplemented by a measure of direct democratic control".[24]

While thus sharing Maine's awareness of the susceptibility of democratic systems to one-man rule, Hobson disagreed with Maine's overall dismissal of democracy and argued rather for an appropriate democratic mechanism as the most promising firewall against Caesaristic ambitions. To that aim, Hobson advocated a parliamentary system guaranteeing true representation, yet complemented by an element of direct-democratic control in order to thwart—or at least contain—any potential excesses of parliamentary party politics.

Not surprisingly, British debates on the consequences of mass democracy had an equivalent outside of Britain and echoed themselves ongoing political developments as well as discussions in that country which had acquired a full-fledged—by nineteenth-century standards—democracy since the late eighteenth century, and with which Britain shared a common language: the United States of America. There, too, the concept of "Caesarism" was not a separate issue of political debate and concern, but featured as part of a wider discourse on the present and future of democratic government, embodying a potential degeneration of—or simply contrasting model to—a sober (democratic) polity. It is in this vein that the term Caesarism is used in 1857 in Orestes Brownson's (1803–1876) equation of "modern Caesarism" with "monarchical absolutism".[25]

Discussions on the risks of dictatorship within democratic frameworks gained momentum as the president's power in the constitutional system of the United States grew, reaching its first zenith under Abraham Lincoln (1809–1865). Throughout his presidential term, and favored by his active and assertive leadership style during the American Civil War as well as his re-election in 1864, Lincoln was faced with allegations of "monarchical pretension" and even dictatorial behavior. Among the starkest pamphlets against Lincoln in this regard was *Abraham Africanus I* (1864), in which the president's style of government was denounced as hubristic, autocratic and an eminent danger to American democracy.[26] At the time, parallels between Lincoln and Julius

Caesar were also being drawn, gaining particular momentum after Lincoln's assassination in April 1865.[27]

Similarly, Lincoln's later successor as US President, Ulysses S. Grant (1822–1885), was faced with accusations of Caesarist intentions, especially when speculation grew in advance of the 1876 elections that he might run for a third term. Caesarism became the favored term for describing Grant's proposed third tenure of office. On July 7, 1873, James Gordon Bennett Jr., editor-in-chief of the by then most popular US newspaper *New York Herald* and a staunch supporter of the Democratic Party, even launched a campaign to alert the nation to its alleged peril. In his editorial of the same date,[28] Bennett asked Americans to put aside such "sentimental and fantastic" issues of politics such as free trade or voting rights and to focus on the only question that truly mattered: "shall we have a republican form of government", or should the country succumb to "Caesarism"? The latter being very probable because the "political situation" was in the hands of Grant:

> He is as completely master as was ever Jefferson, Jackson or Lincoln. Never was a President so submissively obeyed. Never was a party so dominant. Every department of the government, nearly every large State, the army, the navy, the bench [. . .] all, all are in the hands of his followers.

Moreover, Bennett—stressing that "great events are not the works of mere men, but of social and political conditions which daring men ofttimes seize"—saw "many of the elements favorable to Caesarism" present at that time. This included luxury, a spirit of speculation, a loose moral tone, a military spirit and widespread craving for "show and noise". Bennett warned that should Grant be renominated and win the elections, the path to Caesarism would inevitably be paved, and Grant would be "remembered with those daring, ambitious men, like Caesar and Napoleon, who preferred their own gain to the national liberties".[29]

Bennett and others libelling Grant as a perpetrator of Caesarism, however, did not go unchallenged. While supporters of the President rebuked such accusations as inappropriate if not ridiculous,[30] even commentators opposing Grant considered Caesarism to be an inappropriate concept, not least since any true parallels between Caesar and Grant were deemed missing.[31]

With Grant eventually abstaining from running for a third presidential term—not least in view of the accumulated scandals of his presidency, which made even a considerable faction of his Republican Party desire an end to "Grantism"—, the heyday of political discussions on Caesarism in the USA came to an end, although the term and concept remained part of the repertoire of political debate.

The receding of Caesarism discourses after Grant was also due to the fact that the Civil War as the most eminent crisis in the country's history could be considered as having been largely overcome by the late 1870s, despite continuing political and social divisions. After the Reconstruction Era, US domestic politics entered somewhat calmer waters, and with it controversy on the risks of or perhaps need for a "new Caesar" became less pertinent.

The situation was quite different in many continental European states, for which the second half of the nineteenth century marked a time of unrest, politically and otherwise. Accordingly, debate on Caesarism was likely to have a different drive. Yet turbulent times alone did not necessarily make Caesarism a key concern of national political discourses. Italy, faced with the double challenge of dealing with the repercussions of the Revolution of 1848 on the one hand and trying to tackle in parallel its state and nation building on the other, is a case in point.

It was only in the 1860s that Caesarism was taken up by political commentators in Italy. Among the very first—and actually few—to put "Caesarism" front stage of political writing was the previously-mentioned journalist and parliamentarian Giuseppe Lazzaro (1825–1910). His pamphlet *Il cesarismo e l'Italia*, published in 1862, provided a critical assessment of Caesarism, which Lazzaro considered to be a genuinely modern phenomenon.[32] *Cesarismo* rested on the language of "popular will" and could be characterized as "the hypocrisy of the monarchy erected as a system of government". A hybrid of absolutism and universal suffrage, Caesarism for Lazzaro was above all to be admonished for its corrupting and debilitating features: "With Caesarism, the political absurdity of the Etat c'est moi is clothed in legality, with Caesarism, the people commits suicide [*è suicidato*], while with absolutism it is killed."[33] What was particularly alarming for Lazzaro was the fact that Caesarism, while originating in France, was spreading throughout Europe, especially in Germany.[34] Italy, on the other hand, did not seem to be particularly susceptible to Caesarism and could even be considered as a counter-model. In Lazzaro's view it was not figures like Napoleon III or Bismarck, but the Italian statesmen Cavour and Garibaldi who should be seen as real exemplars of modern liberty.[35]

The debate on Caesarism gained some momentum in Italy after the publication of Napoleon III's biography of Caesar in 1865, with the reception of both the book and the concept overwhelmingly negative.[36] Giuseppe Mazzini (1805–1872), for example, objected to the cult of the individual leader, which was the core of Caesarism, since it failed to understand what real leadership was all about, namely: serving God and people under the ideals of truth and morality. Figures such as Alexander the Great, Caesar or Napoleon, however, had misspent their genius by becoming autocratic egoists, and rather than initiating a new era, they had each closed an epoch.[37]

In the following decades, a distinctively critical stance towards Caesarism continued to prevail in the Italian context, yet with only a small number of authors dealing with the concept explicitly and in an analytical manner. Among them was the historian and writer Guglielmo Ferrero (1871–1942), who in his 1898 *Il Militarismo*—appearing in English one year later in a considerably revised and expanded version—examined Caesarism as a phenomenon integrally linked with the (French) Revolution and Jacobinism, and as an enduring legacy in the French Third Republic.[38]

To Ferrero, the fact that contemporary France was nominally a parliamentary and democratic republic could not obscure the fact that "the republican constitution today is what the monarchy and empire were in the past, a mere bark whose nature has changed, but which still covers its original trunk and pith; that is Caesarism".[39] Caesarism was not to be confused with, but actually went beyond, a Napoleonic style of government. In essence, it was the militarism—understood in an encompassing way—of the "Jacobin lay State created by the Revolution in opposition to the Church".[40] The Jacobin State, Ferrero argued, represented a political solution to the problem of the relation between religion and modern society, and had been created by a cultured minority to be the bulwark of liberty. However, "an indissoluble contradiction presided like an unlucky star at its birth". That "original sin of the modern Latin nations, and more especially of France and Italy" was that in order to maintain their authority, the liberal minority—for whom popular sovereignty was a key theoretical concept founded in opposition to monarchical absolutism—imposed their regime tyrannically and by means of force, thus entering into competition with the Church and imitating it in many of its authoritarian ways.[41] Contradictory enough, the Jacobin state— completed by Napoleon—was not just the tyrannical government of a minority, but was by necessity also aristocratic and oligarchic state paternalism, clientelism, bureaucratization, centralization and a mighty executive body seeking legitimacy through the incitement of patriotic fervour and hence inclining towards war were, in Ferrero's eyes, all characteristic features of the (French) Jacobin state. Caesarism as the intrinsic militarist impulse of the Jacobin state had permeated all French regimes of the nineteenth century, including the Third Republic. The only discernible difference was that with Europe's borders changed and France's military capabilities in decline, this impulse had become mainly externalized in the form of French colonialism.

All in all, nineteenth century Italian encounters with Caesarism can be described as subdued and only a niche component of domestic political discourse. Largely perceived as something "foreign", Caesarism served as a warning of possible degenerations of political rule, yet with no immediate implications for Italy. Towards the end of the century, however, a change in perception was looming, as was manifest in Ferrero's approach to the subject. There was an increasing consciousness that Caesarism might be a general concomitant of political modernity, intertwined especially with the challenge of putting the promise of popular sovereignty into practice, and that it was hence not exclusively an issue of French—or German—politics.

Since the concept of Caesarism touched upon the issue of how to organize political leadership in an age of mass politics, there was potential room for a more favorable assessment of "Caesarist" figures and styles of government. Rather than as part of an intensified debate on Caesarism, however, the question of how to mobilize the masses while at the same time taming them, and how to guarantee an organic relationship between the political elite and the "people", were taken up in the proto-fascist discourse emerging in Italy at the turn of the century, with figures such as Gaetano Mosca (1858– 1941) at its forefront.

As a matter of fact, Caesarism never enjoyed the same degree of immediacy in Italy as it did in France and especially Germany, where it continued to be an important reference point beyond the fall of Napoleon III and Bismarck, respectively.

6.1.2 France

It comes as no surprise that the end of the Second Empire brought with it less intensive and particularly less effusive dealings with Caesarist-style rule in France than in the previous two decades. Given that it was mainly Napoleon III and his personalized style of government that were blamed for France's devastating defeat in the Franco- Prussian War, euphoric obeisance to one-man leadership could hardly be expected in the immediate aftermath of 1870. At the same time, however, the Bonapartist movement—represented by followers of the overthrown Emperor and proponents of Napoleonic ideas more generally—continued to be a political force to be reckoned with. A more critical view of Caesarism, but with a hint of admiration for many of its (assumed) features, became characteristic of politico-theoretical discourse in the Third Republic.

Exemplary of this ambivalence prevailing at the time is the entry *Césarisme* in the second edition (1873–1877) of Émile Littré's *Dictionnaire de la langue française*, in which Caesarism is rendered as "domination of the Caesars, that is, the domination of princes brought to government by democracy, but invested with absolute power", and at the same time presented as a "theory of those who think that this form of government is the best."[42] This interpretation did not constitute a fundamental break away from the understanding during the Second Empire, and actually expressed a more positive attitude than, for example, Pierre Larousse's *Grand dictionnaire universel du XIXe siècle* of 1867. Here, *Césarisme* had been defined almost identically as "domination of the sovereigns brought to government by democracy, but invested with absolute power", yet with a distinctively negative undertone. The author acknowledged that "Caesarism necessarily implies the idea of a government that is either good or bad according to the person exercising it, who is always supposed to act providentially in the interest of all and by the will of all", but considered it merely as "one of the progressive forms of despotism, which suits people who cannot or do not know how to govern themselves". Caesarism essentially meant political dictatorship and was an impossible form of government in the long run. This was particularly true for the nineteenth century: "in a society that lives off spirit and work, Caesarism is an impossibility."[43] It was however, telling that any mention of Napoleon III was avoided, thus leaving it up to the readers to decide whether or not to classify his regime as Caesaristic.[44]

The first work in French to explicitly take up Caesarism as an object of interest after the deposition of Louis-Napoléon, *Du césarisme en France*—written by a "M. Jourdeuil", whose biographical details are unknown, and published in June 1871—answered the question as to whether the Second Empire should be qualified as Caesaristic unmistakably in the affirmative, thus setting the tone for later publications in France.

The pamphlet,[45] appearing amidst the Third Republic's process of self-discovery and plans to establish a parliamentary monarchy under Henri d'Artois, Comte de Chambord (1820–1883), grandson of former king Charles X, started its examination of how to deal with the legacy of Caesarism in France with a definition of the term that was as succinct as it was negative: "Caesarism is dictatorship converted into a permanent system of government; It is a discretionary and exceptional sovereignty that establishes itself as a regular power in the interest of the rulers and not the ruled."[46] As far as the author was concerned, the roots of French Caesarism could be traced back to the absolutist regime erected under Louis XIV, even though it only reached its height after the French Revolution. As devastating as the experiences of Caesarism—with the *Ancien Régime*, the First Empire, the Restoration, the July Monarchy and the Second Empire representing only different versions of it—might have been for the country, the lost war now offered a unique chance to reverse them and make France "the most liberal and the best balanced nation in Europe".[47] This was to be achieved by reforms extinguishing Caesarism and eradicating the party system. To that aim, Jourdeuil suggested, among other things, strengthening structures of local government in order to counter the disastrous centralization of political power so typical of Caesarism. Quite astonishingly, however, the two instruments hailed as key remedies had themselves been distinctive for the last stage of French Caesarism in the Second Empire, described by Jourdeuil as *césarisme prolétaire et populacier*[48]—namely direct plebiscitary democracy and universal suffrage:

1. The plebiscite to confer supreme power and decide the great questions of constitutional law;
2. Universal suffrage to delegate a share of executive or legislative power to citizens.[49]

Corresponding to these two instruments perceived as the cornerstones of the country's future political system was the antithetic vision of "a republic with a hereditary president"[50] believed to be the most suitable solution for France, with representative elements left marginalized.

Du césarisme en France is momentous, and one may even say paradigmatic, for French political debate at the time: above all, in that even declared critics of Caesarism—be it defined more broadly as a symptom of French politics going back to even before the Revolution, as Jourdeuil had suggested, or more specifically as a *signum* of the two Napoleonic regimes—could hardly envisage overcoming it without harking back to some of its key features. This went hand in hand with classical republicanism facing a loss of significance and growing confusion with regard to its conceptual and ideological basis. Despite the fact that "republicanism" continued to attract supporters and was almost an inevitable point of reference during the Third Republic, in terms of actual meaning it had only superficial resemblances to earlier predecessors. While classical republicanism had never equated representation to democracy, with the latter typically seen as both unworkable and dangerous, universal suffrage and even plebiscitary government were now regarded as core elements of republicanism. Moreover, the republicanism of the Third Republic had acquired a distinctively social component, with a commitment to educational and social reform, and the establishment of a "just" society. In both cases, analogies with the policies of the Second Empire were evident.

The conceptual transformation process—and indeed conceptual confusion—also found expression in the association of Caesarism with Jacobinism, and Jacobinism with the Third Republic. This connection resulted in political reformers of the Third Republic being accused of Caesarism by—often Catholic—critics such as Eugène Villedieu, who in his *Le Césarisme jacobin, les droits de l'Eglise et le droit national* (1880) blamed the "new Jacobins" for launching a full-scale attack on the Church and thus bereaving citizens of their most fundamental institutional attachment.[51] From the perspective of such critics, Caesarism was "not the negation of republicanism, but—in the metamorphosis of 'Jacobin Caesarism'—its apotheosis".[52] This view of Caesarism as the self-expression and the inevitable result of the Revolution's (Jacobin) doctrines, still alive in the structures of the Third Republic, was not only present in France, but also taken up by foreign commentators such as Guglielmo Ferrero.[53]

A different way of linking the legacy of the Revolution with Caesarism was not necessarily to see the latter as a direct outcome or perpetuation of the Revolution, but rather to declare a miscarried combination of revolutionary idea(l)s—above all that of popular sovereignty—and Caesarist government the root of evil. An example of such a take on the subject is Joseph Ferrand's (1827-1903) book *Césarisme et démocratie* (posthumously published in 1904), with its subtitle *l'incompatibilité entre notre régime administratif et notre régime politique* already referring to the central thrust of the argument. In the wake of the Revolution, Caesarist state centralization had produced a situation of political and administrative debility in France, a fundamental divergence "between our principles and our practices".[54] While on the one hand the national authorities had smothered the potential of local government through an all-encompassing concentration of power at the central level, on the other two pernicious ideas had dominated French political life since the days of the First Consul: firstly, that deliberating is the duty of the many, but that action is the responsibility of the one; secondly, that given that government is claimed to represent the sovereign nation, it was impossible for the people to oppose government, since to do so would be a contradiction in itself. France, in Ferrand's view, had thus institutionalized the *coup d'état*. For while the first idea left the country with a feeble parliamentary system unfit to assume responsibility, the second—together with a dearth of adequate education—generated a body of voters incapacitated to think freely. The consequences were disastrous: not a sovereign people, but an indifferent and spiritless one inept to govern itself, with universal suffrage merely a show of participation.[55]

Parallel to critical engagement with concept and practice of Caesarism—whether in analytical or polemical terms, with *Césarisme* a political battle cry—there was, however, a considerable amount of writings distinctively positive towards Caesarism, too. Motivations and hopes associated with Caesarism certainly varied; but across the board there was, nevertheless, a consensus among the arguments put forward in favor of it: the need to overcome what was perceived as a profound crisis by means of a strong leader enjoying the support of the people. This craving did not have to be explicitly expressed in terms of "Caesarism", but it often was. Such was the case, for example, in an 1888 pamphlet entitled *Le Césarisme*.[56] Its author left no doubt that "Caesarism has become a necessity"; more particularly, that there was the "necessity of an authority, of a master, of a Caesar".[57] The pamphlet sketched a picture of France in dire need of a "saviour",[58] who alone could successfully pursue the renewal of a country faced with a deep and multidimensional crisis: political, economic and moral. The people would clearly sense that what they needed were not "masters", but "*one* master" who "is not afflicted by this plague called parliamentarism—this parliamentarism, which is nothing other than the enactment of the saying: 'speaking to say nothing'. Parliamentarism: a system that produces twenty fools for every competent person". The true wish of the people was clear and unmistakable:

> This is what the people feel and this is why, when one is forced to ask their opinion, they will answer—faced with daily commotion, ministerial instabilities, poverty [which is the] effect of our government, the ongoing lowering of authority, the collapse of all that is grandeur, honesty, elevation—Caesarism! Caesarism![59]

What spoke in favor of Caesarism was not only that such form of government was the one required and desired by the people, but also that all relevant political groups in France could actually approve of it. Bonapartists were naturally in favor of Caesarism and had always fought for it; republicans could not refuse it, since their principal concern—universal suffrage—was guaranteed; and the monarchists' own claimant to the throne, Philippe d'Orléans, Comte de Paris (1838–1894), was a strong advocate of Caesarism.[60] In short, everything spoke for a shift to Caesarism, especially since it could and should not be confused with dictatorship: "The two systems are not at all alike.—Dictatorship rests on nothing solid or legitimate. Caesarism is authority based on an assent to its existence."[61] The looming days of Caesarism, the author concluded full of pathos, would finally mark "the revival of the Fatherland".[62]

This remarkable pro-Caesarism movement in late nineteenth-century France was nurtured by a number of factors: perceived deficits of the political system of the Third Republic, the formal basis of which were the Constitutional Laws of 1875, as well as unresolved social and economic issues; Napoleonic nostalgia, also generating hope for a future equally full of glory and international significance for the nation than the past had been; and not least revanchism directed against Germany to avenge France's humiliating defeat in 1870/1871. Caesarist sentiments at the time were not limited to political writing, but also found concrete political expression. Indeed, the chances of Caesarism (re-)assuming political importance in France were not bad, facilitated by the fact that there were potential points of reference for all relevant political groups in the country and not just the Bonapartists, as recognized also in *Le Césarisme*. The fact that even the monarchists under the leadership of the Comte de Paris showed some sympathy for Caesarist rule—though obviously under the proviso that Philippe d'Orléans would assume the role of the new Caesar himself—provides evidence that by the end of the nineteenth century advocates of monarchism considered (or rather: had to consider) Caesarism as a means to re-gain political power and to generate political legitimacy. This was particularly true for France with its distinctive revolutionary traditions and numerous regime changes since 1789, which had shattered traditional forms of dynastic legitimacy and belief in hereditary monarchy more so than in other parts of Europe. Against this background, and considering the election-based republican framework within which it had to operate for better or worse, it is understandable why French monarchism in the 1880s had a number of programmatic points in common with the "Caesarist idea": above all the acceptance of universal suffrage, coinciding with emphasis on "order" and a strong government, while parliamentarism was rejected as impotent and dangerous.[63]

In the end, however, it was much less the Comte de Paris who became the face and concrete political epitome of the pro-Caesarism movement in France at the time, but another person: Georges Ernest Boulanger (1837–1891). Considering his few years in active politics and the relatively limited importance of the offices actually held by him during that time, huge interest has been paid to Boulanger by French historiography and beyond.[64] This is not only because of his illustrious and at the same time tragic course of life or the difficulties in trying to pigeon-hole him to any one common political scheme (left-right, progressive-reactionary), but also because he stands for a larger political-social movement frequently equated with a specific variant of Caesarism even by contemporaries,[65] namely *Boulangisme*.[66]

Born in Rennes, Georges Ernest Jean-Marie Boulanger graduated from the *École Spéciale Militaire de Saint-Cyr* and made a career in the French army, fighting not just in the Austro-Sardinian and the Franco-Prussian War, but also actively involved in crushing the Paris Commune in April and May 1871. Highly decorated, including the *Légion d'honneur*, Boulanger was appointed general in 1880 and *Directeur de l'infantrie* at the Ministry of War in 1884. In the same year, he became politically active under the tutelage of Georges Clemenceau (1841–1929) and the Radicals—forming the most leftist part of the French Republicans—, who assured Boulanger's appointment as Minister of War in January 1886. It was in this capacity that Boulanger quickly gained popularity, accelerating his military reform agenda by introducing, among other things, improvements for common soldiers, and also by appealing to revanchism through his uncompromising polemics and concrete actions against Imperial Germany, which gained him the nickname *Général Revanche*. In the wake of the so-called "Schnaebele incident" (April 1887), however, which had almost triggered a war with Germany, and with Boulanger increasingly seen as an embarrassment to the government and an incalculable foreign-political risk, he was dismissed on May 30, 1887.

But his removal as minister sparked extraordinary expressions of public support, with Boulanger obtaining 100,000 votes in the partial election in Seine, even though he did not even stand as a candidate. This fuelled his political ambitions and contributed to the creation of a myth surrounding his person. Boulanger's leaving Paris on July 8, 1887 to take command of an army corps in Clermont-Ferrand—all too obvious an attempt of the government to remove him from Paris—grew into a popular demonstration hitherto unknown in France, with tens of thousands of supporters seeing him off at the Gare de Lyon with posters titled *Il reviendra* ("He will come back"). The initial phase of Boulangist enthusiasm, which found its most distinct expression in such rallies, developed into the creation of an elaborate and powerful political organization. This was made possible by Boulanger gathering support, financial and otherwise, from most different political angles: Bonapartists, but also radical leftists and Blanquists as well as monarchists, all of whom considered the general a powerful vehicle to further their own interests. Following his discharge from the armed forces in 1888 under pretextual allegations of misbehavior, having again a contradictory effect on public opinion and boosting Boulanger's popularity, the "Republican Committee of National Protest" (*Comité républicain de protestation nationale*) was formed under the initiative of a group of radicals and leftist backers of Boulanger as an organizational basis to agitate against the government. In addition, Boulanger gained the support of the "League of Patriots" (*Ligue des Patriotes*), originally founded in 1882 as a gymnastics society to instil patriotic pride into the French youth, but gradually assuming a distinctively political character, and by 1888 openly committed to supporting the cause of the general declared to be the saviour of the country. The League played a formative role in the development of the Boulangist movement not just because of its appeal across the political spectrum, resulting from its underlying nationalist values largely shared also on the political left, but also due to the elaborate organizational structure of the League, which could rely on a nationwide network and a high degree of party discipline.[67]

On that organizational basis, the political campaign of the Boulangists focused on one key demand: the installation of an *Assemblée constituante* to revise the existing constitutional framework of 1875, declared as rotten to the core and the key obstacle standing in the way of reinvigorating the nation; notably with a view to introducing direct presidential elections, which would finally subordinate the executive to the sovereign people and brush away the "Republic of notables" despised by radicals and conservatives alike. The principal claim of *révision* was reinforced by a rhetoric of change and a set of demands best described as populist, lacking a clear ideological focus and addressing workers, peasants, the bourgeoisie and intellectuals alike, as manifest in the electoral manifesto *Programme du Général Boulanger* of April 1888. Underlying the vision of a strong nation with a civilizing mission was the explicit desire for "revenge"—mainly, but not exclusively, on the foreign enemy represented by Germany:

> And then, confident in its mission of progress and civilization, seeing an era of justice, calm, order and freedom open before it, France, rid of those who enslave it, will wait, impassive and serene, for the Right, previously misunderstood and violated, to take resounding Revenge on Force![68]

Characteristic of the Boulangists' political campaigning and contributing to its effectiveness was the active usage of new techniques to mobilize support and voters. Rather than relying on traditional forms of exercising personal influence through networks of local dignitaries, the Boulangist movement made wide-ranging use of publicity through different media: campaign leaflets, paintings and photographs of Boulanger, popular histories, and songs extolling the general's virtues, such as the widely-known *C'est Boulanger qu'il nous faut* ("Boulanger is the One We Need").[69] In addition to these propaganda tools used more generally, campaign efforts were consciously directed at potentially receptive audiences and those electoral districts where success was deemed most likely.

The Boulangists' modern form of political campaigning, together with widespread frustration over the *status quo* in the population and *vis-à-vis* the political establishment in particular, allowed for a number of by-elections victories in 1888. These successes increasingly alarmed the government. Boulanger reached his political peak in late January 1889, when he successfully ran as a deputy for Paris, easily winning the seat with an absolute majority. In view of his overwhelming popularity and support at least in the capital, the success of a potential *coup d'état* seemed anything but impossible, and many of his supporters urged Boulanger to seize the opportunity to violently overthrow the government—a possibility Boulanger's critics had publicly warned of in advance of his election victory.[70] Yet Boulanger procrastinated, insisting that power had to be won legally by sweeping the upcoming general elections in 1889. From that moment on, Boulanger's star fell inexorably and quickly.

The government and his political opponents stepped up their efforts to thwart what was now clearly perceived and portrayed as a direct threat to the parliamentary

Republic. On the one hand, doubts were actively nurtured about the candor of Boulanger's political plans and the instruments applied to that aim. His willingness to abstain from a violent regime change was particularly doubted, as was evident in *Le Paris* on February 12, 1889: "Is it by legal means that Mr. Boulanger can come to power? [...] No! He needs a helping hand."[71] These allegations of a plebiscitary despotism looming behind an allegedly "national" party[72] discredited the republican image of Boulanger and added to the alienation of many of his supporters on the political left, who saw in him a possible military dictator. On the other hand, legal measures were taken. Using the existing law, which banned the activities of secret societies, the *Ligue des Patriotes* was prohibited and dissolved in March 1889. Shortly afterwards, and hand in hand with the prosecution of some of his followers, a warrant for Boulanger's own arrest for conspiracy and other treasonable activities was issued. To the astonishment and disappointment of his supporters, Boulanger fled the country in April 1889. The public reputation of Boulanger and his political movement came under further pressure when the secret royalist funding of the Boulangist campaign became public. Faced with such difficulties, the Boulangists lost the general elections held on September 22 and October 6, 1889, respectively, capturing only 72 of the 576 seats in the Chamber of Deputies.

Demoralized by the defeat as well as by the increasingly remote image of leadership Boulanger presented, the various Boulangist fractions descended into quarrelling among themselves in the aftermath of the national elections, and the Boulangist movement eventually vaporized. Boulanger himself—after more than two years in exile—committed suicide in September 1891 at the grave of his mistress in Brussels, who had died a few months earlier, thus drawing a definitive line under the "Boulanger affair".

Boulanger and the "crisis" associated with him occupied only a short yet immensely important period in French history. Boulangism served as a magnifying glass for pressing challenges and ongoing political as well as social transformation processes at the end of the nineteenth century, with considerable ramifications for future politics and political theory alike. Hereafter, three interlinked aspects of Boulangism making it a "political crossroad of France"[73] will be taken into closer consideration:

1. Ideological and programmatic positioning
2. Mass politics
3. Legacy

Leaving aside those who used the term merely in a polemic way—branding it as being one-sidedly as either "radical left" or "radical right", "progressive" or "reactionary", "promise" or "temptation", depending on their respective political position—, open-minded commentators of Boulangism struggled to find a clear definition of what the characteristic features of the movement were, and placing it in terms of ideology and program. Arthur Meyer (1844–1924), director of *Le Gaulois*, made the following attempt in the newspaper's edition of October 11, 1889:

> Boulangism [...]: a nation's vague and mystical desire for a democratic, authoritarian, emancipatory ideal; the mood of a country that, as the result of

various deceptions by the classical parties in which it had faith in the past, is searching, outside the norm, for *something else*, without knowing what or how, and is rallying all the discontented, the deprived and the vanquished in its search for the unknown. This state [of mind], of which we have seen an explosion recently, is nothing new. [...] In old times, it was [...] Messianism, with its added dimension of religion. More recently, it was Bonapartism, with its added dimension of glory. General Boulanger was born of this state of mind. He did not create Boulangism, Boulangism created him.[74]

Meyer's approach to Boulangism is striking in a number of respects. Above all, it underlines the intricacy, indeed arbitrariness, of the material underpinnings of Boulangism, and that it is not a specific ideology or a clear-cut political organization, but first and foremost a "projection surface" for most diverse popular desires. With Boulangism serving as a melting pot of those parts of the population whose wishes and frustrations were not adequately taken up by the existing political class, Meyer saw parallels between Boulanger and Napoleon III, emphasizing that popular ideas would always give birth to someone who actually embodied them. This, at the same time, made it possible for the phenomenon to be associated with more than one specific person. Despite bearing his name, Boulangism was likely destined to survive him, according to Meyer. And while one may want to add that the same can be said of Bonapartism and the two Bonapartes as well, it seems particularly true of Boulanger, who was a less charismatic and "extraordinary" leader than Napoleon I or Napoleon III.[75]

Boulangism as a movement lacking a clear ideological focus provided a home for all those feeling "disgusted" with the current state of affairs: not just Bonapartists who might see the general as a worthy leader following in the steps of the two Napoleons, but also Radicals, Blanquists, nationalists and monarchists, all of whom were keen to instrumentalize the general for their own ends—a presidential system replacing the existing parliamentarism[76] perceived as bourgeois for the Radicals; a social revolution or at least "socialist Caesarism" for the Blanquists; a war of revenge against Germany to regain Alsace-Lorraine for the nationalists; a restoration of kingship for the monarchists.[77] They shared a fundamental rejection of the existing system, and a deep desire for radical change. Whether in the end Boulangism was a vehicle of more left- or of right-wing policies is difficult if not impossible to answer, and might not even be of central importance. What is crucial, however, is that Boulanger and Boulangism represented a possible key to resolving the problem of mass politics as such for politicians on the political left and right alike.

It is worthwhile considering Boulangism as the trailblazer of modern mass politics in France. As an approach to politics which—more consciously than any other political movement before in France—aimed at actively integrating the people into the political process, Boulangism prefigured the mass movements which were to follow in the twentieth century.[78] One central feature of Boulangist mass politics grew directly out of the movement's ideological and programmatic vagueness, or rather "flexibility": its populism; that is, being able to "speak to the people". Rather than promoting a specific ideology or pre-defined program and trying to gain popular support for them, Boulangism chose a different approach, namely creating its political program around the (assumed) "popular will", being receptive to and taking up the wishes and concerns of the masses. In doing so, Boulangism not only eclipsed previous efforts of oppositional forces to acquire political power through a democratic-electoral process in French history, but was also distinct from the other—clearly ideologically framed—form of fundamental critique of the *status quo* at the time, Marxism, with which it was rivalling.

A second central feature of Boulangist mass politics was the way in which it was staged as a political movement not just *for* the masses, but indeed *of* the masses. Overall, political practice in France even during the Third Republic and among essentially all parties had remained highly elitist, susceptible to charges of venality and clientelism. The Boulangist campaigns in the 1880s, however, outlined an alternative style of political practice by offering the "little man" with no party affiliation potential access to the political process. This alternative style was visibly enacted at Boulangist mass rallies, which for some contemporary observers were more central in lending Boulangism its mystique (out of which the legend of Boulanger could grow) than the electoral-plebiscitary successes of the movement.[79] The French writer Auguste-Maurice Barrès (1862–1923), one of the most dedicated and active apologists of the Boulangist cause, later elevated the Boulangist mass rallies to popular celebrations symbolizing France's national(istic) renaissance; notably in the second of his three-volume *Le Roman de l'énergie nationale*, entitled *L'appel au soldat*.[80] But even if one did not share such exaltation and was more inclined to see the Boulangist crowd as an anarchic mob,[81] the fact that the masses had become a collective political force to be reckoned with could no longer be denied.

At the same time, this was also the key legacy of the Boulangist movement, discernible in two main regards; firstly in French politics itself. Boulangism continued to be present in French politics not only through the enduring political activities of Boulangists, especially in parliament, but also through its having had a lasting impact on the established parties and their policies. While Boulangism had already shaken stereotypical thinking that drew a clear line of distinction between political left and right, republicanism and monarchism, the success of the Boulangist movement shaped policies in the forthcoming decades, especially those of socialists and nationalists. For French socialism, the Boulanger crisis did not just mark the beginning of the government taking greater responsibility in providing social and economic welfare, but also helped trigger a change in the methods used for generating political (mass) support, inter alia by attempts to widen popular contacts and thus allowing decisions of socialist leaders to be informed by more "bottom-up input".[82] In turn, Boulangism was significant for French nationalism in that it marked the final breakthrough of militant nationalism becoming an acceptable and even desirable course of action for politicians across the political spectrum, even if this was only because they understood the manipulatory power of nationalistic rhetoric to activate the populace. Nationalism and populism became intrinsically linked, mutually reinforcing each other.

The second key legacy of Boulangism belongs to the field of political theory. More particularly, Boulanger provided a considerable boost to the "scientification" of debates on political leadership, legitimacy of power, and mass democracy. Even in the preceding few decades, the emancipation of theoretical and analytical dealings with Caesarism (in its various facets) from political debate had become discernible. This received a fresh impetus and became a new focus of attention due to the role played by the "masses" in the Boulangist movement. Perhaps the most noteworthy example of the scholarly "processing" of Boulangism and its integration into a general theory is Gustave Le Bon (1841–1931), whose 1895 work *Psychologie des Foules*—published in English one year later under the title *The Crowd: A Study of the Popular Mind*[83]—is considered to be a seminal work on crowd psychology. While many other contemporaries were content to describe "the masses" in tentative terms, Le Bon committed himself to analyzing crowd behavior especially during the "Boulanger crisis" more systematically, namely with a view to drawing conclusions from his findings for the present and future of mass politics.

In his book, Le Bon argues that crowds are not only the sum of their individual parts, but do in fact form new psychological entities. Based on the underlying assumption later taken on board by Sigmund Freud (1856–1939) that human action is dictated by unconscious impulses, Le Bon holds that as part of the mass, each individual loses his or her capacity to reason and acts mainly affectively. Notwithstanding the cultural and societal level of development, Le Bon regards the absence of (critical) judgement and the presence of excitability and credulity as characteristic features of crowds in general. Tending to think and act one-sidedly (whether it be for the good or the bad), crowds—in the context of which opinion formation was mainly carried out by means of emotional contagion—easily succumbed to suggestions and legends, and were correspondingly susceptible to manipulation by talented demagogues. From the point of view of political leadership, understanding the "mental constitution of crowds"[84] and the forces capable of making an impression on them thus allowed for the creation of promising strategies to win crowds over and convey political ideas, ideologies and doctrines.

In the context of Le Bon's theory of the masses and their (political) behavior, the idea and function of a "master" was seminal:

> As soon as a certain number of living beings are gathered together, whether they be animals or men, they place themselves instinctively under the authority of a chief. In the case of human crowds the chief is often nothing more than a ringleader or agitator, but as such he plays a considerable part. His will is the nucleus around which the opinions of the crowd are grouped and attain to identity. A crowd is a servile flock that is incapable of ever doing without a master.[85]

Leaders, who often started out as "followers", tended to be men of action rather than men of words, "recruited from the ranks of those morbidly nervous, excitable, half-deranged persons who are bordering on madness".[86] While nations had never lacked leaders, only few of them were men of ardent convictions stirring the soul of crowds—people like Peter the Hermit, Luther, Savonarola or the key figures of the French Revolution. In Le Bon's view, those capable of arousing faith, "whether religious, political, or social, whether faith in a work, in a person, or an idea"[87] were the only ones to be considered great leaders of crowds. With faith as one of the most tremendous forces at the disposal of humanity, the influence of "apostles of all beliefs"[88] was accordingly great. In terms of leadership style, leaders of crowds wielded despotic authority not only because despotism was a condition of their obtaining a following, but also because crowds were naturally and inherently servile: "It is the need not of liberty but of servitude that is always predominant in the soul of crowds. They are so bent on obedience that they instinctively submit to whoever declares himself their master."[89]

For leaders to imbue the mind of crowds with certain ideas and beliefs, they had recourse to three main expedients, namely affirmation, repetition and contagion—with imitation being the most central effect of the latter.[90] A key factor for any leader's eventual success, however, was their disposing of what Le Bon termed "personal prestige": "It is a faculty independent of all titles, of all authority, and possessed by a small number of persons whom it enables to exercise a veritably magnetic fascination on those around them, although they are socially their equals, and lack all ordinary means of domination."[91] Napoleon was quoted as a particularly enlightening example of this kind of leader, whose prestige alone had made his historical deeds possible, outlived him and was even discernible to the present day.

One of the principal stepping-stones to prestige—if not *the*—was success. This, however, also made for the disappearance of success almost always followed by the disappearance of prestige: "The hero whom the crowd acclaimed yesterday is insulted to-day should he have been overtaken by failure. The re-action, indeed, will be the stronger in proportion as the prestige has been great."[92] Once a hero had fallen, the crowd would consider him a mere equal and take revenge for having bowed to a superiority that no longer existed. While prestige could disappear quickly by want of success, there was also the possibility of prestige being worn away in a longer process, notably by being subjected to discussion. For that reason, "the gods and men who have kept their prestige for long have never tolerated discussion", since "for the crowd to admire, it must be kept at a distance".[93]

For his age, Le Bon stated an important phenomenon that was new in world history: governments' inability to direct opinion. Previously, governments and a small number of writers and newspapers had constituted public opinion. Yet "to-day the writers have lost all influence, and the newspapers only reflect opinion".[94] More and more, the opinion of crowds was developing into *the* guiding principle in politics, which thus became increasingly "swayed by the impulse of changeable crowds, who are uninfluenced by reason and can only be guided by sentiment".[95] Modern crowds were characterized by selfishness and indifference to everything not linked to their immediate interests—to Le Bon unmistakable signs for a civilization in decay. Yet with the modern man being more and more a "prey to indifference" and unattached to ideals, traditions and institutions also had its positive side, considering the power that crowds possessed: "were a single opinion to acquire sufficient prestige to enforce its general acceptance, it would soon be endowed with so tyrannical a strength that everything would have to bend before it, and the era of free discussion would be closed for a long time."[96]

In the last part of his study, Le Bon turned to different types of crowds and their specificities. According to him, a general distinction was to be made between homogeneous crowds (such as sects, castes and classes) and heterogeneous crowds (such as "criminal crowds", juries or parliamentary assemblies), with the latter being the focus of his interests. In times of mass democracy, one group received particular attention: "electoral crowds", defined as collectivities invested with the power of electing the holder of a certain function.

Of the general characteristics specific to crowds, electoral crowds displayed "but slight aptitude for reasoning, the absence of the critical spirit, irritability, credulity, and simplicity",[97] while the influence of the leaders of such crowds and the elements of successful leadership—affirmation, repetition, prestige, and contagion—were perceptible in their decisions. In Le Bon's eyes, electoral crowds were neither better nor worse than other crowds were, but no forthright rejection of universal suffrage or the underlying principle of popular sovereignty was to be derived from this. From a philosophical point of view, the "dogma of the sovereignty of crowds"[98] was as indefensible as the religious dogmas of the Middle Ages, but at this time it enjoyed the same absolute power that they formerly had enjoyed. Time alone could change this. Yet there was also a rational argument to be applied in favor of universal suffrage, bearing in mind the mental inferiority of all collectivities regardless of composition and intellect: "In a crowd men always tend to the same level, and, on general questions, a vote recorded by forty academicians is no better than that of forty water-carriers." Consequently, even if the electorate was solely composed of persons "stuffed with sciences", they would still be mainly guided by their sentiments and party spirit: "We should be spared none of the difficulties we now have to contend with, and we should certainly be subjected to the oppressive tyranny of castes."[99]

Le Bon was not only making a plea for universal suffrage as a lesser evil than any other conceivable alternative, but also for parliamentary government. It was true that the general characteristics of crowds, including the preponderant influence of only a few leaders, were to be found in parliamentary assemblies as well. Fortunately, however, these characteristics were not constantly displayed. Rather, parliamentary assemblies only constituted crowds at certain moments, and the individuals composing them retained their individuality in a great number of cases. This enabled parliaments to sometimes produce excellent legislative work. Correspondingly, and notwithstanding the fact that parliaments tended to waste money and restrict individual liberties, Le Bon concluded that: "In spite of all the difficulties attending their working, parliamentary assemblies are the best form of government mankind has discovered as yet, and more especially the best means it has found to escape the yoke of personal tyrannies."[100]

Overall, Le Bon's ideas were strongly influenced by personal experience, and by the standards of present scholarship, some of his arguments are no longer tenable. This is especially true for the way in which he stressed race as a determining factor for men's actions and crowd behavior, mirroring the *Zeitgeist* of the late nineteenth and early twentieth century. At the same time, however, it is undeniable that Le Bon's work was not only convincing due to its catchy and sharp-witted character, but was also ground-breaking in terms of its sociological-analytical approach, paving the way for future scientific investigations into problems of mass democracy and politics more generally. What distinguishes Le Bon from other writers of his time is the way in which he painted a sober, realistic and at the same time pessimistic panorama of the masses and political leadership, which forgoes any idealism or obvious political stance.[101] Politics and leadership in an era of crowds are portrayed as being characterized not by elements of rationality or sagacity, but emotionality and manipulation. With crowds described as easily excitable, credulous and merely acting by instinct, the toolset of successful leaders was accordingly: leadership was not about intellect or greatness, but merely ability to supply the masses with illusions. Whoever was able to do this had the prerequisite to become their master. Congruently, since crowds were falling for illusion artists rather than truly great and talented men, there was no need for heroism—a crucial element for uniting leaders and the led—to be real: "It is legendary heroes, and not for a moment real heroes, who have impressed the minds of crowds."[102]

Little could be hoped for, even less expected, from an age in which the masses assumed power, and yet Le Bon was unable to identify a true alternative: not just because the idea of popular sovereignty had turned into a *sine qua non*, but also because the erratic behavior of crowds could not simply be contained by limiting the number of those enfranchised or taking part in the political process. Le Bon therefore propagated an early version of the dictum that democracy—particularly, parliamentary democracy—is the worst form of government, except for all the others.

In conclusion, it can be stated that by the turn of the twentieth century debate on "Caesarism" in the literal sense of the word—while still discernible—played a less prominent role in Europe than half a century before. This was also true for France, where the experience of the fall of the Second Empire had marked a major rupture. The material substance of the Caesarism discourse, however, was anything but gone, becoming instead intertwined with and embedded in broader debates on mass politics and its implications. In the French context, Boulangism is a most enlightening case of the continued potency of "Caesarism" within a new discursive framework, which was not least characterized by increasing disintegration of traditional ideological distinctions.[103] What made Boulangism appealing across the political spectrum was the promise of an authoritarian solution by means of the masses—which, however, did not necessarily indicate their actual ability to take effective part in a democratic process, or even the desirability of any truly democratic involvement.

In Germany, which throughout the nineteenth century had been a hub for discussion revolving around the concepts of Bonapartism and Caesarism, the situation was somewhat different from France. In Germany, too, the question of universal suffrage and how to tackle the repercussions of a mass society more generally had taken center stage by the end of the century, and there was also a similar tendency towards a "scientific" understanding of modern politics. More than in other countries, however, the concept of Caesarism continued to be a central reference point for political and theoretical reflection. This was not least due to the specificities of the German Empire's political system.

6.1.3 Germany

By the late nineteenth century, "Caesarism" had become well-established in German lexica and encyclopaedias. Overall, it remained a negatively connoted term and concept, describing a form of government bordering on illegitimacy, which originally dated back to Julius Caesar, but for which the regimes of Napoleon I and even more

Napoleon III in France were considered modern archetypes. The entry *Cäsarismus* in the thirteenth edition of the *Brockhaus* (1883) is paradigmatic in this regard:

> [...] The term C. has become common to characterize the Napoleonic system. In this sense it means a specific kind of monarchy, which is different from the absolute as well as the constitutional [monarchy] because of its democratic basis and the lack of legitimacy, whose core, however, is a personal, autocratic regime, based on the predominance of administration and the ruthless enforcement of state power. The constitutional competences of the legislative bodies are used for its disguise and it tries to surround itself with the dubious glamour of a self-created aristocracy.[104]

It is noteworthy that entries to both Bonapartism and Napoleonism were missing, thus indicating that by then—at least in the German context—Caesarism had achieved the status of an overriding concept into which these other terms had been entirely merged.[105] This is also demonstrated by the second leading German encyclopaedia of the time, *Meyers Konversations-Lexikon*, the fourth edition of which (1886) exclusively referred to *Cäsarismus*. In comparison to the *Brockhaus* entry, however, the one in *Meyers* put a slightly different emphasis, stressing the populist elements of Caesarism and its underlying principle of popular sovereignty:

> [Caesarism is] that political system which seeks to put a form of rule similar to the Caesarean power of ancient Rome in the place of modern constitutional monarchy. The latest example of C. was the second French Empire of Napoleon III. A related notion within the Caesarist style of government is the respect for a certain amount of popular favor and a certain reliance on the fourth estate, whose interests are promoted with a view to counterbalance the power of the parliamentary-minded bourgeoisie.

Moreover, by projecting popular sovereignty back to antiquity, no fundamental difference between traditional Roman and modern Caesarism could be identified by the author of the entry:

> The only differences between the Roman Caesar [...] and the French Emperor were that the latter was answerable to the nation and at the same time hereditary, the former neither the one nor the other. However, since in both cases the people were constitutionally sovereign [...], Roman imperialism [*Imperatorentum*] could be termed a lifelong presidency, the French Empire a hereditary one.[106]

While the latter was an unconventional interpretation not shared by many other commentators at the time, the assessment of Caesarism resting on a bond between leader and fourth estate to the detriment of the middle classes was a view widely held even in the 1850s and 1860s.

Notwithstanding the fact that reference works in the late nineteenth century mainly referred to French examples for modern instances of Caesarism, similar societal and political challenges made for the relevance of the concept in Germany, too. With the introduction of universal (male) suffrage under Bismarck, the *Reich* had unmistakably become a sort of mass democracy, the consequences of which had to be dealt with—often by means of explicit reference to Caesarism. In the German context, the question of how to forge a bridge between the existing monarchical-constitutional system and the masses was of particular concern. Apart from political journalism and writing, this issue was also actively taken up within the emerging social sciences in Germany.

In 1888, Wilhelm Roscher (1817–1894), together with Gustav von Schmoller (1838–1917) founder of the "Historical School of Political Economy" and known for establishing "absolutism" as an epoch designation,[107] made an attempt to institute "Caesarism" as a scientific and universal category in his *Umrisse zur Naturlehre des Cäsarismus*.[108] In the tradition of ancient constitutional theory and Polybios (200–118 BC) in particular, Roscher outlined a cyclical theory of political rule, the final step of which was Caesarism—essentially understood as a monarchical form of military dictatorship, resulting from a degeneration of democracy, which in turn had grown out of absolute monarchy becoming increasingly mixed with democratic features due to the increase of the middle classes.[109]

Criticizing the arbitrary and inflationary use of the term Caesarism, which was widely abused to discredit any powerful monarchy today, Roscher considered the Janus-like character of *Cäsarismus* "with an extremely monarchical, an extremely democratic face" as its distinguishing feature and particular strength.[110] Unavoidably, however, the democratic face obliged any Caesar—the greatest modern representative of which was Napoleon I—to always strive "to outshine everyone, and especially in such traits that please or impress the Everyman".[111] Failure and defeat were accordingly fatal for Caesaristic regimes, the susceptibility to which Roscher did not limit to France. The fact that thus far France had been the only field of Caesaristic experimentation in the nineteenth century was not ascribed to Caesarism being merely a French phenomenon, a view still held by many of Roscher's contemporaries. Rather, it was due to the nature of the French national character that most of the developments to be experienced by all European peoples took place particularly early and with exceptional speed.[112]

Apart from Roscher's work, which found positive reception and severe criticism alike,[113] another attempt to insert Caesarism into a "natural science" of the state had already been made a few years earlier by the political economist and sociologist Albert Schäffle (1831–1903) in his *Bau und Leben des Socialen Körpers*, published in four volumes between 1875 and 1878, with a revised two-volume edition following in 1896.[114] Therein, Caesarism was described as:

> The product of a long, tiring battle between aristocrats and democrats, rich and poor; from the anarchy of the civil war arose, simultaneously "society-rescuing" and democratic, the ancient Greek tyranny, the Roman imperialism [*Imperatorentum*], the modern Caesarie [*Cäsarie*]. It is the iron emergency tire of an inwardly rotten society. In highest potency, its monocrat finally declares himself God, he becomes *divus* Caesar![115]

For Schäffle, the point of departure for a nation's degeneration towards Caesarism was a monarchical system, the ideal form of which was considered to be its constitutional variant. Characterized by a formal dualism between the crown on the one hand and a representative body on the other, constitutional monarchies were equipped with a built-in "check". This dualism, however, was also the potential source of a constitutional monarchy's fall:

If real opposites are powerfully fixed within this dualism, the constitutional state loses unity and falls victim to [...] powerlessness. A state's recovery from the instability of the power center then regularly ends [...] either with absolutism [*Absolutie*], even in the form of a new dynasty of Caesars, or with the formal overthrow of the monarchy, be it by an aristocratic, be it by a democratic republic.[116]

For constitutional monarchies to have a future, Schäffle formulated a clear condition:

[...] the constitutional hereditary monarchy can extend its life by protecting the fourth estate, in multinational states by protecting the equality of nationalities, as its life has been extended by protecting the third estate. If it fails in this task, then it is threatened [...] by the fate of the Bourbons, reduction to the despotisms of restoration, money and the proletariat (Caesarie), decline in popular rule or decline in the social republic. By granting universal suffrage, further development has already been forced into this alternative.[117]

Despite being formulated in general terms, these comments—together with the warning of universal suffrage being an almost irreversible step towards Caesarism—clearly had the political system of the German Empire in mind, with regard to which both Schäffle and Roscher advocated preserving the *status quo*.

Their respective attempts to incorporate Caesarism into a general explanatory framework sketching the perils to which constitutional monarchies were exposed when faced with democratic ambitions are noteworthy. Yet Dieter Groh is right in his observation that the works of Schäffle and Roscher also marked a step back:[118] while Caesarism became part of socio-scientific theory formation, their studies failed to recognize Caesarism as a potentially original and modern phenomenon, as people such as Tocqueville and Lorenz von Stein had underlined long before. By sticking to the idea that the social and political "nature" of men expressing itself in world history followed a perpetual cyclic process, Schäffle and Roscher—like most other political commentators at the time—contented themselves with adapting traditional notions to new frameworks. Accordingly, they showed great awareness for the vital importance of the social question and its solution for the future of (constitutional) monarchy, but lacked any sense for new notions and concepts of political rule.[119]

Such a sense was clearly demonstrated by Max Weber. His central achievement was the development of a universal "sociology of domination" (*Herrschaftssoziologie*), born under the immediate impression of the Wilhelmine Period, when the idiosyncrasies and snags of the *Reich's* political system were becoming progressively accentuated.

6.2 The Wilhelmine Empire: Caesarism's Absorption into a Sociology of Domination

6.2.1 Wilhelm II and the Political System of the Late *Kaiserreich*

Undoubtedly, the accession to the throne in 1888 of the young Wilhelm II (1859–1941), lacking neither self-confidence nor a sense of mission, and even more the dismissal two years later of the "Iron Chancellor", who had so forcefully shaped Prussian and German politics for three decades, marked a historical caesura.[120] Wilhelm II was considerably different from Bismarck in both style and political priority setting—differences engendering at least initially hopes for a new era to dawn among the wider public. Leaving aside later idealized retrojections of Bismarck's unchallenged and almost transcendental nimbus (to which even the retired *Reichskanzler* added an active part),[121] it must not be forgotten that towards its end not only had most of the reformist spirit of the Bismarckian period vanished in favor of authoritarian-reactionary policies, but also much of the personal popularity of the Chancellor.

It is therefore not surprising that the young Emperor captured more sympathies, hopes and expectations than the old Chancellor was able to do at the time of his discharge.[122] Wilhelm II represented a generational and supposedly also epochal change, which seemed to promise a departure from a parochial past and turning to a bright future. Indeed, there was hope that Wilhelm II would be able to recognize the signs and needs of his times, not least with regard to the ever-more dynamic economic and social transformation processes, towards which Bismarck had demonstrated an increasing lack of understanding.

By 1890, Germany had unmistakably turned into a modern industrial society,[123] with the elites of the economic bourgeoisie (*Wirtschaftsbürgertum*) gaining societal influence, as the educated middle-classes (*Bildungsbürgertum*) had done before them. In several respects, Wilhelm II did pay tribute to the ongoing change of society, for example by actively fostering the sciences (especially natural science and engineering), demonstrating proximity to industry and also cultivating an overall bourgeois personal lifestyle. Moreover, and in line with the nationalistic *Zeitgeist*, Wilhelm II induced a radical shift in foreign policy, replacing Bismarck's *raison d'état* with "nation" and "national glory" as guiding principles of the Empire. This was encapsulated in the dictum of Germany's right to a *Platz an der Sonne* ("place in the sun"),[124] and substantiated by Wilhelm's expansionist colonial policy. Not least with regard to the social question, which so many contemporary observers identified as key, Wilhelm raised expectations for a fresh start and a possible durable settling by launching a number of socio-political initiatives. Especially the so-called "February Decrees" of 1890, promising improved social security and workers' representation,[125] seemed to materialize the hope for an organic union of monarchy and democracy, the fourth estate and the Emperor; in short, the hope for a *soziales Kaisertum* ("social empire"), which Friedrich Naumann so astutely proclaimed in 1900,[126] taking up Lorenz von Stein's idea of a "kingship of social reform" uttered half a century before.

The Emperor's socio-political activism, however, was short-lived, and soon replaced by a decidedly anti-socialist stand, alienating both the Social Democratic Party and the working class. In other respects, too, hopes *vis-à-vis* Wilhelm II were dashed, whose person and policies were perceived as increasingly anachronistic the longer his reign lasted. The reasons for this estrangement are many and varied. One central explanatory variable, however, is Wilhelm's particular concept of rulership.

Right from the beginning, the new Emperor left no doubt that he did not intend to take a back seat in political affairs, as his father and grandfather had done during Bismarck's chancellorship. Instead, he was keen on pursuing a "personal regiment" (*persönliches Regiment*)[127] and ruling with as little external interference as possible. Such an autocratic understanding—based on the idea of legitimist-monarchical legitimacy—inevitably clashed with parliament, which claimed a share in exercising the *Reich's* political power, and would not be reconciled with the postulation of popular sovereignty as ultimate source of state authority. The dilemma of Wilhelm's idea of legitimist-monarchical legitimacy being in stark conflict with the given constitutional framework and its democratic features could only be addressed by the Emperor stylizing himself as epitome of the nation, with a sort of *unio mystica* in place between him and the nation. Wilhelm II went to great lengths to propagate this particular kind of "popular emperorship", which was exclusively conceived as "emperorship on behalf the people", and making himself out to be the "born leader" (in a literal sense of the word) of the German nation. Wilhelm was thus claiming a leadership role in the tradition of the two Napoleons, which Bismarck—despite his actively using Caesaristic tools to achieve political objectives—never had and never assumed to have.

Whether Bismarck—as later alleged in *Mr. Punch's History of the Great War*—had actually warned of Wilhelm's "Caesarism" as early as 1888 is doubtful.[128] What is nevertheless clear is that Wilhelm's political style and approach was fundamentally different from that of Bismarck, and that many contemporaries felt compelled to warn of his Caesaristic intentions or even outward *Cäsarenwahnsinn* ("Caesaristic frenzy") with regard to the Emperor. The most prominent writing of the latter kind was Ludwig Quidde's (1858–1941) *Caligula. Eine Studie über römischen Cäsarenwahnsinn* of 1894, which was a weakly disguised frontal attack against Wilhelm II—causing the conservative *Kreuzzeitung* to denounce and scandalize it as *lèse-majesté*—and one of the most successful political pamphlets of the late Empire, seeing more than 30 editions.[129]

In the end, the Caesaristic ambitions of Wilhelm II failed miserably; to a good part, because the Emperor lacked talent and was unable to compellingly embody the "Caesar" he strived to be, neither intellectually nor with regard to physical appearance. Even his being perceived as a symbol of "progress" did not hold for long. Paradoxically, while Germany did indeed represent an *Emergence into the Modern Era*[130] and an "Augustan age" around 1900, its self-proclaimed Augustus Wilhelm II was more a hindrance than a catalyst for it to unfold. Wilhelm II lacked both zeal and political will for change, especially in those areas where action was required most to make the Bismarckian system fit the needs of the twentieth century. This was with regards to the dominant role of army and bureaucracy in the state, the predominance of the nobility, the strong position of the agricultural sector politically represented by the Junkers, and not least the all-pervasive anti-parliamentarism. Worst of all, during the reign of Wilhelm II more than under Bismarck, the German Empire lacked any clear vision for the future other than the arrogant claim of being a "world power".[131] It is therefore not surprising that while Bismarck became increasingly associated with the modern and even "revolutionary" elements of his policies over time, Wilhelm II was regarded more and more as a defender of the *status quo*. "Wilhelminism" thus appears to be not only as a periodical attribution, but also as the expression of a distinct "mentality" and political culture.

Regardless of whether or not one is inclined to follow the hypothesis of the German *Sonderweg* ("special path") in the development of democratic structures having no equivalent in Europe, it can be stated that by the turn of the twentieth century, the economic and social as well as cultural development of the Empire on the one hand, and its political order together with its corroborating institutions on the other, were less and less congruent and drifting further apart. At the time of Bismarck, the gulf was not yet dramatic or at least sufficiently veiled by the euphoria preceding and following the formation of a German nation state. Wilhelm II however, rather than making efforts to bridge the chasm, contributed to its further aggravation by sticking—after a brief intermezzo at the beginning of his rule—to a strictly preservative course of action, the successful pursuit of which might have overtaxed even a more talented statesman than the Emperor.

Bismarck and Wilhelm II alike were faced with the challenges of a political "mass market", which Bismarck seems to have been able to deal with more effectively. Wilhelm II struggled to respond to the changes of politics and the public sphere concomitant with a mass society, but was at best only partly successful in assuming the role of a "media emperor" and being seen as the shining national hero he wished to be.[132] In his case, too, the mass media proved to be a double-edged sword: while they could be used for propaganda and legitimizing rule and ruler, they could also easily turn into a means for criticizing the established order and its representatives, and strip the monarchy of any remaining aura of dignity and "divine nature" it still might dispose of. The often very worldly "scandals" of the Wilhelmine age that found their way into the press and were publicly discussed, especially the Harden-Eulenburg affair, are a case in point.

During the reign of Wilhelm II, the problems of the Bismarckian system escalated and turned into a fully-fledged—though not yet open—systemic crisis, which was "as much a crisis of institutions as it was one of values and aims".[133] The two options that offered themselves to bringing the political constitution of the *Reich* in line with an advancing industrial society were: a parliamentarization of the political system towards a parliamentary monarchy with the Emperor serving only as a depoliticized "dignified" component, or resorting to a plebiscitary-Caesaristic model of government. However, Wilhelm II was strictly opposed to the former, and inept of pursuing the latter.

The incapability of Wilhelm II to be the strong political leader, which his understanding of monarchical rule would have required,[134] together with the chronical weakness of German parliamentarism and the *Reichstag* in particular was finally fatal: it made it not only possible for the army to fill the existing vacuum during the First World War and establish a *de facto* military dictatorship under Paul von Hindenburg (1847–1934) and Erich Ludendorff (1865–1937), but also heralded the downfall of dynasty and Empire in 1918.

It was against the background of the systemic and eventually lethal deficits of the Wilhelmine Empire, with the political constitution of the *Reich* (and an Emperor longing to be more than just a constitutional monarch, but unable to be a Caesar) incongruent with its socio-economic setting and modernity more generally, that Max Weber developed his influential political sociology—a sociology, which was not least meant to provide explanations and potential solutions for the problems specific to Germany that in Weber's eyes had centrally to do with a lack of effective leadership.

6.2.2 Max Weber: Sociology of Domination and "Leader-Democracy"

Karl Emil Maximilian Weber (1864–1920), whose comprehensive work has profoundly influenced social theory and research, was politically engaged throughout his life. This is manifest not only in his political activities, but also in his political writings. Weber accompanied the politics of his time, while at the same time receiving central inputs for his oeuvre thereof. One would not be mistaken in claiming that a central part of Weber's political sociology—embedded in his general sociological framework—is a direct reflection of and immediate answer to the experiences of the German Empire (whose existence is largely congruent with Weber's lifespan), and more particularly the deficits of its *politscher Betrieb* (literally: "political enterprise")[135]. Although becoming ever more visible towards the end of the Wilhelmine period, Weber saw these deficits for the most part already immanent in the Bismarckian system. He pinpointed seven faults in particular:[136]

1. the structural "impotence of parliaments";[137]
2. the supremacy of the civil-service apparatus (*Beamtentum*), which guaranteed good administration, but produced "negative policies";[138]
3. the dominance of "parties of political principle" (*gesinnungspolitische Parteien*), having the character of "minority parties";[139]
4. German career politicians being of a deficient type: "They had no power, no responsibility, and could only play a fairly subaltern role as notables, with the result that they were animated yet again by the instincts which are typically to be found in guilds";[140]
5. an authoritarian-style capitalism, suffocating the potential of modern-liberal capitalism;[141]
6. the existence of rivalling and non-transparent "parallel governments", especially towards the end of the Empire in the shape of the Supreme Army Command (*Oberste Heeresleitung*);[142]
7. the fact of a "democracy without a leader, which means: rule by the 'professional politician' who has no vocation, the type of man who lacks precisely those inner, charismatic qualities which make a leader",[143] becoming most evident at the turn to the Weimar Republic.

In tracing the root of these faults and attempting to identify solutions, the concept of *Cäsarismus* assumed a key role.[144] Corresponding to the—at first somewhat surprising—double function ascribed to Caesarism as source of trouble and salvation alike, the term appears in two overlapping, yet at the same distinct contexts:

I.   as a "political combat term" to condense and express criticism of Bismarck's legacy, mainly (though not exclusively) used in Weber's private correspondences, political journalism and public lectures;
II. as an analytical category—often in guise of "modern" and/or "plebiscitary leadership"—to disclose the very nature of modern politics and its needs.

I. Caesarism as a "combat term"

Weber primarily reproached Bismarck for having thwarted the modernization of the Empire's political institutions along the lines of parliamentarism and true democracy through his "Caesarism". While demonstrating appreciation for Bismarck as an outstanding personality and statesman, Weber denounced the Chancellor's political legacy as disastrous for the nation. This was, for example, with regard to the "Caesarist" abuse of universal suffrage for demagogic and reactionary purposes, which Weber had criticized as early as 1884, and which to him—sharing the views of other liberals, such as Hermann Baumgarten or Heinrich von Sybel—threatened to nullify the great achievement of national unification.[145] But the malign influence of Bismarckian Caesarism went far beyond electoral manipulation.

Weber acknowledged that even liberals had considered "Caesarism—government by a genius—the best political organization for Germany", if there were "the slightest chance of some new Bismarck always emerging to fill the highest position", but in accepting that this was impossible had attempted to secure a strong parliamentary and party system capable of "attracting great political talents".[146] Bismarck, however, had frustrated any such attempts by all possible means. His towering status had cast a shadow over the Empire, which did not allow for the political landscape to flourish. In the end his legacy was:

> a nation without any political sophistication, far below the level which in this regard it had reached twenty years before [i.e. 1870]; a nation without any political will of its own, accustomed to the idea that the great statesman at the helm would make the necessary political decisions [...] a nation accustomed to fatalistic sufferance of all decisions made in the name of "monarchic government", because he had misused monarchic sentiments as a cover for his power interests in the struggle of the parties.

And perhaps worst of all: "The great statesman did not leave behind any political tradition. He neither attracted nor even suffered independent political minds, not to speak of strong political personalities."[147] The consequences of Caesarism in its Bismarckian manifestation were all the more disastrous since they had direct power- and geo-political effects: a nation politically immature and institutionally feeble was incapable of pursuing the imperialist *Machtstaatspolitik* ("power politics") necessary for guaranteeing Germany an adequate status in the world, which Weber fiercely argued for throughout his life.[148]

Another point of Weber's criticism of Bismarckian Caesarism concerned its "illegitimacy"—not understood in terms of normatively (and from the outset) "unjust" or "illegal", but in a rather specific "constitutional" sense, hence already pointing to Weber's sociological valorization of the Caesarism concept. In his *Parlament und Regierung im neugeordneten Deutschland* (1918), Weber argued that in an age of mass democracy, the political leader was no longer determined in traditional ways:

> Active mass democratization means that the political leader [...] gains the trust and the faith of the masses in him and his power with the means of mass demagogy. In substance, this means a shift toward the Caesarist mode of selection. Indeed, every democracy tends in this direction. After all, the specifically Caesarist technique is the plebiscite. It is not an ordinary vote or election, but a profession of faith in the calling of him who demands these acclamations.

The Caesarist leader could rise either in a "military fashion, as a military dictator like Napoleon I, who had his position affirmed through a plebiscite", or in a "bourgeois fashion, through plebiscitary affirmation, acquiesced in by the army, of a claim to power on the part of a non-military politician, such as Napoleon III":

> Both avenues are as antagonistic to the parliamentary principle as they are (of course) to the legitimism of the hereditary monarchy. Every kind of direct popular election of the supreme ruler and, beyond that, every kind of political power that rests on the confidence of the masses and not of parliament—this includes also the position of a popular military hero like Hindenburg[149]—lies on the road to these "pure" forms of Caesarist acclamation.

In particular, this was true of the position of the President of the United States, "whose superiority over parliament derives from his (formally) democratic nomination and election"; but the "hopes that a Caesarist figure like Bismarck attached to universal suffrage and the manner of his antiparliamentary demagogy" would point in the same direction, "although they were adapted, in formulation and phraseology, to the given legitimist conditions of his ministerial position". The circumstances of Bismarck's departure from office demonstrated "the manner in which hereditary legitimism reacts against these Caesarist powers".[150]

For Weber, Caesarism of the Bismarckian kind was thus "illegitimate" in a double sense: on the one hand, because it was void of and betrayed the legitimacy of the hereditary monarchical system; on the other, because it was Caesarism of a "pure" and unrestrained form. In other words, it was all about the dosage of Caesarism. Correctly dosed, Caesarism was not just beneficial, but actually the guarantor and a *sine qua non* for the successful functioning of modern political systems. This refers directly to Weber's more analytical usage of Caesarism especially in his scholarly work.

II. Caesarism as an analytical category

In Weber's scholarly work, Caesarism appears as an inevitable accompaniment to modern politics and as its very soul, even though frequently concealed behind the language of "plebiscitary leadership". What makes his theoretical approach both exceptional and appealing are Weber's endeavors to reconcile "Caesarism" and "parliamentarism"—which until then had been almost exclusively regarded as an antithesis—and amalgamate them to guarantee a balanced, stable and durable political order suiting the needs of modernity. To that he adds democracy as a third component. Within his functional model of parliamentary democracy, the triad democracy—Caesarism—parliamentarism finds its counterpart in the three actors demos—leader—parliament, the close interaction of which is deemed indispensable.

Applying his model to Germany, Weber was hopeful that well-conceived Caesarism offered an opportunity to rekindle the country's parliamentarism and overcome the weaknesses of its political system. But how could that possibly be done? The key for Weber was the cultivation of Caesarism in the context of a solid, vibrant and watchful parliamentary-democratic framework, and to use its potential for mass mobilization as well as national leadership. The "parliamentary Caesarism" he had in mind relied on modern mass parties, "the children of democracy, of mass franchise, of the necessity to woo and organize the masses, and develop the utmost unity of direction and the strictest discipline".[151] Its essence, though, was the principle of the free (s)election of the leader:[152] that was the core of democratic rule (*Herrschaft*). Caesarism was no less than *the* central instrument to guarantee the proper selection of the leader. Pointedly, Weber noted in *Wahlrecht und Demokratie in Deutschland*: "'Caesarism' [is] the election of the leader."[153]

Weber acknowledged differences. While the "Caesarist-plebiscitarian element" was always attenuated in a "democratized hereditary monarchy" such as Britain, for example, it was much stronger in a political system like the United States with an elected president.[154] Nevertheless, that element was always present in any system featuring democratic principles. For Weber, the demos entrusted with providing the "plebiscite" for the Caesar-to-be were the masses: true, that demos had to mature in a genuinely liberal-democratic system, characterized by the postulate of self-determination at all levels, but it comprised the entire population, which should enjoy equal (voting) rights. Weber was consequently not only positioning himself against electoral restrictions such as the one represented by the Prussian three-class franchise; he was also distancing himself from those warning—often by invoking Caesarism—of the danger of "the masses" (mainly represented by the fourth estate) and of the demagogues at their head. As early as in 1895 he stressed to that effect: "The danger does not lie with the masses [. . .]. The deepest core of the socio-political problem is not the question of the economic situation of the ruled but of the political qualifications of the ruling and rising classes."[155]

While accepting the masses as a political force, however, Weber was not at all effusive with regard to their abilities for political participation, and in how far they actually should participate. Acclaiming the leader was the prerogative of the masses—this was their main, but essentially only political function. Weber considered it naïve to believe that (mass) "democracy" could be taken literally as "rule *of* the commoners". That "the great political decisions, even and especially in a democracy, are unavoidably made by a few men", Weber considered as a fact only dogmatists could fail to acknowledge.[156] Even the idea of "choosing" the leader *sensu stricto* was a chimera: "it is not the politically passive 'mass' that produces the leader from its midst, but the political leader [who] recruits his following and wins the mass through 'demagogy'".[157] "Mass democracy, ever since Pericles", Weber summarized in *Parlament und Regierung im neugeordneten Deutschland*, "had always had to pay for its positive successes with major concessions to the Caesarist principle of leadership selection".[158]

In the context of Weber's elitist understanding of the relationship between leader and led, which shows very clear resemblances with Le Bon's assessment of crowds,[159] parliament was anything but redundant—provided it was not a parliament of the Bismarckian and Wilhelmine kind, which only fostered negative selection of the political leadership personnel. As a powerful institution, entrusted with the necessary constitutional rights, parliament was an essential means of Caesarist selection and control, also since it was seen as the breeding ground for responsible Caesarist figures, with their personalities forged in parliamentary life. Likewise, parliamentary Caesarism presented a solution for the "Achilles heel of purely Caesarist domination",[160] namely leadership succession, in assuring that succession would proceed without major disruption, preserving continuity and civil liberties.

From the very beginning, Caesarism was a central concern and component of Weber's political sociology, and it remained such until the end of his life. At the same time, however, it can be observed that Caesarism underwent a process of both transformation and integration in his scholarly work.[161] "Transformation" insofar, as Caesarism as a term became interchangeable with a number of other expressions that essentially superseded it: *plebiszitäre Demokratie* ("plebiscitary democracy"), *Führer-Demokratie* ("leader democracy"), *plebiszitäre Führerdemokratie* ("plebiscitary leadership democracy"), or simply *plebiszitäre Herrschaft* ("plebiscitary rule").[162] "Integration" took place—most discernible in Weber's never-finished magnum opus *Economy and Society* (*Wirtschaft und Gesellschaft*)—in the form that Caesarism's cognates themselves became absorbed into (and understood as expressions of) the sociological concept of "charisma".[163] In his late sociological writings, charisma is portrayed as integral to all modern kinds of rule. Caesarism, rendered now as a form of charisma, became "simply the democratic corollary of an overarching and inescapable iron law of leadership"—a move that allowed "Weber's own value commitments" to be "camouflaged under a scientific rubric".[164]

The latter already anticipates part of the answer to the inevitable question why—if it was so central to his political thought—Weber did not simply make Caesarism, but charisma, the leadership concept par excellence. As has already been demonstrated, Caesarism continually proved to be a polemical and highly charged term throughout its chequered history. Its usability as a "neutral" and "scientific" concept was therefore considerably limited from the outset. Moreover, Caesarism was a notion largely confined to the political arena, whereas Weber was aiming for a universal sociological category embracing all forms of leadership. Finally, Caesarism was associated with illegitimacy; if not necessarily in normative terms, in any case with regard to—in Weber's days still predominant—monarchical-hereditary forms of government. Accordingly, Caesarism proved difficult in being incorporated into Weber's classification of *legitime Herrschaft* (with its three "pure" types of "traditional", "legal", and "charismatic" government),[165] which represented a radical break with traditional concepts of legitimacy by moving *Legitimitätsglaube* ("belief in legitimacy") center stage: the criterion of whether a certain form of rule is legitimate or not is whether those ruled accept this rule as just and valid,[166] thus making antique strains of legitimacy sociologically obsolete. Charisma could thus avail itself of characteristics that were usually attributed to Caesarism, while avoiding connotations of illegitimacy or even tyranny that Caesarism had accumulated over time.[167]

Whether born of frustration[168] or curiosity, Weber's work set standards for political sociology in general and the discourse on Caesarism in particular. His combining parliamentarism on the one hand with "plebiscitary leadership democracy" (that is: Caesarism) on the other was directed at specific German conditions and an intellectual answer to a deep anxiety over the Bismarckian legacy, but was suitable for universalization. Negatively, Caesarism stood for all that could go wrong if authoritarian ambitions of *one* (even and especially if a genius) were not restrained in an environment of mass democratization, for which the system of the German Empire was paradigmatic. Positively, however, it affirmed what political leadership could do in an age of the masses if it were given the proper parliamentary conditions in which to thrive.

Notwithstanding the stringency and persuasiveness of his considerations, towards the end of his life, Weber, too, had to experience first-hand the often challenging relationship between theory and practice—particularly in politics. Following the disastrous end of the First World War for Germany and the collapse of the monarchy, political-constitutional reconstruction of the country was a primary need. Weber committed himself both in writing and practically to that reconstruction, the latter also in his function as a member of the constitutional commission under Hugo Preuß (1860–1925), which was entrusted with the preparation of what was to become the Weimar Constitution. In both contexts, however, Weber was forced to realize that the infant Republic was being torn apart by diverging interests, and that Parliament—in which he had placed so much hope—was unable to fulfill its envisaged role. With an overwhelmingly negative stand towards strong personalities at work in contemporary German parliamentarism, as Weber saw it, Parliament could not be expected to supply nor control the leaders the country was in such dire need of. Under the *de facto* conditions of post-war Germany, the earlier synthesis between leader and Parliament crumbled. In the central debates on how the office of the new *Reichspräsident* should be designed, Weber remained faithful to his politico-theoretical oeuvre and advocated a directly elected and powerful officeholder: the right to directly elect the leader was no less than the "Magna Charta of democracy", a president chosen by the people and entrusted with encompassing rights—including dissolution of parliament and initiate referenda—"the palladium of genuine democracy, which does not mean impotent self-abandonment to cliques but subordination to leaders one has chosen for oneself".[169] Yet since Parliament had tumbled as corrective and guardian, the masses alone were left as arbiters of a supreme leader—the very same masses Weber had always described as gullible and emotional.

Witnessing the practical implications of the new Weimar Constitution coming into force on August 14, 1919[170] was not granted to Weber, whose sudden death in June 1920 abruptly ended a productive scholarly life.

6.3 Conclusions

During the second half of the nineteenth century, the transition to mass politics was no longer something to be feared or hoped for, but an irreversible fact. Mass politics found expression in the extension of franchise and means of broader political participation as well as in the emergence of mass parties and movements across the political spectrum. Crowds were not only becoming a prime factor sustaining political organizations; with their entering the political realm, also new political instruments—and indeed new political narratives and myths—had to be forged in order to cope with the *élan* of the populace.

Late nineteenth-century discourse on "Caesarism" lay under the spell of the accelerating "popularization" of politics, which was going hand in hand with far-reaching economic and societal changes unfolding at a speed unseen before in European history. Traditional elements of debate were perpetuated, especially in how far Caesarism was an illegitimate form or style of government, and whether it was a universal phenomenon or specific to certain nations or cultural environments. However, this was under a considerably different framework, with Caesarism more and more becoming an issue of and even synonym for "politics of crowds".[171] This holds true for all national cases that have been taken into consideration, notwithstanding existing differences of focus and the fact that the intensity of debate varied considerably between countries, with Britain, the United States or Italy comparatively less engaged with Caesarism than France or Germany. As before, Caesarism continued to serve a range of specific purposes: that of a negative foil to contrast a desired political condition or underline the qualities of one's own (national) political system *vis-à-vis* others, as manifest in British and German observers denouncing Caesarism as "French", Italians in turn as "French" and "German"; a polemic notion in domestic day-to-day politics, for example to discredit presidents' or prime ministers' power ambitions in the USA and Britain, respectively; yet also as a political promise and potential solution to break down existing power structures and address the deficiencies of a current political system. But in essentially all instances, Caesarism was now seen in the context of mass democratization and its associated challenges. Concomitant with this shift in perception, Caesarism as both a term and concept was being replaced and taken up by others. This can also be witnessed with regard to France and Germany, where Caesarism had played a prominent role in political theory and practice for a long time.

In France during the 1870s and 1880s, Caesarism quickly evolved from a central concept to characterize the Second Empire—be it its assumed strengths or faults—to an integral part of debates on the political life of the Third Republic and its shortcomings. "Boulangism" epitomized the transformation of Caesarism (and Bonapartism) under the specific French conditions in the wake of the second "Napoleonic experience". Growing out of a claimed need for a more democratic style of politics appropriate to the needs of the modem age, Boulangism as a political tool and power-technique appealed to people from different political quarters, including radical left-wingers and monarchists. "Situated between the revolutionary politics of the past and the mass politics of the future, born of the radical left yet issuing in a radical right [...]",[172] its intrinsic versatility found expression in Boulangism contributing to the rise of (democratic) socialism and (popular) nationalism alike. Thus, though Georges Boulanger was just a short episode in French history, the experience of Boulangism would yield considerable long-term repercussions in French political and intellectual life. Among other things, it fed into—and at the same time generated much of—the emerging social sciences' interest in modern mass politics and leadership, for which Gustave Le Bon is a central representative.

In Germany, developments showed striking parallels to those in France. There, too, the contemporary political environment was the driving force for the "scientification" of debates on modern mass politics. Unlike France, however, it was not the ultimately failed "Caesaristic ambitions" of one general (as well as the movement supporting him) and the challenge they had represented for the existing political order that served as a reflection surface. Rather, it was the existing political-constitutional order itself in its Bismarckian and Wilhelmine version that served this function.

The political system of the *Reich* exhibited a number of structural elements that could be termed "Caesaristic", resulting from the legal and practical dominance of the monarchical principle in the Empire juxtaposed against increasing democratization processes and the weakness of German parliamentarism. In this context, Caesarism—a plebiscitary monarchy—afforded a possible expedient to reconciling monarchical claims to sovereignty and power with a "democratic imperative". The actual form, however, in which Caesarism expressed itself, largely differed between Bismarck and Wilhelm II: while the former had successfully fostered "instrumental Caesarism" as part of the repertoire of *Machtpolitik* in order to achieve concrete political objectives, Wilhelm showed appetite for personal Caesarism, but failed miserably in his desire. Pointedly, the Wilhelmine period can be characterized as an epoch of Caesaristic desire, yet lacking the necessary Caesar, with the Emperor being neither an authentic *Bürger-Kaiser* ("Citizen Emperor")[173] nor a talented populist. In a somnambulistic manner and politically stagnating, with a constitutional system tailored for an autocrat, yet lacking responsible leadership, and the monarchy unable to fulfill the task of lasting "societal integration",[174] the Empire under Wilhelm II steered not only into the catastrophe of the First World War, but also into its own institutional collapse.

It was from the personal experience of the Wilhelmine Empire, in which the deficits immanent in the Bismarckian system became pronounced, that Max Weber drew inspiration for his sociological oeuvre and especially his political sociology. But while his thinking was based on the critical encounter with the specific political and institutional situation in his fatherland, Weber like no other political thinker before him managed to integrate the phenomenon of Caesarism as a centerpiece into an equally compelling and general theoretical framework—an achievement to be aptly condensed to: "from German politics to universal sociology".[175] His role in the theorization of Caesarism and its lasting disentanglement from specific historical cases can therefore hardly be overestimated.

To Weber, Bismarck was the embodiment of a Caesarist ruler—just of the wrong sort, who represented a "pure" and unrestrained version of Caesarism. What proved fatal, however, were much less Bismarck's personal traits than his legacy both personal and institutional. In Weber's eyes, the cruel irony of the state Bismarck established was not only that its leader tolerated no independent politicians as long as he was alive, but also that once the "Iron Chancellor" was dead, there was no one of comparable political ability to replace him. Weber was convinced that political virtues and vices alike were strongly conditioned by institutional factors, and that while political arrangements would not automatically produce great leaders, they could at least facilitate and help cultivate them. It followed therefore that the vital desideratum for Germany was to organize a political system conducive to nurturing leadership qualities and selecting the most gifted leaders. To that aim, Caesarism—the absence of which was unthinkable for Weber in any democratic body politic—was not at all to be removed from the political process. Instead, it had to be carefully nurtured in such a way that those with a vocation for politics could actually practice their art in a manner combining conviction with responsibility. What Weber conceptualized was a functional model of "parliamentary Caesarism".

At its heart was a demos entrusted with the free selection of a leader disposing of charismatic traits; a "Caesar", who—perpetually tested in a democratic process—was subjected to a dynamic bond with the demos. Both were conceived as intrinsically linked in another regard, too: while democratic leadership required both a democratic constitution and a politically interested citizenry, liberty and self-determination of the individual were only to be achieved under the umbrella of Caesaristic-charismatic political leadership. Under the conditions of ever-increasing bureaucratization of all forms of social interaction, only such leadership could guarantee a maximum of political dynamism and an optimum of governance. The third component in Weber's concept was parliament, whose role was twofold: on the one hand, it acted as a second counterbalance to the bureaucratic state administration; on the other, it was the place in which future leaders were "produced", and at the same time the one by which they were controlled and politically framed.

Weber's Caesarism concept was no less than a universal theory of democracy under the conditions of the modern (mass) age. Its thrust, however, was purposively rational. Neither Caesarism nor even democracy were seen as an end in themselves, but mainly as a means to enhance a nation's power. This is one central point of potential normative criticism that can be put against Weber's "plebiscitary leader democracy". Moreover, with hindsight there are a number of analytical shortcomings regarding Weber's theory and conceptualizing of Caesaristic leadership, four of which are particularly worthy of note:[176]

1. Negligence of the complexity and imponderability of politics: Weber paid little attention to the interdependencies between the political system and society, or to those between demos and political leader. Moreover, Weber underestimated the risks inherent in a powerful "Caesar" taking on a life of its own, while overestimating the suitability of democratic competition and parliament for the selection of competent leaders.
2. Distinctively speculative component: The concrete form and functioning of a developed "leadership democracy"—integrating both parliamentary and presidential elements—remained largely untold by Weber, not least since he lacked any clear comparative benchmarks.
3. Reductionist understanding of politics as competition, soliciting allegiance and especially struggle: Weber's understanding that "politics is [...] struggle"[177] and a

"striving to influence the distribution of power between and within political formations"[178] claimed confrontation as the only way to sustainably handle political affairs and provide leadership personnel. He thus neglected the possible shortfalls of a competition-based system—for example candidates lacking public and media impact losing out to those "staging" rather than "doing" politics—and was ignorant of the alternative of a "consensus" and "deliberative democracy".

4. Deficient overall concept of democracy: With a conscious parallelism between parliament and a directly elected leader, Weber opted for an interference-prone political architecture susceptible to latent conflict. His concept of a leadership democracy also lacked clearly defined institutional checks against a unilateral striving for power by either the executive or the legislative body. In an idealistic manner, Weber suggested that the political process itself would guarantee a balance between ruler and ruled, parliament and *Führer*—taking for granted that demos and parliament would be able to muster the required unity and assertiveness if necessary to confront a power-conscious "Caesar" striving for autocracy and dictatorship.

Weber's concept of Caesarism and his democracy theory were clearly not without their faults, yet it seems idle to dwell on them here. Not only, since it is all too easy to raise criticism *a posteriori*, with history and political science having progressed for a century, but also because those faults cannot obscure the intellectual accomplishment of Weber and the innovative nature of his political thinking. It seems justified to claim that Weber marked the final and most decisive break from mainstream dealing with Caesarism in nineteenth-century Europe. The clearest expression of that emancipation is the steering away from the language of illegitimacy, with which Weber's compatriots Roscher and Schäffle and many other thinkers before them, including Auguste Romieu, had essentially characterized Caesarism. Weber, in contrast, erased the normative and condemnatory connotation of illegitimacy as futile (since democracy was just inconceivable without Caesaristic elements) and actually hindering scientific discussion. In his sociological view, Caesarism was genuinely legitimate provided that the ruled believed in the authority of the Caesar and voluntarily complied with his orders.

Weber's analytical and multi-dimensional use of "Caesarism", his reframing of the concept and its active integration into a general synopsis of democracy allowed for a much broader applicability than before. Henceforth, Caesarism was no longer a concept to be exclusively applied to the usual suspects such as the two Napoleons or Bismarck. According to Weber, it could also be used for figures as diverse as the presidents of the United States, a Hindenburg or a Gladstone, all of whom depended on the "trust of the masses rather than that of parliaments" for their political power, durability of rule and legitimacy—notwithstanding the precise technical means through which such trust was obtained.[179] Weber convincingly argued that the real antithesis of modern politics was not parliamentarism vs. Caesarism, but "positive" vs. "negative" Caesarism, leadership democracy vs. leaderless democracy. What he was essentially arguing for was "constitutionalized Caesarism"[180]—one accepting Caesarism as a given fact *and* something beneficial, provided it was institutionally tempered.

But Weber went beyond giving Caesarism a political-democratic meaning; he also "redescribed it in sociological terms under the rubric of charisma, thus stabilizing, and to a degree erasing, a highly contestable idea that now largely disappeared beneath the imposing categories of legitimate *Herrschaft*".[181] Rather than trying to rehabilitate a highly disputed and politicized term for scientific purposes—something also Weber evidently felt unable to do—, he had Caesarism wrapped up in his master concept of charisma, which has had a lasting impact on twentieth and twenty-first century political thought. In so doing, however, Weber also heralded the death knell for Caesarism as an analytical category.

At the time Weber died, the debate on Caesarism was losing the considerable vitality it had enjoyed for most of the nineteenth century. Caesarism gradually disappeared from public discussion, "a once vibrant and visceral term giving way inexorably to specialist usage in political theory and political sociology".[182] The success of the charisma concept on the one hand, Caesarism increasingly turning from common to specialist knowledge on the other, found concrete expression in the former soon becoming incorporated in lexica and encyclopaedias as a modern political concept, while Caesarism was gradually phased out.[183] Irrespective of these conceptual changes, however, the very substance of the Caesarism debate—the question of leadership appropriate to an "age of crowds" and how to reconcile authority and democracy—did not lose any of its acuteness. Instead, nineteenth-century discourse on Caesarism not only found eager—though intricate—reception in political debates during the 1920s and 1930s, but also continued to live on as a central sublayer of political thought throughout the entire twentieth century until today.

7

Outlook: Legacies of Caesarism

While the scientification of the Caesarism discourse in the early twentieth century—closely linked with Max Weber's oeuvre and his attempt at an encompassing "sociology of Caesarism"—induced a turning away from notions and terminologies traditionally used in that context, the intensity of debates now mainly revolving around "leadership", "plebiscitary" or "totalitarian democracy", and "dictatorship" saw an increase rather than a decline in the wake of the First World War. This is by no means surprising. The "Great War" was not just a global conflict of an intensity never seen before in world history, with far-reaching repercussions politically, economically and socially; it also marked a turning point of civilization, which for many contemporaries fundamentally altered the perception of politics and the world more generally—and at the same time increased the appetite for radical (political) solutions to the observed "(identity) crisis", be it real or imagined.

Among the most fervent and influential heralds of a looming "new age" was Oswald Spengler (1880–1936), whose *Der Untergang des Abendlandes* ("The Decline of the West") provided a provocative meta-philosophy of history rejecting Eurocentric and linear concepts of history.[1] The great theme of his two-volume *opus magnum* was a reworking of an older distinction between "culture" and "civilization", with Spengler considering civilization as the result of culture losing its creative impulses and becoming overwhelmed by negative ones. Part of a perpetual cyclical process, "decline" was thus to be seen as the essentially natural termination of an earlier period of prosperity followed by a long-enduring era of decay, yet at the same time also the harbinger of a dawning new "age of culture". In line with this interpretation, which was in sharp contrast to teleological understandings of continuous and inevitable human progress dominating the nineteenth century, Spengler considered Rome as the civilization that followed Greek culture, and the modern West as analogous to Roman antiquity.

In the context of Spengler's edifice of ideas, *Napoleonismus* and *Cäsarismus* were introduced as historical-philosophical notions describing global and atemporal phenomena: "Napoleonism" characterized the "upspringing of formless powers", which introduced the age of civilization, in the modern West embodied by Robespierre and Napoleon Bonaparte.[2] The "beginning of the age of gigantic conflicts", which Spengler associated with the First World War, later marked the "transition from Napoleonism to Caesarism".[3] Caesarism in Spengler's mind was characterized by "great individual powers" becoming the destiny of entire peoples and cultures,[4] and expressed a degeneration of civilization in which democracy had become subject to manipulation, corruption and despotism. Caesarism marked "the end of the politics of intellect [*Geist*] and money" epitomized by the "world-city" (*Weltstadt*), and returned the world to war, primitivism and "formlessness":

> By the term Caesarism I mean that kind of government which, irrespective of any constitutional formulation, is in its inward self a return to thorough formlessness. [...] all institutions, however carefully maintained, [are] thenceforth destitute of all meaning and weight. Of importance is exclusively the wholly personal power exercised by the Caesar [...] It is the homecoming from a form-fulfilled world into primitivism, into the cosmic-historyless. Biological stretches of time once more take the place of historical periods.[5]

For Spengler, Caesarism grows on the soil of democracy—particularly the emergence of the masses equipped with the right to vote, but always remaining an "object for a subject",[6]—yet "its roots stretch deeply into the soil of blood and tradition". What could be witnessed now, as before in history, was "the final battle between Democracy and Caesarism, between the leading forces of a dictatorial money-economy and the purely political will-to-order of the Caesars".[7]

Spengler's ideologically charged and somewhat esoteric use of "Caesarism" in the framework of a world-historical analysis no longer ascribed much intrinsic analytical value to the term, especially in the understanding of concrete political phenomena, and made for the "Caesarism" concept becoming one of the elements of his work that found least eager reception. By contrast, in identifying an age of decay, characterized by depravity and embodied by a corrupted and degenerated democracy doomed to perish, and suggesting the inevitable need for a fundamental (re-)ordering of things, Spengler had the finger on the pulse of the time.

The widespread understanding of the First World War as a rupture of historical dimensions and the need to rebuild Europe after 1918 provided space for "political experimentation", and increased a susceptibility to authoritarian solutions in particular. This is especially true for the big loser of the War: Germany. Yet the fact that the "anti-democratic discourse" after 1918 was particularly intensive in that European nation in which the debate on Caesarism had been cultivated throughout the nineteenth century more than anywhere else, and in which Hitler was to come to power in the 1930s, inescapably raises the question as to the potential link between Caesarism and another "-ism" that proves no less conceptually challenging: totalitarianism. What is the relationship between the two? Is totalitarianism—especially Fascism and National Socialism—perhaps a radicalized version of Caesarism? Or are they distinct phenomena in their own right?

These questions will be taken up in the following section, with a focus on debates in the Weimar Republic. This enables discussions on the deficits and the possible future of Germany's political system during the late Empire portrayed in the previous chapter to be further pursued.

7.1 From Caesarism to Totalitarianism?

The loss of the First World War was traumatic for Germany in a number of respects, not least intellectually. Not only had Germany's claim to a world status fatally foundered; the War also left a nation economically ruined and politically divided, faced with a perpetuated "cold civil war" even after the revolutionary upheavals of 1918/1919 and the suppression of leftist uprisings. A society torn apart and bogged down with stark social tensions did not bode well for the new Weimar Republic, which from the very beginning was stigmatized by the lost war, and radically challenged both from the political left and right. The Weimar Republic was a democracy that lacked a true democratic spirit.[8] The widespread repudiation of (Western) parliamentary democracy and republicanism is encapsulated in Thomas Mann's (1875-1955) *Betrachtungen eines Unpolitischen*: "Germany as a republic, as a virtue-state with a social contract, democratic popular government and 'complete absorption of the individual in the totality' [...] that would be the horror!"[9]

The unifying element of the fundamental criticism put forward against the Weimar Republic and its institutions from both extremes of the political spectrum was its distinct anti-liberalism. Yet while "liberalism" served as a bogeyman and (negative) combat term both on the political left and on the right, the—often militant—polemics against it and the counter-concepts put forward had a different thrust. While the (radical) political left advocated the ideal of a classless society ending the rule of the bourgeoisie, if required by means of a "dictatorship of the proletariat", the opposition against Weimar from what is usually referred to as the "German right" had a less distinct focus. Nevertheless, it was eventually even more potent than the opposition from the left—and at the same time demonstrates the difficulties of upholding clear-cut left-right distinctions in German politics after the First World War.

Among the currents of "right-wing" opposition against "liberalism" as represented by the Weimar Republic, two large groups can be distinguished: adherents of a more traditional nationalism, adhering to the model of the Bismarckian "power state"; and the representatives of a—for the most part younger—generation receiving much of the impetus for their fight against the new republic from their war experiences, and combining their anti-liberalism with a distinctly anti-bourgeois and anti-capitalist (not to say "socialist") component.

Especially for the latter, the term "Conservative Revolution" has become established in scholarly literature.[10] It indicates a general orientation towards the "past" and "tradition", yet unlike traditional forms of conservatism one explicitly linked with the aim of a revolutionary systemic change. Thus, it is an intrinsically dynamic and modern conception of conservatism, largely based on an "invention" of tradition: what is deemed worth preserving still needs to be created before it can then be maintained. Or, as one of the key representatives of the Conservative Revolution, Arthur Moeller van den Bruck (1896-1925), put it: "conservative is to create things worth preserving."[11] As a matter of fact, many authors of the Conservative Revolution did not advocate a conservative restauration, but a radical renewal of society. Their political thought was not anti-modern, but aimed rather at a different, "German" modernity.

Anti-Westernism, and setting Western liberalism and democracy—often associated with England and France—against a suggested "German political principle", was a distinctive feature of the Conservative Revolution. Its most important conceptual juxtapositions included: constitutional formalism vs. expression of a popular will; anonymous bureaucracy vs. leadership; party interests vs. service to the people; society (*Gesellschaft*) vs. community (*Gemeinschaft*); civilization vs. culture.[12]

Politically, the efforts of the Conservative Revolution were directed at overthrowing the constitutional system of the Weimar Republic in favor of a new state order. These attempts to safeguard *Deutschtum* ("Germandom") against the perils of Western liberalism and democracy were fully compatible and connected with the central features of the older Caesarism discourse: crisis, masses, leader(ship), and authority. In this context, nationalism and authoritarianism were not considered incompatible with (revolutionary) socialism, quite to the contrary, as Ernst Jünger (1895–1998) expressed in June 1926 with regard to the characteristics of the future state: "It will be national. It will be social. It will be able to defend itself. It will be structured authoritatively. [. . .] It is not reactionary, but revolutionary from the bottom up."[13]

Within the overarching anti-liberalism, there were a number of other recurring *topoi*, with anti-parliamentarism and the repudiation of representative democracy being perhaps the most pervasive ones. Anti-parliamentarism at the time—which had a long tradition in Germany, but was by no means specific to Germany alone in the interwar period—needs to be seen against the background of a rapidly changing party system from parties of notables to modern mass parties. The consequences of this transition had been clearly addressed by the sociologist Robert Michels (1876–1936) as early as 1911 in his influential *Zur Soziologie des Parteiwesens in der modernen Demokratie* ("On the Sociology of Political Parties in Modern Democracy"), in which he had formulated his "iron law of oligarchy": any complex political organization, no matter how democratic or representative it may claim to be, eventually develops into a rule by a small elite (oligarchy).[14] These characteristics of mass parties could easily be taken as an argument against modern representative democracy and parliamentarism as a whole, with which such parties were inseparably linked.

Carl Schmitt's *Die geistesgeschichtliche Lage des heutigen Parlamentarismus* (1923) reasoned exactly along these lines: since "in the actual practice of parliamentary business, openness [*Öffentlichkeit*] and discussion have become an empty and trivial formality", parliament as it had developed in the nineteenth century—namely as a political instrument of the bourgeoisie, supposedly based on the principle of general discussion—had "lost its previous foundation and its purpose".[15] For Schmitt, parliamentarism stood in the way of that form of democracy fitting the needs of the industrial age, namely plebiscitary mass democracy. Parliaments in his view were anachronistic institutions no longer suited to expressing a nation's political will. Parliamentarism understood thus, as the product of liberalism in decline, was contrasted with a particular concept of democracy as *volonté générale*—the identity of the ruler and the ruled. It was hence not democracy *per se* which Schmitt and others were fiercely criticizing, but "parliamentary", "party" and "liberal" democracy. Parties were not seen to be a necessary or even useful means for guiding the political process in a society of increasing plurality, but merely as a disintegrating force driven by selfish interests and as such endangering the body politic.[16] According to the protagonists of the Conservative Revolution, a true democracy was hallmarked by the nexus between a "strong leader" and the "masses". The Conservative Revolution invoked the replacement of the contract-based "liberal" society, whose form of government was the parliamentary democracy, by an inwardly—and almost spiritually—united *Volksgemeinschaft* ("people's community"), be it defined by "culture", "blood" or "race". Such an understanding corresponded with an authoritarian, if not totalitarian, conception of the state:

> The people is the unity of those who have lived, who live and who will live; it is a whole that unfolds in generations. One does not grasp the will of the people through the ever more thorough development of a statistical election machinery [...]. It is quite conceivable that the real will of the people [*Volkheit*] be expressed more genuinely in a simple acclamation, in the self-evident and uncontested existence [*Dasein*] of an active political leadership and formation [*Gestaltung*]. The essence of democracy consists in the fact that the people emerge as a political whole. A democracy is only possible among equals, and it does not stop being a democracy when it dominates over unequals within the [same] state and puts them under a lesser law.[17]

Despite its featuring so centrally, however, more often than not the "masses" were perceived negatively by the proponents of the Conservative Revolution, and *Führertum* seen as a means to tame and guide the crowd. Accordingly, while it was consistently stressed that "it is not the form of the state that constitutes a democracy, but the participation of the people in the state", there was rarely any doubt about the ideal of a "guided democracy—not parliamentarism"; one, in which a leader acted "as if his will was theirs and their will his, while in reality he gives them direction".[18] Or, to put it in the words of the Austrian author Karl Anton Prinz Rohan (1898–1975): "Not spineless subordination of followers to the leader's *potestas patris*, but devoted subordination to the brotherly leader, recognised as strongest realisation of themselves."[19]

The ideal of a *Führer-Demokratie* ("leader democracy") manifests a genuinely elitist understanding, with the qualitative principle of leadership destined to prevail against the quantitative principle of majority rule by the masses. Moreover, it reveals a paradox element of the Conservative Revolution: while parliamentary democracy is attacked because of the presumed remoteness from the people of what today might be branded as "the establishment", the Conservative Revolution is arguing for an exclusive rather than inclusive concept of politics itself.

In conceptual terms, by understanding democracy first and foremost as acclamation and by stripping it of its liberal elements, Schmitt and others not only arrive at a sharp conceptual distinction between liberalism and democracy, but actually suggest a sameness—or at least compatibility—between democracy and dictatorship. Accordingly, also the terminological construct "democratic dictatorship" was not perceived as a contradiction in terms, as Edgar Julius Jung (1894–1934) outlined in his programmatic work *Die Herrschaft der Minderwertigen*: "The call for a democratic dictatorship is understandable, because such a dictatorship seems suitable for re-establishing the contact between leader and people."[20] Yet while most authors did not go into too much scholarly reasoning in their advocating "right dictatorship", Carl Schmitt aimed to provide a sound politico-theoretical foundation, which deserves closer attention.[21]

Schmitt's *Die Diktatur* (1921) is based on the distinction between "commissarial" dictatorship on the one hand, "sovereign" dictatorship on the other, and focuses on the historical transition of the one to the other in the modern age.[22] While traditional commissarial dictatorship as practised in ancient Rome was limited to emergency circumstances only—characterized by the limitation of its exercise with regard to both time and specified tasks—and merely an instrument to restore the previously existing order that had come to peril, sovereign dictatorship was of a fundamentally different character. According to Schmitt, the latter was inextricably linked with the development of the modern notion of popular sovereignty:

> In the 18th century, an understanding of dictatorship appears for the first time in the history of the Christian West according to which the dictator still remains a commissar, but as a consequence of the constitutive, and not the constituted, nature of the people's power, a direct commissar of the people [*Volkskommissar*]—a dictator who also dictates to his principal [*Auftraggeber*], without ceasing to legitimise himself through that principal.[23]

Unlike its commissarial predecessor, sovereign dictatorship—represented by individuals, but also political bodies like those of revolutionary France—was unlimited in its parameters and essentially set out to establish a completely new order. The central distinction between the two was therefore that while commissarial dictatorship must seek to make itself superfluous, sovereign dictatorship seeks to perpetuate itself. Schmitt accused the "*bürgerliche* political literature"—in as much as it paid attention at all—to completely misconstrue dictatorship. Liberals characterized dictatorship as "personal rule of one", a feature they would consider inherently linked with two others:

> firstly, that this rule is based on consensus of the people, however induced or assumed, and thus rests on democratic foundations; secondly, that the dictator avails himself of a strongly centralized governing apparatus, characteristic of the rule and government of a modern state. Napoleon I is the prototype of the modern dictator within such a conception.[24]

Distinctive for the modern understanding of dictatorship was "the abolition [*Aufhebung*] of democracy on democratic grounds", resulting in that "there is mostly no difference between dictatorship and Caesarism anymore and that [consequently] an essential element, namely [...] the commissarial character of the dictatorship, drops out".[25] Thus, Caesarism was clearly associated with (modern) sovereign dictatorship, yet no longer assumed the role of a central analytical category,[26] but rather served as a placeholder for demonstrating the unreflective usage of dictatorship. This was a clear indication of the turning point of Caesarism's conceptual application, especially marked by Max Weber's work.[27]

What did alarm Schmitt was that the communists with their doctrine of the "dictatorship of the proletariat" were the only ones seeming to take the concept of dictatorship seriously and to recognize its real essence, namely being "a means to reach a certain goal". For that very reason, "because its content is only determined by the interest of the intended outcome, in other words by a set of specific circumstances, [dictatorship] cannot be genuinely defined as the abolition of democracy".[28] Yet while the communists would recognize the purely technical and temporary nature of dictatorship, which for them was the means to implement the transition to communism, one could not neglect the one crucial difference from the classical concept: whereas the dictatorship of the proletariat was a provisional instrument to create a new situation, classical commissarial dictatorship had been employed to restore a previously existing one. All in all, Schmitt considered the communists to be the true heirs of the French Revolution: not just because they represented a radical elite willing to use violent means in line with what they claimed to be a world-historical need and supposedly sanctioned by the masses, to which they could never effectively be held accountable; but also because "the dictatorship of the proletariat, identified with the people, as a transition to an economic situation in which the state is 'withering away', presupposes the concept of a sovereign dictatorship",[29] as Schmitt outlined in the conclusion of *Die Diktatur*.

In Schmitt's later works, his strict distinction between commissarial and sovereign dictatorship is less pronounced. Whether one should go so far as to interpret this as an attempt to formulate a right-wing version of sovereign dictatorship by countering the communist "dictatorship of the proletariat" with a "dictatorship of the nation"[30] remains open to discussion. Nevertheless it is true that Schmitt plays a part in the—previously criticized—fusing of "(commissarial) dictatorship" with "Caesarism" as the expression of a post-revolutionary dictatorship based on popular sovereignty. In *Die Diktatur*, Schmitt had defined dictatorship as "necessarily a 'state of exception'",[31] understood in the literal German sense of *Ausnahme* ("exception"). Yet his famous introductory sentence in *Politische Theologie* (1922) one year later suggested the possibility of a "perpetuated state of exception", and signalled the endorsement of something resembling much more sovereign than commissarial dictatorship: "Sovereign is he who decides on the exception" (*Souverän ist, wer über den Ausnahmezustand entscheidet*).[32] Rather than having a particular actor restoring a previous order in a crisis, the crisis actor now *is* the order itself.

"Exception", and the intermingling of ordinary rule of law with governmental absolutism, is also characteristic of Schmitt's more practical political treatises dealing with the constitution of the Weimar Republic, and the emergency powers of the President of the Reich in particular, including *Die Diktatur des Reichspräsidenten* (1924), *Der Hüter der Verfassung* (1929, extended edition in 1931) and *Legalität und Legitimität* (1932).[33] Therein, Schmitt interprets the Reich as facing a sustained crisis, from which only the plebiscitary-legitimized President might provide salvation: "The President of the Reich stands at the center of an entire plebiscitary-based system of party-political neutrality and independence."[34]

Schmitt derived the right for presidential dictatorial action from Art. 48 of the Weimar Constitution, which granted emergency powers to the *Reichspräsident*,[35] but he was increasingly inclined to justify a—if necessary lasting—state of emergency on the grounds of an assumed pre-constitutional sovereign will of the people rather than the principles enshrined in the constitution. In his writings of the late 1920s and early 1930s—drafted under the impression of a dramatic economic crisis and widespread political unrest—Schmitt argued that since the President of the Reich was elected plebiscitarily by the nation, there was no need for additional checks, constitutional or otherwise; simply because the President as a charismatic leader embodied the unity of the people's sovereign will, thus also legitimizing any emergency action deemed necessary.[36]

According to the logic of Schmitt and others, dictatorship was invested with legitimacy by virtue of the fact that it was associated with "action", that is the exact opposite of the despised "debate" considered the soul of liberal parliamentarism. This was to be condensed in the formula: "Dictatorship is the opposite of discussion."[37] "Action" (that is: "dictatorship"), in turn, was indispensable within a framework in which all true politics was considered to be *Kampf* ("struggle") and based on the distinction between friend and enemy.[38] For, as Schmitt had already written in 1922 about the *Bürgertum* as a merely "deliberating class" in reference to Donoso Cortés: "A class that concentrates all political activity in discussion, in press and parliament, is no match for an age of social struggles."[39] Yet by invoking a struggle for the very survival of the state, it was possible to even justify a dictatorship as legitimate and in fact democratic which for the benefit of some abstract "public weal" and mystic *Volkheit* ("people-ness") did not necessarily represent the will of the entire population: "That is why a dictatorship can be 'democratic' as a temporary necessity, if it corresponds to state necessity and thus to the will of the people [*Volkheit*], even if it does not correspond to the will of all private individuals."[40]

The concept of a powerful "*Führer*" state", entrusted with safeguarding an organically construed body politic, in which the individual was subordinated to the community and its charismatic leader, and in which national authority, heroism and glory should flourish again, inevitably raises the question as to whether the Conservative Revolution prepared the intellectual ground for National Socialism. Undoubtedly, the political thought of the "right" opposition against the Weimar Republic was for a good part compatible with the Fascist and National Socialist belief system. Many representatives of the Conservative Revolution arranged themselves with the Nazi regime after 1933, or even actively corroborated the regime's ideology and policies. Perhaps the most famous example is Carl Schmitt himself, who has earned himself the unflattering title of a "crown jurist" of the Third Reich. Joining the NSDAP in May 1933, Schmitt defended Hitler's seizure of power in *Staat, Bewegung, Volk. Die Dreigliederung der politischen Einheit* (1933) as both legal *and* desirable. Other than having served as the legal framework within which the *Machtergreifung* ("seizure of power") had taken place, however, and for the good of the nation, the Weimar Constitution was a system that had been overcome.[41] Schmitt praised the new "strong state", which "raises and secures the whole of political unity beyond all forms of diversity", and an all-pervasive *Führertum* as its guardian: "The strength of the National Socialist state lies in the fact that from top to bottom and in every atom of its existence it is dominated and permeated by the idea of *Führertum*."[42]

Schmitt's writings and his instrumental use of constitutional history provided a scholarly legitimation for the regime, which he supported unconditionally even in day-to-day politics. After the "Röhm Putsch" in 1934 (also "Night of the Long Knives"),

Schmitt not only defended the purge, but actually described it as imperative and an act of necessity in *Der Führer schützt das Recht*. The judiciary emanated from *Führertum*, and a true leader was always the ultimate judge as well: "The *Führer* protects the law from the worst abuse when, in moments of danger, he creates law directly as supreme judge by virtue of his *Führertum*."[43]

Nevertheless, such propinquity to the Nazi regime—with Schmitt inspiring it to use notions such as *totaler Staat* ("total state") or *totaler Krieg* ("total war")[44]—was not discernible among all representatives of the Conservative Revolution. Many of the right-wing critics of liberalism and representative democracy during the Weimar Republic, who had fought for a plebiscitary-authoritarian "*Führer* state", were in clear opposition to National Socialism. Among them were also Oswald Spengler and Edgar Julius Jung, who despised National Socialism as something spiritless and shallow, criticizing it not least for its obsession with a primitive form of anti-Semitism and political fanaticism— an attitude which they did not change even after Hitler's seizure of power, as Spengler's *Jahre der Entscheidung* and Jung's *Sinndeutung der deutschen Revolution* (both 1933) testify.[45] Rather than Hitler, Spengler and Jung were inclined to see Benito Mussolini as the personification of their anti-democratic and anti-liberal ideals; as one of the "leaders of the future" who epitomized an age in which "[there is] disgust for all liberal and socialist party systems, for every popular form, which always compromises its object, for everything that appears *en masse* and wants to have its say".[46]

Yet the fact that the repudiation of National Socialism could easily go hand in hand with strong sympathies for Italian Fascism underlines the ambivalence of the Conservative Revolution. Criticism of National Socialism was specific and mainly directed against those elements perceived as excesses of crude ideology and political hubris. To many, Fascism appeared to be the better alternative merely because it embodied a more "pragmatic" materialization of the common ideals of anti-liberalism and authoritarianism than National Socialism with its traits of a fully-fledged "political religion"; indeed something closer to conventional "Caesarism" with a powerful and charismatic leader disposing of plebiscitary legitimacy governing the destinies of the nation at its center.

Perhaps the one who most forcefully interpreted and legitimized Italian Fascism along those lines, however, was someone outside the conservative-revolutionary school of thought, and socialized on the left of the political spectrum: Robert Michels, whose political thought dwelled on the social psychology of Gustave Le Bon and the charisma concept of Weber, while at the same time inspiring the work of Weber, with whom Michels was closely related both biographically and intellectually.[47] Even in his well-received work *On the Sociology of Political Parties in Modern Democracy* of 1911— tellingly dedicated to Weber—Michels had been keenly interested in what he termed "Bonapartism" and "(plebiscitary) Caesarism" respectively. *Bonapartismus* to him was:

> the theory of governance by the individual will, originally emergent from the general will but emancipated from it and become sovereign, whose democratic history protects it against the dangers of its anti-democratic present. In [Bonapartism] the rule of the Caesars [...] becomes the real organ of popular sovereignty. [...] It is the synthesis of democracy and autocracy.[48]

Since the elected leader represented the majority of the people, every opposition must be thus undemocratic. Conceived as "infallible", he was entitled—indeed obliged—to crush any opponent of the government with reference to popular sovereignty, "since the chosen one can claim by right to represent popular sovereignty, which has been freely entrusted to him".[49]

In the context of his analysis, Michels—similar to Weber—considered a Caesaristic moment inherent in all modern-day politics, which was characterized by mass democracy and mass parties:

> With democratically sympathetic crowds, Bonapartism always has a favorable chance of success, because it allows them to remain under the illusion of being masters of their masters, and it gives this illusion a legal [*rechtliche*] colour—that is, one suitable to the masses struggling for their "right" [*Recht*]—by introducing the practice of delegation [*Mandatsübertragung*] via the broad masses of the people.[50]

The leader appeared "to be put in his place by a free act of will, indeed at the pleasure of the masses, [and] to be their creature", thus flattering the crowds, yet actually providing the leader with legitimacy and power hitherto unseen:

> By virtue of the democratic process of his election, the elected leader is more qualified to regard himself as an expression of the general will, and as such to claim obedience and submission to his own will, than the born leader of the aristocracy. Whenever being accused of undemocratic behavior, the modern party leaders, like Napoleon, refer to the will of the masses, who would tolerate them, that is, their capacity as elected and chosen ones.

Traditionally, criticism of rulers was countered with the argument that disobeying their orders meant sinning against God; "modern democracy holds that no one may disobey the order[s] of the oligarchs, for in doing so man would sin against himself, against his own will that he has voluntarily transferred to a representative." Leadership in a democracy, Michels reasoned, was built on the fiction of a democratic omnipotence of the masses. As theoretically sound the idea of a free decision of the people might be, practice would prove that: "If not always the election, then reliably the re-election of leaders is executed by such methods and under the influence of such powerful suggestions and other coercive practices [*Zwangsvorstellungen*], that freedom of choice appears considerably impaired."[51]

In 1911, Michels examined Bonapartism mainly out of analytical interest for its featuring traits that were characteristic of the history and present state of modern democratic and revolutionary parties. In the 1920s, however, when he was drawn to Italian Fascism, an increasingly personal sympathy for a Caesaristic form of rule became discernible. Michels, who had become an Italian citizen in 1913, applauded Mussolini's seizure of power in 1922/1923 as an instructive case in point of Weber's charisma concept, and aimed to convey this concept to Italian readers by sketching an idealized image of the nation's new leader. In Mussolini, Fascism—to Michels "absolutely Carlylian" and a "prototypical example of the inner desires of the crowd for heroship"—had found a "leadership character of great style", as he outlined in 1924.[52] Three years later, Michels described Mussolini as the ideal of a "charismatic leader":

> Today, another image of a believer and prophet [...] stands before the eyes of the sociological researcher, that of Benito Mussolini. [...] firstly, he is so to speak the only undisputed leader of a major party; secondly, he is also the dictatorial head of a great people and state. In him, the maxim of the identification of leader and state (L'Etat c'est moi) [...] has reached the maximum of its potential for development in practice.[53]

After taking up a newly created chair at the University of Perugia in 1928— supposedly fostered by Mussolini himself—Michels intensified his efforts to provide scientific validation for Fascism by developing a Fascist theory of corporatism and leadership, and he became an open apologist of the regime and its *Duce*.[54]

Michels' transition from a sharp critic of elitist tendencies in all mass organizations to a worshipper of a Caesaristic *"Führer* principle" embodied by Fascism may appear surprising. However, it is already inherent in his 1911 study of oligarchic tendencies in modern-day politics and his basic understanding of democracy as a deceptive illusion. In such framework, charismatic leadership appeared to be the most authentic and unequivocal transfer of the will of the many to the one, and "Bonapartism"— characterized by the demolition of parliamentarism and the construction of a "strong state"—the only salvation for modern nations from degenerating into non-democracies.

The fact that Michels continued to randomly use "Bonapartism" and "Caesarism" as analytical categories even in his writings of the 1920s and 1930s, while now conscious only to apply the concept of "charismatic leadership" whenever affirming Fascism and Mussolini, underlines two things: the eminent influence of Weber, and the acknowledged inadequacy of those terms as descriptors for concrete contemporary phenomena, be it because of their being so discredited, or because the historical associations evoked by them were deemed unsuitable.

It is, therefore, not surprising that in the propaganda and self-representation of National Socialism and even Fascism connections to Caesar(ism) and Napoleon(ism) were only cautiously established, if at all. In the case of Italian Fascism, the link to ancient Rome was evident in terminological terms alone, and Caesarism played an obvious part in the Fascist vision of the resurrection and the re-establishment of the *Imperium Romanum*. In this context, Mussolini undoubtedly saw himself in the tradition of Caesar and also Augustus,[55] yet at the same time—like Napoleon before him—he seemed to waver between welcoming and rejecting the Caesar label.[56] In the end, going beyond the aim of creating national myths and constructing identity by recalling the splendour and glory of antiquity and stressing direct parallels between the *Duce* and the Roman Caesars—particularly with respect to the concrete organization and exercise of power—remained a rare exception.

In Nazi Germany, actively fostering historical analogies between the *Führer* and "great men" of the past was no less tricky, with the two Napoleons in the focus. Occasionally, during the Third Reich writers set out to describe Napoleon I as a harbinger of a fundamental reshuffling of Europe that was now being accomplished by

National Socialism, and to portray Napoleon III as a "socialist Emperor" and precursor of the National Socialist *Führerstaat*:

> The form of the state was new: an authoritarian and total *Führertum* of the people's Emperor; class interests and previous party-political ideas had drifted so far apart that only through the Napoleonic principle could France be saved from anarchy and decay: prohibition of all parties and rule of the entire interest of the entire people by the person of the non- and supra-partisan emperor. He received his authority by plebiscite from the entire people. [...] Napoleon prevailed in tattered France as a "Messiah of Order".[57]

Yet concomitantly, the shortcomings of Bonapartism were explicitly underlined as to leave no doubt about the historical references being inferior to the historical ingenuity of Hitler, the nation's charismatic[58] leader:

> Napoleon [III] did not achieve, nor even earnestly strive for, consistent integration of the national will and inner connection with his people [...] Napoleon has missed what was crucial, adding the spiritual [*ideelle*] bond to material care.[59]

Similar was the thrust of *Napoleon. Kometenbahn eines Genies* (1942) by the senior Nazi Party official Philipp Bouhler (1899–1945): Bouhler depicted Napoleon I as a model for "Europe's lasting reorganization", endowed him with the nimbus of genius like Hitler, and drew parallels between the history of the Napoleonic Empire and that of the National Socialist *Reich*. Notwithstanding, he discovered a structural difference between the two regimes: Napoleon had lacked "an organization of the [entire] people", which was the "iron foundation" of National Socialism and Fascism alike and guarantor of the "the unconditional execution of the commands of a leader, for the penetration of his will to the very last cells".[60]

Overall, however, parallels between the Bonapartes and Hitler were avoided by partisans of National Socialism: firstly, because of the *topos* of France as Germany's *Erbfeind*; and secondly, because the eventual fall of both Napoleons and their regimes did not seem to be a particularly good omen, even less an historical example worthy of pursuing. Occasionally, National Socialists even felt obliged to explicitly denounce such parallels and the relevance of the "Napoleonic legacy" for National Socialism more generally—manifest, for example, in the historian Walter Frank (1905–1945) vehemently repudiating any comparability of Hitler and Boulanger in 1931,[61] which had been suggested by the Jewish lawyer Bruno Weil (1883–1961) in his *Glück und Elend des Generals Boulanger* (1931).[62]

Reluctance to emphasize congruence of Caesarism and Bonapartism on the one hand, and Fascism and National Socialism on the other, by partisans of the latter was not only based on a fear of negative associations, and due to Caesarism and Bonapartism losing conceptual significance more generally; there was also a sense of peerlessness and singularity of the contemporary phenomena *vis-à-vis* anything world history had seen before, partly rooted perhaps in sheer arrogance, yet also in the genuine conviction that the totalitarian movements of the twentieth century were unlike Caesarism and

Bonapartism, respectively. This is also the gist of one of the few known instances in which "Caesarism" was actively used by Fascist leaders in public appearances, namely Oswald Mosley's (1896–1980) address to the English-Speaking Union in March 1933. In outlining an "anti-determinist" version of Spenglerism and stressing the tremendous progressive implications of "modern science and mechanical development", Mosley described Fascism as a synthesis of left and right adapted to the needs of the modern age—and different from (ancient) Caesarism:

> It is, of course, true that fascism has an historical relation to Caesarism, but the modern world differs profoundly from the forms and conditions of the ancient world. Modern organization is too vast and too complex to rest on any individual alone, however gifted. Modern Caesarism, like all things modern, is collective. The will and talent of the individual alone is replaced by the will and ability of the disciplined thousands who comprise a fascist movement. Every blackshirt is an individual cell of a collective Caesarism. The organized will of devoted masses, subject to a voluntary discipline, and inspired by the passionate ideal of national survival, replaces the will to power and a higher order of the individual superman. Nevertheless, this collective Caesarism, armed with the weapons of modem science, stands in the same historic relationship as ancient Caesarism to reaction on the one hand and to anarchy on the other. Caesarism stood against Spartacism on the one hand and the Patrician Senate on the other. That position is as old as the history of the last two thousand years. But they lacked, in those days, the opportunities for constructive achievement which are present today [. . .][63]

According to Mosley, Fascism's "modern Caesarism"—distinct from ancient Caesarism, but implicitly also nineteenth-century Bonapartism—together with modern science would deliver "order and progress" to the world, and promote the evolution of "Faustian man; a civilization which could renew its youth in a persisting dynamism".[64]

The perception of Fascism and National Socialism as being different from Caesarism is corroborated by post-1945 scholarship on totalitarianism, which in itself is part of Caesarism's broader (intellectual) long-term legacy. Without wanting to enter into the ongoing debate on the usefulness and practicability of the totalitarianism concept as such, the specific features defining totalitarian regimes, and the question in how far certain regimes may or may not be termed "totalitarian" in the light of their political practice,[65] there is widespread consensus in at least one regard: that conceptually as ideal types, totalitarian movements are fundamentally different from autocratic regimes— which is also the thrust of the perhaps most prominent work in the field, Hannah Arendt's (1906–1975) *The Origins of Totalitarianism* (1951).[66] Autocratic regimes, frequently referred to as "authoritarian regimes" in the social sciences, are denoted by the monopolization of political power by a single power-holder aiming to suppress opposition, but otherwise willing to afford society a degree of liberty. In contrast, totalitarian regimes seek to not only gain absolute political power, but also attempt to seize control of virtually all aspects of social life in order to command the thoughts and actions of their citizens completely. In other words, it is the attempt to dominate every aspect of everyone's life with a view to change the world and human nature.

Caesarism throughout the nineteenth century had undoubtedly tended more towards authoritarianism than totalitarianism, both as concrete practice of rule and as politico-theoretical concept. When considering the specific criteria, which scholars have employed to define totalitarian regimes over time, it becomes clear that most criteria are not—or only to a limited extent—applicable to what can be associated with Caesarism. Of the six constitutive and mutually supporting characteristics of totalitarianism pinpointed in the classic 1956 work *Totalitarian Dictatorship and Autocracy* by Carl Joachim Friedrich and Zbigniew Brzeziński, for example, none seems to entirely fit the nineteenth-century Caesaristic regimes and concepts of Caesarism/Bonapartism examined so far:

1. all-encompassing and generally binding ideology aimed at the creation of a new society with strong utopian and pseudo-religious elements;
2. single, hierarchically organized mass party, monopolizing all formal power, intertwined with state bureaucracy and typically led by a dictator;
3. elaborate system of terror, making extensive use of violence against both real and potential enemies to control both the population and party;
4. almost complete state monopoly on the means of mass communication;
5. almost complete state monopoly on weapons;
6. coordinated direction and control of the economy through central state planning.[67]

Against this background, an essential difference between Caesarism and totalitarianism can legitimately be argued for, a view also widely held in specialized literature.[68] Nevertheless, while it would be misleading to consider totalitarianism merely as an offshoot of Caesarism, there is an unmistakable nexus between the two phenomena. Among the things they have in common, the following are particularly noteworthy:

- a distinctive revolutionary component aimed either at reshuffling the *status quo* or, conversely, preserving and stabilizing certain political and social conditions, with the revolution mainly conceptualized as one "from above";
- the justification of crossing boundaries—legal, ethical or otherwise—with reference to a fundamental crisis, manifest, e.g., in the active use (or at least evocation as a possibility) of a coup to trigger a regime change or firming up an already established regime;
- (charismatic) leader figures appearing as "deliverer" or even "saviour" and "political Messiah";
- an ideological-institutional layout connecting authoritarianism with anti-parliamentarism, and streamlining the plebiscitary principle for a largely unrestricted personal rule;
- instrumentalization of a centralist-bureaucratic state apparatus;
- ideological flexibility, borrowing both from the political right and left, and a distinct combination of jingoism and social—or even socialist—policies;
- central importance of programs and programmatic works suitable for a mass market, and active use of (mass) media; in connection herewith;

- aura—and partly also living practice—of a "popular" or "mass movement";
- character of an international movement with trans-national and even global repercussions on public opinion and (foreign) policy.

In short: Caesarism is not totalitarianism. There is, however, considerable compatibility in some respects. Totalitarianism is akin to Caesarism, which by nature does tend towards the totalitarian. Both can be interpreted as an outcome of and reaction to the "modern age": an age dynamizing all aspects of human existence, fundamentally altering existing patterns of social and economic life and challenging traditional forms of legitimacy, with the masses increasingly assuming the role of *the* central political "kingmaker", but also facing alienation due to ever-fewer certainties.

Since the challenges associated with these changes continue to exist until today, it is not surprising that even the traumatic experiences with totalitarian regimes in the first half of the twentieth century have not made issues of authoritarian crisis management and strong charismatic leadership—in a nutshell: "Caesarism"—evaporate.

7.2 Caesarism's Legacy in the Twentieth and Twenty-first Century

As has been demonstrated in the previous section, Caesarism continued to be a relevant and substantial issue after the First World War. By extending the examination of the long-term legacy of Caesarism in the twentieth and twenty-first century beyond German debates of the interwar period and the question of how Caesarism relates to Fascism and National Socialism, two central levels are discernible:

I.   Firstly, Caesarism as an explicit "theoretical-analytical legacy", characterized by attempts—of a more or less elaborate kind—to (re-)use and (re-)interpret Caesarism as a social-scientific concept and tool.
II. Secondly, Caesarism as a more implicit "substantial legacy", living on in transmuted form as a pointed marker of a politico-cultural debate that spotlights fundamental problems and challenges of modern politics.

Let us turn to the "**explicit legacy**" of Caesarism first, in which two main strands can be distinguished: Caesarism used in the context of general political theory on the one hand, and as a tool for comparative study—namely to assess the extent to which politicians of the twentieth and twenty-first centuries have followed the example of nineteenth-century predecessors—on the other.

When it comes to the use of Caesarism for and within **political theory**, it is not surprising that in view of the pervasive historical experience of Fascism, Nazism and Stalinism, studies have tended to assess Caesarism *vis-à-vis* those modes of domination that have come to be called "totalitarian" one way or another. Rarely is there a claim for the concept of Caesarism to be adequate for understanding the enormities perpetrated before and during the Second World War; but often, "totalitarianism" serves the function of an underlying "benchmark" and as the actual motivation to make Caesarism an object of research.

This also holds true for twentieth-century Marxist receptions of Caesarism under the impact of the totalitarian experience, an early example of which is Antonio Gramsci (1891–1937). Penned during his imprisonment in the 1930s, Gramsci's variegated and at the same time truncated reflections on the subject are undoubtedly—and indeed heavily—influenced by Mussolini's rule in Italy, yet are not explicitly concerned with Fascism and do aim at sketching a more universal "political theory" of Caesarism.[69] Gramsci sketched Caesarism as the expression of "the particular solution in which a great personality is entrusted with the task of 'arbitration' over a historico-political situation characterized by an equilibrium of forces heading towards catastrophe".[70] Notwithstanding, the historical formation and significance of Caesarism varied over time and space, with progressive and reactionary forms of Caesarism distinguishable:

> Caesarism is progressive when its intervention helps the progressive force to triumph, albeit with its victory tempered by certain compromises and limitations. It is reactionary when its intervention helps the reactionary force to triumph—in this case too with certain compromises and limitations, which have, however, a different value, extent, and significance than in the former.[71]

For Gramsci, Caesar and Napoleon I were examples of progressive, Napoleon III and Bismarck of reactionary Caesarism—a dualism complemented and partly correlated by the juxtaposition of "qualitative" and "quantitative" Caesarism, the former so innovatory that it marked the transformation of one type of state into another, while the latter represented merely an evolution of the same type of state.[72] Thus, Gramsci considered Caesarism first and foremost to be both a "situation" and the "solution" to that situation, with a "great personality" as the instrument to that aim. Fundamentally deviating from mainstream thinking about Caesarism, however, he qualified his position by suggesting that a "Caesarist solution can exist even without a Caesar, without any great, 'heroic' and representative personality". Parliamentary systems provided a mechanism for such "compromise solutions", and Gramsci cited the British Labour governments of Ramsay MacDonald (1866–1937) as examples, with the degree of Caesarism claimed to have "increased when the government was formed which had MacDonald as its head and a Conservative majority",[73] referring to the British National Government of 1931. Besides his suggesting that even governments without charismatic leaders, and especially coalition governments, could be of a Caesaristic nature, a second feature of Gramsci's analysis of Caesarism is worthy of comment; namely his claim that the conditions of Caesarism after Napoleon III, and its military element in particular, were considerably different from earlier versions of the phenomenon due to the nature of modern (civil) society and the existence of mass organizations:

> In the modern world, with its great economic-trade-union and party-political coalitions, the mechanism of the Caesarist phenomenon is very different from what it was up to the time of Napoleon III. In the period up to Napoleon III, the regular military forces or soldiers of the line were a decisive element in the advent of Caesarism, and this came about through quite precise *coups d'état*, through military actions, etc. In the modern world trade-union and political forces, with

the limitless financial means which may be at the disposal of small groups of citizens, complicate the problem. The functionaries of the parties and economic unions can be corrupted or terrorized, without any need for military action in the grand style—of the Caesar or 18 Brumaire type.[74]

Alluding to the struggle between labor and capital, bourgeoisie and proletariat, Gramsci argued that in the modern world "the equilibrium with catastrophic prospects" occurred not between forces which previously were able to fuse and unite—albeit after what was always a wearisome and bloody process—, but "between forces whose opposition is historically incurable and indeed becomes especially acute with the advent of Caesarist forms".[75] The central lesson to be learnt was the following: since the whole nature of politics had changed, not only were the means different through which Caesarism maintained itself, but also the strategies by which Caesarism could possibly be countered—an assumption feeding directly into Gramsci's principal concern to conceptualize a political theory fitting the complexity of state and society in the modern age.

Gramsci's considerations on Caesarism were inventive, mainly in that he identified it as a structural problem embedded in class struggles and an issue also for parliamentary systems without the need for a proper "Caesar", but also evasive and not particularly practical. Gramsci's work, too, as Weber's before him, is thus symptomatic for Caesarism becoming transformed from a common term of political discussion into a theoretical and at times highly specialized notion.

In line with the trend of it losing out as a common term and being used in more abstract and scientific terms, Caesarism has been processed mainly within political sociology and political science after 1945. In this context, Caesarism frequently features as part of a wider taxonomy of "democracy" and "dictatorship", with varying degrees of importance ascribed to the term, and more or less analytical clarity and depth being demonstrated. Among the richest and most sophisticated efforts to come up with a social-scientific concept of Caesarism is the essay *Notes on the Theory of Dictatorship* of the German-American political scientist Franz Neumann (1900–1954), who died before his manuscript was finished.[76] Unwilling to use "despotism", Neumann's preferred designation of Caesarism is "dictatorship", which he defines as "rule of a person or a group of persons who arrogate to themselves and monopolize power in the state, exercising it without restraint".[77] Outlining three kinds of dictatorship, Neumann depicts Caesarism as the one type occupying an intermediate position between the two others: "simple dictatorship" and "totalitarian dictatorship". "Simple dictatorships" were those in which power was exercised by either an individual or a group disposing of "absolute control of the traditional means of coercion only, i.e., the army, police bureaucracy and judiciary". It was typical of countries and times distinguished by minimal mass involvement in politics and relatively low political awareness, and characterized by only limited social control exercised by the regime.[78] "Totalitarian dictatorships", on the other hand, were all-encompassing. Though Neumann abstained from seeing totalitarian dictatorship as an exclusively modern phenomenon, considering regimes such as those of ancient Sparta or the rule of Diocletian as earlier versions of it, he argued that totalitarian dictatorships would only develop their full potential in the framework of an industrial society and by means of modern technology and science. Largely following Arendt, Friedrich and Brzeziński in characterizing totalitarianism, Neumann, too, considered pervasive social control, a quasi-abolition of any rule of law, and the monopolization of power by one state party together with the absorption of the private sphere into the state apparatus permeated by a strictly hierarchical leadership principle as defining features.[79] Distinct from both "simple" and "totalitarian" were "Caesaristic" dictatorships, which would arise in situations where an individual was "compelled to build up popular support, to secure a mass base, either for his rise to power or for the exercise of it, or for both".[80] What, therefore, distanced Caesarism from "simple" dictatorship was dependence on the masses; or, to put it another way: its being contingent on "democratic" conditions, in which the crowds must be reckoned with as a political force. With regard to totalitarianism, in turn, "Caesaristic dictatorship"—which to Neumann was always personal in form—differed in that it was not an entirely unchecked police state, and that the division between the private and public sphere remained vaguely intact. Neumann admitted that totalitarian regimes indeed possessed a "Caesaristic element", not least in that "the masses' identification with a leader, the hero" was to be witnessed "in all Caesaristic and totalitarian movements". However: "Up to the nineteenth century at least, Caesaristic dictatorship does not necessarily lead to a totalitarian system, nor is the totalitarian state necessarily the result of a genuine Caesaristic movement. Totalitarianism is thus a separate problem."[81]

Ipso facto, Neumann's reasoning implied that in the modern age dictatorship was only possible either in the form of Caesarism or totalitarianism, since with the rise of the masses, "simple dictatorship" had become largely unfeasible. Two other aspects of Neumann's analysis are worth noting as well: firstly, claiming a pan-historical applicability of Caesarism, which was especially, but not exclusively, a phenomenon of the period after the "Great Revolutions" of the eighteenth century; secondly, his emphasizing the role of specific class relationships for the actual function of (Caesaristic) dictatorship, with three possible constellations being distinguished: a) an insurgent, disenfranchised social class aspiring to gain power, with the existing political system being resistant to such aspirations, in which case dictatorship arises as a "conflict resolution" either transitorily (if the aspiring class is politically mature) or indefinitely (if that class is immature); b) a social class threatened by demise striving to preserve its power, in which case dictatorship functions as a guarantor for the preservation of the *status quo*; and c) a "doomed" class aiming to restore their previous pre-eminence, in which case dictatorship is a means to reversing the existing social and economic order to that aim.[82]

Neumann's efforts to establish Caesarism as a politico-theoretical ideal type within a general theory of dictatorship were ambitious and not lacking in sophistication, but they were not without shortcomings either. While one might want to condone certain inconsistencies in the text due to its fragmentary nature, at least one point of criticism nevertheless remains: Neumann's ahistorical approach, with Caesarism almost completely detached from concrete historical contexts and at the same time somewhat arbitrarily applied as a brand to most different figures from antiquity through to the twentieth century.

The ahistoricity of Neumann's essay, partly owing to the need for high abstraction in order to be able to arrive at a "general theory", is symptomatic for "attempts to 'operationalize' Caesarism"—namely by transforming it from a vernacular term of public discussion into an analytical tool of social science—having in general been "largely unsuccessful or implausible on various counts. Some are factually inaccurate or anachronistic; others are too general, or speculative or teleological; still others fail to bear any clear relationship to Caesar himself", as Peter Baehr judges harshly yet on the whole accurately.[83] Overall, such attempts have remained small in number after 1945, manifest also in the fact that "Caesarism" or "Bonapartism" had at best led a shadowy existence in increasing efforts to come up with a modern typology of rule and regime types after the Second World War. By and large, these efforts have two commonalities: firstly, they continue to consider the (nation) state as the main place and frame of political rule, though with "state" increasingly becoming replaced by "political system" in order to go beyond a merely legal understanding of "state", cover also socio-political and socio-cultural dimensions and underline the "organic" interactions of the political with other spheres of modern societies; secondly, modern typologies of political rule are decisively marked by a pervasive dichotomy between democracy and dictatorship.[84] Starting from this general dichotomy, which has become almost hegemonic in the second half of the twentieth century, different subtypes are then derived, frequently following a double division as well: parliamentarian vs. presidential democracy, authoritarian vs. totalitarian dictatorship, etc. Hardly ever, however, does Caesarism play a noteworthy role in these (sub-)typologies or is even mentioned.

One of the few examples is Karl Loewenstein's (1891–1973) influential work *Political Power and the Governmental Process* (1957), wherein he classifies political systems according to the way in which power is applied and controlled, distinguishing between "constitutionalism as the shared, and autocracy as the concentrated, exercise of political power",[85] and convinced that all types of government both of the past and present could be fitted into one of the two categories. Within the group of autocratic systems, Loewenstein not only distinguishes between authoritarian and totalitarian regimes, but also further differentiates, albeit without too much theorizing, "three patterns of autocracy": "absolute monarchy", "neopresidentialism" and "Napoleon's plebiscitary Caesarism".[86] The power mechanisms of the latter, according to Loewenstein, would present "an authoritarian power configuration administratively just as efficient as that of the *Ancien Régime*", which was "hidden behind a façade elaborately decorated in the style of the democratic ideology inherited from the antecedent French Revolution".[87]

As seldom as Caesarism was incorporated into political theory and political typology, as rarely was it employed in the Spenglerian tradition as integral part of a philosophy of history after the Second World War. One exception is Amaury de Riencourt's (1918–2005) *L'ère des nouveaux césars* of 1957.[88] In a variation of Spengler's thought, de Riencourt portrayed the Western World as being on the brink of Caesarism, the result of European "culture" having been superseded by American "civilization" and now in irreversible political, economic and moral decline. Considering European culture (which was ending) and American civilization (which was emerging) merely as different phases of the same society, his argument rested on two key assumptions: one, that expanding democracy would lead "unintentionally to imperialism, and imperialism inevitably end in destroying the republican institutions of earlier days"; second, that the greater the social equality, the dimmer the prospects of liberty, and that "as society becomes more equalitarian, it tends increasingly to concentrate absolute power in the hands of one single man". Against this background, Caesarism for de Riencourt was neither an ideology, nor a specific form or style of government, but the particular expression of a historical development in which human society followed the eternal biological rules of birth, growth, blooming, decaying and eventually death:

> Caesarism is not dictatorship, not the result of one man's overriding ambition, not a brutal seizure of power through revolution. It is not based on a specific doctrine or philosophy. It is essentially pragmatic and untheoretical. It is a slow, often century-old, unconscious development that ends in a voluntary surrender of a free people escaping from freedom to one autocratic master.[89]

With the twentieth century identified as the "dramatic watershed separating the culture behind us from the civilization that lies ahead",[90] Caesarism—the concentration of power in the office and person of the chief executive—would increasingly become an issue, epitomized especially by the United States of America and its president. The dawning "(American) Caesarism" was growing organically, nurtured by internal and international factors alike. As for internal factors, today's Western society and above all American society, following the example of previous civilizations, tended towards democratic equality, producing mediocrity and anonymity in its wake. The more uniform the level of society was, de Riencourt argued, the greater the compact emotional power of the multitude of like-minded people—a power that would need to be "concentrated and personalized by one man who acts as its articulate spokesman". Today, no one else than the "incumbent of the most powerful office in the most powerful state in the world" could be that man.[91] Representative parliamentary bodies such as the US Congress were unsuited to providing an alternative to the masses' craving for a personal leader, since the larger a community would become, the less it would respect an assembly, and the more it would be attracted by an individual man. The underlying reason for this was plain, as de Riencourt outlined:

> The larger the masses, the more they display *feminine* traits by emphasizing emotional reactions rather than rational judgement. They instinctively tend to look for masculine leadership as a compensation—the leadership they can find in a strong man but never in an assembly, which is after all only a reproduction in miniature of their own faults and weaknesses. Instinct always prevails in the end.[92]

Besides internal factors were such of an international nature that accompanied the growth of democratic civilization and prepared the ground for Caesarism, namely "the development of imperial expansion, military might, and foreign commitments"[93] that would further increase the power of the executive body. With regard to the United States, de Riencourt stated that while the trend towards an all-powerful executive was still hidden at the time when Alexis the Tocqueville had examined the US, it was unmistakable today, with the president disposing of extensive powers both at home and in foreign affairs, while Congress was left with very little means to actually check the government and its actions. The first fully-fledged American Caesar was still to come, but the path to that was predestined and more obstacle-free than that of the ancient Caesars, since democratic equality with its concomitant conformism was much more strongly developed in modern societies and especially in the US than anytime before in world history:

> Future crises will inevitably transform [the President of the United States] into a full-fledged Caesar [...] Today he wears ten hats—as Head of State, Chief Executive, Minister of Foreign Affairs, Chief Legislator, Head of Party, Tribune of the People, Ultimate Arbitrator of Social Justice, Guardian of Economic Prosperity, and World Leader of Western Civilization. Slowly and unobtrusively, these hats are becoming crowns and this pyramid of hats is slowly metamorphosing itself into a tiara, the tiara of one man's world imperium.[94]

Overall, the future thus looked bleak to de Riencourt, who nevertheless saw a possible ray of hope: while in modern times man's technical knowledge made it possible for him to either build a heaven on earth or destroy his planet, "his historical knowledge makes it possible, for the first time, to avoid those deadly shoals on which every other Civilization has destroyed itself".[95] In other words: while Caesarism might be inevitable, mankind's responses to it were not predetermined—and might actually be informed not only by the lessons to be learnt from the past, but also by the sheer fact that modern technological power no longer allowed for those mistakes to be made which past civilizations had been free to indulge in.

Slightly more active than in political typology and political philosophy was the use of Caesarism as a tool for **comparative study**—a second strand of Caesarism's explicit legacy in the twentieth century. Characteristically, historical-comparative studies of "concrete" contemporary Caesarism and especially Caesar figures after 1945 were focused on France. These studies were mainly concerned with analyzing the extent to which (French) politicians of the twentieth century had followed the example of their nineteenth century predecessors.[96] Among those who became objects of comparison was Philippe Pétain (1856–1951), whose role as *Chef de l'État Français* from 1940 to 1944 evoked parallels with the two Bonapartes: not only his nimbus of the alleged saviour in a fundamental national crisis, nurtured by a distinct personal charisma resting on past deeds,[97] and his personalized style of government made for Pétain being considered a potential twentieth-century expression of Caesarism; also—and in particular—the "Bonapartist" model of the regime change of 1940 facilitated a comparison with 1799 and 1851, respectively.

More still than Pétain, however, it was another military leader who was associated with Caesarism and seen in the tradition of nineteenth-century French Bonapartism: Charles de Gaulle (1890–1970). Since his establishing the Fifth Republic and becoming its first president, thus making him the most central political figure in post-war France, it has been observed that Gaullism and Bonapartism have a number of elements in common: a quasi-monocratic political regime, supported by a centralized administration; pro-business policies going hand in hand with "social concerns"; a visionary modernization agenda paired with Saint-Simonian technocratic reformism; assertive foreign (and military) policies in the national interest; and attempts to control the media of mass communication. What is particularly characteristic for both de Gaulle and the two Napoleons are their attempts to constitutionalize a crisis(-born) form of strong and leader-centered government—notably by means of plebiscite. In other words, to legitimize the "heroic leader"[98] underlying the new institutional order by appealing to popular sovereignty. The Constitution of the Fifth French Republic, approved in a constitutional referendum on September 28, 1958 with an overwhelming 82.6 percent of the votes in favor, is such that can be associated with Bonapartism and Caesarism.[99] Clearly, a predominance of the executive *vis-à-vis* the legislative branch is discernible, with the President of the Republic disposing of a number of constitutional powers and prerogatives, such as:

- being the guardian of the Constitution and the Nation, entrusted to guarantee the proper functioning of the public authorities and the continuity of the State, national independence, territorial integrity and observance of treaties (Art. 5);
- appointment of the Prime Minister and the other members of the Government (Art. 8);
- presiding over the Council of Ministers (Art. 9);
- promulgation of all Acts of Parliament, combined with a (suspensive) veto (Art. 10);
- dissolution of the National Assembly and calling of new elections (Art. 12);
- commander-in-chief of the armed forces (Art. 15);
- granting of pardon (Art. 17).

Particularly momentous for the role ascribed by the Constitution to the President as a mighty and quasi "extra-constitutional" authority are the provisions of Art. 16, granting him exceptional and almost dictatorial emergency powers whenever "there exists a serious and immediate threat to the institutions of the Republic, the independence of the Nation, the integrity of its territory or the fulfilment of its international obligations", and when the "regular functioning of the constitutional public authorities has been interrupted". In this case, the President is free to "take the measures required by the circumstances". Perhaps the most "Caesarist" feature of the Constitution, however, is the President's right specified in Art. 11 to submit government bills to a referendum, thus putting him in a position to circumvent parliament and directly appeal to the sovereign nation. The significance of that stipulation is manifest in that it has not only been applied to matters of ordinary legislation, but also used as a means to foster constitutional change—famously in 1962 by de Gaulle himself in order to enforce direct election of the President of the Republic. The politically most controversial and eventually successful constitutional referendum of October 28, 1962 further strengthened the executive at the expense of parliament, providing the President with more status and thus greater influence even without infringing upon constitutional powers: with the President now disposing of political legitimacy in his own right and independent of parliament, it was he who could now claim to embody the sovereign will of the entire nation.

In view of a constitutional system deliberately concentrating power and prestige in the president while marginalizing parliament, the French Fifth Republic has frequently been characterized as a "monarchical republic". Emerging as a reaction against the failings—real and perceived—of the parliamentary systems of the preceding Third and Fourth Republics, both of which stood for weakness, instability and lack of leadership, the constitutional order of 1958/1962 gave authority to a potent leader embodying national unity and keeping political factions in check: a "republican monarch"[100] disposing of constitutional powers far greater than those of most other office holders in modern democratic systems, including the President of the United States.

The widespread perception of the Fifth Republic as essentially a "monarchy" made polemical analogy with Bonapartism irresistible, especially among the (leftist) critics of de Gaulle. Most prominently, it was François Mitterand (1916–1996), who in 1964 launched a fierce attack against what he considered *Le coup d'état permanent*.[101] For Mitterand, de Gaulle was the true successor of the two Napoleons, both in spirit and in deed:

> Like the first Bonaparte, he would only hold the crown for himself, and tore it from the hands that brought it to his brow. Like the second Bonaparte, he desired only one form of consent to the omnipotent gesture: the consent of the people. Duly conditioned by the tested formulas of the Napoleonic plebiscite, universal suffrage acquiesced.[102]

Mitterand's political pamphlet harshly criticized the imbalanced constitutional order erected by and around de Gaulle no less than the latter's inability—indeed unwillingness—to fill the promised role of the President as an arbiter, and his dangerously depoliticizing the nation: "by replacing the representation of the nation with the infallibility of the leader, General de Gaulle focuses the interest, curiosity, and passions of the Nation on himself, and depoliticizes the rest."[103] Paradoxically, however, it was later Mitterand himself who, once in office, more than any other of de Gaulle's successors as President of the French Fifth Republic stretched the powers of the office and did his utmost to maintain the aura of the French Presidency as a sacred institution—telling evidence of perceptions being always subject to one's own position, and the attraction of power more generally.

In as much as the powerful and all-pervasive presidency enshrined in the Constitution may be taken as an argument for de Gaulle's Fifth Republic being an institutionalized version of twentieth-century Bonapartism in the tradition of Napoleon I and Napoleon III, it is the Constitution which also demonstrates the challenges of simple historical analogies, and the shortcomings of Caesarism as a tool for comparative study more particularly. Not only were the specific framework conditions under which de Gaulle seized power and had the Constitution of 1958 approved by a referendum considerably different from both the situation in 1799 and 1851. The political system of 1958/1962 also provided for a synthesis of Bonapartist and genuinely republican traditions within a constitutional order that since its establishment has allowed for the actual expression of citizens' democratic free will, rather than just serving as a vehicle for confirming or strengthening personal power of the nation's leader—which was characteristic for the regimes of both Napoleon I and Napoleon III.

The periods of *cohabitation* since 1958, during which the president did not dispose of a majority in parliament and government was thus divided between him and the prime minister, can be seen as an expression of the limits of the office of the Fifth Republic's "Caesar", and his being embedded in a genuinely democratic political culture. This is also manifest in that since de Gaulle's fundamental reshuffling of France's political system, none of the French Presidents has made an attempt to perpetuate power claims beyond their terms, neither by abusing the office's powerful legal instruments—above all plebiscite—nor even less so by violent means. Quite on the contrary: de Gaulle himself set the example for his successors, taking the consequences of the rejection of his proposed reform of the Senate and local governments in a nationwide referendum on April 27, 1969, and resigning the presidency outright one day later, in the middle of his second seven-year term. De Gaulle's voluntarily renouncing power after what he considered a personal vote of no-confidence was in sharp contrast to Napoleon I and Napoleon III, who were swept away by external force—together with their respective regimes as such.

Indeed, what can be considered a *signum* of the Fifth Republic and made it fundamentally different from the Bonapartist regimes of the nineteenth century was the successful and overall stable institutionalization of the political system, which was no longer at the mercy of the *one* individual leader. In other words, the Fifth Republic had found means to resolve the problem of succession in a genuinely leader-centered system—may it be described as Bonapartist or not. De Gaulle himself was keenly aware of the need to allow for at least some moving away "from heroic toward humdrum leadership"[104] in the long run, and his forcing through direct elections of the President in 1962 can be seen from this particular angle. For, as de Gaulle confided to his *aide-de-camp* in April 1961, full of self-confidence, but also anxious about his succession:

> In fact I re-established the monarchy [*sic*!] in my favor; but after me there will be no one to impose himself on the country. I was elected without the need of a referendum; after me it will not be the same. So it will be necessary to establish a presidential system to avoid returning to the struggles of the past. The president of the Republic must be elected by universal suffrage. Elected in this way, he will—whatever his personal qualities—have some semblance of authority and power during his mandate.[105]

The problems arising even in the French setting of "Bonapartism" and "Caesarism" being used as an analytical tool to draw systematic and direct historical comparisons were likely to be even more distinct in other national contexts. It is therefore not surprising that such scholarly attempts have rarely been made.

In a less "scientific" manner, however, the element of (historical) comparison has played out significantly in yet another respect: Caesarism being used not so much as an instrument of research, but a means to describe and often harshly criticize contemporary political conditions and challenges—especially real and perceived deviations from (representative) democratic government—by evoking historical analogies. This refers to the second layer of Caesarism's legacy today, namely its "**substantial legacy**": in its being polemically employed without a conscious analytical purpose, "Caesarism" proves to have become a negative *topos* of political discourse—and indeed political practice—meant to mark crisis phenomena of modern politics. This is, for example, when commentators of US, Russian or Israeli politics and their leadership today talk of "symptoms of creeping Caesarism" and state that "Caesarism is on the rise"[106] in order to capture in a catchphrase certain features and trends of these political systems and their representatives.

After all, its "substantial" legacy may be considered the most sustained bequest of "Caesarism", though that legacy tends to be subdued and harder to discern. More often than not it is of an implicit kind, with the term "Caesarism" (or "Bonapartism") not necessarily used explicitly. Instead, Caesarism lives on in transmuted form, and its "substantial legacy" today mainly crystallizes around a number of alternative key terms and concepts: (charismatic) "leadership"; "direct democracy" favored over parliamentarism (often accompanied by a denunciation of "elites" and/or the "establishment"); ideas of "managed", "directed" or "steered" democracy; and "populism". Contemporary debate on populism in particular takes up many of the elements and concerns present in past discourses on Caesarism, especially those of the late nineteenth and early twentieth century with the advent of universal suffrage and modern mass democracy. Today's populism debate[107] in all its discernible ambivalence, too, reflects the insight of Weber and others that modern (democratic) political systems are neither conceivable nor viable without a Caesaristic moment, given the fundamental shifts in political legitimacy in the post-revolutionary age with politicians increasingly required to prevail in democratic procedures inner-party and beyond, and the gaining and preserving of the masses' trust turning into a *sine qua non* for exercising political power; but that in the end it is the form and intensity of the Caesaristic element which is decisive, the latter being necessary and positive as an instrument to guarantee competent and efficient governance, yet of utmost danger and negative if merely a means to the end of authoritarian (one-man) rule and qualifying (representative) democracy as such. Thus, populism—as Caesarism, too—might be more appropriately characterized in terms of "mirror of democracy"[108] than "counter-democracy".[109]

Among the features of populism, the delineation of a profound "crisis" (real or alleged) combined with a clear concept of an enemy as well as harsh criticism of the existing political elite and/or system by self-proclaimed "underdogs" ("Us against them"), the passionate plea for determined leadership to overcome the status quo by charismatic figures actively instrumentalizing mass media, the discernible ideological indeterminacy with authoritarian traits combined with leftist policies, and the preparedness to reshuffle political institutions and "cross frontiers"—rhetorically and otherwise—are the ones that demonstrate clearest resemblance with Caesarism discourses of the past. It is true that in other respects populism certainly features elements unknown to or less relevant in past debates on Caesarism,[110] and it would be wrong to equate the one with the other. Debates on the potential need or dangers of a "Caesar" in the nineteenth and early twentieth century largely took place in the context of democracy still emerging or solidifying itself, while today's populism is essentially a "post-democratic" phenomenon nurtured by dwindling faith in the problem-solving competence of existing democratic systems, more particularly parliamentary government, its checks and balances and basic freedoms. Moreover, while "personalization of rule" in the context of past Caesarism discourses still clung to reminiscences of traditional monarchical forms of government and could be seen as "rule by one" becoming merely transmuted under the auspices of the Revolution's paradigm of "popular sovereignty", today's *penchant* for strong leaders is first and foremost an expression of politics and polities perceived as too abstract or anonymous becoming "re-personalized".

What both phenomena undoubtedly have in common, however, is discontentment with the *status quo* and the search for *the one*: a figure (charismatic or not)[111] who promises to solve problems, and on whom hopes can be pinned particularly in times of peril and despair—even, or perhaps especially, in an age of popular sovereignty. The search for mastery, which all too often is hardly more than an "illusion of mastery",[112] seems to have been equally as pervasive in the past as it is in the present and is likely to be in the future.

8

Concluding Remarks

Among the most pervasive ideas of political thought in the second half of the twentieth century was that of (Western-style) liberal democracy as a universal model with no other true alternative. In the wake of the Second World War, democracy was increasingly seen not just as the only legitimate, but also as the only viable form of government in the long term, as the norm and *ultima ratio* of human development. Alternative forms of government and rule—most frequently summed up under the generic term "dictatorship"—were more or less explicitly interpreted as exception and aberration. Scholars might acknowledge the development of democracy as an often long and not always successful struggle; however, the main question was essentially why certain societies had become Western-style democracies,[1] while others had not (yet), and how existing dictatorships could effectively be transformed into democracies. In the wake of the so-called "third wave of democratization" from the 1970s onwards,[2] the latter question became formally institutionalized through numerous political transformation theories,[3] which in their overwhelming majority were concerned with conceiving systemic changes as if the transition from absolutism or dictatorship to democracy was a natural one-way street.

It was in the logic of this goal-directed understanding of democracy that on a conceptual level the dichotomy democracy vs. dictatorship became narrowed down to democracy vs. "non-democracy", as in Adam Przeworski's work *Democracy and Development*.[4] The collapse of the communist regimes in Central and Eastern Europe did its part to increase the belief in the superiority of democratic systems, and some theorists—most famously Francis Fukuyama—were even tempted to declare that the progression of human history as a struggle between ideologies was largely at an end, with the world settling on Western liberal democracy after 1989.[5]

The widespread teleological assumption of democracy as the ultimate goal of history—hereby surmising the illegitimacy, defectiveness and transience of "non-democratic" regimes—also put into perspective the progress made in studying authoritarian and dictatorial political systems, and how democracies might turn into such systems. What was disregarded in particular for most of the second half of the twentieth century was the possibility of "democratic dictatorship"; that is, a hybrid system equally featuring elements of democracy and dictatorship. It was only after the millennium with the "Western model" proving to be anything but an "end of history" and instead becoming increasingly challenged, and with liberal and representative democracy globally on the defensive, that scholarly interest has been growing: not only with regard to the threats to democracy due to its immanent deficiencies, but also the political, social and economic conditions under which democracy and dictatorship might potentially become merged. What has become more evident in recent decades is an incongruity between democracy as an ideal type, and democracy's often sobering (political) practice around the globe. This is particularly notable with respect to the principle of popular sovereignty as *the* center of modern democratic statehood, the meaning of which, however, has become largely distorted over time, and which today is instrumentalized by authoritarian and dictatorial systems alike as a source of legitimacy.

The present study has turned to a historical dimension of that field of tension between democracy and dictatorship discernible today, encapsulated by the concept of "(modern) Caesarism". More particularly, it has been concerned with providing a long-term analysis of Caesarism discourse and practice in the nineteenth and twentieth century, with three overlaying features deemed characteristic of this political and politico-theoretical phenomenon:

1. fusing both "dictatorial" and "democratic" elements, namely authoritarian—often charismatic—leadership by one person and an underlying popular legitimization, while aiming to neutralize intermediary representative bodies;
2. gaining full acuteness in the period during and after the American and French Revolutions only, when traditional patterns of political legitimacy shifted towards democratic ones; and
3. being always concomitant with a moment of distinct "crisis".

The aim has not been to come up with a fully-fledged "master theory" of Caesarism, nor to provide a clear-cut set of criteria defining "Caesarism", which would possibly allow certain historical or contemporary political systems and figures to be unequivocally qualified as "Caesarist(ic)". Rather, the overall objective has been to contribute towards pinning down and assessing Caesarism as an inherently dynamic and at the same time elusive phenomenon of public and scholarly discourse. This has been with a view to also demonstrating the intrinsic historicity of contemporary debates on democracy and dictatorship and their compatibility. Thus, two goals have essentially been pursued in parallel: on the one hand, to provide a "history of discourses", i.e., examining why, when, by whom and with which purpose Caesarism and related concepts were used to describe certain rulers and regimes; on the other hand, to distil elements for a historically grounded theory of Caesarism as a natural concomitant of all modern politics from the analysis of past discourses. Past and present equally demonstrate that the appeal of monocratic rule has not necessarily been disappearing in an age devoted to the principle of popular sovereignty. Quite to the contrary: it seems that the rise of the masses has created new leeway and possibilities for individuals striving for power—*prima facie* a paradox that has been at the core of the Caesarism discourse since the late eighteenth century. It is worth recapitulating the main stages of that vibrant discourse, which has seen quite a few shifts.

What has been formative for the genesis and future development of Caesarism both as a concept and as political practice was the age of the French Revolution. This is for two reasons: a) because the question as to the compatibility of the paradigm of popular sovereignty and rule by one arose in an unprecedented manner in that age, and b) because of the person of Napoleon Bonaparte, who shaped future debates on Caesarism by becoming established as a point of reference. Revolutionary language and policies of fundamental political and social renewal clearly heralded a new age, yet were soon confronted with experiences of fundamental "crises": war, economic disorder, domestic terror. Against the background of these experiences, demands for a domestication of the Revolution were soon gaining ground, as was a "negative great parallel" with antiquity, in which contemporary commentators such as Edmund Burke or Joseph de Maistre portrayed the masses as new barbarians, and militarism as a distinctive feature of the time. However, in view of a Revolution increasingly getting out of control and devouring its own children, a potential "new Caesar" could—and indeed was by many—also be seen as "saviour", or at least a necessary evil. While there were other potential candidates for that role, it was Napoleon Bonaparte who eventually assumed it, combining talent, will to power, favorable framework conditions and luck.

The 18 Brumaire and the Consular Constitution following in its wake deviated from prior (constitutional) practice in both the American and French Revolution in as much as the sovereign will of the nation was now primarily projected on the head of the executive branch rather than on a representative legislative body. Correspondingly, plebiscites—rather than elections—assumed the role of central manifestations of the popular will. Napoleon and his regime thus embodied *the* central feature of what was later characterized as and associated with Caesarism: namely the principle that confidence comes from below while authority comes from above—with much of the political system being tailored to ensure that public confidence is given to the right man. With a view to "steer" the popular will, votes mainly served an instrumental purpose and were hardly more than a "seemly façade for dictatorship".[6] The plebiscitary model, which in itself was nurtured by his nimbus as a military genius, allowed Napoleon to steadily increase his authority and power via lifelong Consulate to hereditary Empire. Yet the structural fragility of the Napoleonic system became blatantly obvious when Napoleon's star began to decline from late 1812 onwards, resulting in the Emperor's deposition in 1814. Tellingly, however, Napoleon's demise did not put an end to the "Napoleonic myth".

To the contrary: the more time passed, the more the image of Napoleon as the nation's rescuer, its glorious hero, reformer and visionary, became firmly established. Favorable analogies with other "great" figures of world history and especially Caesar could hence easily be drawn. Simultaneously, the ambivalence of Napoleon, his embodying pre-revolutionary, revolutionary and counter-revolutionary elements at the same time, his representing authority, progressiveness and (relative) stability alike, also allowed for him and his political regime to be seen as a singular and new phenomenon of human history. "Bonapartism" thus became established as a descriptor of a putatively new type of post-revolutionary rule even before the emergence of "Caesarism", underlying the central importance of Napoleon as a person for nineteenth-century discourse on (new) forms of government. Among the first attempting to establish Bonapartism as a new illegitimate model in political theory was Benjamin Constant, who distinguished "monarchy" as a regular regime type from what he termed "usurpation": an illegitimate type embodied in Napoleon Bonaparte, with earlier though not entirely comparable precedents in Oliver Cromwell and Julius Caesar. Yet what contemporaries such as Constant—whose scholarly efforts actually anticipated many of the themes of the later "Caesarism" debate—fundamentally underestimated was the long-term potential immanent in the "Napoleonic model".

Once the "revolutionary crisis" had abated and Napoleon's rule come to an end, the debate on "Bonapartism" started to lose some of its vigor, but by no means its general significance. Even if 1814/1815 might mark a victory of the anti-revolutionary powers, the legacy of the Revolution had to be dealt with by nations and governments throughout Europe. Turning the clock back and pursuing strict neo-absolutist policies was in most cases not an option—or at least only a dangerously daring one, as the Spanish example demonstrated, where the restoration of autocracy by Ferdinand VII was soon followed by the 1820 revolt in favor of restoring the Cadiz Constitution of 1812. Organizing the body politic after the Napoleonic period obviously necessitated some form of reconciliation between Revolution and Reaction.

The most pervasive attempt to that aim was "constitutional monarchism"—that is, making constitutional concessions and allowing for limited political participation of the people through representative bodies, in order to defend monarchical power and above all "monarchical sovereignty" against the revolutionary encroachments of popular sovereignty. Parallels between constitutional monarchism and Bonapartism are discernible, not just at the meta-level of trying to reconcile what appears to be irreconcilable. It can also be argued that in both cases a traditional monocratic element of rule is revered, though with a different emphasis: while constitutional monarchism can be seen as the attempt to merge monocracy with constitutionalism as the one key innovation of the Revolution, Bonapartism aims at combining monocracy with popular sovereignty as the other. Yet while constitutional monarchism—following the example of the French *Charte constitutionnelle* of 1814—developed into a successful European model during the Restoration period, Bonapartism and the underlying principle of the "sovereign nation" faced open resentment by the ruling classes, thus being of almost no practical political relevance in the decades after Napoleon's fall.

At the level of political thought, however, the assessment of Napoleon's regime and Bonapartism was actively taken further, particularly in the context of ongoing debates on the legitimacy of political rule. For the most part, the Napoleonic legacy was seen critically: as the epitome of a specific form of despotism resultant from some misguided "popular will" coinciding with the unrestrained hubris of a political upstart. Nonetheless, the repudiation of Napoleon and the political "radicalism" he represented was not unanimous. In the orbit of Hegelian philosophy, the widely held view that it was "great men" that made history and brought societies forward was further corroborated. This idea found particularly fertile ground during the period of European Restoration, characterized by an increasingly perceived "stagnation" of political and social life. Especially in *Vormärz* Germany, political and national expectations— liberalization, constitutionalization and national unification—remained largely unaccomplished. The longer attempts were made to merely preserve the *status quo*, also by means of oppression, the more frustration grew in the "age of Metternich", and the more positive the image of the former pariah Napoleon became. Especially the movement of the Young Germans advocated radical change, considering a "national dictatorship" to be a possible—perhaps the only—alternative in a situation that was seen as no less than a fundamental crisis both intellectually and politically. What Germany desperately needed in the eyes of contemporary observers like Heinrich Heine was a "Germanic Napoleon".

Even among those repudiating the "Napoleonic model" there was growing awareness after 1815 that Bonapartism might not have been a one-off experience only, but that this phenomenon was intrinsic to and typical of modernity. The perhaps most important analytical contribution to understanding Bonapartism as structurally inherent in post-revolutionary societies was provided by Alexis de Tocqueville. Assessing an age which to him was above all characterized by the paradigm of increasing egality, Tocqueville offered sharp insights into the—for the most part hidden—dialectic of "popular sovereignty" and despotic rule, and the "fragility" of democracy in view of ever-present desires for leadership and guidance.

It was due to the scholarly work of Tocqueville and others that Bonapartism became more and more detached from the person of Napoleon and established as the designation of a particular and new type of regime; that is, Bonapartism turned from a predominantly ideological to a more politico-theoretical term. Accordingly, despite the debate losing some of the immediacy it had enjoyed during and in the immediate aftermath of the Napoleonic age, the 1820s, 1830s and 1840s are most instructive for the dynamic development of a concept that in the wake of the Revolution of 1848 was suddenly in the spotlight again.

The mid-nineteenth century represented the second "formative period" of the discourse on Caesarism. While the Revolution of 1789 and Napoleon Bonaparte had laid the ground—though not yet by explicitly using the term "Caesarism"—and provided it with a lasting spin, the Revolution of 1848 and its repercussions corroborated and redefined the discourse: not just conceptually, with Caesarism becoming durably established besides Bonapartism and slowly superseding it due to the former representing greater universality and smacking less of French exclusiveness; but also in terms of determining the substance and role of Caesarism. Perhaps the single most important factor in Caesarism assuming new meaning and focus was the growing importance of the "social question", which in the early 1800s had not been the vital issue it was a few decades later. With existing political systems becoming increasingly challenged by dynamic socio-economic transformation processes, it was again France that in 1848 assumed the role of a European vanguard, proving the supposed stability of the European Restoration a chimera.

The collapse of the July Monarchy and the establishment of the Second Republic in February 1848—which served as the initial spark for a wave of revolutionary upheavals throughout Europe—inspired hopes of democratization and social change. At the same time, however, political disorder and uncertainty following in the wake of the regime change prompted fears of a radicalization of the Revolution. Public desires for a progressive reformer and crisis manager were thus equally present at the time. The one politician who in the French context was best able to stage himself as embodying both roles *in persona* was again a Bonaparte: Louis-Napoléon. It was not just the aura of his legendary uncle which helped him win the presidential elections in late 1848, but also the fact that he was hard to pin down ideologically, claiming for himself both reformism and conservatism, republican and democratic values as much as stability and order. Meanwhile, in view of a perceived "red menace", the conservatory element of modern political rule perceptibly gained importance in political thought in France and beyond. Fervent calls were made for a "new Caesar" as the only means to prevent ochlocracy and tame the mob by writers like Donoso Cortés and François-Auguste Romieu. Romieu in particular was instrumental in establishing "Caesarism" as an integral part of political debate, describing *Césarisme* as a modern rule of force indispensable in view of impending civil war. Napoleon's *coup d'état* of December 1851 and the Second Empire emerging from it were almost instantly labelled with this new terminology, which hence became swiftly prominent throughout Europe.

Louis-Napoléon's seizure and consolidation of power—resulting in a regime that, following the lead of the first Napoleon, was essentially a plebiscitary monocracy, characterized by a concentration of power in the executive branch monopolized by the Emperor and a largely marginalized parliament—found eager reception in Europe, above all in Germany: there, the events in the neighboring country found particularly strong reception not least due to Germany's unresolved national and constitutional question, which made debate about Caesarism in France a proxy arena for debate about the future of Germany. Similar to France, in Germany, too, strong polemics was distinctive of the contemporary discourse on Caesarism, ranging from strict opposition to a model which some saw as the epitome of "Romanism" opposed to "Germanism" (Gustav Diezel), to favorable endorsement (Constantin Frantz) or even depiction as *the* future model for all of Europe (Philipp Anton von Segesser). At the same time, while there continued to be assessments of Bonapartism and Caesarism as the result of specific, yet non-recurring historical settings, a more "structural"—and accordingly more universal—interpretation clearly gained ground; one acknowledging Caesarism to be the expression of a new socio-economic and political reality characterized by a growing importance of the masses and the proletariat, respectively. Consideration of the phenomenon in these terms, most famously done so by Karl Marx, did its part to further detach Bonapartism[7] and Caesarism from individual figures.

Aside from the sphere of political thought, the constitutional practice of the Second Empire demonstrated the challenges inherent in Caesaristic rule in general, and its institutionalization in particular. A central requirement was to secure democratic legitimacy for the Caesar on a permanent basis: not just on the occasions of national plebiscites being applied to authorize the takeover of power or constitutional revision (1851, 1852 and 1870), but also in regular (parliamentary) elections. In times of universal (male) suffrage either being or at least becoming the norm, and society and economy concurrently undergoing radical change, this was a most delicate endeavor, as demonstrated in France in the 1860s, when even the massive "steering" of elections was no longer a sufficient means to guarantee complacent majorities in parliament. Accordingly, losing electoral support had to be compensated for by a cautious liberalization of the political system, culminating in the constitutional change of early 1870. Yet even a few months later, putative steadiness turned out to be an illusion. Within a remarkably short time, the regime became delegitimized and was swept away by its defeat in the Franco-Prussian War; a war into which Napoleon had not least been forced by the *vox populi* with which his regime identified itself—the very same voice that shortly thereafter did not show any mercy with the Emperor once he had proved unable to embody success and guarantee stability.

Overall, the debate on Caesarism reached a new degree of differentiation and intensity with Napoleon III, also marking increasing difficulty to clearly locate the phenomenon in ideological terms. Diversity was the distinctive element in the assessment of the Second Empire; yet also the political practice of the regime, which did not pursue any clear-cut leftist or rightist policies, but rather a mixture of both, could be characterized in terms of heterogeneity. Nevertheless, there was a clear element of conformity as well both in political thought and practice, manifest in the central role played by the issue of "political legitimacy" and its link both with the "social question" and the "masses" more generally. Clearer perhaps than the reign of Napoleon I, it was that of Napoleon III which threw advantages and disadvantages of Caesaristic government into sharp relief: identifiability of political action and responsibility, swift decision-making processes, relative programmatic flexibility appealing to a fairly broad social basis, and the aura of "heroism" and exceptionality being among the "selling arguments"; transience of personal charisma and stark—eventually often fatal—dependency on public opinion, requiring elaborate mechanisms of propaganda, coercion or corruption, as immanent deficits. In the end, the fate of Louis-Napoléon equally epitomized the potential and dilemma of a new form of authoritarian-monocratic rule relying on and deriving its legitimacy from the masses.

The more the masses became a political factor to be reckoned with, the more Caesarism was likely to become an issue not to be dismissed in traditional monarchical systems either. Germany in the second half of the nineteenth century was a point in case, with debates on "Germanic Caesarism" mainly fuelled by the developments in France, and revolving around the person of Otto von Bismarck in particular.

Though deeply rooted in conservative thought, Bismarck was keenly aware that in view of traditional sources of political legitimacy—and especially the doctrine of divine right—forfeiting appeal and bonding strength in the modern age, the existing monarchical order had to be secured by other means. Against the background of this realization, Bismarck demonstrated a striking openness to pursue "new" and "unorthodox" forms of governance once in power, which placed him in clear opposition to traditional legitimist circles in Germany. Far-sightedly, Bismarck acknowledged the populace to be a political factor which to ignore was simply impossible and indeed dangerous. Yet accepting a political role for the masses did by no means imply their being perceived as an overwhelmingly positive, even less so rational force. Instead, Bismarck—like many others of his time—contended an intrinsic irrationality of the masses and their exertion of a destructive force on existing political systems. At the same time, however, he was deeply convinced that the unreasoning masses would keenly feel a need of order, too—something that for Bismarck was the key explanatory variable for people's readiness to give up on liberties and succumb to Caesarism:

> if they do not recognise this need [of order] *a priori*, they always realise it eventually after manifold arguments *ad hominem*; and to purchase order from a dictatorship and Caesarism they cheerfully sacrifice that justifiable amount of freedom which

ought to be maintained, and which the political society of Europe can endure without ill-health.[8]

Bismarck considered the appetites for dictatorship and Caesarism to be an integral part of a historical cycle: "desire"—"revolution and destruction of the existing order"—"desire for order"—"trading freedom for order". While Bismarck regarded that cycle as most clearly represented by modern French history, he also acknowledged it to be essentially universal and accordingly recognized the risk for Germany if it entered such cycle as well. With a view to reinforcing the existing monarchy standing for order and stability, the "Iron Chancellor" therefore pursued proactive policies aimed at preventing revolution and mob rule by appealing to the masses and strengthening their allegiance to the crown; notably by making occasional concessions to public opinion and the revolutionary legacy, which earned him the title "white revolutionary".[9] While publicly distancing himself from French Bonapartism and not representing Caesarism in any traditional sense of the word, Bismarck nevertheless applied a Caesaristic toolkit that allows for a comparison with Napoleon III; a toolkit that was, among other things, characterized by authoritarian leadership, ideological flexibility mixing conservative and reformist paradigms, and an active social policy. In short: Bismarck actively applied Caesaristic methods without being—or even aiming to be—a Caesar proper.

Discourse on Caesarism, both in politics and political thought, reached its peak in the late nineteenth and early twentieth century, when the consolidation of industrial society and mass democracy became ever-more discernible. As Caesarism was widely seen as being related to or even synonymous with "mass politics", debates at the time had a truly international dimension, even though the concept enjoyed different degrees of relevance and immediacy in different national contexts, and a broad range of meanings and values were attached to it. While negative connotations of Caesarism as an unwanted form of political rule or leadership continued to prevail overall, there was also widespread understanding of Caesarism being a natural and perhaps indispensable concomitant of democratization and universal suffrage. Even contemporaries beyond suspicion of adhering to dictatorship saw some need for a "democratic tyranny",[10] or at least political leaders and the demos establishing closer links with each other. In this vein, Georg Jellinek, for example, considered in his 1906 *Verfassungsänderung und Verfassungswandlung* the ongoing process "that beyond parliaments, beyond these artificial creations of recent times in so many states, the two only indestructible powers of the state begin to face each other directly: government and people" as one of the most crucial of modern history; notably because it was the perhaps most immediate expression of "direct democracy", more of which Jellinek was clearly favorable to.[11]

The two nations in which debates on Caesarism proved the most intense at the time were France and Germany; and it was also there that the most important contributions to the "scientification" of the concept originated. These attempts to incorporate Caesarism into the emerging (social) sciences took place against the background of and were largely informed by contemporary political developments in these two nations; in particular, the experiences of Boulangism in France and Wilhelminism in Germany, both of which expounded the actuality and the challenges of "Caesarism" in a specific way. The case of Georges Boulanger equally demonstrated the susceptibility of the masses to popular *homines novi* and alleged heroes promising radical political change, but also the fragility of personal Caesaristic ambitions. In turn, the reign of Emperor Wilhelm II revealed the fundamental problems emerging from a political system essentially tailored for a Caesaristic leader if that system failed to provide the leader(ship) required by the existing institutional setting in an age of mass politics.

It was with these political experiences in mind that Gustave Le Bon and Max Weber developed their "mass sociology" and "sociology of domination" respectively, in both of which crowds and their leaders featured as essential elements of modern political life. Weber did not content himself with describing Caesarism as naturally belonging to modern societies and went one step further, moving Caesarism to the center of a universal theory of (mass) democracy, the ideal of which was a plebiscitary leadership democracy (*Führerdemokratie*): "above parliament there stands [...] the [...] plebiscitary dictator, who rallies the masses behind him by means of the 'machine' [...]".[12] Considering the conditions of modern society as he understood it, and especially the emotionality of the masses as demonstrated by Le Bon and others, democracy to Weber was simply inconceivable without Caesaristic elements. This allowed for a much broader application of the concept of Caesarism to political figures not usually associated with the term, such as US Presidents or William Gladstone. Weber's political theory also was innovative in that Caesarism was not portrayed in traditional terms as an antithesis of parliamentary government, but rather as something that could function well within a parliamentary system. Ultimately, the envisaged "leader democracy" even asked for no less than a balanced equilibrium of Caesarism and parliamentarism. Such a reinterpretation required Weber to imagine Caesarism quite differently from its Napoleonic or Bismarckian and Wilhelmine manifestations, which to him were examples of ill-conceived Caesarism.

Aware of how historically charged and disputed the term was, however, Weber abstained from vindicating Caesarism, and had the concept rather being wrapped up in his master concept of "charisma" that did not evoke the same emotions and suggested novelty and scholarly objectivity instead. Weber's largely successful efforts to universalize the concept thus also marked the beginning of the end of Caesarism as a vibrant and widespread notion of political discourse, which from the early 1920s onwards increasingly diminished in importance.

Notwithstanding its forfeiting significance as a term and concept, the legacy of Caesarism has been palpable far beyond the early twentieth century, since the fundamental issues fuelling the Caesarism discourse have anything but vanished.

As far as the interwar period and the political debates on Fascism and National Socialism are concerned, a strong tie with the previous Caesarism discourse was still discernible, even if one must be vigilant against deriving any simplistic "from Caesarism to totalitarianism" assumptions from that fact. Totalitarianism is after all a phenomenon distinct from Caesarism, but not only are the intellectual continuities between the two noteworthy, as represented by figures such as Carl Schmitt and Robert Michels; also the compatibility of much of their substance, especially the *topos* of "people" and "leader(ship)" entering a sort of new democratic *unio mystica*, cannot be neglected and proves evidence that Fascism and National Socialism belong to the same set of political responses to Western modernity.

Even after 1945, the explicit use of Caesarism did not entirely vanish: there have been attempts to revitalize Caesarism as an analytical tool within the emerging political science, particularly in attempts to generate typologies of different forms of government, an element of a meta-philosophy of history, and a reference point for historical comparison. The latter has been prominent in and with regard to France. There, the disaster of 1940 and the ensuing Vichy regime, but especially the crisis of the Fourth Republic in its seeming to prove the inability of parliamentarism to guarantee national survival and being eventually overturned by Charles de Gaulle, prompted comparisons with nineteenth century experiences of Bonapartism.[13] Overall more significant than its explicit legacy, however, is Caesarism's implicit legacy: be it as an undercurrent of debates on dictatorship and different manifestations thereof, or the nature of modern politics more generally.

Today, Caesarism together with the earlier Bonapartism has been largely superseded by alternative terminologies. Yet what all of them have in common is their revolving around what might be termed the "post-revolutionary dilemma of the political";[14] that is, how to organize and legitimize stable political rule in modern mass societies penetrated by the all-pervasive premise of "popular sovereignty". Caesarism is a pointed expression of and reaction to that dilemma, offering a potential way to reconcile the claim of political participation of the many with that for decisive political leadership, especially in times of crisis. Caesarism can be condensed to the formula: "synthesis of democracy and autocracy".[15] As such, it is an expression of a timeless endeavor in the realm of politics to make the apparently incompatible compatible, and a phenomenon pertinent not only to nascent or young democracies, in which reminiscences of monarchical rule or entrenched authoritarian sentiments might persist, but also to long-standing democratic systems.

But from where does the potentiality of "Caesarism" emerge even in long-standing democracies? One may be inclined to answer: perhaps from an unrealistic and overly idealistic understanding of democracy. While any in-depth scholarly discussion would go beyond the bounds of this study, a few general reflections may be allowed on this point.

Above all, it needs to be acknowledged that democracy comes with a degree of manipulation, too: some "art of seduction" needs to be cultivated by politicians of all leanings and ethical standards in order to gain the voters' support, especially since large parts of any given body politic tend to be what might be characterized as "politically passive", demonstrating only limited or selective interest in the actual business of politics. Against this background, emotions play a crucial role in gaining citizens' attention and eventually votes, since reasoning and rational arguments alone tend to be insufficient to attract the many; all the more so since education—political and otherwise—rarely comes up to the ideal of elevating citizens to feel "responsible" in an encompassing way, to be competent to emerge from nonage entirely, or to be able to take fully-informed decisions.

In as much as democratic politics is always about manipulation, it is also about power. Politics—including its democratic version—is hardly conceivable without any pursuit for at least a portion of power or influencing the division of power, as is politics without leadership and hence leaders. This also goes for liberal democracies. In the end, as elsewhere too, it is sort, dosage and direction that are decisive for power and leadership to unfold either in a positive or negative manner. "Post-truth" politics today demonstrates the latter, more particularly the vulnerability of societies throughout the world to politicians who emotionalize and radicalize the political sphere, disguise their unrestrained craving for status and influence behind their self-staging as the true mouthpiece of "the people", and thereby accidentally—or willingly—shatter the foundations of liberal democracy. What facilitates post-truth politics and the life of contemporary populists are symptoms of fatigue on the part of parliamentarism and representative democracy, which find themselves associated with what is condemned as "system" or "establishment". After such desires had crumbled for some time in the wake of the Second World War, there now seems to be a new craving for personalized "trouble shooters": heroes and saviours of the nation, or maybe just wreckers doing what is deemed necessary to dispose of political systems that are perceived as unjust or rotten. In times such as ours where crisis appears to be almost omnipresent, pinning hopes and expectations on individuals rather than collective bodies or institutions such as parliaments is particularly appealing; especially if those individuals do not shy away from making sparkling yet untenable promises, and staging themselves as "underdogs" and fighters against noxious "political correctness".

Declaring today's populism to be merely rehashed nineteenth-century Caesarism would clearly be too simplistic an equation, and would neglect the specific conditions under which contemporary populism flourishes: the economic and cultural repercussions of globalization that are fundamentally challenging long-grown socio-economic structures and identities; perceived inefficiencies especially in Western democracies, with long decision-making processes and difficulties to advance necessary reforms in a timely manner; and the capabilities offered by modern technology. Having said that, however, it would be short-sighted not to recognize the similarities between many populists today and nineteenth-century politicians applying Caesaristic methods: their being leaders presenting themselves as radical opponents of established institutions; their rhetorically stressing to be the executors of the popular will in its entirety; or their penchant for social policies.

To conclude: Caesarism may have lost the public presence it had enjoyed in the nineteenth and early twentieth century, when it was central to a general debate about dangers, opportunities and pathologies of a fundamentally changing political and social environment people had to make sense of. Nevertheless, Caesarism is more than just a political terminology and a social-scientific concept of the past hinging on the great parallel with antiquity; notably an incisive formula reminding of the very kernel and the resulting challenges of our post-Enlightenment and post-revolutionary world. A world, in which since the eighteenth century the claims to "self-determination"— politically and otherwise—and "democracy" in its literal Greek meaning have been radically pushed forward and materialized; yet a world in which there is still appetite for authority, indeed a "longing for the leader".[16]

That longing—which determined political figures have always been more than willing to fulfill—thrives because the desire for, but in many cases also the ability to, self-definite and self-determine is not always as developed as one might expect or wish. Instead, to this day and also in established democracies there continues to be considerable willingness to give oneself up to the "pleasures of servitude".[17] One may find that deplorable and deem it unworthy of modern societies, but neglecting man's falling for "irresponsibility" would be tantamount to self-deception. As long as humans are ready to put their destiny into the hands of others and yield decision-making power to them, there will always be the risk of the former being manipulated and instrumentalized, and the latter abusing the power they have been entrusted with. In other words: as long as there is a readiness to be ruled, there is a chance of Caesarism. Attempting to avoid any danger of democracy degenerating into Caesarism would require no less than relinquishing our common understanding and practice of democratic politics altogether: a prospect which is neither realistic nor necessarily desirable.

Notes

1 Introduction

1   According to the 2018 *Freedom in the World* report by Freedom House, global freedom has seen no less than 12 consecutive years of decline. See Freedom House 2018. For the complete analysis see https://freedomhouse.org/report/freedom-world/freedom-world-2018.

2   In this vein, see, e.g., the article *Orbáns Handschrift* in the [FAZ] on April 19, 2011.

3   See Zick/Küpper/Hövermann 2011, especially p. 115f. Eight countries were taken into closer consideration: Britain, France, Germany, Portugal, Italy, the Netherlands, Poland and Hungary. Besides Portugal, the support for a one-man rule was strongest in Poland (60.8 percent) and Hungary (56.6 percent).

4   Schmitt 1996 [1923], p. 42. In English, the title is usually—though not quite accurately—referred to as *The Crisis of Parliamentary Democracy*.

5   Cf., e.g., the entry "Cäsarismus" in the German *Lexikon der Politik* (Nohlen/Schultze/Schüttemeyer 1998) or the entry "Bonapartism" in the *Dictionary of the Social Sciences* (Calhoun 2002).

6   "Bonapartism", "democratic dictatorship", "democratic monocracy" or "electoral autocracy" might have been terminological alternatives, yet some arguments can be made in favor of Caesarism: on the one hand, the term has not only been used by contemporaries in the nineteenth and twentieth century and hence avoids being a purely artificial *ex post* construction (such as "democratic monocracy" or the like would be), but is still familiar enough in the present; on the other, the term signals sufficient "neutrality" to be used as a heuristic device, at least compared to highly charged terms such as "dictatorship". Compared to "Bonapartism" as the most obvious alternative to be chosen, "Caesarism" disposes of greater universality by not suggesting an immediate entrenchment with France and one family.

7   On the problems of applying a rigid concept of Caesarism or Bonapartism for assessing individual statesmen see, e.g., Pflanze 1982, p. 598f.

8   A lexical conceptual history of Caesarism and related political and social concepts is only available in German. See the entries "Cäsarismus, Napoleonismus, Bonapartismus, Führer, Chef, Imperialismus" by Dieter Groh and "Diktatur" by Ernst Nolte in *Geschichtliche Grundbegriffe* (Brunner/Conze/Koselleck 1972–1997 Vol. 1, pp. 726–771 and pp. 900–924). For the reception history of the (ancient) term "Caesarism" in particular see the entry "Cäsarismus" in *Der Neue Pauly* (Kloft/Köhler 1999; for the English translation in *Brill's New Pauly* see Kloft/Köhler 2006).

9   In this study, monocratic and monocracy, respectively, are understood in their literal Greek sense of the word (*mónos* = "alone", "single"; *krateîn* = "to rule") to designate any "rule by one", whether that rule may be considered legitimate or illegitimate.

10 See Weber 1980 [1922], pp. 122–176.

11 Rotteck 1829–1835 Vol. 2 (1830), p. 172.

12 According to Weber, "charisma" can be defined as a certain quality of an individual, by virtue of which one is set apart from ordinary people and treated as endowed with supernatural, superhuman, or at least specifically exceptional powers or qualities. See Weber 1980 [1922], pp. 140–142, especially p. 140. On charisma as a "master concept" of Weber's sociology and its relation to "Caesarism" cf. Chapter 6.2.

13 See, e.g., Gacon 1958, Chatelain 1970, Lacour 1971, Mangoni 1976, Mitchell 1977a, Chandler 1989, Thody 1989, Magraw 1997, Gluck 2001.

14 See, among others, such influential works as Voegelin 1996 [1938] or Arendt 2004 [1951].

15 See, e.g., the scholarly work of Peter Baehr and Melvin Richter (Baehr 1998, Baehr/ Richter 2004, Richter 2005, Baehr 2008).

16 This goes in particular for the nineteenth century. See Osterhammel 2009, p. 1281.

17 On the concept of "futures past" see Koselleck 2004.

18 See, e.g., Fehrenbach 1977, p. 39f.

19 One of the terminological attempts to capture that period is "saddle period" (see Koselleck 1972), set between 1750 and 1850.

20 For the term see especially Voegelin 1952.

2 Revolution and Crisis

1 For details on the Federal Constitution see Kurland/Lerner 1996 [1987].

2 See Sieyès 1789.

3 Ibid., p. 1.

4 *Constitution française* (3 September 1791). In: Berlia 1952 [1898], pp. 1–33.

5 Cf. the speech of Chrétien-François de Lamoignon (1735-1789) on the principles of the French monarchy, delivered at a royal sitting of the *Parlement* of Paris on November 19, 1787. In: [AP] 1862ff. [1787-1799] Vol. I, pp. 265–269, quote p. 265.

6 On the distant relation of the American political class towards popular sovereignty see Benjamin Rush's *On the Defects of the Confederation* (1787): "It is often said that 'the sovereign and all other powers is seated in the people'. This idea is unhappily expressed. It should be—'all power is derived from the people'. They possess it only on the days of their elections. After this, it is the property of their rulers." In: Rush 1947, pp. 26–31, quote p. 28.

7 On differences between American and French revolutionary constitutionalism see Dippel 1989.

8 Cf. Furet/Halévi 1996, title.

9 See, e.g., Krause 2008.

10 [AP] 1862ff. [1787-1799] Vol. XLVII, p. 645. On the deposition of Louis XVI as an act proving "the limits of constitutionalism" see Sellin 2004, pp. 268–277, quote p. 268.

11 On the idea of a "second Revolution" see already François Mignet: Mignet 1856 [1824], p. 153f.

12 *Acte constitutionnel et Déclaration des droits de l'homme et du citoyen.* In: Berlia 1952 [1898], pp. 62–73.

13 *Constitution de la République française*, 5 fructidor an III (August 22, 1795). In: ibid., pp. 73–109.

14 A contemporary evaluation of the Directory including relevant sources is, e.g., Henry 1801.

15 On the dynamic of what he calls the "Great Revolutions" and their early roots in the cultures of "axial age" (Karl Jaspers) see especially Eisenstadt 1992, Eisenstadt 2006.

16 What had been shattered in Weberian terms was the characteristic traditional legitimization source of monarchical rule, based on the "established belief in the sanctity of immemorial traditions and the legitimacy of those exercising authority under them" (Weber 1978 Vol. 1, p. 215).

17 See Thamer 2000, p. 122.

18 Concerning the development of the "Caesar question" see Baehr 1998, especially pp. 29–88. On the (after-)life of Caesar in Western imagination during the last two millennia see Wyke 2007.

19 Guicciardini 1965, p. 77.

20 Montesquieu 1788 [1748], Book X 14, p. 251f.

21 Ibid., Book VIII *De la corruption des principes des trois gouvernements*, pp. 188–216, quote VIII 2, p. 190.

22 See, e.g., Hooke 1738–1771.

23 See Stürmer 1977b, pp. 104–106.

24 See Koselleck 2006 [1959], pp. 115–120.

25 See Thamer 1973, especially pp. 37–130. Envisaging a new Caesar went usually hand in hand with a positive evaluation of ancient Caesarism as a whole. See, e.g., Linguet 1777 [1766], bluntly praising Roman-style tyrannical rule under the Caesars.

26 Eighteenth century proponents of this "negative parallel" were, e.g., Diderot (1713–1784), Frederick II of Prussia (1712–1786) and Friedrich Karl von Moser (1723–1798). Moser concluded in 1787 from the decline of absolute monarchy: "Es geht auf eine Römisch-militärische Verfassung los, wie unter den Cäsarn [*sic!*] [. . .]" Moser 1787, p. 166.

27 See Burke 2001 [1790].

28 Among the authors influenced by Burke is Chateaubriand. See, e.g., Chateaubriand 1797. Among the rejoinders to Burke, the most prominent are Thomas Paine's *Rights of Man* (Paine 1925 [1791–1792]) and Mary Wollstonecraft's *A Vindication of the Rights of Men* (1790; In: Wollstonecraft 1995, pp. 1–64).

29 Burke 2001 [1790], p. 388.

30 In: Maistre 1821, p. 161.

31 See especially Schmitt 2006 [1921]. For Schmitt's theory of dictatorship cf. Chapter 7.1.

32 Cf. Bernier 1983, title. Giuseppe Garibaldi (1807–1882) was later praised in the same terms (*eroe dei due mondi*).

33 See Charavay 1898, pp. 236–238.

34 See Unger 2002, p. 268. Yet when La Fayette ceded military control of the nation to civil governance, even contemporary observers were assuming that "the time will come perhaps when he will repent having not seized that opportunity [. . .]" William Short (1759–1847) to Gouverneur Morris (1752–1816), July 27, 1790. In: Morris 1939 Vol. 1, pp. 565–567, quote p. 565f.

35 See Gilcher-Holtey 1995, p. 257f.

36 On the enduring "myth of Napoleon" see Hazareesingh 2005 [2004].

37 The number of biographies of Napoleon alone has become immense. More recent works in English include Ellis 1997, Schom 1997, McLynn 1997, Asprey 2000–2001, Alexander 2001, Johnson 2002, Englund 2005. Nineteenth-century biographies (e.g., Abbott 1855) and histories of the Consulate and Empire in general keep their value, too, particularly due to their often detailed account of events and as sources for material. See, e.g., Thiers 1845–1862.

38 Bonaparte 1908, p. 567.

39 Cf. his corresponding remarks to Count Las Cases in September 1815 on St. Helena (Las Cases 1823 Vol. 1, p. 150f.).

40 See Thody 1989, p. 20.

41 Cf. Napoleon's account of the events in a letter to his brother Joseph, dated October 6, 1795. In: Bonaparte 1858–1869 Vol. 1 Doc. 72, p. 91. A new comprehensive (critical) edition of Napoleon's correspondence, edited by the *Fondation Napoléon*, is under way (see Bonaparte 2004ff.).

42 On the genesis of Napoleonic propaganda between 1796 and 1799 see Hanley 2005.

43 Wieland 1777, p. 132.

44 Wieland 1800 [1798], p. 91f.

45 Ibid., p. 94.

46 Napoleon to Talleyrand, September 19, 1797. In: Bonaparte 1858–1869 Vol. 3 Doc. 2223, pp. 417–420.

47 Ibid., p. 418f.

48 Hunt/Lansky/Hanson 1979, title.

49 Tulard 1999, title.

50 See Thody 1989, p. 24.

51 Woloch 2001, p. 3. On the preparation of the coup see ibid., pp. 3–18.

52 On the decisive role of Lucien Bonaparte see Boudon 2009. A personal account of the events is provided in Bonaparte 1845.

53 See *Proclamation*, Paris, 19 Brumaire an VIII (November 10, 1799). In: Bonaparte 1858–1869 Vol. 6 Doc. 4389, p. 5f.

54 See Woloch 2001, p. 30.

55 On the reactions to the Brumaire events in the provinces see Woloch 1997. However, not even among Jacobins opposition against the *coup d'état* was unanimous. See, e.g., Thuillier 2005.

56 *Constitution de la République française*, 22 frimaire an VIII (December 13, 1799). In: Berlia 1952 [1898], pp. 109–118.

57 Address of Garat in the sitting of the Legislative Commissions on 23 Frimaire (December 14). In: Lombard de Langres 1799, pp. 425–431, quote p. 426.

58 For details see Lentz 1997.

59 See Sellin 2018, pp. 167–171, especially p. 168.

60 For a theoretical discussion of referendum and plebiscite as two forms of "popular democracy" see Denquin 1976.

61 The official results showed 3,011,007 *oui* and 1,562 *non* votes. For details see Langlois 1972.

62 Tellingly, the "Constitution of the Year VIII" was not only the shortest since the outbreak of the Revolution with only 95 articles (compared to, e.g., 207 in the Constitution of 1791 and 377 in the Constitution of 1795), but also the first without a formal Declaration of Rights.

63 To cover the origin of the work, the subtitle reads *fragment traduit de l'anglais*. The pamphlet is reprinted in Bourrienne 1829 Vol. 6, pp. 73–85. A detailed analysis of the pamphlet in Thiers 1845–1862 Vol. 2, pp. 210–215. See also ibid., p. 250f.

64 In: Bourrienne 1829 Vol. 6, p. 80.

65 In: ibid. Vol. 6, p. 81f.

66 In: ibid. Vol. 6, p. 82.

67 In: ibid. Vol. 6, p. 83.

68 In: ibid. Vol. 6, p. 83.

69 See, e.g., Thiers 1845–1862 Vol. 2, p. 214.

70 See Bonaparte 1911–1913 Vol. 1, pp. 96–98.

71 See Bourrienne 1829 Vol. 3, p. 74. Even before his stormy confrontation with the Council of Five Hundred, Napoleon had already attempted to discount similar historical analogies in the Council of Ancients: "I know that Caesar and Cromwell are talked of—as if this day could be compared with past times. No, I desire nothing but the safety of the Republic, and to maintain the resolutions to which you are about to come." Bonaparte 1823–1824 Vol. 1, p. 92.

72 Lenormand 1848 Vol. 1, p. 240.

73 Goethe's conversation with Napoleon was recorded by Friedrich von Müller (1779–1849). In: Goethe 1966, p. 72. Also in Bonaparte 1911–1913 Vol. 2, p. 30. While Napoleon's admiration for Caesar continued to reveal itself rather blatantly in less guarded instants, he always emphasized that "never had he the thought of becoming a Cromwell" (Lenormand 1848, p. 264).

74 *Sénatus-consulte qui proclame Napoléon Bonaparte Premier Consul à vie*, 14 thermidor an X (August 2, 1802). In: Berlia 1952 [1898], p. 120.

75 *Sénatus-consulte organique*, 28 floréal an XII (May 18, 1804). In: ibid., pp. 131–151.

76 On the role of Napoleon's servitors in the erection of the Empire see Woloch 2004. See also Woloch 2001, pp. 90–119.

77 His main argument was that the public will had to be heard. In a private conversation with Antoine Claire Thibaudeau (1765–1854) Napoleon remarked that "the plebiscite has the advantage of legalizing my extension of office and to purify the origin of my power" (Thibaudeau 1827, p. 264).

78 See Woloch 2004, p. 33.

79 See, e.g., Willms 2009 [2005], p. 360.

80 This was in July 1800. In: Roederer 1942, p. 126f., p. 129. On the question of a hereditary monarchy see also pp. 203–211 (November 1804).

81 *Projet de déclaration pour l'établissement de l'Empire, proposé au Conseil d'état par les présidents des sections en 1804.* In: Capefigue 1840 Vol. 8, pp. 278–281, quote p. 281.

82 Berlier 1838, p. 94.

83 Ibid., p. 95.

84 Reinhard 1952, p. 271f.

85 On the debates in the *Tribunat* see Woloch 2001, pp. 104–110, Woloch 2004, pp. 40–44. All the speeches are reproduced in [Gazette nationale] 1789–1810 Nr. 221–225, 11-15 floréal an XII (1 to May 5, 1804), pp. 1003–1028.

86 See, e.g., *Discours du C. Carret.* In: ibid. Nr. 225, 15 floréal an XII, p. 1025f.

87 The draft was first presented in the *Tribunat* by Louis Alexandre Jard-Panvillier (1757–1822) on 13 floréal. In: ibid. Nr. 224, 14 floréal an XII, p. 1020. Napoleon used a similar argument in a conversation with Jean-Antoine Chaptal (1756–1832), successor of Lucien Bonaparte as Minister of the Interior (see Chaptal 1893, p. 308f.).

88 *Discours du C. Albisson.* In: [Gazette nationale] 1789–1810 Nr. 225, 15 floréal an XII, p. 1023.

89 [Gazette nationale] 1789–1810 Nr. 226, 16 floréal XII (May 6, 1804).

90 The term goes back to Max Weber (*Veralltäglichung*) and describes the process by which charismatic rule is turned into a "daily practice", thus losing its "elevatedness". See Weber 1980 [1922], pp. 142–148 and pp. 661–681.

91 On Napoleon's coronation see Cabanis 2007 [1970].

92 Thibaudeau 1827, p. 252.

93 See Englund 2005, p. 245.

94 On Napoleon's strategy to legitimise his own rule by instrumentalizing the
    coronation of Charlemagne in 800 see Kraus 2000. In his correspondence and
    writings, Napoleon frequently refers to his famous imperial precursor. See,
    e.g., Napoleon to Cardinal Fesch, Munich, January 7, 1806. In: Bonaparte
    1858–1869 Vol. 11 Doc. 9656, p. 528f.

95 *Sénatus-consulte organique de la Constitution*, 16 thermidor an X (August 4, 1802). In:
    Berlia 1952 [1898], pp. 120–128.

96 See Campbell 1958, pp. 54–56.

97 On Napoleon's shift "from saviour to despot" see Tulard 1987 [1977], pp. 307–324.

98 Napoleon to Joseph-Napoléon Bonaparte, Reims, March 14, 1814. In: Bonaparte 1854
    Vol. 10, p. 198f., quote p. 199.

99 See Broers 2008.

100 On the Napoleonic state cult see Sellin 2013.

101 See also Erbe 1995, especially pp. 135–139.

102 Notes on the Proposed Inscriptions for the Arc de Triomphe, Schönbrunn, October 3,
    1809. In: Bonaparte 1858–1869 Vol. 19 Doc. 15894, p. 545.

103 See Bonaparte 1911–1913 Vol. 2, p. 227.

104 See ibid. Vol. 1, p. 204.

105 See *Déclaration des Puissances Alliées* (March 25, 1814). In: Chod'zko 1863 Vol. 1,
    pp. 143–146.

106 On the regime change in 1814 and the restoration of the Bourbon dynasty see Sellin
    2001, Prutsch 2006, pp. 13–55.

107 *Sénatus-consulte portant que Napoléon Bonaparte est déchu du trône, et que le droit
    d'hérédité établi dans sa famille est aboli* (April 3, 1814). In: [BL] 1814 Vol. 1 No.°8,
    pp. 7–9.

108 Ibid. Vol. 1 No.°8, p. 7.

109 For details on Napoleon's abdication see Sellin 2001, pp. 173–194.

110 2 November 1816. In: Bonaparte 1955, p. 273f.

111 Memoirs dictated to Count Las Cases, 9/10 April 1816. In: Las Cases 1823 Vol. 2,
    p. 29. On Napoleon's (self-)depiction as "Prince of Liberal Ideas" see Hazareesingh
    2005 [2004], pp. 151–183.

112 See, e.g., Napoleon to Count Las Cases, November 11, 1816. In: Las Cases 1823 Vol. 4,
    p. 134.

113 August 24, 1816. In: ibid. Vol. 3, p. 267.

114 See Bonaparte 1823–1824 Vol. 1, pp. 53–100. According to Napoleon, the French
    nation looked for a saviour, its own "tutelary genius" (Ibid., p. 54) to deliver it from its
    misery: "It was not like the return of a citizen to his country, or a general at the head
    of a victorious army, but like the triumph of a sovereign restored to his people." Ibid.,
    p. 57.

115 November 11, 1816. In: Las Cases 1823 Vol. 4, p. 139.

116 Bonaparte 1836b, p. 219.

117 Ibid., p. 218.

118 Extract of a speech at Lyon, September 20, 1852. In: Girard 1977, p. 23.

119 See Harvey 1998, p. 27.

120 [Parliamentary Debates] 1803–1820 Vol. 17 (1810), p. 223.

121 On Napoleon as a successor of Alexander—and Caesar—see Stendhal [= Marie-
    Henri Beyle] 1876 [1817-1818], p. 1. On the contrast between Alexander and
    Napoleon see [European Magazine] 1782–1825 Vol. 65 (January to June 1814),
    p. 396.

122 On Charlemagne and Napoleon see, e.g., Woltmann 1804b, Guizot 1828–1832 Vol. 2, p. 267.
123 On Cromwell and Napoleon see, e.g., Macaulay 1828.
124 See Groh 2004 [1972], p. 734.
125 The Caesar-Napoleon parallelism has continued to be applied up to the present day. Two examples from the twentieth century are Ferrero 1933 and Ford 1970.
126 Cited in: Harvey 1998, p. 28.
127 *Caracter of Buonaparte.* In: [European Magazine] 1782–1825 Vol. 65 (January to June 1814), p. 395.
128 Chateaubriand 1849–1850 Vol. 6, p. 240. To take another example, the poet Robert Southey (1774–1843), even though a declared enemy of Napoleon, willingly acknowledged that at least until his takeover of power he had been "a soldier of fortune, who had faithfully served the cause in which he engaged, and whose career had been distinguished by a series of successes unexampled in modern times" (Southey 1861 [1813], p. 165).
129 Görres 1854 [1800], p. 42f.
130 Woltmann 1804a, p. 245f.
131 On Hegel's concept of *weltgeschichtliche Individuen* and their role see especially his *Lectures on the Philosophy of History* (Hegel 1999 [1837], explicitly pp. 45–51).
132 See Hegel 1999 [1800–1802], p. 580.
133 Buchholz 1805, p. 152f. On his distinction between "sovereignty" and "despotism" with respect to Napoleon see also Buchholz 1804.
134 See Seume 1962, p. 1287, 1309, 1387.
135 See Groh 2004 [1972], p. 736.
136 Among the most passionate anti-Napoleonic German writers was Gustav von Schlabrendorf (1750–1824), sometimes also ironically referred to as the "Diogenes of Paris", who lived in the French capital. See especially Schlabrendorf 1804, Schlabrendorf/Bergk 1806, Schlabrendorf/Bergk 1814.
137 Luden 1814, p. 76.
138 Ibid.
139 See Constant 1814. A recent English translation in Constant 2002 [1988], pp. 43–167.
140 For a comparison of the two see Baehr 1998, pp. 97–100.
141 Constant 2002 [1988], p. 88.
142 Ibid., p. 88f.
143 Ibid., p. 89.
144 Ibid., p. 90f.
145 "The governments, be they republican, be they monarchical, which it [the Napoleonic regime; MJP] had destroyed, were without apparent hope or visible resources: yet they survived in the hearts of their peoples. Twenty lost battles could not dislodge them from there: one single battle was won and usurpation was seen to be put to flight on all sides." Ibid., p. 100f.
146 Ibid., p. 95.
147 Ibid., pp. 95–97.
148 Ibid., p. 97.
149 Ibid., p. 115.
150 See ibid., pp. 142–146, explicitly p. 142.
151 On the causes which would make despotism impossible see ibid., pp. 140–142.
152 See ibid., p. 140.
153 Ibid., p. 99.

154 Ibid., p. 158.
155 Ibid., p. 159.
156 Ibid., pp. 161–164.
157 See ibid., p. 165.
158 Quote from the draft of a never published pamphlet by the English poet Samuel
     Taylor Coleridge (1772–1834), most likely written in 1812. In: Calleo 1960, pp. 88–90,
     here p. 89.
159 This is the main message throughout Constant's political writing, particularly in his
     *Principes de politique, applicables à tous les gouvernements représentatifs et
     particulièrement à la constitution actuelle de la France* (Constant 1815). A recent
     English translation in Constant 2002 [1988], pp. 169–305, quote p. 180.
160 Constant was charged with the drafting of the *Acte additionnel aux Constitutions de
     l'Empire* (April 22, 1815). In: [BL] 1815 Vol. 1 No. 19 (No. 112), pp. 131–140.
161 According to Immanuel Kant's famous quotation in his treatise *Zur Frage: Was ist
     Aufklärung?* (Kant 1999 [1784], p. 20).
162 Woloch 2004, p. 30.
163 See Metternich 1880–1884 Part 1 Vol. 1, p. 151.
164 There are good reasons to doubt whether Napoleon actually made these utterances
     (see Sellin 2001, pp. 62–64). It also strikes one's eye that Metternich's claim of
     Napoleon saying that while traditional monarchs could suffer twenty defeats, he
     could not dare to lose a single battle, appears similarly in Constant's characterization
     of Napoleon's rule (cf. note 145 above).
165 *Caracter of Buonaparte.* In: [European Magazine] 1782–1825 Vol. 65 (January to June
     1814), p. 395.
166 Koppe 1815, p. 45.
167 Napoleon thereby emphasized having neither the red heel which distinguished the
     aristocrats at Versailles, nor the red bonnet of liberty worn by the extreme *sans-
     culottes* during the Revolution.
168 Ferrero 1903 [1899], p. 207. Cf. also Chapter 6.1.1.
169 The term "usurpation" had been used before, but in a much narrower and slightly
     different way than by Constant, e.g. by John Locke in his *Second Treatise of
     Government* (see Locke 2004 [1689], p. 397f.).
170 In: Constant 2002 [1988], p. 147.
171 Staël-Holstein 1964, p. 129.

3 "Bonapartism" as Hazard and Promise

1 On the Restoration as a "European project" see Sellin 2001, Sellin 2017.
2 Anderson/Anderson 1967, p. 39f., p. 78f.
3 *Charte constitutionnelle* (June 4, 1814). In: [BL] 1814 Vol. 1 No. 133, pp. 197–207.
4 On the *Charte constitutionnelle* and "constitutional monarchism" as a model in the
   post-Napoleonic age see Prutsch 2009a, Prutsch 2013, Grotke/Prutsch 2014.
5 See Sellin 1996, pp. 348–350.
6 See *Saint-Pétersbourg, 6/18 juillet 1814.* In: Maistre 1860 Vol. 1, p. 379.
7 See Maistre 1980 [1797], p. 184.
8 See, e.g., Kirsch 2007.
9 *Political State of Prussia.* In: [Edinburgh Review] 1802–1929 Vol. 83 No. 167 (January
   1846), pp. 224–239, quote p. 229.

10 *Rapport fait au Roi pendant son voyage de Gand à Paris* (June 1815). In: Pallain 1881, pp. 436–484.
11 In: ibid., p. 464.
12 In: ibid., p. 467.
13 In: ibid., p. 469.
14 See Constant 1814.
15 See Richter 2005, p. 235, talking about a "family of political concepts".
16 See Guizot 1828, Guizot 1829–1832 [1828–1830]. A contemporary English translation is Guizot 1846 [1828–1830].
17 Guizot 1828, 9th lecture (June 13, 1828), p. 13. Translation follows Guizot 1846 [1828–1830] Vol. 1, p. 166.
18 Guizot 1828, 4th lecture (May 9, 1828), p. 20. Translation follows Guizot 1846 [1828–1830] Vol. 1, p. 73f.
19 Cf. Guizot 1828, 9th lecture (June 13, 1828), p. 21f.
20 Guizot 1851 [1820–1822] Vol. 2, p. 139f. Translation follows Guizot 1852 [1820–1822], p. 341.
21 Guizot 1829–1832 [1828–1830] Vol. 2, 20th lecture, p. 263f. Translation follows Guizot 1846 [1828-1830] Vol. 2, p. 183f.
22 Guizot 1829–1832 [1828–1830] Vol. 2, 20th lecture, p. 264f. Translation follows Guizot 1846 [1828-1830] Vol. 2, p. 184.
23 Guizot 1829–1832 [1828–1830] Vol. 2, 20th lecture, p. 266f. Translation follows Guizot 1846 [1828-1830] Vol. 2, p. 185.
24 Cf. Guizot's review of *De la monarchie française depuis la seconde restauration jusqu'à la fin de la session de 1816* by Francois Dominique de Reynaud, Comte de Montlosier (1755–1838), appearing in the third volume of the *Archives Philosophiques, Politiques et Littéraires* (Guizot 1818, p. 396).
25 On the July Revolution of 1830 and the revision of the *Charte constitutionnelle* in 1830 see Rosanvallon 1994, Prutsch 2006, Prutsch 2008, Prutsch 2009b. The revised *Charte constitutionnelle* (June 4, 1814) in: [BL] 1830–1848 Vol. 1 No. 133, pp. 197–207.
26 Both works were only published posthumously: *Mémoires sur Napoléon* as part of Stendhal's *Œuvres complètes* in 1876 (misleadingly titled *Vie de Napoléon*; see Stendhal [= Marie-Henri Beyle] 1876 [1817–1818]), *Vie de Napoléon* as late as 1929 (Stendhal [= Marie-Henri Beyle] 1930 [1836–1837]).
27 Stendhal [= Marie-Henri Beyle] 1930 [1817–1818] Chapter XIX, p. 61.
28 Ibid. Chapter LXXXVII, p. 335.
29 Stendhal [= Marie-Henri Beyle] 1930 [1836–1837] Chapter I, p. 29.
30 On the "Napoleonic myth" in Germany see Beßlich 2007.
31 The Federal Act of 1815 (*Deutsche Bundesakte vom 8. Juni 1815*. In: Huber 1978 [1961], pp. 84–90) had been a disappointment for both the national and constitutional movement in Germany.
32 The Karlsbad Decrees were enacted on 20 September 1819. The text of the decrees in ibid., pp. 101–105.
33 *Schlußakte der Wiener Ministerkonferenzen* (May 15, 1820). In: ibid., pp. 91–100.
34 In: Perthes 1861 Vol. 3, p. 307.
35 In: ibid. Vol. 3, p. 311.
36 In: ibid. Vol. 3, p. 311f.
37 *Zweiter Bundesbeschluß über Maßregeln zur Aufrechterhaltung der gesetzlichen Ordnung und Ruhe in Deutschland* (July 5, 1832). In: Huber 1978 [1961], p. 134f.

38 *Bundesbeschluß über Maßregeln zur Aufrechterhaltung der gesetzlichen Ordnung und Ruhe in Deutschland* (28 May 1832). In: ibid., p. 132f.

39 *Schlußprotokoll der Wiener Ministerkonferenzen* (June 12, 1834). In: ibid., p. 137–149.

40 In: Perthes 1861 Vol. 3, p. 346.

41 See Groh 2004 [1972], p. 740f.

42 Heine 1861–1866 Vol. 3 (*Englische Fragmente. Shakespeare's Mädchen und Frauen*), p. 139f.

43 Ibid. Vol. 8 (*Französische Zustände. Erster Theil*), p. 359f. (Dieppe, August 20, 1832). Heine had also used the term earlier, however less consciously. See, e.g., his description of popular Bonapartist poets under the July Monarchy as "Tyrtäen des Bonapartismus". Ibid. Vol. 8 (*Französische Zustände. Erster Theil*), p. 154 (Paris, March 25, 1832).

44 Mackintosh 1835 Vol. 2, p. 314f. (November 25, 1814).

45 Thomas Jefferson to Marquis de La Fayette (Monticello, February 14, 1815). In: Jefferson 1830 Vol. 4, Letter CXXI, pp. 246–252, quote p. 247.

46 The transformation into a political concept can also be seen in an 1831 letter of the British educator and historian Thomas Arnold (1795–1842) to the Prussian diplomat Christian Karl Josias von Bunsen (1791–1860). He argued that "Nothing can be more opposite than Liberalism and Bonapartism", while expressing confidence that "the whole power of the [English] nation would be heartily put forth to strangle in the birth the first symptoms of Napoleonism". Thomas Arnold to Chevalier Bunsen (Rugby, March 20, 1831). In: Arnold 1844 Vol. 1, pp. 288–291, quote p. 290.

47 Given the "success story" to come of "Bonapartism" and slightly after also "Casearism", later authors have mistakenly re-projected these terminologies to authors of the early nineteenth century. See, for example, Johnson 1963, p. 56, putting "Bonapartism" into Guizot's mouth notwithstanding that Guizot had not yet applied the term, but rather the notion "system of Bonaparte" (*système de Buonaparte*). See Guizot 1818, p. 396.

48 Heine 1861–1866 Vol. 3 (*Englische Fragmente. Shakespeare's Mädchen und Frauen*), p. 212.

49 Ibid. Vol. 8 (*Französische Zustände. Erster Theil*), p. 360. (Dieppe, August 20, 1832).

50 Ibid. Vol. 10 (*Französische Zustände. Dritter Theil*), p. 55f. (June 20, 1842).

51 Ibid. Vol. 10 (*Französische Zustände. Dritter Theil*), p. 57 and 59f. (July 12, 1842).

52 The "defending" and "preserving" role of Bonapartism shines through also in Heine's later appreciation of Louis-Napoléon Bonaparte. See, e.g., Heine to Gustav Kolb (Paris, April 21, 1851). In: Holzhausen 1903, p. 216.

53 Heine's attitude towards the idea of radical change of state and society was not without inconsistencies, as was his personality in general: Ideologically close to the young Hegelian movement, Heine acknowledged the need for a destruction of the existing order for political renewal. At the same time, however, he dreaded the equalizing tendencies of a new social order and never actually subscribed to it. See Groh 2004 [1972], p. 742f.

54 Quote in: ibid., p. 743.

55 Böhmer 1868 Vol. 1, p. 279.

56 The other uses of "Caesarism" in the work are most likely *ex post* applications by the editor, Johannes Janssen, who published Böhmer's *Leben, Briefe und kleinere Schriften* in 1868, when the term had become widely used.

57 Perthes 1861 Vol. 3, p. 449.

58 *Dictator, Dictatur*. In: Rotteck/Welcker 1834–1843 Vol. 4, pp. 392–396.

59 Schulz-Bodner 1837, p. 395f.

60 The *Historismus* school of writing about the past, too, which was about to unfold under the influence of Leopold von Ranke (1795–1886), reflected this interest in great men and their deeds.

61 Carlyle 1840, p. 233.

62 On Tocqueville's politico-theoretical contribution to the concepts of political legitimacy and the regimes of Napoleon I and Napoleon III in particular see, e.g., the works of Melvin Richter: Richter 1988, Richter 2004.

63 *Quelle espèce de despotisme les nations démocratiques ont à craindre* (Vol. IV Chapter 6). In: Tocqueville 2010 [1835–1840] Vol. 4, pp. 1245–1261. The discussion of this issue was continued in *Suite des chapitres précédents* (Ibid., pp. 1262–1277), preparing for the final chapter of *De la démocratie en Amérique* (Vol. IV Chapter 8: *Vue générale du sujet*; ibid., pp. 1278–1285).

64 Ibid. Vol. 4, p. 1245f.

65 See ibid. Vol. 4, p. 1280.

66 Ibid. Vol. 4, p. 1248f. An alternative he was thinking of "for lack of anything better" was "administrative despotism". Ibid., p. 1249, notes.

67 Ibid. Vol. 4, p. 1247f.

68 It is worth noting that the conclusions drawn by Tocqueville in 1840 regarding the greatest danger to modern democracies were considerably different from those in the earlier 1835 volume of *Democracy in America*. In 1835 he had depicted modern liberty threatened by a return to the oppressive regime exercised by the Caesars. In the following years, however, Tocqueville changed his mind and came to acknowledge that historical analogies were not quite helpful, as a manuscript note of 7 March 1838 reveals (Ibid. Vol. 4, p. 1247, notes).

69 See Constant 1814 and the previous chapter.

70 Tocqueville 2010 [1835-1840] Vol. 4, p. 1249f.

71 Ibid. Vol. 4, p. 1252.

72 Ibid. Vol. 4, p. 1255f.

73 Ibid. Vol. 4, p. 1262.

74 Ibid. Vol. 4, p. 1265.

75 Ibid. Vol. 4, p. 1275.

76 Ibid. Vol. 4, p. 1276.

77 Ibid. Vol. 4, p. 1280.

78 In January 1831, Louis-Philippe summarized the program of the July Monarchy in the famous statement that he would attempt to remain in a *juste milieu* with equal distance from the excesses of popular power and the abuses of royal power.

79 See Weber 1980 [1922], pp. 122–124.

80 Therein, one can see a clear echo of the classical discourse on "mixed government", keeping its charm throughout time. In his memoirs, even Lucien Bonaparte fancied a "throne surrounded [. . .] with democratic and aristocratic institutions, wisely balanced", and considered "mixed governments" as "the only ones where the constitutional liberties, precious fruits of our civilization, can live and prosper in the midst of the inequalities and passions inseparable from humanity" (Bonaparte 1836a, p. 302f.).

81 See Hegel 1999 [1837].

82 On Bonapartism emancipating itself from Napoleon Bonaparte and its becoming part of a "national patrimony" in France, and the transformation of Napoleon's political legacy into a wider concept of Caesarism, see Alexander 2000 and Bruyère-Ostells 2013.

4 From Bonapartism to Caesarism:
The Mid-Century and Louis-Napoléon

1   Price 2001, p. 10.
2   See ibid., p. 10.
3   Due to the lack of exact statistical material, the numbers vary in the literature. Most
     works, however, indicate a number between 9 and 10 million.
4   See Tocqueville 1896 [1893], p. 98.
5   Ibid., p. 94.
6   6.9 of 8.2 million registered voters cast their votes. See Rosanvallon 2008 [1992],
     p. 381.
7   *Constitution de la République française* (November 4, 1848). In: [BL] 1848–1852 Vol. 2
     No. 87, pp. 575–605.
8   See Discourse of Grévy in the National Constituent Assembly (October 6, 1848). In:
     Grévy 1888 Vol. 1, pp. 38–61.
9   On the role of the "Napoleonic legend" in 1848 see Tudesq 1957.
10 See ibid., p. 71f.
11 The writings of Louis-Napoléon are collected in the *Œuvres de Napoléon III*
     (Bonaparte 1856). For his political works see the first two volumes. An early English
     translation is Bonaparte 1852.
12 See Price 2001, p. 16.
13 *Des Idées Napoléoniennes* (1839). In: Bonaparte 1856 Vol. 1, pp. 15–233, quote p. 172. In
     a short pamphlet one year later, he summarized the cornerstones of his political vision
     in similar terms. See *L'Idée Napoléonienne* (1840). In: ibid. Vol. 1, pp. 1–13.
14 *Extinction du paupérisme* (1844). In: ibid. Vol. 2, pp. 107–151.
15 Ibid., p. 122.
16 All in all, around 7.5 million French made use of their right to vote, that is around
     76 percent of the registered voters. See Anceau 2008, p. 142f.
17 Proudhon 1850, p. 248.
18 Even in Paris, Louis-Napoléon gained a comfortable majority of 58 percent of the
     votes. See Price 2001, p. 19.
19 See Stein 1842.
20 See Stein 1850.
21 Ibid. Vol. 1, p. IVf.
22 Ibid. Vol. 1, p. V and VII.
23 Ibid. Vol. 1, p. Vf.
24 Ibid. Vol. 3, p. 76.
25 Ibid. Vol. 3, p. 47f.
26 Ibid. Vol. 1, p. 241.
27 Ibid. Vol. 1, p. 243f.
28 Ibid. Vol. 1, p. 245.
29 Ibid. Vol. 3, pp. 417–420.
30 See ibid. Vol. 3, p. 420f.
31 Ibid. Vol. 3, p. 422f.
32 A short English biography of Donoso Cortés is Herrera 1995.
33 His writings and programmatic speeches are collected in Donoso Cortés 1854–1855, a
     selection in English in Donoso Cortés 2007. On his political thought see Galindo
     Herrero 1957, on his theory of dictatorship in particular Beneyto Pérez 1988.

34 In: Donoso Cortés 1854–1855 Vol. 3, pp. 253–274. The general debate was on the emergency law (*Ley de poderes extraordinarios*) passed by parliament in March 1848.

35 Ibid. Vol. 3, p. 259 and 261.

36 Ibid. Vol. 3, p. 266 and 270.

37 Ibid. Vol. 3, p. 268.

38 Ibid. Vol. 3, p. 271.

39 Ibid. Vol. 3, p. 273.

40 Ibid. Vol. 3, p. 274.

41 In: ibid. Vol. 3, pp. 303–325.

42 Ibid. Vol. 3, p. 316.

43 Ibid. Vol. 3, p. 317.

44 Ibid. Vol. 3, p. 317.

45 See Beyme 2002, p. 559f. For Donoso Cortés' assessment of the political situation in France 1851/1852 cf. his reports from Paris. In: Donoso Cortés 1854–1855 Vol. 5, pp. 235–370. The comparison between Napoleon III and Augustus can be found in a letter dated December 10, 1851. In: ibid., pp. 320–326, especially p. 321.

46 In: ibid. Vol. 4, pp. 13–297, appendix pp. 299–406. A translated English edition is Donoso Cortés 1879 [1851].

47 Romieu is regularly described as the "father" of "Caesarism". See, e.g., Groh 2004 [1972], p. 751f., Baehr 1998, pp. 106–112. On Romieu and his concept of Caesarism see Janssen Perio 1972.

48 See Romieu 1850.

49 Ibid., p. 200.

50 See ibid., p. 102.

51 Ibid., p. 6.

52 See ibid., p. 8f.

53 Ibid., p. 19f.

54 Ibid., p. 13. Further portrayals of Napoleon as Caesar on p. 34, p. 44 and p. 130. The successors of Caesar and Napoleon alike, Romieu underlined, would profit from the "magic of the [predecessors'] names" (ibid., p. 34).

55 See ibid., pp. 109–116, especially p. 115.

56 Ibid., p. 116.

57 See ibid., p. 118f.

58 Ibid., p. 122.

59 See ibid., p. 29f.

60 Ibid., p. 193f.

61 Ibid., p. 196f.

62 Ibid., p. 200.

63 Ibid., p. 206f.

64 See, e.g., ibid., p. 156f.

65 Romieu 1851c, p. 2.

66 Ibid., p. 3f.

67 Ibid., p. 17f. and p. 46f.

68 Ibid., p. 10.

69 Ibid., p. 25.

70 Ibid., p. 65f.

71 Ibid., p. 68 and p. 70.

72 Ibid., p. 91.

73 Ibid., pp. 95–97.

74 Ibid., p. 100.

75 Romieu was acquainted with the writings of the Spaniard not least through his close friendship with Louis Veuillot (1813–1883), editor of Juan Donoso Cortés' writings in France.

76 Of the later Emperor's entourage, Persigny is often described as the most passionate ideologue of Bonapartism. On Persigny's role as a political mastermind of the Second Empire see Clément 2006.

77 See, e.g., Romieu 1851c, p. 99.

78 The right-left division corresponded with strong regional discrepancies of the election results. See Salmon 2001, p. 6f.

79 *Loi qui modifie la loi électorale du 15 mars 1849* (May 31, 1850). In: [BL] 1848–1852 Vol. 5 No. 266, pp. 605–609.

80 *Inauguration de la section du chemin de fer de Lyon entre Tonnerre et Dijon* (June 1, 1851). In: Bonaparte 1856 Vol. 3, pp. 210–212, quote p. 210.

81 See ibid. Vol. 3, p. 211.

82 On the preparation and execution of the coup see, e.g., Anceau 2009.

83 See *Proclamation du Président de la République. Appel au Peuple* (December 2, 1851). In: [BL] 1848–1852 Vol. 8 No. 465, p. 988f.

84 See Bonaparte 1856 Vol. 3, p. 273.

85 Ibid. Vol. 3, p. 272 and p. 274.

86 On the role of the "Imperial Legend" for Louis-Napoléon see Hazareesingh 2005 [2004], pp. 184–208.

87 Unlike for the plebiscites of Napoleon Bonaparte, which had been exclusively termed *appels au peuple*, for those of Louis-Napoléon *plébiscite* was (re-)used as a technical term after having been applied earlier for the referenda of 1793 and 1795. See *Décret sur la présentation d'un Plébiscite à l'acceptation du Peuple français* (December 2, 1851). In: [BL] 1848–1852 Vol. 8 No. 465, p. 991f. The use, however, was not entirely consistent, as the President's call for an *appel au peuple* in his personal address to the nation that very same day proves: *Proclamation du Président de la République. Appel au Peuple* (December 2, 1851). In: ibid. Vol. 8 No. 465, p. 988f.

88 *Extrait du registre des Délibérations de la Commission consultative. Recensement général des votes émis sur le plébiscite présenté à l'acceptation du Peuple français* (December 31, 1851). In: ibid. Vol. 8 No. 474, pp. 1229–1232. Even if 1.5 million abstentions are considered as expressions of passive resistance and therefore added to the "No" votes, still a majority of around 78 percent of all registered voters had cast their ballot in favor of Louis-Napoléon.

89 See Ménager 1988, pp. 112–114.

90 *Constitution faite en vertu des pouvoirs délégués par le Peuple français à Louis-Napoléon Bonaparte, par le vote des 20 et 21 Décembre 1851* (January 14, 1852). In: [BL] 1848–1852 Vol. 9 No. 479, pp. 49–72.

91 See ibid., p. 50.

92 Ibid., p. 51f.

93 Ibid., p. 53.

94 One of the most striking similarities is between Article 6 of the 1852 Constitution and Article 14 of the former *Charte*.

95 See *Discours de Bordeaux* (October 9, 1852). In: Bonaparte 1856 Vol. 3, pp. 341–344.

96 See ibid. Vol. 3, pp. 342–344.

97 *Sénatus-consulte portant modification à la Constitution* (November 7, 1852). In: [BL] 1848–1852 Vol. 10 No. 587, pp. 677–680.

98 *Recensement général des Votes émis sur le projet de Plébiscite présenté les 21 et 22 novembre 1852 à l'acceptation du Peuple français* (December 1, 1852). In: [BL] 1852–1870 Vol. 1 No. 1, pp. 1–5.

99 *Sénatus-consulte portant interprétation et modification de la Constitution du 14 janvier 1852* (December 25, 1852). In: ibid. Vol. 1 No. 5, pp. 57–59.

100 A detailed analysis of the Second Empire, focusing on its "anatomy of power", is Price 2001.

101 *Caractère de Bonaparte*. In: Chateaubriand 1849–1850 Vol. 3, pp. 415–419, quote p. 418.

102 "Quoi ! après Auguste, Augustule ! ... Quoi ! Parce-ce que nous avons eu Napoléon-le-Grand, il faut que nous ayons Napoléon-le-petit !" (July 17, 1851). In: [Moniteur universel] 1811–1868 No. 199 (July 18, 1851), pp. 2041–2052, quote p. 2050.

103 See Hugo 1852a. Hugo's pamphlet found immediately translation into English under the title *Napoleon the Little* (Hugo 1852b). The following quotations are largely based on the English edition.

104 Hugo 1852a, p. 351; Hugo 1852b, p. 228.

105 Hugo 1852a, p. 343; Hugo 1852b, p. 222f.

106 Hugo 1852a, p. 253f; Hugo 1852b, p. 171.

107 Hugo 1852a, p. 275; Hugo 1852b, p. 185.

108 [Westminster Review] 1824–1914 No. CXIV (October 1852), p. 336.

109 Marx's remarks are from the introduction to the second edition of the *Eighteenth Brumaire*: Marx 1869 [1852], p. IV.

110 See Schoelcher 1852.

111 [Westminster Review] 1824–1914 No. CXIV (October 1852), p. 336. In the 1870s, Hugo eventually published a more "factual" two-volumes account of the coup (Hugo 1877–1878).

112 See Proudhon 1852.

113 Ibid., p. 88f.

114 Ibid., p. 93.

115 Ibid., p. 265f.

116 Ibid., p. 278.

117 See Tocqueville 1856. A commented and annotated edition in, e.g., Tocqueville 1986, pp. 893–1105, notes pp. 1154–1160.

118 For the *Recollections* see Tocqueville 1896 [1893]. Much of Tocqueville's correspondence was printed already in Tocqueville 1864–1866, namely in the volumes 5 to 7. A viable collection in English translation is Tocqueville 1985.

119 Tocqueville to the editor of the London *Times* (December 11, 1851). In: Tocqueville 1985, pp. 266-278, quotes p. 276.

120 Senior 1871 Vol. 2, pp. 226–228.

121 See Tocqueville to Henry Reeve (January 9, 1852). In: Tocqueville 1985, pp. 283–285.

122 Tocqueville to Gustave de Beaumont (November 28, 1849). In: ibid., pp. 239–245, quote p. 242.

123 Tocqueville to Sophie Swetchine (January 7, 1856). In: ibid., pp. 325–327, quote p. 326.

124 Tocqueville to Arthur de Gobineau (September 16, 1858). In: ibid., pp. 374–377, quote p. 376.

125 Tocqueville to Arthur de Gobineau (January 24, 1857). In: ibid., pp. 342–348, quotes p. 347.

126 See Romieu 1851b and Romieu 1851a.

127 In an article published in the *Rheinische Zeitung* in 1866, Ludwig Bamberger
     (1823–1899) stressed that "the concept of Caesarism, as it passes from hand to hand
     today, first came into the world with the dawn of the second French Empire. Romieu
     [...] gave the first impetus". *Der Cäsarismus* (1866). In: Bamberger 1894–1898 Vol. 3,
     pp. 328–336, quote p. 333.

128 On the perception of the Caesarism of Napoleon III in Germany see Gollwitzer 1952.
     An English translation appeared 35 years later (Gollwitzer 1987), then commented
     and located in more recent scholarly discussions.

129 See Frantz 1852. A more recent and commented edition is Frantz 1990.

130 See Frantz 1852, p. 3.

131 The term and concept of "Napoleonism" appears throughout the book, but is
     explicitly dealt with in Chapters VII (*Der Napoleonismus*) and VIII (*Der
     Napoleonismus und Europa*). See ibid., pp. 74–95.

132 Ibid., p. 31.

133 Ibid., p. 74.

134 Ibid., p. 32.

135 Ibid., p. 76f.

136 Ibid., p. 77.

137 Ibid., p. 78.

138 Ibid., p. 79.

139 See ibid., p. 80.

140 Ibid., p. 81.

141 Ibid., p. 4.

142 See ibid., p. 98.

143 Ibid., p. 101.

144 See ibid., p. 104f.

145 Ibid., p. 109.

146 See Groh 2004 [1972], p. 752.

147 *Provincial und Gesammt-Vertretung* (1851). In: Radowitz 1852–1853 Vol. 4,
     pp. 259–261, quote p. 259.

148 See *Die Strömungen* (1852). In: ibid. Vol. 4, p. 312f.

149 *Louis Napoleon und die Partheien* (1851). In: ibid. Vol. 4, p. 257f.

150 *Deutschland und der Napoleonismus* (1860). In: Planck 1922, pp. 3–65. Though
     written in 1860, the piece was only published in 1922.

151 Especially in jurisprudence that distinction had been used for some time, namely in
     the German "Historical School of Law" (*Historische Rechtsschule*) in the tradition of
     Friedrich Carl von Savigny.

152 See Diezel 1852, Diezel 1853.

153 Explicitly, e.g., Diezel 1852, p. 75f.

154 Diezel 1853, p. 215.

155 Ibid., p. 230.

156 Ibid., p. 261.

157 See Diezel 1852, p. 208.

158 Diezel 1853, p. 267f.

159 Diezel 1852, p. 391.

160 See Lieber 1853, especially pp. 335–351.

161 Ibid., p. 343.

162 See Mommsen 1853, p. 431.

163 Ibid., p. 432.

164   Mommsen 1857 [1853], p. 458.

165   Ibid., p. 459.

166   Mommsen 1858, p. 240.

167   Ibid., p. 241.

168   See Gollwitzer 1952, p. 60.

169   See Bonaparte 1865–1866.

170   See ibid. Vol. 1, p. VI. Tellingly, Caesar's bloody end was omitted in the work.

171   Quoted in: Wickert 1959–1980 Vol. 4, p. 153f.

172   *Das Vorwort Napoleon's III*. In: [Zeitung des Judenthums] No. 11 (March 14, 1865), pp. 162–164, continued in No. 12 (March 21, 1865), pp. 175–178. Quote p. 163f.

173   Ibid., p. 164.

174   "[…] die Verwandlung des Bonapartismus in den Cäsarismus gehört erst Napoleon III. an." Ibid., p. 175.

175   Ibid., p. 163.

176   See Gollwitzer 1952, pp. 40–44.

177   Segesser 1877, p. 339.

178   Ibid., p. 23.

179   Ibid., p. 138.

180   See Mundt 1857 Vol. 2, pp. 147–191, quote p. 148.

181   Ibid. Vol. 1, introduction.

182   Ibid. Vol. 1, p. 34.

183   Mundt 1858 Vol. 2, p. 176.

184   *Extinction du paupérisme* (1844). In: Bonaparte 1856 Vol. 2, pp. 107–151.

185   Mundt 1857 Vol. 1, p. 132.

186   See Mundt 1858 Vol. 2, p. 241.

187   Diezel 1852, p. 110f.

188   See Marx 1985 [1852], for an English translation Marx 1979 [1852]. On Marx's *Eighteenth Brumaire* see, e.g., Carver 2004.

189   Marx 1979 [1852], p. 103.

190   Marx 1869 [1852], p. IV.

191   Ibid., p. Vf.

192   Marx 1979 [1852], p. 187.

193   Ibid., p. 107f.

194   Ibid., p. 184f.

195   Ibid., p. 197.

196   *Discours sur les principes politiques de l'Empire* (August 26, 1863). In: Persigny 1865, pp. 157–167.

197   Ibid., p. 160.

198   See ibid., p. 164f.

199   Ibid., p. 166.

200   Ibid., p. 167.

201   See Price 2001, pp. 214–220.

202   See ibid., pp. 227–230.

203   See McMillan 1991, p. 138f.

204   Sellin 2018, p. 239.

205   Boon 1936, p. 91.

206   Ibid., p. 69.

207   Ibid., p. 73.

208   *Lettre au ministre d'État* (January 5, 1860). In: Bonaparte 1869 Vol. 5, pp. 107–112.

209 See Price 2001, p. 236f.

210 On the "management" of elections during the Second Empire see ibid., pp. 95–133.

211 Cf. Art. 5 of the 1852 Constitution.

212 Barni 1868, p. 113.

213 See, e.g., Rosanvallon 2008 [1992] and Rémond 1982 [1954], especially 106f.

214 See Hazareesingh 2004, especially pp. 140–145.

215 See Plessis 1979 [1973], p. 209.

216 Quoted in: Price 2001, p. 395f.

217 *Sénatus-consulte du 8 septembre 1869, qui modifie divers articles de la Constitution, les articles 3 et 5 du sénatus-consulte du 22 décembre 1852 et l'article 1er du sénatus-consulte du 31 décembre 1861* (September 8, 1869). In: [Staatsarchiv] 1861–1916 Vol. 18 (January to June 1870) No. 3946, pp. 17–19.

218 See Proclamation of Napoleon III to the French Nation (April 23, 1870). In: ibid. Vol. 18 (January to June 1870) No. 3956, p. 54.

219 *Sénatus-consulte fixant la Constitution de l'Empire* (May 21, 1870). In: [BL] 1852–1870 Vol. 35 No. 1802, pp. 519–530.

220 Imperial Sitting on the occasion of the proclamation of the official results of the plebiscite (May 21, 1870). In: [Staatsarchiv] 1861–1916 Vol. 18 (January to June 1870) No. 3965, pp. 68–71, quote p. 70f.

221 Price 2001, p. 400.

222 See Constant 1814.

223 See Sellin 2001, pp. 143–171.

224 See *Eigenhändiges Mémoire, betr. die Beziehungen Preußens zu Frankreich* (June 2, 1857). In: Poschinger 1882–1884 Vol. 4, pp. 274–280. Also in Bismarck 1924–1935 Vol. 2 No. 253, pp. 227–232 (headed *Denkschrift für Minister v. Manteuffel*).

225 Barni 1868, p. 246.

226 *Discours prononcé à l'ouverture du Congrès international de la paix* (September 9, 1867). In: ibid., pp. 259–263, quote p. 260.

227 On the "European Concert" after 1815 see Schulz 2009. The "Vienna System" can also be interpreted as the first in a series of European post-war peace utopias in the nineteenth and twentieth century (see Stråth 2016).

228 On the origins of the Franco-Prussian War see Wetzel 2001.

229 Price 2001, p. 406.

230 Quoted in: ibid., p. 409.

231 Quoted in: Fimiani 1995, p. 284.

5 "Germanic Caesarism" and the *Bismarckreich*

1 Diezel 1852, p. 133f.

2 Blankenburg 1870, p. 730.

3 Ibid., p. 724.

4 Ibid., p. 722.

5 Ibid., p. 725.

6 See Gollwitzer 1952, p. 58.

7 *Die Revolution und die Reaktion* (*Hartungsche Zeitung* Nr. 118, May 22, 1848). In: Rosenkranz 1919, pp. 105–110, quote p. 109.

8 See Rohmer 1848.

9 See ibid., p. 20.

10 Ibid., p. 23f.

11 Rochau 1853–1869 Vol. 1, p. 2.

12 Ibid. Vol. 1, p. 208.

13 Bollmann uses both the expressions "napoleonischer" and "französischer Cäsarismus".
    E.g., Bollmann 1858, p. 36, p. 47, p. 90.

14 Ibid., p. 47f.

15 See ibid., p. 58.

16 Ibid., p. 101.

17 Ibid., p. 102.

18 See Duncker, Max. In: [Allgemeine Deutsche Biographie] 1875–1912 Vol. 48,
    pp. 171–199, especially p. 184.

19 Duncker to Graf Maximilian von Schwerin-Putzar (Berlin, February 18, 1862).
    In: Duncker 1923, pp. 315–317, quotes p. 315 and 317.

20 In: Baumgarten 1894, p. XLVIII.

21 *Der deutsche Liberalismus. Eine Selbstkritik.* In: ibid., pp. 76–216.

22 See Gollwitzer 1952, p. 64f. The term *Cavourismus* is actually one of the nineteenth
    century and was actively used in Germany as early as in the 1860s. Cf., e.g., the article
    Zur Erwiderung. In: [Neue Preußische Zeitung] 1848–1939 No. 303 (December 30,
    1863), Beilage. For a comparison of "Cavourism" with "Bismarckism" see Rusconi 2013,
    especially pp. 129–155.

23 Baumgarten 1894, p. 181.

24 On the attitudes of Prussian conservatives towards Bonapartism particularly in the
    1850s see Barclay 2004, which has inspired the following section.

25 See Haller 1816–1825.

26 See Stahl 1845.

27 Ibid., p. 34.

28 Schlegelmilch 2009, p. 67.

29 Friedrich Wilhelm to Prince Johann von Sachsen (May 31, 1832). Quoted in: Barclay
    2004, p. 68.

30 Leopold von Gerlach to Otto von Bismarck (December 20, 1851). In: Gerlach 1912,
    pp. 4–6, quotes p. 5f.

31 Gerlach 1891–1892 Vol. 1 (December 26, 1851), pp. 710–713, quote p. 710f.

32 Ibid. Vol. 1 (January 2, 1852), p. 716f., quote p. 716.

33 Ibid. Vol. 2 (June 21, 1855), pp. 322–325, quote p. 323.

34 Leopold von Gerlach to Otto von Bismarck (June 5, 1857). In: Gerlach 1912,
    pp. 216–221, quote p. 218.

35 Ernst Ludwig von Gerlach to Leopold von Gerlach (February 3, 1853). Quoted in:
    Barclay 2004, p. 67.

36 Ibid., p. 76.

37 Leopold von Gerlach to Otto von Bismarck (January 23, 1855). In: Gerlach 1912,
    pp. 131–133, quote p. 132.

38 Leopold von Gerlach to Otto von Bismarck (May 21, 1857). In: ibid., pp. 213–216,
    quote p. 213.

39 See, for example, the letters of Leopold von Gerlach to Bismarck on January 4 and 23,
    1855, in which Gerlach characterized Manteuffels literally as "principaliter
    Bonapartist" and "völlig Bonapartist". In: ibid., pp. 126–129 and 131–133, quotes p. 127
    and p. 133.

40 See Leopold von Gerlach to Otto von Bismarck (February 25, 1853). In: ibid.,
    pp. 38–41, especially p. 39.

41 Leopold von Gerlach to Otto von Bismarck (November 13, 1852). In: ibid., pp. 27–30, quote p. 29.
42 Leopold von Gerlach to Otto von Bismarck (February 1854). In: ibid., pp. 79–83, quote p. 82.
43 See Riehl 1851, quotes p. 198.
44 Leopold von Gerlach to Otto von Bismarck (June 5, 1857). In: Gerlach 1912, pp. 216–221, quote p. 219. In English translation also in Bismarck 1898 [1890] Vol. 1, pp. 203–208, quote p. 206.
45 It remains unclear how, in the light of such criteria, Gerlach could disqualify Manteuffel as a Bonapartist (cf. note 39 above).
46 Barclay 2004, p. 79.
47 On this issue see, e.g., Stürmer 1974, Gall 1976 (re-edition: Gall 1996), Fehrenbach 1977, Mitchell 1977a (in German: Mitchell 1977b), Wolter 1977, Kuhn 1978, Pflanze 1982.
48 The argument of the non-comparability of Bismarck and the Bonapartes can be found, e.g., in Gall 1976 (explicitly p. 207) or Blanning 2004 (especially p. 65).
49 See, e.g., Gall 2008 [1980], p. 75.
50 Privatschreiben an Minister v. Manteuffel (April 26, 1856). In: Bismarck 1924–1935 Vol. 2, pp. 138–145.
51 Leopold von Gerlach to Otto von Bismarck (April 29, 1857). In: Gerlach 1912, pp. 205–208, quote p. 206.
52 See Otto von Bismarck to Leopold von Gerlach (May 2, 1857). In: Bismarck 2007 [1890], pp. 130–137, quote p. 131. English translation in Bismarck 1898 [1890] Vol. 1, pp. 170–180.
53 Leopold von Gerlach to Otto von Bismarck (May 6, 1857). In: Gerlach 1912, pp. 208–213, quote p. 211.
54 See Otto von Bismarck to Leopold von Gerlach (May 11, 1857). In: Gerlach/Bismarck 1893, p. 335f.
55 Leopold von Gerlach to Otto von Bismarck (May 21, 1857). In: Gerlach 1912, pp. 213–216, quote p. 213f.
56 *Eigenhändiges Mémoire, betr. die Beziehungen Preußens zu Frankreich* (2 June 1857). In: Poschinger 1882–1884 Vol. 4, pp. 274–280.
57 See Otto von Bismarck to Leopold von Gerlach (May 30, 1857). In: Gerlach/Bismarck 1893, pp. 337–345, especially p. 337 and p. 339.
58 Ibid., p. 340f.
59 Otto von Bismarck to Leopold von Gerlach (May 2, 1860). In: ibid., pp. 352–355, quote p. 354.
60 Ibid., p. 353.
61 See, e.g., Pflanze 1982.
62 See especially Wehler 1969.
63 Friedrich Engels to Karl Marx (April 13, 1866). In: Marx/Engels 1956–1990 Vol. 31 No. 104, p. 208f., quote p. 208.
64 See Lazzaro 1862, quote p. 17.
65 See, e.g., Fehrenbach 1977, p. 39.
66 See, e.g., Gall 1976, Mitchell 1977a.
67 See, e.g., Blanning 2004, Althammer 2009, p. 59f., Leonhard 2010, p. 312f.
68 See *Monsieur de Bismarck*. In: Bamberger 1894–1898 Vol. 3, pp. 337–443. See also Bamberger's article *Der Cäsarismus*, published in the *Rheinische Zeitung* in August 1866 (In: ibid. Vol. 3, pp. 328–336).
69 Cf. also Chapter 3.1.

70 For this view see already, e.g., Horn 1672 [1664] Book 1 Ch. 10 Para. 7.

71 Cf. Art. 57 of the *Schlußakte der Wiener Ministerkonferenzen* (May 15, 1820). In: Huber 1978 [1961], pp. 91–100.

72 See Kirsch 2007, p. 85. See also Kirsch 1999, pp. 210–218.

73 *Constitution faite en vertu des pouvoirs délégués par le Peuple français à Louis-Napoléon Bonaparte, par le vote des 20 et 21 Décembre 1851* (January 14, 1852). In: [BL] 1848–1852 Vol. 9 No. 479, pp. 49–72.

74 *Verfassungs-Urkunde für den Preußischen Staat* (January 31, 1850). In: [Preußische Gesetzessammlung] 1810–1906 1850 No. 3 (3212), pp. 17–35.

75 *Gesetz, betreffend die Verfassung des Deutschen Reichs* (April 16, 1871). In: [Bundesgesetzblatt des Deutschen Bundes] 1871 No. 16 (628), pp. 63–85.

76 *Sénatus-consulte fixant la Constitution de l'Empire* (May 21, 1870). In: [BL] 1852–1870 Vol. 35 No. 1802, pp. 519–530.

77 See Morsey 1957, p. 321.

78 See Fehrenbach 1977, p. 49.

79 Bismarck 1924–1935 Vol. 15, p. 179.

80 See Stürmer 1969.

81 See, e.g., Oeschey 1944, p. 388.

82 Stahl 1845, p. 18.

83 Ibid., p. 21. See also ibid., p. 30.

84 See Kuhn 1978, p. 290.

85 *Gesetz betreffend die Ertheilung der Indemnität in Bezug auf die Führung des Staatshaushalts vom Jahre 1862 ab und die Ermächtigung zu den Staatsausgaben für das Jahr 1866* (September 14, 1866). In: Huber 1978 [1961] Vol. 2, p. 102f.

86 On the exchanges between Bismarck and Lasalle see Mayer 1928.

87 See Robert von der Goltz (1817–1869) to Bismarck (Paris, January 29, 1863). In: Stolberg-Wernigerode 1941, p. 310f., here p. 311. More generally on the relations between Napoleon III and Bismarck: Geuss 1959.

88 Bismarck to Heinrich Alexander von Redern (1804–1888) (Berlin, April 17, 1866). In: Bismarck 1924–1935 Vol. 5, pp. 455–458, quote p. 457.

89 Quoted in: Fehrenbach 1977, p. 50.

90 In: [SBVRND] 1867–1870 Vol. 1, pp. 477–480, quote p. 479.

91 See Rein 1957, p. 106. In a conversation with the Austrian ambassador in Paris, Richard Klemens von Metternich (1829–1895), Napoleon III described universal suffrage as the single most important of the "principes sur lesquels repose mon pouvoir". Metternich to Alexander Graf von Mensdorff-Pouilly (Paris, April 14, 1866). In: Oncken 1967 [1926], pp. 133–135, quote p. 134.

92 See Althammer 2009, p. 45.

93 On Bismarck's stance towards suffrage see Augst 1917.

94 See Fehrenbach 1969, pp. 65–67.

95 See *Tischgespräch am 30. Januar 1871 in Versailles*. In: Bismarck 1924–1935 Vol. 7 (*Gespräche. Erster Band: Bis zur Aufrichtung des Deutschen Reiches*), pp. 491–494, especially p. 493f.

96 In: ibid. Vol. 15 (*Erinnerung und Gedanke*), p. 324.

97 In: ibid. Vol. 6b (*Politische Schriften: 1869 bis 1871*), p. 578 (introduction to *Schreiben an den bayrischen Ministerpräsidenten Grafen von Bray-Steinburg*, ibid. pp. 577–580).

98 See *Sitzung der Budgetkommission des Hauses der Abgeordneten* (September 30, 1862). In: Bismarck 1969–1970 [1892–1905] Vol. 2, pp. 20–38.

99   On the relation between foreign policies and Bismarckian "Bonapartism" see Wolter 1977.

100 Cf. Chapter 4.4.3.

101 In: [RGBl.] 1871–1945 1878 No. 34, pp. 351–358.

102 Bismarck, December 1880. In: Bismarck 1924–1935 Vol. 6c (*Politische Schriften: 1871 bis 1890*), p. 230.

103 Conversation of Bismarck with the English Writer William Harbutt Dawson (Friedrichsruh, April 18, 1892). In: ibid. Vol. 9 (*Gespräche. Dritter Band der Abteilung Gespräche: Von der Entlassung bis zum Tode Bismarcks*), pp. 194–197, quote p. 195f.

104 See Lassalle to Bismarck (Berlin, June 3, 1863). In: Mayer 1928, pp. 59–62, quote p. 60.

105 *Einleitung (1895) zu Karl Marx' „Die Klassenkämpfe in Frankreich 1848 bis 1850".* In: Marx/Engels 2010, pp. 330–351, quotes p. 338f.

106 Eyck 1968, p. 116f.

107 Fehrenbach 1977, p. 49.

108 See Jansen 2004, title.

109 Speech in the German *Reichstag* (February 24, 1881). In: Bismarck 1924–1935 Vol. 12 (*Reden 1878 bis 1885*), pp. 188–195, quote p. 195.

110 See Naumann 1905 [1900].

6 Mass Democracy and "Scientification": Caesarism at the Turn of the Century

1   Hillebrand 1873, p. 195. Hillebrand considered (democratic) *Tyrannis* and *Cäsarismus* to have essentially been France's form of government since the French Revolution, at times hidden, openly in the last 25 years (Ibid., p. 194 and p. 196).

2   This distinction had already been made earlier, among others by Karl von Rotteck in 1826 (see Rotteck 1826 Vol. 9, p. 83).

3   Mosse 1971, p. 167.

4   See also Baehr 2008, p. 51.

5   *Der Cäsarismus* (1866). In: Bamberger 1894–1898 Vol. 3, pp. 328–336, quote p. 328.

6   *France under Louis Napoleon.* In: [Westminster Review] 1824–1914 No. CXXXVIII (October 1858), pp. 167–194, quote p. 174.

7   See Russell 1865 [1821].

8   *The Coming Session.* In: [London Quarterly Review] 1809–1883 No. CXIX (January 1866), pp. 131–148, quote p. 147. Quoted in Murkens 2014, p. 369f.

9   *On Liberty* (1859). In: Mill 1989, pp. 1–115, quote p. 66.

10   *Caesarism as it now exists* (1865). In: Bagehot 1965–1986 Vol. 4, pp. 111–116.

11   Ibid., p. 111.

12   Ibid., p. 112.

13   Ibid., p. 113.

14   Ibid., p. 114.

15   Ibid., p. 115f.

16   *The Collapse of Caesarism* (1870). In: Bagehot 1965–1986 Vol. 4, pp. 155–159; quote p. 155f.

17   Ibid., p. 156.

18   Ibid., p. 158f. Unlike many other contemporaries, who draw a comparison between Napoleon III and Bismarck, Bagehot considered the French Second Empire very

distinct from the Prussian system of "personal government". The latter had "not in any sense been Caesarism, but indeed a system as strongly contrasted with Caesarism as our own system of parliamentary omnipotence", for "an hereditary king, strong in the affection of an aristocracy near his throne, and of a middle class that shows an educated preference for the old dynasty, has no need to fear the displeasure of the lowest among the population" (Ibid., p. 157 and p. 159).

19 Maine 1886 [1885], p. vii.
20 Ibid., p. x.
21 Ibid., p. 88f.
22 Ibid., p. 30.
23 See Hobson 1909.
24 Ibid., p. 12 and p. 14.
25 Brownson 1857, p. 434: "[...] monarchical absolutism, or what I choose to call modern Caesarism."
26 See [Abraham Africanus I] 1864.
27 The fact of John Wilkes Booth (1838–1865), Lincoln's assassinator, noting in his diary that he had shouted *Sic semper tyrannis*—attributed to Marcus Iunius Brutus during the murder of Caesar—proves evidence of the parallelization of Lincoln and Caesar being prominent especially among opponents of the President.
28 *What We May Learn from the Old World—The War against Caesarism in France and Spain—Have We a Republican Form of Government?* In: [New York Herald] 1835–1924 (July 7, 1873), p. 4.
29 Ibid.
30 See, e.g., Smith 1873.
31 See, e.g., *Grantism versus Caesarism.* In: [National Quarterly Review] 1860–1880 Vol. XXIX (June and September 1874), pp. 256–267.
32 See Lazzaro 1862, explicitly p. 5.
33 Ibid., p. 7.
34 Ibid., p. 16.
35 Ibid., p. 23f.
36 See Baehr 2008, p. 34f.
37 *Il Cesarismo* (1865). In: Mazzini 1938–1939 Vol. 2, pp. 791–807.
38 See Ferrero 1903 [1899], especially Chapter VII on *Militarism and Caesarism in France*, pp. 199–237.
39 Ibid., p. 201.
40 Ibid., p. 202.
41 Ibid., p. 203f.
42 *Césarisme.* In: Littré 1873–1877 [1863–1872] Vol. 1, p. 534.
43 *Césarisme.* In: Larousse 1866–1876 Vol. 3 (1867), p. 812.
44 It is worth mentioning that while Caesarism became an established term in French lexica and dictionaries in the second half of the nineteenth century, this was not consistently the case. *La grande encyclopédie: inventaire raisonné des sciences, des lettres et des arts*, for example, lacked an entry *Césarisme*, and also *Bonapartisme* was exclusively defined as "tendance politique qui s'efforce de rétablir ou de maintenir à la tete de la France la dynastie des Bonaparte". *Bonapartisme.* In: Dreyfus/Berthelot 1886–1902 Vol. 7 (1889), pp. 263–266, quote p. 263.
45 See Jourdeuil 1871.
46 Ibid., p. 5.
47 Ibid., p. 32.

48 The previous stages are termed "Le césarisme nobiliaire et clérical ; Le césarisme militaire et administratif ; Le césarisme bourgeois et parlementaire" (Ibid., p. 30).

49 Ibid., p. 20.

50 Ibid., p. 31, cf. also p. 27.

51 See Villedieu 1880.

52 Baehr 2008, p. 48.

53 Cf. the previous section.

54 See Ferrand 1904, quote p. 5.

55 See ibid., especially pp. 8–15.

56 See Pagès du Port 1888.

57 Ibid., p. 14f.

58 Ibid., p. 17.

59 Ibid., p. 18.

60 See ibid., p. 22. The author of the pamphlet is referring to the much noticed 1887 manifesto of the Comte de Paris, in which he had formally embraced universal manhood suffrage while simultaneously rejecting the principle of parliamentary government. Cf. note 63 below.

61 Pagès du Port 1888, p. 23.

62 Ibid., p. 24.

63 The programmatic guidelines of the monarchist movement in France were outlined by the Comte de Paris in 1887 as *Instructions de Mgr le Comte de Paris aux représentants du parti monarchiste en France* (see Orléans 1887).

64 See, e.g., Garrigues 1991.

65 See, e.g., Lafargue 1887, Pagès du Port 1888.

66 See, e.g., Pelletier 1986, Garrigues 1992.

67 See Hutton 1976, p. 93f.

68 [Programme du Général Boulanger] 1888.

69 On Boulangist propaganda see, e.g., Spoiden 2012.

70 See Garrigues 2009.

71 Quote in: ibid., p. 46.

72 See, e.g., [Le Temps] 1861–1942 No. 10131 (January 29, 1889), p. 1.

73 See Seager 1969, title.

74 *Le Boulangisme.* In: [Gaulois] 1868–1929 No. 2600 (October 11, 1889), p. 1.

75 See Hutton 1976, p. 90.

76 On the role of anti-parliamentarism for the Boulangist movement see Garrigues 2013.

77 See Doty 1970, p. 250.

78 See Hutton 1976, p. 86.

79 See, e.g., Morphy 1891.

80 See Barrès 1900.

81 For such an interpretation see, e.g., Adam 1895.

82 See Hutton 1976, p. 97f.

83 See Le Bon 1896 [1895].

84 Ibid., p. 117.

85 Ibid., p. 118.

86 Ibid., p. 118f., quote p. 119.

87 Ibid., p. 120.

88 Ibid., p. xxi.

89 Ibid., p. 122.

90   The importance of imitation had already been stressed by Le Bon in his earlier work
     L'homme et les Sociétés (see Le Bon 1881 Vol. 2, p. 116).
91   Le Bon 1896 [1895], p. 136.
92   Ibid., p. 145.
93   Ibid., p. 146.
94   Ibid., p. 158.
95   Ibid., p. 159.
96   Ibid., p. 162f.
97   Ibid., p. 190.
98   Ibid., p. 199.
99   Ibid., p. 200f.
100 Ibid., p. 221.
101 This is despite the fact that socialism—which Le Bon describes as "the last illusion
     that is still vital [to-day]" (Ibid., p. 109)—is considered a particularly threatening
     development.
102 Ibid., p. 33.
103 Even in the 1891 pamphlet *Le Boulangisme du people* (Copin-Albancelli 1891), the
     potential of Boulangism serving as a bridge between conservatism and republicanism
     was recognized.
104 *Cäsarismus*. In: [Brockhaus] 1882–1887 Vol. 4, p. 37f., quote p. 38. A literally identical
     characterization of "modern Caesarism" appeared in the *Cäsarismus* entry of the
     Brockhaus' fourteenth edition (1894), which otherwise was just slightly shorter than
     the one from the thirteenth, since the passages on ancient Roman Caesarism had
     been pruned. This might be taken as an argument for Caesarism becoming even
     more seen as a mainly modern phenomenon. See *Cäsarismus*. In: [Brockhaus]
     1893–1897 Vol. 3, p. 978.
105 Bonapartism and Napoleonism remained missing also in the following decades,
     such e.g. in the fourteenth edition (1894–1896) of the *Brockhaus* and its condensed
     edition of 1911. Therein, *Cäsarismus* was briefly characterized as follows:
     "Cäsarismus, das von Caesar eingeführte demokrat.-autokratische Staatssystem;
     absolute Militärherrschaft mit parlamentarischen Formen (2. Franz. Kaiserreich)."
     Cäsarismus. In: [Brockhaus] 1911 Vol. 1, p. 313.
106 *Cäsarismus*. In: [Meyers] 1885–1890 Vol. 3, p. 842. This fairly unique approach of
     claiming Roman and Napoleonic Caesarism to be merely different forms of
     "presidency" was not kept in later editions of *Meyers Konversations-Lexikon*. See, e.g.,
     the corresponding entry in the sixth edition of 1905 (*Cäsarismus*. In: [Meyers]
     1902–1908 Vol. 3, p. 792). Alike in the *Brockhaus*, specific entries for Bonapartism
     and/or Napoleonism remained absent in *Meyers*, too. In *Meyers Kleines Lexikon* of
     1933, Caesarism and Bonpartism were explicitly equated, with only a cross-reference
     to *Cäsarismus* under the entry *Bonapartismus*. See *Cäsarismus*. In: [Meyers] 1933
     Vol. 1, p. 800.
107 See Roscher 1874, p. 380f.
108 See Roscher 1888.
109 See ibid., p. 642.
110 See ibid., p. 646f., quote p. 646.
111 Ibid., p. 647f.
112 See ibid., p. 737.
113 E.g., Roscher's study was quoted as a reference work for the entry *Cäsarismus* in the
     fourteenth edition of the *Brockhaus* ([Brockhaus] 1893–1897 Vol. 3, p. 978), and

influences can be traced both to Max Weber and Georg Jellinek. See, e.g., Weber 1980 [1922], p. 156; Jellinek 1914 [1900], p. 525. At the same time, harsh criticsm towards Roscher's approach was uttered from other sides, e.g. by Otto Hintze (1861–1940). See, e.g., Hintze 1982 [1897].

114 See Schäffle 1896 [1875–1878]. The parts dealing with Caesarism remained unchanged in the second edition.

115 Ibid. Vol. 2, p. 486f.

116 Ibid. Vol. 2, p. 484.

117 Ibid. Vol. 2, p. 485.

118 See Groh 2004 [1972], p. 766.

119 In the same vain, e.g., Pöhlmann 1895, especially p. 266 and p. 284. Even radical socialists who did not tire warning of Caesarism as the fate of the working classes shared the view of Caesarism being an essentially ancient phenomenon (see, for example, Most 1878).

120 On Wilhelm II and his epoch see, e.g., Röhl 1993–2008.

121 On the Bismarck cult and myth starting to grow shortly after the Chancellor's dismissal and his legacy more generally see, e.g., Frankel 2003, Hardtwig 2005, Müller 2008.

122 See, e.g., Kessler 1962 [1935], pp. 251–266.

123 See, e.g., Gall 2001 [2000], p. 7.

124 This wording itself goes back to a speech of the later Chancellor Bernhard von Bülow (1849–1929), by then Secretary of State in the Foreign Ministry, in the *Reichstag* on December 6, 1897, in which he defended the Empire's colonial policy. In: [SBVR] 1871–1918 IX. Legislaturperiode V. Session Vol. 1, p. 60.

125 In: [RANZ] 1871–1918 1890 No. 34 (February 5, 1890), p. 1.

126 See Naumann 1905 [1900], especially pp. 221–229.

127 See, e.g., Hull 1991.

128 "If Mr. Punch's awakening was gradual he at least recognised the dangerous elements in the Kaiser's character as far back as October, 1888, when he underlined Bismarck's warning against Caesarism." Graves 1919, p. x.

129 See Quidde 1894. In a satirical manner, Quidde—who later received the Nobel Peace Prize in 1927 for his achievements in the German peace movement—branded the self-complacency and hubris of the "Emperor" (purportedly the Roman emperor Caligula, but essentially Wilhelm II), while ridiculing his personality. On Quidde's pamphlet see, e.g., Holl/Kloft/Fesser 2001.

130 See Kroll 2013, title (*Aufbruch in die Moderne*).

131 See Plessner 1982 [1959], p. 48.

132 On the question how far Wilhelm II was a *Medienkaiser* see, e.g., Glaab 2008. On the "charisma" of Wilhelm see, e.g., Sieg 2004.

133 Stürmer 1977a, p. 206.

134 On the "failure of leadership" see Dietrich 1981.

135 Weber 1988 [1919]-b, p. 541. In what follows, Johannes Winckelmann's edition of Weber's (scattered) political writings (Weber 1988) and *Wirtschaft und Gesellschaft* (Weber 1980 [1922]) are the standard reference works for quotes. The English translations are largely based on Weber 1946, Weber 1978 and Weber 1996.

136 See Schmidt 2000 [1995], pp. 181–185.

137 Weber 1988 [1919]-b, p. 541.

138 Weber 1988 [1918]-b, p. 351.

139 Weber 1988 [1919]-b, p. 542.

140 Ibid., p. 542. Translation follows Weber 1996, p. 349.

141 On Weber's criticism in this regard, see, e.g., Schluchter 1980.

142 See, e.g., Weber 1988 [1918]-a, p. 445.

143 Weber 1988 [1919]-b, p. 544. Translation follows Weber 1996, p. 351.

144 Extensive work in disclosing Caesarism as a central element of Weber's political sociology has been done by Peter Baehr (see especially Baehr 2004 and Baehr 2008).

145 See Weber to Hermann Baumgarten, November 8, 1884. In: Weber 1936, pp. 139–148, especially p. 143.

146 Weber 1988 [1918]-b, p. 314 (translation follows Weber 1978 Vol. 2, p. 1387).

147 Weber 1988 [1918]-b, p. 319 (translation: Weber 1978 Vol. 2, p. 1392). Weber never publicly branded Wilhelm II as Caesarist. This is most likely because Weber simply did not see much of a Caesaristic leader in the Emperor, but at best a pale administrator of the Bismarckian system. In private correspondence Weber did refer to Wilhelm as "Caesar", though. See, e.g., Weber to Hermann Baumgarten (January 3, 1891). In: Weber 1936, pp. 324–330, especially p. 328. In another letter a few days earlier, Weber had also identified "Boulangist-Bonapartist" elements in Wilhelm's understanding and practice of politics. Weber to Hermann Baumgarten (December 31, 1889). In: ibid., pp. 322–324, quote p. 323.

148 See, e.g., Weber's inaugural lecture at the University of Freiburg in May 1895 (*The Nation State and Economic Policy*. In: Weber 1996, pp. 1–28, especially p. 16).

149 On the *Hindenburgmythos*, which sprang in particular from Hindenburg's nimbus as the glorious victor of the Battle of Tannenberg in 1914 and was decisive for his winning the German presidential elections in 1925, see, e.g., Hoegen 2007.

150 Weber 1988 [1918]-b, p. 393f. (translation: Weber 1978 Vol. 2, p. 1451f).

151 Weber 1988 [1919]-b, p. 532 (translation: Weber 1946, p. 102f.).

152 The German term *Auslese*, resonating also a moment of "elitism", better reflects Weber's ideas than the English "selection" (*Auswahl*) or "election" (*Wahl*).

153 Weber 1988 [1917], p. 291 (translation: Weber 1996, p. 128).

154 Weber 1988 [1918]-b, p. 394 (translation: Weber 1978 Vol. 2, p. 1452).

155 Weber 1988 [1895], p. 23 (translation: Weber 1996, p. 26).

156 Weber 1988 [1918]-b, p. 395 (translation: Weber 1978 Vol. 2, p. 1452).

157 Weber 1988 [1918]-b, p. 401 (translation: Weber 1978 Vol. 2, p. 1457).

158 Weber 1988 [1918]-b, p. 395 (translation: Weber 1978 Vol. 2, p. 1452).

159 See Le Bon 1896 [1895], discussed in the previous chapter. On Weber's idea of the "irrationality of masses", following Le Bon's traits and a common *topos* of nineteenth-century debate on Caesarism, see Baehr 1998, pp. 236–242.

160 Weber 1988 [1918]-b, p. 401 (translation: Weber 1978 Vol. 2, p. 1457).

161 For more details see Baehr 2008, pp. 89–104.

162 See, e.g., Weber 1980 [1922], p. 156f. This "transformation" can be best exemplified in the drafting of *Wirtschaft und Gesellschaft*: while Caesarism still emerges twice in the 1913 draft of the typology of legitimate domination, it has vanished entirely from its 1918 and 1919 counterparts. For a critical edition of the early version of Weber's sociology of domination see Vol. I/22,4 of the *Max-Weber-Gesamtausgabe* currently being finalized (Weber 1984ff.). On the genesis of *Wirtschaft und Gesellschaft* see Vol. I/24 thereof.

163 See, for instance, Weber 1980 [1922], p. 156 (translation: Weber 1978 Vol. 1, p. 268): "Plebiscitary democracy—the most important type of leader democracy—is a variant of charismatic authority, which hides behind a legitimacy that is formally derived from the will of the governed."

164 Baehr 2008, p. 168.

165 See Weber 1980 [1922], pp. 122–176.

166 On his concept of *Legitimitätsglaube* see ibid., pp. 122–124.

167 The usefulness of applying a less biased terminology than Caesarism becomes
     particularly evident in Weber's 1919 essay *Politik als Beruf* (Weber 1988 [1919]-b):
     there, by using the language of charisma, Weber could convey his conviction that
     Caesaristic traits were *the* quality attribute of modern politicians without provoking
     immediate opposition for using "Caesarism".

168 On this note see, e.g., Eliaeson 1991, p. 318.

169 Weber 1988 [1919]-a, p. 501 (translation: Weber 1996, p. 308). See also his remarks in
     Politik als Beruf that only a president elected "in a plebiscitarian way and not by
     parliament" could become "the safety-valve of the demand for leadership" (Weber
     1988 [1919]-b, p. 544).

170 For a detailed account of the Weimar Constitution see Gusy 1997.

171 See Borch 2012.

172 Hutton 1976, p. 86.

173 Among the few ascribing Wilhelm II the qualities of a "citizen emperor" is
     Pintschovius 2008.

174 See, e.g., Wienfort 1993, p. 210.

175 Baehr 2008, p. 59.

176 See Schmidt 2000 [1995], pp. 194–197.

177 Weber 1988 [1918]-b, p. 329, Weber's footnote ("Politik ist: Kampf"). Cf. also ibid.,
     p. 392: "all politics is essentially struggle" ("alle Politik [ist] dem Wesen nach Kampf").

178 Weber 1988 [1919]-b, p. 512 (translation: Weber 1996, p. 316).

179 Weber 1988 [1918]-b, pp. 393–395, quote p. 394 (translation: Weber 1996, p. 221). See
     also Weber 1988 [1919]-b, pp. 532–540.

180 On the idea of constitutional(ized) Caesarism see, e.g., Eliaeson 2000.

181 Baehr 2004, p. 173.

182 Baehr 2008, p. 104.

183 The fifteenth edition of the *Brockhaus* appearing between 1929 and 1935 is a case in
     point. While *Cäsarismus* had been integral part both of the thirteenth and fourteenth
     edition, it no longer featured in the fifteenth edition. Neither can a specific entry on
     Napoleonismus be found (only such on *Napoleon* and *Bonaparte*). In turn, *Charisma*
     had now become a specific entry (as had *Chef* and *Demagog*). See [Brockhaus]
     1928–1935. This shift of attention in reference works was not specific to Germany,
     but actually a more universal phenomenon. The first edition of the *Enciclopedia
     italiana di scienze, lettere ed arti*, for example, contained an entry *Carisma* (as well as
     such on *Bonaparte* and *Cesaropapismo*), while both *Cesarismo* and *Bonapartismo*
     were missing. See [Enciclopedia Italiana] 1929–1937.

7 Outlook: Legacies of Caesarism

1   See Spengler 1922.

2   Ibid. Vol. 2, p. 505.

3   Ibid. Vol. 2, p. 521.

4   Ibid. Vol. 2, p. 523.

5   Ibid. Vol. 2, p. 541f.

6   Ibid. Vol. 2, p. 572.

7   Ibid. Vol. 2, p. 583. Cf. also ibid., p. 634. In an article for the *Preußische Jahrbücher* in 1921 Spengler expressed his conviction that "We Germans will never again produce a Goethe, but a Caesar" (Spengler 1967 [1921], p. 154).
8   See, e.g., Sontheimer 1957, p. 42f.
9   Mann 1920 [1918], p. 265f. Mann soon distanced himself from the views expressed in *Reflections of a Nonpolitical Man*, becoming a fierce defender of the Weimar Republic. See, e.g., his speech *Von deutscher Republik* on October 13, 1922 in Berlin.
10 See especially Sontheimer 1962.
11 Moeller van den Bruck 1926 [1923], p. 291.
12 See Sontheimer 1957, p. 44.
13 Jünger 1926, p. 223.
14 See Michels 1989 [1911].
15 Schmitt 1996 [1923], p. 63.
16 See, e.g., Spengler 1924, especially pp. 3–27.
17 Günther 1932, p. 177.
18 Moeller van den Bruck 1926 [1923], p. 154, p. 171 and p. 183.
19 *Führertum* (1930). In: Rohan 1930, pp. 56–63, quote p. 62.
20 Jung 1930 [1927], p. 333.
21 On Schmitt's concept of dictatorship see, e.g., Kelly 2016. Tellingly, when calling for a "democratic dictatorship", Jung himself references Carl Schmitt's characterization of "Caesarism" (Schmitt 1996 [1923], p. 42; see also footnote 4), though without using the term "Caesarism": Jung 1930 [1927], p. 333.
22 See Schmitt 2006 [1921].
23 Ibid., p. XIX.
24 Ibid., p. XIIIf.
25 Ibid., p. XIVf.
26 Schmitt is using Caesarism only randomly in *Die Diktatur*, and also not very consistently throughout, since the term is occasionally also referring to the Roman imperial period.
27 On Schmitt's intellectual relationship with Weber see, e.g., Engelbrekt 2009.
28 Schmitt 2006 [1921], p. XVI.
29 Ibid., p. 202.
30 See McCormick 2004.
31 Schmitt 2006 [1921], p. XVI.
32 Schmitt 2004 [1922], p. 13.
33 See Schmitt 1924, Schmitt 1929, Schmitt 1969 [1931], Schmitt 2005 [1932].
34 Schmitt 1969 [1931], p. 158.
35 Especially Art. 48 Par. 2 of the Constitution was pertinent: *Die Verfassung des Deutschen Reiches* (1919). In: [RGBl.] 1871–1945 1919 No. 152, pp. 1383–1418.
36 See especially Schmitt 1969 [1931]. In direct response to Schmitt's *Der Hüter der Verfassung*, Hans Kelsen (1881–1973) felt encouraged to draft his *Wer soll der Hüter der Verfassung sein?* (Kelsen 1931), in which he made a plea for constitutional courts as defenders of the constitutional order.
37 Schmitt 2004 [1922], p. 67.
38 For the friend-enemy distinction as the key characteristic of politics see Schmitt 2002 [1932], p. 26.
39 Schmitt 2004 [1922], p. 64.
40 Günther 1932, p. 177f.
41 See Schmitt 1933, especially p. 8.

42 Ibid., p. 33.
43 Schmitt 1934, column 946.
44 *Totaler Feind, totaler Krieg, totaler Staat* (1937) In: Schmitt 1940, pp. 235–239.
45 See Spengler 1933, Jung 1933. Spengler characterized the Nazis' *Machtergreifung*—
    using analogies to the situation in France 1793—in less than flattering terms (see
    Spengler 1933, p. IX).
46 Ibid., p. 140.
47 On the relation between Weber and Michels see, e.g., Wang 1997, pp. 56–61. Michels
    paid tribute to Weber's achievements throughout his life. See, e.g., Michels 1927,
    pp. 109–118.
48 Michels 1989 [1911], p. 210.
49 Ibid., p. 210.
50 Ibid., p. 211f.
51 Ibid., p. 213.
52 *Der Aufstieg des Fascismus in Italien* (1924). In: Michels 1987, pp. 265–295, quote p. 293.
53 *Über die Kriterien der Bildung und Entwicklung politischer Parteien* (1927). In: ibid.,
    pp. 298–304, quote p. 299.
54 See especially Michels 1930. For an analysis of Mussolini's personal charisma and his
    personality cult see, e.g., Melograni 1976, Gentile 1998. On the applicability of Weber's
    charisma concept to interwar Fascism more generally see, e.g., Kallis 2006, Pinto/
    Eatwell/Larsen 2007.
55 See, e.g., Nelis 2007.
56 See, e.g., Seldes 1935, p. 371f. Mussolini is claimed to have said: "Julius Caesar. The
    greatest man that ever lived. [...] Yes, I have a tremendous admiration for Caesar. Still
    [...] I myself belong rather to the class of the Bismarcks." Ibid., p. 371.
57 Bremer 1938, p. 163.
58 On Hitler's personal charisma and the role of charisma for National Socialism in
    general see, e.g., Kershaw 2002, Nolzen 2005, Lepsius 2006, Wehler 2007, Herbst 2010,
    Pyta 2010.
59 Windelband 1936, p. 103.
60 See Bouhler 1942, quotes p. 9 and p. 403. Hitler actually commented favorably on
    Bouhler's book (cf. Hitler's corresponding comments on March 23, 1942. In: Picker
    1965 [1963], p. 199f.) and compared himself with Napoleon at times, especially with
    respect to their plans for global domination. See, e.g., Speer 2002 [1975], p. 86. In
    retrospect, Speer admitted that he, too, had seen Hitler as a "great man" and heroic
    personality in the tradition of Napoleon (Ibid., 501f.).
61 *Hitler-Boulanger?* In: [Angriff] 1927–1945 (November 23, 1931) (1. Beilage).
62 See Weil 1931. Weil was not the only one discerning parallels between Boulanger and
    Hitler. See, e.g., *Boulanger, der vor Hitler war...* In: [Abendblatt Berlin] 1848–1938
    (February 11, 1932).
63 Mosley 1968, pp. 320–326, quote p. 323f. The speech is reproduced in Mosley's
    autobiography *My Life*, namely as a centerpiece of Chapter 17 "The Ideology of
    Fascism—Science and Caesarism" (Ibid., pp. 316–335).
64 Ibid., p. 324f. In his autobiography, Mosley fully reaffirmed his views uttered in the
    1930s: "After this lapse of time it still seems to me a very considerable thesis—now
    reinforced by the subsequent development of science—that for the first time executive
    men could find the means to do something truly great and enduring. The union of a
    revolutionary movement, which is a modern Caesarism, with the force of modern
    science could be nothing less than this." Ibid., p. 326f., quote p. 326.

65 See, e.g., Kershaw 2000 [1985], p. 45f.
66 See Arendt 1951. Cf. also Arendt's comment that "everything we know of totalitarianism demonstrates a horrible originality which no farfetched historical parallels can alleviate". *Understanding and Politics* (1954). In: Arendt 1994, pp. 307–327, quote p. 309.
67 See Friedrich/Brzeziński 1956.
68 See, e.g., Dülffer 1976.
69 Fascism is not mentioned in that part of the *Prison Notebooks* in which Gramsci mainly developed his thoughts on Caesarism (Gramsci 1971, pp. 219–223). The term "Caesarism" seems to have been suggested to Gramsci by the analogies drawn in Italy at the time to ancient Rome (see Gramsci 1974 [1951], p. 189f.).
70 Gramsci 1971, p. 219.
71 Ibid., p. 219.
72 See ibid., p. 222.
73 Ibid., p. 220.
74 Ibid., p. 220.
75 Ibid., p. 222.
76 See Neumann 1957 [1954].
77 Ibid., p. 233.
78 See ibid., p. 235f., quote p. 235.
79 See ibid., pp. 243-247.
80 See ibid., pp. 236–243, quote p. 236.
81 Ibid., p. 253 and p. 243f.
82 See ibid., p. 250f.
83 Baehr 1998, p. 284.
84 Compared to the predominant distinction between democracy and dictatorship (sometimes also autocracy or monocracy), the practical importance of suggested alternative typologies (see, e.g., Finer 1997 Vol. 1, p. 37, Brinkmann 1994 [1991]) is negligible.
85 Loewenstein 1965 [1957], p. 29.
86 See ibid., pp. 61–69.
87 Ibid., p. 63.
88 An English translation appeared in the same year: de Riencourt 1957.
89 Ibid., p. 5. Cf. also ibid., p. 8.
90 Ibid., p. 11.
91 Ibid., p. 328.
92 Ibid., p. 329.
93 Ibid., p. 329.
94 Ibid., p. 330f.
95 Ibid., p. 12.
96 See, e.g., Zeldin 1979, Rémond 1982 [1954], Thody 1989.
97 Pétain's charisma mainly resulted from his military achievements, notably during the First World War, which gained him the status of a national hero (*le héros de Verdun*). In this regard, Pétain had much in common with Hindenburg. See Goltz/Robert 2009.
98 On Bonapartist and Gaullist "heroic leadership" as a variant of Weber's charismatic leadership see Hayward 2004.
99 *Constitution [du 4 octobre 1958].* In: [JO] 1870ff. October 5, 1958, pp. 9151–9172.
100 It was as early as 1945 that Michel Debré (1912–1996)—a close aide of de Gaulle—had used the term *monarque républicain* (cf. Debré 1945, p. 122). On Debré's constitutional ideas see Wahl 1959.

101 See Mitterrand 1964.
102 Ibid., p. 79.
103 Ibid., p. 167f.
104 Hayward 2004, p. 230.
105 Flohic 1979, p. 58.
106 Cf., e.g., the online articles *Vladimir Putin and Donald Trump Are Symptoms of Creeping Caesarism* (Hui 2016) and *Forget Fascism: In the U.S. and Israel, Caesarism Is on the Rise* (Ilany 2016).
107 Out of the rich literature on contemporary populism see, e.g., Wodak/KhosraviNik/ Mral 2013, Moffitt 2016, Rovira Kaltwasser/Taggart/Ochoa Espejo/Ostiguy 2017.
108 Panizza 2005, title.
109 Rosanvallon 2008, title.
110 Among the features that seem to be genuine to modern populism is, e.g., the conscious playing with and deviating from "political correctness", which is a fairly recent concept largely unknown before the 1980s, or the active use of social media to repeatedly convey the same plain political messages.
111 In contemporary scholarship, especially social scientists tend to move away from making "charisma" central to the phenomenon of populism.
112 Dooren 1995, title.

8 Concluding Remarks

1 See, for example, Moore 1993 [1966], p. 413f.
2 See Huntington 1991.
3 "Transformation" competes and is often synonymously used with alternative terms such as "system change", "regime change", and "transition".
4 See Przeworski 2000, explicitly, e.g., p. 18.
5 See Fukuyama 1989, Fukuyama 1992.
6 Campbell 1958, p. 57.
7 Bonapartism continued to be prominent on the political left until the second half of the twentieth century, especially in Marxist historiography. See, e.g., Giertz 1970, Seeber/Dewitz 1977.
8 Bismarck 1898 [1890] Vol. 2, p. 66 (Original: Bismarck 2007 [1890], p. 321).
9 See Kissinger 1968, title.
10 For that term see, e.g., Zweig 1909, p. 481f. (*demokratische Tyrannis*).
11 Jellinek 1906, p. 80.
12 Weber 1988 [1919]-b, p. 536.
13 More than in other national contexts, it is in France that the concept of Caesarism in its articulations of Bonapartism and also Boulangism continues to be used explicitly to make sense of contemporary political life and figures. See, e.g., Hewlett 2007, Goodliffe 2012.
14 Leonhard 2010, p. 315.
15 Michels 1989 [1911], p. 210.
16 Wirth 2007, title. See also, e.g., Tänzler 2007.
17 Boesche 1996, p. 201.

Bibliography

[Abendblatt Berlin]. 1848–1938. *8-Uhr-Abendblatt*. Berlin.

[Abraham Africanus I]. 1864. *Abraham Africanus I. His Secret Life, as Revealed under Mesmeric Influence. Mysteries of the White House*. New York, NY.

[Allgemeine Deutsche Biographie]. 1875–1912. *Allgemeine Deutsche Biographie*. 56 Vols. Leipzig.

[Angriff]. 1927–1945. *Der Angriff*. Berlin.

[AP]. 1862ff. [1787–1799]. *Archives parlementaires de 1787 à 1860: recueil complet des débats législatifs & politiques des chambres françaises. Première série (1787 à 1799)*. Paris.

[BL]. 1814. *Bulletin des lois du Royaume de France, 5e série*. Paris.

[BL]. 1815. *Bulletin des lois, 6e série*. Paris.

[BL]. 1830–1848. *Bulletin des lois du Royaume de France, 9e série*. Paris.

[BL]. 1848–1852. *Bulletin des lois de la République française, 10e série*. Paris.

[BL]. 1852–1870. *Bulletin des lois de l'Empire français, 11e série*. Paris.

[Brockhaus]. ^{13}1882–1887. *Brockhaus' Conversations-Lexikon*. 16 Vols. Leipzig.

[Brockhaus]. ^{14}1893–1897. *Brockhaus' Konversations-Lexikon*. 16 Vols. Leipzig; Berlin; Wien.

[Brockhaus]. ^{5}1911. *Brockhaus' Kleines Konversations-Lexikon*. 2 Vols. Leipzig.

[Brockhaus]. ^{15}1928–1935. *Der Große Brockhaus. Handbuch des Wissens in zwanzig Bänden*. 20 Vols. Leipzig.

[Bundesgesetzblatt des Deutschen Bundes]. 1871. *Bundesgesetzblatt des Deutschen Bundes*. Berlin.

[Edinburgh Review]. 1802–1929. *The Edinburgh Review*. London.

[Enciclopedia Italiana]. 1929–1937. *Enciclopedia Italiana di scienze, lettere ed arti*. 35 Vols. Roma.

[European Magazine]. 1782–1825. *The European Magazine, and London Review, Containing Portraits and Views; Biography, Anecdotes, Literature, History, State Papers, Parliamentary Journal, Gazettes, Politics, Arts, Manners, and Amusement of the Age [. . .]*. London.

[FAZ]. *Frankfurter Allgemeine Zeitung*. Frankfurt/Main.

[Gaulois]. 1868–1929. *Le Gaulois*. Paris.

[Gazette nationale]. 1789–1810. *Gazette nationale ou le Moniteur universel*. Paris.

[JO]. 1870ff. *Journal officiel de la République française*. Paris.

[Le Temps]. 1861–1942. *Le Temps*. Paris.

[London Quarterly Review]. 1809–1883. *The London Quarterly Review. American Edition*. New York, NY.

[Meyers]. ^{4}1885–1890. *Meyers Konversations-Lexikon. Eine Encyklopädie des allgemeinen Wissens*. 16 [17] Vols. Leipzig.

[Meyers]. ^{6}1902–1908. *Meyers Großes Konversations-Lexikon. Ein Nachschlagewerk des allgemeinen Wissens*. 20 Vols. Leipzig; Wien.

[Meyers]. ^{9}1933. *Meyers Kleines Lexikon*. 3 Vols. Leipzig.

[Moniteur universel]. 1811–1868. *Le Moniteur universel*. Paris.

[National Quarterly Review]. 1860–1880. *The National Quarterly Review*. New York, NY.

[Neue Preußische Zeitung]. 1848–1939. *Neue Preußische Zeitung*. Berlin.

[New York Herald]. 1835–1924. *The New York Herald*. New York, NY.

[Parliamentary Debates]. 1803–1820. *The Parliamentary Debates from the Year 1803 to the Present Time [First Series]*. 25 Vols. London.

[Preußische Gesetzessammlung]. 1810–1906. *Gesetz-Sammlung für die Königlichen Preußischen Staaten*. Berlin.

[Programme du Général Boulanger]. 1888. *Programme du Général Boulanger*. Paris.

[RANZ]. 1871–1918. *Deutscher Reichs-Anzeiger und Königlich Preußischer Staats-Anzeiger*. Berlin.

[RGBl.]. 1871–1945. *Reichs-Gesetzblatt*. Berlin.

[SBVR]. 1871–1918. *Stenographische Berichte über die Verhandlungen des Reichstags*. Berlin.

[SBVRND]. 1867–1870. *Stenographische Berichte über die Verhandlungen des Reichstages des Norddeutschen Bundes*. Berlin.

[Staatsarchiv]. 1861–1916. *Das Staatsarchiv. Sammlung der officiellen Actenstücke zur Geschichte der Gegenwart [ed. by Ludwig Carl Aegidi and Alfred Klauhold]*. 86 Vols. Hamburg; Leipzig [from vol. 22].

[Westminster Review]. 1824–1914. *Westminster Review*. London.

[Zeitung des Judenthums]. *Allgemeine Zeitung des Judenthums. Ein unparteiisches Organ für alles jüdische Interesse*. Bonn.

Abbott, John S.C. 1855. *The History of Napoleon Bonaparte with Maps and Illustrations*. 2 Vols. London; New York, NY.

Adam, Paul. 1895. *Le mystère des foules*. 2 Vols. Paris.

Alexander, Robert S. 2000. "The Hero as Houdini: Napoleon and 19th-century Bonapartism". In: *Modern & Contemporary France* 8 (4), 457–467.

Alexander, Robert S. 2001. *Napoleon*. London.

Althammer, Beate. 2009. *Das Bismarckreich 1871–1890*. Paderborn [etc.].

Anceau, Éric. 2008. *Napoléon III: un Saint-Simon à cheval*. Paris.

Anceau, Éric. 2009. "Le coup d'État du 2 décembre 1851 ou la chronique de deux morts annoncées et l'avènement d'un grand principe". In: *Parlement[s]. Revue d'histoire politique* 12 (2), 24–42.

Anderson, Eugene N.; Anderson, Pauline R. 1967. *Political Institutions and Social Change in Continental Europe in the Nineteenth Century*. Berkeley, CA.

Arendt, Hannah. 1951. *The Origins of Totalitarianism*. New York, NY.

Arendt, Hannah. 1994. *Essays in Understanding 1930–1954: Formation, Exile, and Totalitarianism [ed. by Jerome Kohn]*. New York, NY.

Arendt, Hannah. 2004 [1951]. *The Origins of Totalitarianism*. New York, NY.

Arnold, Thomas. ²1844. *The Life and Correspondence of Thomas Arnold, D.D., Late Head Master of Rugby School, and Regius Professor of Modern History in the University of Oxford [ed. by Arthur Penrhyn Stanley]*. 2 Vols. London.

Asprey, Robert B. 2000–2001. *The Rise and Fall of Napoleon Bonaparte*. 2 Vols. London.

Augst, Richard. 1917. *Bismarcks Stellung zum parlamentarischen Wahlrecht*. Leipzig.

Baehr, Peter. 1998. *Caesar and the Fading of the Roman World: A Study in Republicanism and Caesarism*. New Brunswick, NJ; London.

Baehr, Peter. 2004. "Max Weber and the Avatars of Caesarism". In: Baehr, Peter; Richter, Melvin (Ed.). *Dictatorship in History and Theory: Bonapartism, Caesarism, and Totalitarianism*. Cambridge, 155–174.

Baehr, Peter. 2008. *Caesarism, Charisma and Fate: Historical Sources and Modern Resonances in the Work of Max Weber.* New Brunswick, NJ; London.

Baehr, Peter; Richter, Melvin (Ed.). 2004. *Dictatorship in History and Theory: Bonapartism, Caesarism, and Totalitarianism.* Cambridge.

Bagehot, Walter. 1965–1986. *The Collected Works of Walter Bagehot [ed. by Norman St. John-Stevas].* 15 Vols. London.

Bamberger, Ludwig. 1894–1898. *Gesammelte Schriften.* 5 Vols. Berlin.

Barclay, David E. 2004. "Prussian Conservatives and the Problem of Bonapartism". In: Baehr, Peter; Richter, Melvin (Ed.). *Dictatorship in History and Theory: Bonapartism, Caesarism, and Totalitarianism.* Cambridge, 67–81.

Barni, Jules. 1868. *La morale dans la démocratie.* Paris.

Barrès, Maurice. 1900. *L'appel au soldat.* Paris.

Baumgarten, Hermann. 1894. *Historische und politische Aufsätze und Reden [ed. by Erich Marcks].* Straßburg.

Beneyto Pérez, José María. 1988. *Apokalypse der Moderne. Die Diktaturtheorie von Donoso Cortés.* Stuttgart.

Berlia, Georges [et al.] (Ed.). ⁷1952 [1898]. *Les constitutions et les principales lois politiques de la France depuis 1789.* Paris.

Berlier, Théophile. 1838. *Précis de la vie politique de Théophile Berlier écrit par lui même et adressé à ses enfans.* Dijon.

Bernier, Olivier. 1983. *Lafayette: Hero of Two Worlds.* New York, NY.

Beßlich, Barbara. 2007. *Der deutsche Napoleon-Mythos. Literatur und Erinnerung 1800–1945.* Darmstadt.

Beyme, Klaus von. 2002. *Politische Theorien im Zeitalter der Ideologien. 1789–1945.* Wiesbaden.

Bismarck, Otto von. 1898 [1890]. *Bismarck: The Man and the Statesman. Being the Reflections and Reminiscences of Otto Prince von Bismarck [ed. by A.J. Butler].* 2 Vols. London.

Bismarck, Otto von. 1924–1935. *Die gesammelten Werke [ed. by Herman von Petersdorff].* 15 [19] Vols. Berlin.

Bismarck, Otto von. 1969–1970 [1892–1905]. *Die politischen Reden des Fürsten Bismarck: Historisch-kritische Gesamtausgabe [ed. by Horst Kohl].* 14 Vols. Aalen.

Bismarck, Otto von. 2007 [1890]. *Gedanken und Erinnerungen [ed. by Hermann Proebst].* München.

Blankenburg, Heinrich. 1870. "Verfassung und innere Politik des zweiten Kaiserreichs. Historisch-kritischer Essay". In: *Unsere Zeit. Deutsche Revue der Gegenwart. Monatsschrift zum Conversations-Lexikon* 6 (1), 721–750.

Blanning, Timothy C.W. 2004. "The Bonapartes and Germany". In: Baehr, Peter; Richter, Melvin (Ed.). *Dictatorship in History and Theory: Bonapartism, Caesarism, and Totalitarianism.* Cambridge, 53–66.

Boesche, Roger. 1996. *Theories of Tyranny from Plato to Arendt.* University Park, PA.

Böhmer, Johann Friedrich. 1868. *Johann Friedrich Böhmer's Leben, Briefe und kleinere Schriften [ed. by Johannes Janssen].* 3 Vols. Freiburg/Breisgau.

Bollmann, Karl. 1858. *Vertheidigung des Macchiavellismus.* Quedlinburg.

Bonaparte, Joseph-Napoléon. 1854. *Mémoires et correspondance politique et militaire du Roi Joseph [ed. by A. du Casee].* 10 Vols. Paris.

Bonaparte, Louis. 1852. *The Political and Historical Works of Louis Napoleon Bonaparte, President of the French Republic. Now First Collected with an Original Memoir of His Life, Brought Down to the Promulgation of the Constitution of 1852, and Occasional Notes.* 2 Vols. London.

Bonaparte, Louis. 1856. *Œuvres de Napoléon III*. 4 Vols. Paris.

Bonaparte, Louis. 1865–1866. *Histoire de Jules César*. 2 Vols. Paris.

Bonaparte, Louis. 1869. *Œuvres de Napoléon III*. 5 Vols. Paris.

Bonaparte, Lucien. 1836a. *Memoirs of Lucien Bonaparte (Prince of Canino). Part the First (From the year 1792, to the year 8 of the Republic)*. New York, NY.

Bonaparte, Lucien. 1845. *Révolution de brumaire, ou Relation des principaux évévenments des journées des 18 et 19 brumaire, par Lucien Bonaparte, prince de Canino. Suivi d'une notice nécrologique sur ce Prince, et d'une ode intitulée: l'Amérique, extraite du Recueil de ses Poésies posthumes*. Paris.

Bonaparte, Napoléon. 1823–1824. *Memoirs of the History of France During the Reign of Napoleon, dictated by the Emperor at Saint Helena to the Generals who Shared his Captivity, and Published from the Original Manuscripts Corrected by Himself*. 7 Vols. London.

Bonaparte, Napoléon. 1836b. *Précis des guerres de César, par Napoléon, écrit par M. Marchand, à l'île Sainte-Hèlène, sous la dictée de l'Empereur, suivi des plusieurs fragmens inédits*. Paris.

Bonaparte, Napoléon. 1858–1869. *Correspondance de Napoléon Ier. Publiée par ordre de l'Empereur Napoléon III*. 32 Vols. Paris.

Bonaparte, Napoléon. 1908. *Napoléon: manuscripts inédits 1786–1791. Publiés d'après les originaux autographes [ed. by Frédéric Masson and Guido Biagi]*. Paris.

Bonaparte, Napoléon. ²1911–1913. *Gespräche Napoleons des Ersten [ed. by F.M. Kircheisen]*. 3 Vols. Stuttgart.

Bonaparte, Napoléon. 1955. *The Mind of Napoleon: A Selection from his Written and Spoken Words [ed. by H.J. Christopher]*. New York, NY.

Bonaparte, Napoléon. 2004ff. *Correspondance générale [ed. by Fondation Napoléon]*. Paris.

Boon, Hendrik Nicolaas. 1936. *Rêve et réalité dans l'oeuvre économique et sociale de Napoléon III*. 's-Gravenhage.

Borch, Christian. 2012. *The Politics of Crowds: An Alternative History of Sociology*. Cambridge [etc.].

Boudon, Jacques-Olivier. 2009. "Lucien Bonaparte et le coup d'État de Brumaire". In: *Parlement[s]. Revue d'histoire politique* 12 (2), 8–23.

Bouhler, Philipp. 1942. *Napoleon. Kometenbahn eines Genies*. München.

Bourrienne, Louis Antoine Fauvelet de. 1829. *Mémoires de M. de Bourrienne, ministre d'État, sur Napoléon, le Directoire, le Consulat, l'Empire et la Restauration*. 10 Vols. Bruxelles.

Bremer, Karl-Heinz. 1938. "Der sozialistische Kaiser". In: *Die Tat* 30 (1), 160–171.

Brinkmann, Karl. ²1994 [1991]. *Verfassungslehre*. München; Wien.

Broers, Michael. 2008. "The Concept of 'Total War' in the Revolutionary-Napoleonic Period". In: *War In History* 15 (3), 247–268.

Brownson, Orestes Augustus. 1857. *The Convert: or, Leaves from my experience*. New York, NY.

Brunner, Otto; Conze, Werner; Koselleck, Reinhart (Ed.). 1972–1997. *Geschichtliche Grundbegriffe. Historisches Lexikon zur politisch-sozialen Sprache in Deutschland*. 8 [9] Vols. Stuttgart.

Bruyère-Ostells, Walter. 2013. "De l'héritage politique napoléonien à la formulation du césarisme démocratique (1814–1848)". In: *French Politics, Culture & Society* 31 (2), 1–14.

Buchholz, Paul Ferdinand Friedrich. 1804. "Ueber den Unterschied des Despotismus und der Souveränität, in Beziehung auf Bonaparte". In: *Geschichte und Politik. Eine Zeitschrift* 1, 265–286.

Buchholz, Paul Ferdinand Friedrich. 1805. *Der neue Leviathan*. Tübingen.

Burke, Edmund. 2001 [1790]. *Reflections on the Revolution in France: A Critical Edition [ed. by J.C.D. Clark]*. Stanford, CA.

Cabanis, José. 2007 [1970]. *Le sacre de Napoléon: 2 décembre 1804*. Paris.

Calhoun, Craig (Ed.). 2002. *Dictionary of the Social Sciences*. Oxford [etc.].

Calleo, David. 1960. "Coleridge on Napoleon". In: *Yale French Studies* (26), 83–93.

Campbell, Peter. 1958. *French Electoral Systems and Elections since 1789*. London.

Capefigue, Baptiste. 1840. *L'Europe pendant le Consulat et l'Empire de Napoléon*. 10 Vols. Paris.

Carlyle, Thomas. 1840. *On Heroes, Hero-Worship, and the Heroic in History*. London.

Carver, Terrell. 2004. "Marx's Eighteenth Brumaire of Louis Bonaparte: Democracy, Dictatorship, and the Politics of Class Struggle". In: Baehr, Peter; Richter, Melvin (Ed.). *Dictatorship in History and Theory: Bonapartism, Caesarism, and Totalitarianism*. Cambridge, 103–127.

Chandler, David G. 1989. "Napoleon as Man and Leader". In: *Consortium on Revolutionary Europe 1750-1850: Proceedings* 19 (1), 582–605.

Chaptal, Jean Antoine Claude de. 1893. *Mes souvenirs sur Napoléon [ed. by Antoine Chaptal]*. Paris.

Charavay, Étienne. 1898. *Le général La Fayette, 1757–1834: notice biographique*. Paris.

Chateaubriand, François René Auguste vicomte de. 1797. *Essai historique, politique et moral, sur les révolutions anciennes et modernes, considérées dans leurs rapports avec La Révolution Françoise*. London.

Chateaubriand, François René Auguste vicomte de. 1849–1850. *Mémoires d'outre-tombe*. 12 Vols. Paris.

Chatelain, Jacques. 1970. "Du Bonapartisme intégral au Bonapartisme libéral: Latour du Moulin, député du Doubs". In: *Politique* (49), 167–208.

Chod'zko, Leonard Jakób Borejko [= Comte d'Angeberg] (Ed.). 1863. *Le congrès de Vienne et les traités de 1815, précédé et suivi des actes diplomatiques qui s'y rattachent. Avec une introduction historique par M. Capefigue*. 2 Vols. Paris.

Clément, Pascal. 2006. *Persigny: l'homme qui a inventé Napoléon III*. Paris.

Constant, Benjamin. ⁴1814. *De l'esprit de conquête et de l'usurpation dans leurs rapports avec la civilisation européenne*. Paris.

Constant, Benjamin. 2002 [1988]. *Political Writings [ed. by Biancamaria Fontana]*. Cambridge.

Constant, Benjamin [= Constant de Rebecque, Henri-Benjamin]. 1815. *Principes de politique, applicables à tous les gouvernements représentatifs et particulièrement à la constitution actuelle de la France*. Paris.

Copin-Albancelli, Paul. 1891. *Le Boulangisme du peuple*. Paris.

de Riencourt, Amaury. 1957. *The Coming Caesars*. London.

Debré, Michel; Monick, Emmanuel [= Jacquier-Bruère]. 1945. *Refaire la France: l'effort d'une génération*. Paris.

Denquin, Jean-Marie. 1976. *Référendum et plébiscite: essai de théorie générale*. Paris.

Dietrich, Donald. 1981. "Kaiser Wilhelm II.: Crisis and the Failure of Leadership". In: *Journal of Psychohistory* 8 (4), 465–484.

Diezel, Gustav. 1852. *Deutschland und die abendländische Civilisation. Zur Läuterung unserer politischen und socialen Begriffe*. Stuttgart.

Diezel, Gustav. 1853. *Frankreich, seine Elemente und ihre Entwicklung. Mit einer Einleitung über Form und Freiheit in der Geschichte*. Stuttgart.

Dippel, Horst. 1989. "Popular Sovereignty and the Separation of Powers in American and French Revolutionary Constitutionalism". In: *Amerikastudien-American Studies* 34 (1), 21–31.

Donoso Cortés, Juan. 1854–1855. *Obras de Don Juan Donoso Cortés, Marqués de Valdegamas [ed. by Don Gavino Tejado].* 5 Vols. Madrid.

Donoso Cortés, Juan. 1879 [1851]. *Essays on Catholicism, Liberalism and Socialism: Considered in their Fundamental Principles [translated by William McDonald].* Dublin.

Donoso Cortés, Juan. 2007. *Donoso Cortes: Readings in Political Theory [ed. by Robert A. Herrera].* Ave Maria, FL.

Dooren, Ron van. 1995. "Charismatic Leadership: The Illusion of Mastery". In: *Politics, Groups and the Individual. International Journal of Political Psychology and Political Socialization* 5 (2), 31–36.

Doty, C. Stewart. 1970. "Parliamentary Boulangism after 1889". In: *Historian* 32 (2), 250–269.

Dreyfus, Ferdinand-Camille; Berthelot, André (Ed.). 1886–1902. *La grande encyclopédie: inventaire raisonné des sciences, des lettres et des arts.* 31 Vols. Paris.

Dülffer, Jost. 1976. "Bonapartism, Fascism and National Socialism". In: *Journal of Contemporary History* 11 (4), 109–128.

Duncker, Maximilian Wolfgang. 1923. *Politischer Briefwechsel aus seinem Nachlaß [ed. by Johannes Schultze].* Stuttgart; Berlin.

Eisenstadt, Shmuel N. 1992. "Frameworks of the Great Revolutions: Culture, Social Structure, History and Human Agency". In: *International Social Science Journal* 133, 385–401.

Eisenstadt, Shmuel N. 2006. *The Great Revolutions and the Civilizations of Modernity.* Leiden [etc.].

Eliaeson, Sven. 1991. "Between Ratio and Charisma—Max Weber's Views on Plebiscitary Leadership Democracy". In: *Statsvetenskaplig Tidskrift* 94 (4), 317–339.

Eliaeson, Sven. 2000. "Constitutional Caesarism: Weber's Politics in their German Context". In: Turner, Stephen (Ed.). *The Cambridge Companion to Weber.* Cambridge, 131–148.

Ellis, Geoffrey. 1997. *Napoleon.* London [etc.].

Engelbrekt, Kjell. 2009. "What Carl Schmitt Picked Up in Weber's Seminar: A Historical Controversy Revisited". In: *European Legacy* 14 (6), 667–684.

Englund, Steven. 2005. *Napoleon: A Political Life.* New York, NY [etc.].

Erbe, Michael. 1995. "Der Caesarmythos im Spiegel der Herrschaftsideologie Napoleons I. und Napoleons III.". In: Stupperich, Reinhard (Ed.). *Lebendige Antike. Rezeptionen der Antike in Politik, Kunst und Wissenschaft der Neuzeit. Kolloquium für Wolfgang Schiering.* Mannheim, 135–142.

Eyck, Erich. ³1968. *Bismarck and the German Empire.* London.

Fehrenbach, Elisabeth. 1969. *Wandlungen des deutschen Kaisergedankens 1871–1918.* München; Wien.

Fehrenbach, Elisabeth. 1977. "Bonapartismus und Konservatismus in Bismarcks Politik". In: Hammer, Karl; Hartmann, Peter Claus (Ed.). *Le Bonapartisme. Phénomène historique et mythe politique. Actes du 13e colloque historique franco-allemand de l'Institut Historique Allemand de Paris à Augsbourg du 26 jusqu'au 30 septembre 1975/ Der Bonapartismus. Historisches Phänomen und politischer Mythos. 13. deutsch-französisches Historikerkolloquium des Deutschen Historischen Instituts Paris in Augsburg vom 26. bis 30. September 1975.* Zürich; München, 39–55.

Ferrand, Joseph. 1904. *Césarisme et démocratie: l'incompatibilité entre notre régime administratif et notre régime politique.* Paris.

Ferrero, Guglielmo. 1903 [1899]. *Militarism: A Contribution to the Peace Crusade.* Boston, MA.

Ferrero, Guglielmo. 1933. *The Life of Caesar.* New York, NY.

Fimiani, Enzo. 1995. "Per una storia delle teorie e pratiche plebiscitarie nell'Europa moderna e contemporanea". In: *Annali dell'Istituto storico italo-germanico in Trento* 21, 267–333.

Finer, Samuel E. 1997. *The History of Government from the Earliest Times*. 3 Vols. Oxford; New York, NY.

Flohic, François. 1979. *Souvenirs d'outre-Gaulle*. Paris.

Ford, Franklin L. 1970. *Europe: 1780–1830*. London.

Frankel, Richard. 2003. "From the Beer Halls to the Halls of Power: The Cult of Bismarck and the Legitimization of a New German Right, 1898–1945". In: *German Studies Review* 26 (3), 543–560.

Frantz, Constantin. 1852. *Louis Napoleon*. Berlin.

Frantz, Constantin. 1990. *Louis Napoléon. Masse oder Volk [ed. by Günter Maschke]*. Wien; Leipzig.

Freedom House (Ed.). 2018. *Freedom in the World 2018: Democracy in Crisis*. Washington, D.C.

Friedrich, Carl J.; Brzeziński, Zbigniew. 1956. *Totalitarian Dictatorship and Autocracy*. Cambridge, MA.

Fukuyama, Francis. 1989. "The End of History?". In: *The National Interest* 16, 3–18.

Fukuyama, Francis. 1992. *The End of History and the Last Man*. New York, NY.

Furet, François; Halévi, Ran. 1996. *La monarchie républicaine: La Constitution de 1791*. Paris.

Gacon, Jean. 1958. "Les tentations du bonapartisme et le mythe de la grandeur". In: *La Pensee* (80), 6–16.

Galindo Herrero, Santiago. 1957. *Donoso Cortés y su teoría política*. Badajoz.

Gall, Lothar. 1976. "Bismarck und der Bonapartismus". In: *Historische Zeitschrift* 223 (3), 618–637.

Gall, Lothar. 1996. "Bismarck und der Bonapartismus". In: Gall, Lothar (Ed.). *Bürgertum, liberale Bewegung und Nation: ausgewählte Aufsätze [ed. by Dieter Hein]*. München, 256–271.

Gall, Lothar. ²2001 [2000]. "Otto von Bismarck und Wilhelm II.: Repräsentanten eines Epochenwechsels?". In: Gall, Lothar (Ed.). *Otto von Bismarck und Wilhelm II.: Repräsentanten eines Epochenwechsels?* Paderborn [etc.], 1–12.

Gall, Lothar. ³2008 [1980]. *Bismarck. Der weiße Revolutionär*. Berlin.

Garrigues, Jean. 1991. *Le Général Boulanger*. Paris.

Garrigues, Jean. 1992. *Le boulangisme*. Paris.

Garrigues, Jean. 2009. "Le Général Boulanger et le fantasme du coup d'État". In: *Parlement[s]. Revue d'histoire politique* 12 (2), 43–48.

Garrigues, Jean. 2013. "Le boulangisme est-il antiparlementaire?". In: *Parlement[s], Revue d'histoire politique* (3), 49–58.

Gentile, Emilio. 1998. "Mussolini's Charisma". In: *Modern Italy* 3 (2), 219–235.

Gerlach, Ludwig Friedrich Leopold von. 1891–1892. *Denkwürdigkeiten aus dem Leben Leopold von Gerlachs, Generals der Infanterie und General-Adjutanten König Friedrich Wilhelms IV. [ed. by Ulrike Agnes von Gerlach]*. 2 Vols. Berlin.

Gerlach, Ludwig Friedrich Leopold von. 1912. *Briefe des Generals Leopold von Gerlach an Otto von Bismarck [ed. by Horst Kohl]*. Stuttgart; Berlin.

Gerlach, Ludwig Friedrich Leopold von; Bismarck, Otto von. ³1893. *Briefwechsel des Generals Leopold von Gerlach mit dem Bundestags-Gesandten Otto von Bismarck*. Berlin.

Geuss, Herbert. 1959. *Bismarck und Napoleon der Dritte: Ein Beitrag zur Geschichte der preußisch-französischen Beziehungen 1851–1871*. Köln.

Giertz, Horst. 1970. "Zu einigen Fragen des Stolypinschen Bonapartismus. Gedanken zu zwei Büchern von A. Ja. Avrech". In: *Jahrbuch für Geschichte der Sozialistischen Länder Europas* 14 (2), 167–177.

Gilcher-Holtey, Ingrid. 1995. "Robespierre: Die Charismatisierung der Vernunft". In: *Geschichte und Gesellschaft* 21, 248–258.

Girard, Louis. 1977. "Caractères du Bonapartisme dans la seconde moitié du XIXe siècle". In: Hammer, Karl; Hartmann, Peter Claus (Ed.). *Le Bonapartisme. Phénomène historique et mythe politique. Actes du 13e colloque historique franco-allemand de l'Institut Historique Allemand de Paris à Augsbourg du 26 jusqu'au 30 septembre 1975/ Der Bonapartismus. Historisches Phänomen und politischer Mythos. 13. deutsch-französisches Historikerkolloquium des Deutschen Historischen Instituts Paris in Augsburg vom 26. bis 30. September 1975.* Zürich; München, 22–28.

Glaab, Sonja. 2008. "Wilhelm II. und die Presse—ein Medienkaiser in seinem Element?". In: *Publizistik* 53 (2), 200–214.

Gluck, Leopold. 2001. "On the Various Meanings of Bonapartism". In: *Kultura i społeczeństwo* 45 (1), 7–38.

Goethe, Johann Wolfgang von. 1966. *Goethe: Conversations and Encounters [ed. by David Luke and Robert Pick].* London.

Gollwitzer, Heinz. 1952. "Der Cäsarismus Napoleons III. im Widerhall der öffentlichen Meinung Deutschlands". In: *Historische Zeitschrift* 173 (1), 23–75.

Gollwitzer, Heinz. 1987. "The Caesarism of Napoleon III as seen by Public Opinion in Germany". In: *Economy and Society* 16 (3), 357–404.

Goltz, Anna von der; Robert, Gildea. 2009. "Flawed Saviours: The Myths of Hindenburg and Pétain". In: *European History Quarterly* 39 (3), 439–464.

Goodliffe, Gabriel. 2012. *The Resurgence of the Radical Right in France: From Boulangisme to the Front National.* Cambridge.

Görres, Joseph von. 1854 [1800]. "Resultate meiner Sendung nach Paris im Brumaire des achten Jahres". In: Görres, Joseph von. *Gesammelte Schriften. Erste Abtheilung. Politische Schriften. Erster Band [ed. by M. Görres].* München, 25–112.

Gramsci, Antonio. 1971. *Selections from the Prison Notebooks [ed. by Quintin Hoare and Geoffrey Nowell Smith].* London.

Gramsci, Antonio. 1974 [1951]. *Passato e presente.* Torino.

Graves, Charles Larcom. 1919. *Mr. Punch's History of the Great War.* New York, NY.

Grévy, François Paul Jules. 1888. *Discours politiques et judiciaires, rapports et messages de Jules Grévy. Recueillis, accompagnés de notices historiques, et précédés d'une introduction par Lucien Delabrousse.* 2 Vols. Paris.

Groh, Dieter. 2004 [1972]. "Cäsarismus, Napoleonismus, Bonapartismus, Führer, Chef, Imperialismus". In: Brunner, Otto; Conze, Werner; Koselleck, Reinhart (Ed.). *Geschichtliche Grundbegriffe. Historisches Lexikon zur politisch-sozialen Sprache in Deutschland. Band 1: A-D. Studienausgabe.* Stuttgart, 727–771.

Grotke, Kelly L.; Prutsch, Markus J. (Ed.). 2014. *Constitutionalism, Legitimacy, and Power: Nineteenth-Century Experiences.* Oxford [etc.].

Guicciardini, Francesco. 1965. *Selected Writings [ed. by C. Grayson].* London [etc.].

Guizot, François. 1818. "De la monarchie française depuis la seconde restauration jusqu'à la fin de la session de 1816, par M. le comte de Montlosier". In: *Archives Philosophiques, Politiques et Littéraires* 3, 385–409.

Guizot, François. 1828. *Cours d'histoire moderne. Histoire générale de la civilisation en Europe depuis la chute de l'Empire Romain jusqu'à la Révolution française.* Paris.

Guizot, François. 1828–1832. *Histoire de la civilisation en France depuis la chute de l'Empire Romain jusqu'en 1789.* 5 Vols. Paris.

Guizot, François. 1829–1832 [1828–1830]. *Cours d'histoire moderne. Histoire de la civilisation en France depuis la chute de l'Empire Romain jusqu'en 1789.* 5 Vols. Paris.

Guizot, François. 1846 [1828–1830]. *The History of Civilization, from the Fall of the Roman Empire to the French Revolution [translated by William Hazlitt].* 3 Vols. London.

Guizot, François. 1851 [1820–1822]. *Histoire des origines du gouvernement représentatif en Europe.* 2 Vols. Paris.

Guizot, François. 1852 [1820–1822]. *History of the Origin of Representative Government in Europe [translated by Andrew R. Scoble].* London.

Günther, Gerhard. 1932. *Das werdende Reich: Reichsgeschichte und Reichsreform.* Hamburg.

Gusy, Christoph. 1997. *Die Weimarer Reichsverfassung.* Tübingen.

Haller, Karl Ludwig von. 1816–1825. *Restauration der Staats-Wissenschaft, oder, Theorie des natürlich-geselligen Zustands, der Chimäre des künstlich-bürgerlichen entgegengesetzt.* 6 Vols. Winterthur.

Hanley, Wayne. 2005. *The Genesis of Napoleonic Propaganda, 1796 to 1799.* New York, NY.

Hardtwig, Wolfgang. 2005. "Der Bismarck-Mythos. Gestalt und Funktionen zwischen politischer Öffentlichkeit und Wissenschaft". In: Hardtwig, Wolfgang (Ed.). *Politische Kulturgeschichte der Zwischenkriegszeit 1918–1939.* Göttingen, 61–90.

Harvey, A. D. 1998. "Napoleon—the Myth". In: *History Today* 48 (1), 27–32.

Hayward, Jack. 2004. "Bonapartism and Gaullist Heroic Leadership: Comparing Crisis Appeals to Impersonated People". In: Baehr, Peter; Richter, Melvin (Ed.). *Dictatorship in History and Theory: Bonapartism, Caesarism, and Totalitarianism.* Cambridge, 221–239.

Hazareesingh, Sudhir. 2004. "Bonapartism as the Progenitor of Democracy: The Pardoxical Case of the French Second Empire". In: Baehr, Peter; Richter, Melvin (Ed.). *Dictatorship in History and Theory: Bonapartism, Caesarism, and Totalitarianism.* Cambridge, 129–152.

Hazareesingh, Sudhir. 2005 [2004]. *The Legend of Napoleon.* London.

Hegel, Georg Wilhelm Friedrich. 1999 [1800–1802]. "Die Verfassung Deutschlands". In: Hegel, Georg Wilhelm Friedrich. *Werke Bd. 1. Frühe Schriften.* Frankfurt/Main, 461–581.

Hegel, Georg Wilhelm Friedrich. 1999 [1837]. *Vorlesungen über die Philosophie der Geschichte.* Frankfurt/Main.

Heine, Heinrich. 1861–1866. *Heinrich Heine's Sämmtliche Werke. Rechtmäßige Original-Ausgabe.* 21 Vols. Hamburg.

Henry, Pierre François. 1801. *Histoire du Directoire Exécutif de la République Française depuis son installation jusqu'au dix-huit Brumaire inclusivement, suivie de pieces justificatives.* 2 Vols. Paris.

Herbst, Ludolf. 2010. *Hitlers Charisma: Die Erfindung eines deutschen Messias.* Frankfurt/Main.

Herrera, Robert A. 1995. *Donoso Cortés: Cassandra of the Age.* Grand Rapids, MI; Cambridge.

Hewlett, Nick. 2007. "Nicolas Sarkozy and the Legacy of Bonapartism: The French Presidential and Parliamentary Elections of 2007". In: *Modern & Contemporary France* 15 (4), 405–422.

Hillebrand, Karl. 1873. *Frankreich und die Franzosen in der zweiten Hälfte des XIX. Jahrhunderts: Eindrücke und Erfahrungen.* Berlin.

Hintze, Otto. 1982 [1897]. "Roschers politische Entwicklungstheorie". In: Hintze, Otto (Ed.). *Soziologie und Geschichte. Gesammelte Abhandlungen zur Soziologie, Politik und Theorie der Geschichte [ed. by Gerhard Oestreich].* Göttingen, 3–45.

Hobson, John Atkinson. 1909. *The Crisis of Liberalism: New Issues of Democracy.* London.

Hoegen, Jesko von. 2007. *Der Held von Tannenberg: Genese und Funktion des Hindenburg-Mythos.* Köln; Weimar.

Holl, Karl; Kloft, Hans; Fesser, Gerd. 2001. *Caligula—Wilhelm II. und der Caesarenwahnsinn: Antikenrezeption und wilhelminische Politik am Beispiel des "Caligula" von Ludwig Quidde.* Bremen.

Holzhausen, Paul. 1903. *Heinrich Heine und Napoleon I.* Frankfurt/Main.

Hooke, Nathaniel. 1738–1771. *The Roman History: From the Building of Rome to the Ruin of the Commonwealth.* 4 Vols. London.

Horn, Johann Friedrich. 1672 [1664]. *Politicorum pars architectonica de civitate [ed. by A. Epstein].* Frankfurt/Main.

Huber, Ernst Rudolf (Ed.). ³1978 [1961]. *Deutsche Verfassungsdokumente 1803–1850.* Stuttgart [etc.].

Hugo, Victor. 1852a. *Napoléon le Petit.* London; Brussels.

Hugo, Victor. 1852b. *Napoleon the Little.* London.

Hugo, Victor. 1877–1878. *Histoire d'un crime: déposition d'un témoin.* 2 Vols. Paris.

Hui, Keith K.C. 2016. *Vladimir Putin and Donald Trump Are Symptoms of Creeping Caesarism [June 2, 2016]* (accessed May 13, 2017). Available from http://fpif.org/vladimir-putin-donald-trump-symptoms-creeping-caesarism/.

Hull, Isabel V. 1991. "Persönliches Regiment". In: Röhl, John C.G. (Ed.). *Der Ort Kaiser Wilhelms II. in der deutschen Geschichte.* München, 3–23.

Hunt, Lynn; Lansky, David; Hanson, Paul. 1979. "The Failure of the Liberal Republic in France, 1795–1799: The Road to Brumaire". In: *Journal of Modern History* 51 (4), 734–759.

Huntington, Samuel P. 1991. *The Third Wave: Democratization in the Late Twentieth Century.* Norman, OK.

Hutton, Patrick H. 1976. "Popular Boulangism and the Advent of Mass Politics in France, 1886–90". In: *Journal of Contemporary History* 11 (1), 85–106.

Ilany, Ofry. 2016. *Forget Fascism: In the U.S. and Israel, Caesarism Is on the Rise [16 December 2016]* (accessed February 13, 2018). Available from http://www.haaretz.com/opinion/.premium-1.759311.

Jansen, Christian. 2004. "Otto von Bismarck: Modernität und Repression, Gewaltsamkeit und List. Ein absolutistischer Staatsdiener im Zeitalter der Massenpolitik". In: Möller, Frank (Ed.). *Charismatische Führer der deutschen Nation.* München, 63–83.

Janssen Perio, Evert Maarten. 1972. "Auguste Romieu en het Caesarisme". In: *Tijdschrift voor Geschiedenis* 85 (1), 38–55.

Jefferson, Thomas. ²1830. *Memoir, Correspondence and Miscellanies, from the Papers of Thomas Jefferson [ed. by Thomas Jefferson Randolph].* 4 Vols. Boston, MA; New York, NY.

Jellinek, Georg. 1906. *Verfassungsänderung und Verfassungswandlung. Eine staatsrechtlich-politische Abhandlung.* Berlin.

Jellinek, Georg. ³1914 [1900]. *Allgemeine Staatslehre [ed. by Walter Jellinek].* Berlin.

Johnson, Douglas. 1963. *Guizot: Aspects of French History 1787–1874.* London; Toronto.

Johnson, Paul. 2002. *Napoleon.* London.

Jourdeuil, M. 1871. *Du césarisme en France.* Paris.

Jung, Edgar Julius. ²1930 [1927]. *Die Herrschaft der Minderwertigen. Ihr Zerfall und ihre Ablösung durch ein Neues Reich.* Berlin.

Jung, Edgar Julius. 1933. *Sinndeutung der deutschen Revolution.* Oldenburg.

Jünger, Ernst. 1926. "Schließt Euch zusammen!". In: *Die Standarte. Wochenstschrift des neuen Nationalismus* 1 (10), 222–226.

Kallis, Aristotle A. 2006. "Fascism, 'Charisma' and 'Charismatisation': Weber's Model of 'Charismatic Domination' and Interwar European Fascism". In: *Totalitarian Movements and Political Religions* 7 (1), 25–43.

Kant, Immanuel. 1999 [1784]. "Zur Frage: Was ist Aufklärung?". In: Kant, Immanuel. *Was ist Aufklärung? Ausgewählte kleine Schriften*. Hamburg, 20–27.

Kelly, Duncan. 2016. "Carl Schmitt's Political Theory of Dictatorship". In: Meierhenrich, Jens; Simons, Oliver (Ed.). *The Oxford Handbook of Carl Schmitt*. New York, NY, 217–244.

Kelsen, Hans. 1931. "Wer soll Hüter der Verfassung sein?". In: *Die Justiz* 6, 5–56.

Kershaw, Ian. ⁴2000 [1985]. *The Nazi Dictatorship: Problems and Perspectives of Interpretation*. London.

Kershaw, Ian. 2002. *Der Hitler-Mythos: Volksmeinung und Propaganda im Dritten Reich*. Stuttgart.

Kessler, Harry Graf. ²1962 [1935]. *Gesichter und Zeiten: Erinnerungen*. Berlin.

Kirsch, Martin. 1999. *Monarch und Parlament im 19. Jahrhundert. Der monarchische Konstitutionalismus als europäischer Verfassungstyp—Frankreich im Vergleich*. Göttingen.

Kirsch, Martin. 2007. "Die Funktionalisierung des Monarchen im 19. Jahrhundert im europäischen Vergleich". In: Fisch, Stefan; Gauzy, Florence; Metzger, Chantal (Ed.). *Machtstrukturen im Staat in Deutschland und Frankreich/Les structures de pouvoir dans l'État en France et en Allemagne*. Stuttgart, 82–98.

Kissinger, Henry A. 1968. "The White Revolutionary: Reflections on Bismarck". In: *Daedalus* 97 (3), 888–924.

Kloft, Hans; Köhler, Jens. 1999. "Cäsarismus". In: Landfester, Manfred (Ed.). *Der Neue Pauly. Enzyklopädie der Antike. Band 13: Rezeptions- und Wissenschaftsgeschichte*. Stuttgart [etc.], 623–629.

Kloft, Hans; Köhler, Jens. 2006. "Caesarism". In: *Brill's New Pauly. Brill Online*. <http://www.brillonline.nl/subscriber/uid=1497/entry?entry=bnp_e1306730>

Koppe, Karl Wilhelm. 1815. *Die Stimme eines Preußischen Staatsbürgers in den wichtigsten Angelegenheiten dieser Zeit. Veranlaßt durch die Schrift des Herrn Geh. Raths Schmalz: Ueber politische Vereine etc*. Köln.

Koselleck, Reinhart. 1972. "Über die Theoriebedürftigkeit der Geschichtswissenschaft". In: Conze, Werner (Ed.). *Theorie der Geschichtswissenschaft und Praxis des Geschichtsunterrichts. Acht Beiträge*. Stuttgart, 10–28.

Koselleck, Reinhart. 2004. *Futures Past: On the Semantics of Historical Time*. New York, NY.

Koselleck, Reinhart. ¹⁰2006 [1959]. *Kritik und Krise. Eine Studie zur Pathogenese der bürgerlichen Welt*. Frankfurt/Main.

Kraus, Thomas R. 2000. "Napoleon—Aachen—Karl der Große. Betrachtungen zur napoleonischen Herrschaftslegitimation". In: Kramp, Mario (Ed.). *Krönungen: Könige in Aachen—Geschichte und Mythos. Katalog der Ausstellung. Band 2*. Mainz, 699–707.

Krause, Skadi. 2008. *Die souveräne Nation. Zur Delegitimierung monarchischer Herrschaft in Frankreich 1788–1789*. Berlin.

Kroll, Frank-Lothar. 2013. *Geburt der Moderne: Politik, Gesellschaft und Kultur vor dem Ersten Weltkrieg*. Berlin.

Kuhn, Axel. 1978. "Elemente des Bonapartismus im Bismarck-Deutschland". In: *Jahrbuch des Instituts für Deutsche Geschichte* 7, 277–297.

Kurland, Philip B.; Lerner, Ralph (Ed.). ²1996 [1987]. *The Founder's Constitution*. 5 Vols. Chicago, IL [etc.].

Lacour, René. 1971. "Le Bonapartisme sous la IIIe République". In: *Cahiers d'Histoire* 16 (1), 81–87.

Lafargue, Paul. 1887. "La question Boulanger". In: *Le Socialiste* (23 July 1887).

Langlois, Claude. 1972. "Le plébiscite de l'an VIII ou le coup d'Etat du 18 pluviôse an VIII". In: *Annales Historiques de la Révolution Française* 44, 43–65, 231–246, 391–415.

Larousse, Pierre (Ed.). 1866–1876. *Grand dictionnaire universel du XIXe siècle*. 15 Vols. Paris.

Las Cases, Emmanuel-Augustin-Dieudonné-Joseph de. 1823. *Mémorial de Sainte Hélène. Journal of the Private Life and Conversations of the Emperor Napoleon at Saint Helena*. 8 [4] Vols. London.

Lazzaro, Giuseppe. 1862. *Il cesarismo e l'Italia*. Napoli.

Le Bon, Gustave. 1881. *L'homme et les sociétés*. 2 Vols. Paris.

Le Bon, Gustave. 1896 [1895]. *The Crowd: A Study of the Popular Mind*. New York, NY.

Lenormand, Marie Anne Adelaide. 1848. *Historical and Secret Memoirs of the Empress Josephine, First Wife of Napoleon Bonaparte*. 2 Vols. Philadelphia, PA.

Lentz, Thierry. 1997. *Le 18 brumaire: les coups d'État de Napoléon Bonaparte (novembre-décembre 1799)*. Paris.

Leonhard, Jörn. 2010. "Das Präsens der Revolution: Der Bonapartismus in der europäischen Geschichte des 19. und 20. Jahrhunderts". In: Daum, Werner (Ed.). *Kommunikation und Konfliktaustragung: Verfassungskultur als Faktor politischer und gesellschaftlicher Machtverhältnisse*. Berlin, 293–317.

Lepsius, M. Rainer. 2006. "The Model of Charismatic Leadership and its Applicability to the Rule of Adolf Hitler". In: *Totalitarian Movements and Political Religions* 7 (2), 175–190.

Lieber, Francis. 1853. *On Civil Liberty and Self-Government*. London.

Linguet, Simon-Nicholas Henri. 1777 [1766]. *Histoire des révolutions de l'empire romain, pour servir de suite à celle des Révolutions de la République*. 2 Vols. Liège.

Littré, Émile (Ed.). ^{2}1873–1877 [1863–1872]. *Dictionnaire de la langue française*. 4 Vols. Paris.

Locke, John. 2004 [1689]. *Two Treatises of Government [ed. by P. Laslett]*. Cambridge [etc.].

Loewenstein, Karl. ^{2}1965 [1957]. *Political Power and the Governmental Process*. Chicago, IL.

Lombard de Langres, Vincent. 1799. *Le dix-huit brumaire, ou tableau des événemens qui ont amené cette journée; des moyens secrets par lesquels elle a été préparée; des faits qui l'ont accompagnée, et des résultats qu'elle doit avoir; auquel on a ajouté des anecdotes sur les principaux personnages qui étaient en place; et les pièces justificatives, etc.* Paris.

Luden, Heinrich. 1814. "Die Buonapartisten in Teutschland". In: *Nemesis. Zeitschrift für Politik und Geschichte* 3, 72–77.

Macaulay, Thomas Babington. 1828. "The Constitutional History of England, from the Accession of Henry VII. to the Death of George II. By Henry Hallam". In: *The Edinburgh Review* 48 (95), 96–169.

Mackintosh, James. 1835. *Memoirs of the Life of the Right Honorable Sir James Mackintosh [ed. by Robert James Mackintosh]*. 2 Vols. London.

Magraw, Roger. 1997. "The People's Emperor? Louis Napoleon and Popular Bonapartism". In: *Modern History Review* 8 (3), 28–30.

Maine, Henry Sumner. ^{3}1886 [1885]. *Popular Government: Four Essays*. London.

Maistre, Joseph Marie comte de. 1821. *Considérations sur la France. Nouvelle édition, la seule revue et corrigée par l'auteur; suivie de l'Essai sur le principe générateur des constitutions politiques et des autres institutions humaines. Troisième édition, revue et corrigée. Par le même*. Paris.

Maistre, Joseph Marie comte de. 1860. *Correspondance diplomatique de Joseph de Maistre 1811–1817 [ed. by Albert Blanc].* 2 Vols. Paris.

Maistre, Joseph Marie comte de. 1980 [1797]. *Considérations sur la France [ed. by Jean-Louis Darcel].* Genève.

Mangoni, Luisa. 1976. "Cesarismo, bonapartismo, fascismo". In: *Studi Storici* 17 (3), 41–61.

Mann, Thomas. 1920 [1918]. *Betrachtungen eines Unpolitischen.* Berlin.

Marx, Karl. 1869 [1852]. *Der Achtzehnte Brumaire des Louis Bonaparte.* Hamburg.

Marx, Karl. 1979 [1852]. "The Eighteenth Brumaire of Louis Bonaparte". In: Cohen, Jack [et al.] (Ed.). *Karl Marx Frederick Engels Collected Works. Volume 11: Marx and Engels: 1851–53.* London, 99–197.

Marx, Karl. 1985 [1852]. "Der achtzehnte Brumaire des Louis Bonaparte". In: Institut für Marxismus-Leninismus beim Zentralkomitee der Kommunistischen Partei der Sowjetunion; Institut für Marxismus-Leninismus beim Zentralkomitee der Sozialistischen Einheitspartei Deutschlands (Ed.). *Karl Marx Friedrich Engels-Gesamtausgabe (MEGA). Erste Abteilung: Werke, Artikel, Entwürfe. Band 11: Werke, Artikel, Entwürfe Juli 1851 bis Dezember 1852. Text.* Berlin, 96–189.

Marx, Karl; Engels, Friedrich. 1956–1990. *Marx Engels Werke [ed. by Institut für Marxismus-Leninismus beim Zentralkomitee der SED/Institut für Geschichte der Arbeiterbewegung].* 43 [45] Vols. Berlin.

Marx, Karl; Engels, Friedrich. 2010. *Karl Marx Friedrich Engels Gesamtausgabe (MEGA). Erste Abteilung: Werke, Artikel, Entwürfe. Band 32. Friedrich Engels: Werke, Artikel, Entwürfe März 1891 bis August 1895 [ed. by Internationale Marx-Engels-Stiftung Amsterdam].* Berlin.

Mayer, Gustav. 1928. *Bismarck und Lassalle: Ihr Briefwechsel und ihre Gespräche.* Berlin.

Mazzini, Giuseppe. 1938–1939. *Opere [ed. by Luigi Salvatorelli].* 2 Vols. Milano; Roma.

McCormick, John P. 2004. "From Constitutional Technique to Caesarist Ploy: Carl Schmitt on Dictatorship, Liberalism, and Emergency Powers". In: Baehr, Peter; Richter, Melvin (Ed.). *Dictatorship in History and Theory: Bonapartism, Caesarism, and Totalitarianism.* Cambridge, 197–219.

McLynn, Frank. 1997. *Napoleon: A Biography.* London.

McMillan, James F. 1991. *Napoleon III.* London [etc.].

Melograni, Piero. 1976. "The Cult of the Duce in Mussolini's Italy". In: *Journal of Contemporary History* 11 (4), 221–237.

Ménager, Bernard. 1988. *Le Napoléon de Peuple.* Paris.

Metternich, Clemens Wenzel Lothar Fürst von. 1880–1884. *Aus Metternich's nachgelassenen Papieren [ed. by Richard Clemens Lothar Fürst von Metternich-Winneburg].* 8 Vols. Wien.

Michels, Robert. 1927. *Bedeutende Männer. Charakterologische Studien.* Leipzig.

Michels, Robert. 1930. *Italien von heute. Politische und wirtschaftliche Kulturgeschichte von 1860 bis 1930.* Zürich; Leipzig.

Michels, Robert. 1987. *Masse, Führer, Intellektuelle. Politisch-soziologische Aufsätze 1906–1933 [ed. by Joachim Milles].* Frankfurt/Main; New York, NY.

Michels, Robert. ⁴1989 [1911]. *Zur Soziologie des Parteiwesens in der modernen Demokratie. Untersuchungen über die oligarchischen Tendenzen des Gruppenlebens [ed. by Frank R. Pfetsch].* Stuttgart.

Mignet, François Auguste Marie. 1856 [1824]. *History of the French Revolution from 1789 to 1814.* London.

Mill, John Stuart. 1989. *On Liberty with The Subjection of Women and Chapters on Socialism [ed. by Stefan Collini].* Cambridge [etc.].

Mitchell, Allan. 1977a. "Bonapartism as a Model for Bismarckian Politics". In: *The Journal of Modern History* 49 (2), 181–199.

Mitchell, Allan. 1977b. "Der Bonapartismus als Modell der Bismarckschen Reichspolitik". In: Hammer, Karl; Hartmann, Peter Claus (Ed.). *Le Bonapartisme. Phénomène historique et mythe politique. Actes du 13e colloque historique franco-allemand de l'Institut Historique Allemand de Paris à Augsbourg du 26 jusqu'au 30 septembre 1975/ Der Bonapartismus. Historisches Phänomen und politischer Mythos. 13. deutsch-französisches Historikerkolloquium des Deutschen Historischen Instituts Paris in Augsburg vom 26. bis 30. September 1975.* Zürich; München, 56–76.

Mitterrand, François. 1964. *Le coup d'état permanent.* Paris.

Moeller van den Bruck, Arthur. ²1926 [1923]. *Das dritte Reich.* Berlin.

Moffitt, Benjamin. 2016. *The Global Rise of Populism: Performance, Political Style, and Representation.* Stanford, CA.

Mommsen, Christian Matthias Theodor. 1853. *Römische Geschichte. Dritter Band. Von Sullas Tode bis zur Schlacht von Thapsus.* Berlin.

Mommsen, Christian Matthias Theodor. ²1857 [1853]. *Römische Geschichte. Dritter Band. Von Sullas Tode bis zur Schlacht von Thapsus.* Berlin.

Mommsen, Christian Matthias Theodor. 1858. "Thiers und die Kaiserzeit". In: *Preußische Jahrbücher* 1, 225–244.

Montesquieu, Charles-Louis de Secondat baron de. 1788 [1748]. *Œuvres de Montesquieu. Tome premier.* Paris.

Moore, Barrington. 1993 [1966]. *Social Origins of Dictatorship and Democracy: Lord and Peasant in the Making of the Modern World.* Boston, MA.

Morphy, Michel. 1891. *Mon rôle dans le boulangisme.* Paris.

Morris, Gouverneur. 1939. *A Diary of the French Revolution by Gouverneur Morris 1752–1816, Minister to France during the Terror [ed. by Beatrix Cary Davenport].* 2 Vols. Boston, MA.

Morsey, Rudolf. 1957. *Die oberste Reichsverwaltung unter Bismarck: 1867—1890.* Münster.

Moser, Friedrich Karl von. 1787. *Ueber die Regierung der geistlichen Staaten in Deutschland.* Frankfurt und Leipzig [= Mannheim].

Mosley, Oswald. 1968. *My Life.* London [etc.].

Mosse, George L. 1971. "Caesarism, Circuses, and Monuments". In: *Journal of Contemporary History* 6 (2), 167–182.

Most, Johann. 1878. *Die socialen Bewegungen im alten Rom und der Cäsarismus.* Berlin.

Müller, Frank Lorenz. 2008. "Man, Myth and Monuments: The Legacy of Otto von Bismarck (1866–1998)". In: *European History Quarterly* 38 (4), 626–636.

Mundt, Theodor. 1857. *Pariser Kaiser-Skizzen.* 2 Vols. Berlin.

Mundt, Theodor. 1858. *Paris und Louis Napoleon. Neue Skizzen aus dem französischen Kaiserreich.* 2 Vols. Berlin.

Murkens, Jo Eric Khushal. 2014. "Unintended Democracy: Parliamentary Reform in the United Kingdom". In: Grotke, Kelly L.; Prutsch, Markus J. (Ed.). *Constitutionalism, Legitimacy, and Power: Nineteenth-Century Experiences.* Oxford [etc.], 351–370.

Naumann, Friedrich. ⁴1905 [1900]. *Demokratie und Kaisertum. Ein Handbuch für innere Politik.* Berlin-Schöneberg.

Nelis, Jan. 2007. "Constructing Fascist Identity: Benito Mussolini and the Myth of Romanità". In: *Classical World* 100 (4), 391–415.

Neumann, Franz. 1957 [1954]. "Notes on the Theory of Dictatorship". In: Neumann, Franz. *The Democratic and the Authoritarian State: Essays in Political and Legal Theory [ed. by Herbert Marcuse].* London, 233–256.

Nohlen, Dieter; Schultze, Rainer-Olaf; Schüttemeyer, Suzanne S. (Ed.). 1998. *Lexikon der Politik. Band 7. Politische Begriffe*. München.

Nolzen, Armin. 2005. "Charismatic Legitimation and Bureaucratic Rule: The NSDAP in the Third Reich, 1933–1945". In: *German History* 23 (4), 494–518.

Oeschey, Rudolf. 1944. "Montesquieu und die Verfassungen des deutschen Frühkonstitutionalismus". In: *Zeitschrift für die gesamte Staatswissenschaft* 104, 361–388.

Oncken, Hermann. 1967 [1926]. *Die Rheinpolitik Kaiser Napoleons III. von 1863–1870 und der Ursprung des Krieges von 1870/1871. Nach den Staatsakten von Österreich, Preußen und den süddeutschen Mittelstaaten*. 3 Vols. Osnabrück.

Orléans, Louis-Philippe-Albert d'. 1887. *Instructions de Mgr le Comte de Paris aux représentants du parti monarchiste en France*. Paris.

Osterhammel, Jürgen. 2009. *Die Verwandlung der Welt. Eine Geschichte des 19. Jahrhunderts*. München.

Pagès du Port, G. 1888. *Le Césarisme*. Paris.

Paine, Thomas. 1925 [1791–1792]. *Rights of Man [ed. by William M. van der Weyde]*. New Rochelle, NY.

Pallain, Georges (Ed.). ³1881. *Correspondance inédite du Prince de Talleyrand et du Roi Louis XVIII. pendant le Congrès de Vienne. Publiée sur les manuscrits conservés au dépôt des Affaires étrangères, avec préface, éclaircissements et notes*. Paris [etc.].

Panizza, Francisco (Ed.). 2005. *Populism and the Mirror of Democracy*. London [etc.].

Pelletier, Georges. 1986. "La naissance du boulangisme". In: *Gavroche: Revue d'Histoire Populaire* (27/28), 17–26.

Persigny, Jean Gilbert Victor Fialin duc de. 1865. *Le duc de Persigny et les doctrines de l'empire précédé d'une notice [ed. by Joseph Delaroa]*. Paris.

Perthes, Clemens Theodor (Ed.). ⁵1861. *Friedrich Perthes' Leben nach dessen schriftlichen und mündlichen Mittheilungen*. 3 Vols. Gotha.

Pflanze, Otto. 1982. "Bismarcks Herrschaftstechnik als Problem der gegenwärtigen Historiographie". In: *Historische Zeitschrift* 234 (3), 561–600.

Picker, Henry. ²1965 [1963]. *Hitlers Tischgespräche im Führerhauptquartier 1941–1942 [ed. by Percy Ernst Schramm]*. Stuttgart.

Pinto, António Costa; Eatwell, Roger; Larsen, Stein Ugelvik (Ed.). 2007. *Charisma and Fascism in Interwar Europe*. London [etc.].

Pintschovius, Joska. 2008. *Der Bürger-Kaiser: Wilhelm II.* Berlin.

Planck, Karl Christian. 1922. *Deutsche Zukunft: ausgewählte politische Schriften [ed. by Mathilde Planck]*. München.

Plessis, Alain. 1979 [1973]. *De la fête impériale au mur des fédérés 1852–1871*. Paris.

Plessner, Helmuth. 1982 [1959]. *Die verspätete Nation*. Frankfurt/Main.

Pöhlmann, Robert von. 1895. "Die Entstehung des Cäsarismus". In: Pöhlmann, Robert von (Ed.). *Aus Altertum und Gegenwart: Gesammelte Abhandlungen*. München, 245–291.

Poschinger, Heinrich von (Ed.). 1882–1884. *Preußen im Bundestag 1851 bis 1859. Documente der K. Preuß. Bundestagsgesandtschaft*. 4 Vols. Leipzig.

Price, Roger. 2001. *The French Second Empire: An Anatomy of Political Power*. Cambridge [etc.].

Proudhon, Pierre-Joseph. 1850. *Les confessions d'un révolutionnaire pour servir à l'histoire de la Revolution de Février*. Paris.

Proudhon, Pierre-Joseph. ⁴1852. *La Révolution sociale démontrée par le coup d'état du 2 décembre*. Paris.

Prutsch, Markus J. 2006. *Die Charte constitutionnelle Ludwigs XVIII. in der Krise von 1830. Verfassungsentwicklung und Verfassungsrevision in Frankreich 1814 bis 1830*. Marburg.

Prutsch, Markus J. 2008. "Die Revision der französischen Verfassung im Jahre 1830. Zur Frage der Bewährung des Verfassungssystems der *Charte constitutionnelle* von 1814". In: *Der Staat. Zeitschrift für Staatslehre und Verfassungsgeschichte, deutsches und europäisches öffentliches Recht* 47 (1), 85–107.

Prutsch, Markus J. 2009a. "The Legal 'Model' of the Charte Constitutionnelle and the 1818 Baden Constitution". In: Beck Varela, Laura; Gutiérrez Vega, Pablo; Spinosa, Alberto (Ed.). *Crossing Legal Cultures*. München, 383–398.

Prutsch, Markus J. 2009b. "The Revision of the Charte Constitutionnelle in the Crisis of 1830". In: Hornyák, Szabolcs [et al.] (Ed.). *Turning Points and Breaklines*. München, 393–410.

Prutsch, Markus J. 2013. *Making Sense of Constitutional Monarchism in Post-Napoleonic France and Germany*. Basingstoke [etc.].

Przeworski, Adam [et al.] 2000. *Democracy and Development: Political Institutions and Well-Being in the World, 1950–1990*. Cambridge.

Pyta, Wolfram. 2010. "Charisma und Geniezuschreibung: Strategien der Herrschaftslegitimation Hitlers". In: Assmann, Jan (Ed.). *Herrscherkult und Heilserwartung*. München, 213–234.

Quidde, Ludwig. 1894. *Caligula. Eine Studie über römischen Cäsarenwahnsinn*. Leipzig.

Radowitz, Joseph Maria Ernst Christian Wilhelm von. 1852–1853. *Gesammelte Schriften*. 5 Vols. Berlin.

Rein, Gustav Adolf. 1957. *Die Revolution in der Politik Bismarcks*. Göttingen.

Reinhard, Marcel. 1952. *Le grand Carnot. II: L'organisateur de la victoire: 1792–1823*. Paris.

Rémond, René. ⁴1982 [1954]. *Les Droites en France*. Paris.

Richter, Melvin. 1988. "Tocqueville, Napoleon, and Bonapartism". In: Eisenstadt, Abraham S. (Ed.). *Reconsidering Tocqueville's Democracy in America*. New Brunswick, NJ; London, 110–145.

Richter, Melvin. 2004. "Tocqueville and French Nineteenth-Century Conceptualizations of the Two Bonapartes and Their Empires". In: Baehr, Peter; Richter, Melvin (Ed.). *Dictatorship in History and Theory: Bonapartism, Caesarism, and Totalitarianism*. Cambridge, 83–102.

Richter, Melvin. 2005. "A Family of Political Concepts: Tyranny, Despotism, Bonapartism, Caesarism, Dictatorship, 1750–1917". In: *European Journal of Political Theory* 4 (3), 221–248.

Riehl, Wilhelm Heinrich. 1851. *Die bürgerliche Gesellschaft*. Stuttgart; Tübingen.

Rochau, Ludwig August von. 1853–1869. *Grundsätze der Realpolitik, angewendet auf die staatlichen Zustände Deutschlands*. 2 Vols. Stuttgart; Heidelberg.

Roederer, Pierre-Louis. 1942. *Mémoires sur la Révolution, le Consulat et l'Empire [ed. by Octave Aubry]*. Paris.

Rohan, Karl Anton Prinz. 1930. *Umbruch der Zeit: 1923–1930—Gesammelte Aufsätze [ed. by Rochus Freiherr von Rheinbaben]*. Berlin.

Röhl, John C. G. 1993–2008. *Wilhelm II*. 3 Vols. München.

Rohmer, Friedrich. ²1848. *Die Monarchie und der vierte Stand*. München.

Romieu, Auguste. ²1850. *L'ère des Césars*. Paris.

Romieu, Auguste. 1851a. *Das rothe Gespenst von 1852. Mit einem Preußischen Nachworte*. Berlin.

Romieu, Auguste. 1851b. *Der Cäsarismus oder die Nothwendigkeit der Säbelherrschaft dargethan durch geschichtliche Beispiele von den Zeiten der Cäsaren bis auf die Gegenwart*. Weimar.

Romieu, Auguste. ³1851c. *Le Spectre rouge de 1852*. Paris.

Romieu, Auguste. 1993. *Der Cäsarismus. Das rote Gespenst von 1852 [ed. by Günter Maschke]*. Wien; Leipzig.

Rosanvallon, Pierre. 1994. *La monarchie impossible. Les Chartes de 1814 et de 1830*. Paris.

Rosanvallon, Pierre. 2008. *Counter-Democracy: Politics in an Age of Distrust*. Cambridge [etc.].

Rosanvallon, Pierre. 2008 [1992]. *Le sacre du citoyen: Histoire du suffrage universel en France*. Paris.

Roscher, Wilhelm Georg Friedrich. 1874. *Geschichte der Nationalökonomik*. München.

Roscher, Wilhelm Georg Friedrich. 1888. "Umrisse zur Naturlehre des Cäsarismus". In: *Abhandlungen der philologisch-historischen Classe der Königlich Sächsischen Gesellschaft der Wissenschaften* 10 (9), 639–753.

Rosenkranz, Johann Karl Friedrich. 1919. *Politische Briefe und Aufsätze 1848–1856 [ed. by Paul Herre]*. Leipzig.

Rotteck, Carl von. 1826. *Allgemeine Geschichte vom Anfang der historischen Kentniss bis auf unsere Zeiten*. 9 Vols. Freiburg/Breisgau.

Rotteck, Carl von. 1829–1835. *Lehrbuch des Vernunftsrechts und der Staatswissenschaften*. 4 Vols. Stuttgart.

Rotteck, Carl von; Welcker, Carl Theodor Georg Philipp (Ed.). 1834–1843. *Staats-Lexikon oder Encyklopädie der Staatswissenschaften in Verbindung mit vielen der angesehensten Publicisten Deutschlands*. 15 Vols. Altona.

Rovira Kaltwasser, Cristóbal [et al.] (Ed.). 2017. *The Oxford Handbook of Populism*. Oxford.

Rusconi, Gian Enrico. 2013. *Cavour und Bismarck. Zwei Staatsmänner im Spannungsfeld von Liberalismus und Cäsarismus*. München.

Rush, Benjamin. 1947. *The Selected Writings of Benjamin Rush [ed. by Dagobert D. Runes]*. New York, NY.

Russell, John. 1865 [1821]. *An Essay on the History of the English Government and Constitution from the Reign of Henry VII to the Present Time. New Edition*. London.

Salmon, Frédéric. 2001. *Atlas électoral de la France 1848–2001*. Paris.

Schäffle, Albert. ²1896 [1875–1878]. *Bau und Leben des Socialen Körpers: Encyclopädischer Entwurf einer realen Anatomie, Physiologie und Psychologie der menschlichen Gesellschaft*. 2 Vols. Tübingen.

Schlabrendorf, Gustav. 1804. *Napoleon Bonaparte und das französische Volk unter seinem Consulate*. Germanien [= Hamburg].

Schlabrendorf, Gustav; Bergk, Johann Adam. 1806. *Napoleon Bonaparte wie er leibt und lebt, und das französische Volk unter ihm. Aus dem Englischen*. Petersburg [= Hamburg].

Schlabrendorf, Gustav; Bergk, Johann Adam. 1814. *Napoleon Bonaparte wie er leibt und lebt, und das französische Volk unter ihm. Zweiter Theil*. Petersburg [= Hamburg].

Schlegelmilch, Arthur. 2009. *Die Alternative des Monarchischen Konstitutionalismus. Eine Neuinterpretation der deutschen und österreichischen Verfassungsgeschichte des 19. Jahrhunderts*. Bonn.

Schluchter, Wolfgang. 1980. "Der autoritär verfasste Kapitalismus. Max Webers Kritik am Kaiserreich". In: Schluchter, Wolfgang. *Rationalismus der Weltbeherrschung. Studien zu Max Weber*. Frankfurt/Main, 134–160.

Schmidt, Manfred G. ³2000 [1995]. *Demokratietheorien*. Opladen.

Schmitt, Carl. 1924. "Die Diktatur des Reichspräsiden nach Art. 48 der Reichsverfassung". In: Vereinigung der Deutschen Staatsrechtslehrer (Ed.). *Der deutsche Föderalismus. Die Diktatur des Reichspräsidenten. Verhandlungen der Tagung der deutschen Staatsrechtslehrer zu Jena am 14. und 15. April 1924. Mit Eröffnungsansprache und einer Zusammenfassung der Diskussionsreden*. Berlin; Leipzig, 63–139.

Schmitt, Carl. 1929. "Der Hüter der Verfassung". In: *Archiv des öffentlichen Rechts* NF 16, 161–232.

Schmitt, Carl. 1933. *Staat, Bewegung, Volk. Die Dreigliederung der politischen Einheit.* Hamburg.

Schmitt, Carl. 1934. "Der Führer schützt das Recht". In: *Deutsche Juristen-Zeitung* 39 (15), 945–950.

Schmitt, Carl. 1940. *Positionen und Begriffe im Kampf mit Weimar-Genf-Versailles. 1923–1939.* Hamburg.

Schmitt, Carl. ²1969 [1931]. *Der Hüter der Verfassung.* Berlin.

Schmitt, Carl. ⁸1996 [1923]. *Die geistesgeschichtliche Lage des heutigen Parlamentarismus.* Berlin.

Schmitt, Carl. ⁷2002 [1932]. *Der Begriff des Politischen. Text von 1932 mit einem Vorwort von drei Corollarien.* Berlin.

Schmitt, Carl. ⁸2004 [1922]. *Politische Theologie. Vier Kapitel zur Lehre von der Souveränität.* Berlin.

Schmitt, Carl. ⁷2005 [1932]. *Legalität und Legitimität.* Berlin.

Schmitt, Carl. ⁷2006 [1921]. *Die Diktatur. Von den Anfängen des modernen Souveränitätsgedankens bis zum proletarischen Klassenkampf.* Berlin.

Schoelcher, Victor. 1852. *Histoire des crimes du 2 décembre.* 2 Vols. Bruxelles.

Schom, Alan. 1997. *Napoleon Bonaparte.* New York, NY.

Schulz-Bodner, Wilhelm. 1837. "Dictator, Dictatur". In: Rotteck, Carl von; Welcker, Carl Theodor Georg Philipp (Ed.). *Staats-Lexikon oder Encyklopädie der Staatswissenschaften in Verbindung mit vielen der angesehensten Publicisten Deutschlands. Vierter Band.* Altona, 392–396.

Schulz, Matthias. 2009. *Normen und Praxis. Das Europäische Konzert der Großmächte als Sicherheitsrat, 1815–1860.* München.

Seager, Frederic H. 1969. *The Boulanger Affair: Political Crossroad of France 1886–1889.* Ithaca, NY.

Seeber, Gustav; Dewitz, Horst (Ed.). 1977. *Bismarcks Sturz: Zur Rolle der Klassen in der Endphase des preussisch-deutschen Bonapartismus 1884/85 bis 1890.* Berlin.

Segesser, Philipp Anton von. 1877. *Sammlung kleiner Schriften. Erster Band: Studien und Glossen zur Tagesgeschichte. 1859–1875.* Bern.

Seldes, George. 1935. *Sawdust Caesar: The Untold History of Mussolini and Fascism.* New York, NY; London.

Sellin, Volker. 1996. " 'Heute ist die Revolution monarchisch'. Legitimität und Legitimierungspolitik im Zeitalter des Wiener Kongresses". In: *Quellen und Forschungen aus Italienischen Archiven und Bibliotheken* 76, 335–361.

Sellin, Volker. 2001. *Die geraubte Revolution. Der Sturz Napoleons und die Restauration in Europa.* Göttingen.

Sellin, Volker. 2004. "The Breakdown of the Rule of Law. A Comparative View of the Depositions of George III, Louis XVI and Napoleon I". In: Friedeburg, Robert von (Ed.). *Murder and Monarchy: Regicide in European History, 1300–1800.* Houndmills [etc.], 259–289.

Sellin, Volker. 2013. "Der Napoleonische Staatskult". In: Braun, Guido [et al.] (Ed.). *Napoleonische Expansionspolitik: Okkupation oder Integration?* Berlin; Boston, MA, 138–159.

Sellin, Volker. 2017. *European Monarchies from 1814 to 1906: A Century of Restorations.* Berlin; Boston, MA.

Sellin, Volker. 2018. *Violence and Legitimacy: European Monarchy in the Age of Revolutions.* Berlin; Boston, MA.

Senior, Nassau William. 1871. *Journals Kept in France and Italy from 1848 to 1852. With a Sketch of the Revolution of 1848 [ed. by Mary Charlotte Mair Simpson]*. 2 Vols. London.

Seume, Johann Gottfried. 1962. *Prosaschriften [ed. by W. Kraft]*. Köln.

Sieg, Ulrich. 2004. "Wilhelm II.—ein "leutseliger Charismatiker"". In: Möller, Frank (Ed.). *Charismatische Führer der deutschen Nation*. München, 85–108.

Sieyès, Emmanuel Joseph. 1789. *Qu'est-ce que le Tiers-État?* Paris.

Smith, Matthew Hale. 1873. *Caesarism: General Grant for a Third Term*. Cambridge, MA.

Sontheimer, Kurt. 1957. "Antidemokratisches Denken in der Weimarer Republik". In: *Vierteljahrshefte für Zeitgeschichte* 5 (1), 42–62.

Sontheimer, Kurt. 1962. *Antidemokratisches Denken in der Weimarer Republik. Die politischen Ideen des deutschen Nationalismus zwischen 1918 und 1933*. München.

Southey, Robert. 1861 [1813]. *Life of Nelson*. London.

Speer, Albert. 2002 [1975]. *Spandauer Tagebücher*. Berlin; München.

Spengler, Oswald. 1922. *Der Untergang des Abendlandes. Umrisse einer Morphologie der Weltgeschichte*. 2 Vols. München.

Spengler, Oswald. 1924. *Neubau des deutschen Reiches*. München.

Spengler, Oswald. 1933. *Jahre der Entscheidung. Erster Theil: Deutschland und die weltgeschichtliche Entwicklung*. München.

Spengler, Oswald. 1967 [1921]. "Pessimism?". In: Spengler, Oswald. *Selected Essays [ed. by Donald O. White]*. Chicago, IL, 133–154.

Spoiden, Stéphane. 2012. "La réclame du général Boulanger". In: *Contemporary French Civilization* 37 (1), 23–37.

Staël-Holstein, Anne Louise Germaine de. 1964. *Madame de Staël on Politics, Literature, and National Character [ed. by Morroe Berger]*. Garden City, NY.

Stahl, Friedrich Julius. 1845. *Das Monarchische Princip. Eine staatsrechtlich-politische Abhandlung*. Heidelberg.

Stein, Lorenz von. 1842. *Der Socialismus und Communismus des heutigen Frankreichs. Ein Beitrag zur Zeitgeschichte*. Leipzig.

Stein, Lorenz von. 1850. *Geschichte der socialen Bewegung in Frankreich von 1789 bis auf unsere Tage*. 3 Vols. Leipzig.

Stendhal [= Marie-Henri Beyle]. 1876 [1817–1818]. *Vie de Napoléon. Fragments*. Paris.

Stendhal [= Marie-Henri Beyle]. 1930 [1817–1818]. *Napoléon. I: Vie de Napoléon [ed. by Henri Martineau]*. Paris.

Stendhal [= Marie-Henri Beyle]. 1930 [1836–1837]. *Napoléon. II: Mémoires sur Napoléon [ed. by Henri Martineau]*. Paris.

Stolberg-Wernigerode, Otto zu. 1941. *Robert Heinrich Graf von der Goltz: Botschafter in Paris 1863–1869*. Oldenburg.

Stråth, Bo. 2016. *Europe's Utopias of Peace: 1815, 1919, 1951*. London [etc.].

Stürmer, Michael. 1969. "Staatsstreichgedanken im Bismarckreich". In: *Historische Zeitschrift* 209 (3), 566–615.

Stürmer, Michael. 1974. *Regierung und Reichstag im Bismarckstaat 1871–1880. Cäsarismus oder Parlamentarismus*. Düsseldorf.

Stürmer, Michael. 1977a. "Caesar's Laurel Crown—the Case for a Comparative Concept". In: *The Journal of Modern History* 49 (2), 203–207.

Stürmer, Michael. 1977b. "Krise, Konflikt, Entscheidung. Die Suche nach dem neuen Cäsar als europäisches Verfassungsproblem". In: Hammer, Karl; Hartmann, Peter Claus (Ed.). *Le Bonapartisme. Phénomène historique et mythe politique. Actes du 13e colloque historique franco-allemand de l'Institut Historique Allemand de Paris à Augsbourg du 26 jusqu'au 30 septembre 1975/Der Bonapartismus. Historisches Phänomen und politischer*

Mythos. 13. deutsch-französisches Historikerkolloquium des Deutschen Historischen Instituts Paris in Augsburg vom 26. bis 30. September 1975. Zürich; München, 102–118.

Tänzler, Dirk. 2007. "Politisches Charisma in der entzauberten Welt". In: Gostmann, Peter; Merz-Benz, Peter-Ulrich (Ed.). *Macht und Herrschaft.* Wiesbaden, 107–137.

Thamer, Hans-Ulrich. 1973. *Revolution und Reaktion in der französischen Sozialkritik des 18. Jahrhunderts: Linguet, Mably, Babeuf.* Frankfurt/Main.

Thamer, Hans-Ulrich. 2000. "Napoleon—Der Retter der revolutionären Nation". In: Nippel, Wilfried (Ed.). *Virtuosen der Macht. Herrschaft und Charisma von Perikles bis Mao.* München, 121–136.

Thibaudeau, Antoine Claire. 1827. *Mémoires sur le Consulat. 1799 à 1804. Par un ancien conseiller d'état.* Paris.

Thiers, Louis Adolphe. 1845–1862. *Histoire du Consulat et de l'Émpire, faisant suite à l'Histoire de la Révolution française.* 20 Vols. Paris.

Thody, Philip. 1989. *French Caesarism from Napoleon I to Charles de Gaulle.* Basingstoke.

Thuillier, G. 2005. "Une relation inédite du 18 brumaire: le Coup d'oeil sur la révolution consulaire de Parent l'aîné (frimaire an VIII)". In: *La revue administrative* 58 (347), 462–473.

Tocqueville, Alexis de. 1856. *L'Ancien Régime et la Révolution.* Paris.

Tocqueville, Alexis de. 1864–1866. *Œuvres complètes [ed. by Marie Clérel de Tocqueville].* 9 Vols. Paris.

Tocqueville, Alexis de. 1896 [1893]. *The Recollections of Alexis de Tocqueville. Edited by the Comte de Tocqueville and Now First Translated into English by Alexander Teixeira de Mattos.* London.

Tocqueville, Alexis de. 1985. *Selected Letters on Politics and Society [ed. by Roger Boesche].* Berkeley, CA; Los Angeles, CA; London.

Tocqueville, Alexis de. 1986. *De la démocratie en Amérique; Souvenirs; L'Ancien Régime et la Révolution [ed. by Jean-Claude Lamberti and Françoise Mélonio].* Paris.

Tocqueville, Alexis de. 2010 [1835–1840]. *Democracy in America: Historical-Critical Edition of De la démocratie en Amérique. A Bilingual French-English Edition [ed. by Eduardo Nolla].* 4 Vols. Indianapolis, IN.

Tudesq, André-Jean. 1957. "La légende napoléonienne en France en 1848". In: *Revue Historique* 218, 64–85.

Tulard, Jean. 1987 [1977]. *Napoléon: ou, Le mythe du sauveur.* Paris.

Tulard, Jean. 1999. *Le 18 brumaire: comment terminer une révolution.* Paris.

Unger, Harlow G. 2002. *Lafayette.* Hoboken, NJ.

Villedieu, Eugène. 1880. *Le Césarisme jacobin, les droits de l'Eglise et le droit national.* Paris.

Voegelin, Eric. 1952. *The New Science of Politics: An Introduction.* Chicago, IL.

Voegelin, Eric. 1996 [1938]. *Die Politischen Religionen [ed. by Peter J. Opitz].* München.

Wahl, Nicholas. 1959. "Aux Origines de la Nouvelle Constitution". In: *Revue française de science politique* 9 (1), 30–66.

Wang, Rongfen. 1997. *Cäsarismus und Machtpolitik. Eine historisch-biobliographische Analyse von Max Webers Charismakonzept.* Berlin.

Weber, Max. 1936. *Jugendbriefe [ed. by Marianne Weber].* Tübingen.

Weber, Max. 1946. *From Max Weber: Essays in Sociology [ed. by H.H. Gerth and C. Wright Mills].* New York, NY.

Weber, Max. 1978. *Economy and Society: An Outline of Interpretive Sociology [ed. by Guenther Roth and Claus Wittich].* 2 Vols. Berkeley, CA; Los Angeles, CA; London.

Weber, Max. ⁵1980 [1922]. *Wirtschaft und Gesellschaft. Grundriss der verstehenden Soziologie [ed. by Johannes Winckelmann].* Tübingen.

Weber, Max. 1984ff. *Max-Weber-Gesamtausgabe [ed. by Horst Baier, Gangolf Hübinger, M. Rainer Lepsius, Wolfgang J. Mommsen, Wolfgang Schluchter and Johannes Winckelmann]*. Tübingen.

Weber, Max. ⁵1988. *Max Weber. Gesammelte politische Schriften [ed. by Johannes Winckelmann]*. Tübingen.

Weber, Max. 1988 [1895]. "Der Nationalstaat und die Volkswirtschaftspolitik". In: Weber, Max. *Max Weber. Gesammelte politische Schriften [ed. by Johannes Winckelmann]*. Tübingen, 1–25.

Weber, Max. 1988 [1917]. "Wahlrecht und Demokratie in Deutschland". In: Weber, Max. *Max Weber. Gesammelte politische Schriften [ed. by Johannes Winckelmann]*. Tübingen, 245–291.

Weber, Max. 1988 [1918]-a. "Die nächste innerpolitische Aufgabe". In: Weber, Max. *Max Weber. Gesammelte politische Schriften [ed. by Johannes Winckelmann]*. Tübingen, 444–446.

Weber, Max. 1988 [1918]-b. "Parlament und Regierung im neugeordneten Deutschland. Zur politischen Kritik des Beamtentums und Parteiwesens". In: Weber, Max. *Max Weber. Gesammelte politische Schriften [ed. by Johannes Winckelmann]*. Tübingen, 306–443.

Weber, Max. 1988 [1919]-a. "Der Reichspräsident". In: Weber, Max. *Max Weber. Gesammelte politische Schriften [ed. by Johannes Winckelmann]*. Tübingen, 498–501.

Weber, Max. 1988 [1919]-b. "Politik als Beruf". In: Weber, Max. *Max Weber. Gesammelte politische Schriften [ed. by Johannes Winckelmann]*. Tübingen, 505–560.

Weber, Max. 1996. *Political Writings [ed. by Peter Lassman and Ronald Speirs]*. Cambridge [etc.].

Wehler, Hans-Ulrich. 1969. *Bismarck und der Imperialismus*. Köln; Berlin.

Wehler, Hans-Ulrich. 2007. "Das analytische Potential des Charisma-Konzepts: Hitlers charismatische Herrschaft". In: Anter, Andreas; Breuer, Stefan (Ed.). *Max Webers Staatssoziologie: Positionen und Perspektiven*. Baden-Baden, 175–189.

Weil, Bruno. 1931. *Glück und Elend des Generals Boulanger*. Berlin.

Wetzel, David. 2001. *A Duel of Giants: Bismarck, Napoleon III, and the Origins of the Franco-Prussian War*. Madison, WI [etc.].

Wickert, Lothar. 1959–1980. *Theodor Mommsen. Eine Biographie*. 4 Vols. Frankfurt/Main.

Wieland, Christoph Martin. 1777. "Ueber das göttliche Recht der Obrigkeit oder: Ueber den Lehrsatz: 'Daß die höchste Gewalt in einem Staat durch das Volk geschaffen sey'". In: *Der Teutsche Merkur* 4, 119–145.

Wieland, Christoph Martin. 1800 [1798]. *Gespräche unter vier Augen*. Karlsruhe.

Wienfort, Monika. 1993. *Monarchie in der bürgerlichen Gesellschaft. Deutschland und England von 1640 bis 1848*. Göttingen.

Willms, Johannes. 2009 [2005]. *Napoleon. Eine Biographie*. München.

Windelband, Wolfgang. 1936. "Die historische Figur Napoleons III.". In: *Deutsche Rundschau* 248, 97–103.

Wirth, Hans-Jürgen. 2007. "Macht, Narzissmus und die Sehnsucht nach dem Führer". In: *Aus Politik und Zeitgeschichte* 11, 13–18.

Wodak, Ruth; KhosraviNik, Majid; Mral, Brigitte (Ed.). 2013. *Right-wing Populism in Europe: Politics and Discourse*. London [etc.].

Wollstonecraft, Mary. 1995. *A Vindication of the Rights of Men and A Vindication of the Rights of Woman [ed. by Sylvana Tomaselli]*. Cambridge; New York, NY.

Woloch, Isser. 1997. "Réflexions sur les réactions à Brumaire dans les milieux républicains provinciaux". In: Bertaud, Jean-Paul (Ed.). *Mélanges Michel Vovelles. Volume de l'Institut d'Histoire de la Révolution Française. Sur la Révolution: approches plurielles.* Paris, 309–318.

Woloch, Isser. 2001. *Napoleon and his Collaborators: The Making of a Dictatorship.* New York, NY; London.

Woloch, Isser. 2004. "From Consulate to Empire: Impetus and Reistance". In: Baehr, Peter; Richter, Melvin (Ed.). *Dictatorship in History and Theory: Bonapartism, Caesarism, and Totalitarianism.* Cambridge, 29–52.

Wolter, Heinz. 1977. "Zum Verhältnis von Außenpolitik und Bismarckschem Bonapartismus". In: *Jahrbuch für Geschichte* 16, 119–137.

Woltmann, Karl Ludwig von. 1804a. "Die Feldherrn der Französischen Republik". In: *Geschichte und Politik. Eine Zeitschrift* 1, 240–246.

Woltmann, Karl Ludwig von. 1804b. "Karl der Große und Bonaparte". In: *Geschichte und Politik. Eine Zeitschrift* 1, 67–84.

Wyke, Maria. 2007. *Caesar: A Life in Western Culture.* London.

Zeldin, Theodore. 1979. *France 1848–1945: Politics and Anger.* Oxford.

Zick, Andreas; Küpper, Beate; Hövermann, Andreas. 2011. *Die Abwertung der Anderen. Eine europäische Zustandsbeschreibung zu Intoleranz, Vorurteilen und Diskriminierung [ed. by Friedrich-Ebert-Stiftung].* Bonn.

Zweig, Egon. 1909. *Die Lehre vom Pouvoir Constituant. Ein Beitrag zum Staatsrecht der französischen Revolution.* Tübingen.

Index